Readings from

CHILDHOOD EDUCATION

Articles of Lasting Value

Readings from

CHILDHOOD EDUCATION

Articles of Lasting Value

Editor: MARGARET RASMUSSEN

Assistant Editors:
Sylvia Sunderlin
Lucy Prete Martin

D. KEITH OSBORN, *Chairman*,
Anthology Committee

Association for Childhood Education International
3615 Wisconsin Avenue, N.W., Washington, D. C. 20016

1966

©Copyright 1966 by Association for Childhood Education International, 3615 Wisconsin Avenue, N.W., Washington, D. C. 20016. All rights reserved. Without permission in writing from the Association for Childhood Education International, no part of this book may be reproduced in any form, by mimeograph or any other means.

Library of Congress Catalog Card Number: 66-24209.

Printed in the United States of America

Price: $3.75

Dedication: to MARY E. LEEPER, whose wisdom and vision inspired all to undertake great responsibilities in working *with* and *for* children; who believed CHILDHOOD EDUCATION to be the Association's "voice" which could move education forward.

288811

Dedication: to WILLIAM HEARD KILPATRICK, whose philosophy influenced the accomplishments of the Association and the contents of CHILDHOOD EDUCATION, on whose Editorial Board he served for forty years.

FOREWORD

OVER THE YEARS THERE HAVE BEEN REQUESTS FOR AN ANTHOLOGY OF articles from CHILDHOOD EDUCATION. The occasion of the fortieth anniversary of the Journal, CHILDHOOD EDUCATION, seemed an appropriate time to bring forth such a book as a commemoration of that anniversary.

The ACEI Executive Board set up an Anthology Committee to make selections of articles of lasting value. This committee consisted of most of the CHILDHOOD EDUCATION Editorial Board chairmen from 1924-1964, three editors, a few Editorial Board members and ACEI Advisory Board members. For me, as chairman of the Committee, the work has been a pleasant task although not an easy one.

How does one select about seventy-five articles from more than 3,000 articles published between 1924 and 1964? What are the criteria for selection? Committee members suggested a number of plans for the organization of the book, and some began reading articles to fit the plan. It was discovered this was not feasible; they later reverted to the original question, "Is this article of lasting value?"

At this juncture, a core committee (some from Anthology Committee and others) read and re-read the selections and narrowed the selections down to 500 titles. These were reduced to a master list of 150 titles. Most of the titles in the book were chosen by four (or more) of the Committee members. Although there is overlapping, the titles seemed to fall into sections—beliefs, the child, the teacher, the classroom, past inspirations and a glimpse into the future.

A criticism of this book might be that some of the reader's favorite articles are omitted—I know that a few of my favorites are missing. Another criticism might be that some areas of interest have either been omitted or treated slightly. I had to keep reminding myself that a book of readings was *not* a textbook but a volume of articles with wide appeal.

As you read this book you will find some all-time favorites—Claudia Lewis' delightful experiment in children's language as told in "Deep as a Giant," Mauree Applegate's "Hoppity, Skippity—Serendipity" and the "Declaration of Faith," by Erna Christensen, Jennie Wahlert and Laura Zirbes. Ralph Witherspoon's article, "Teacher, Know Thyself," serves as an excellent check-up for both teachers and students in education. I think it should be "must" reading every fall prior to school opening. Your fall reading should also include Zirbes' "What Creative Teaching Means" and the Committee's favorite article, Winifred Bain's "With Life So Long, Why Shorten Childhood?"

My appreciation goes to each Committee member who read the selections, to those who tabulated them, and to the editorial staff at ACEI headquarters, who have seen this book through to production.

It is hoped readers will find the time-tested articles useful.—*By* D. KEITH OSBORN, *Chairman, Community Services, The Merrill-Palmer Institute, Detroit, and Chairman, ACEI Anthology Committee.*

ACKNOWLEDGMENTS TO COMMITTEES

Former CHILDHOOD EDUCATION Editorial Board Chairmen 1924-1964

DOROTHY E. WILLY,* Evanston, Illinois
WINIFRED E. BAIN, Boston, Massachusetts
LAURA ZIRBES, Columbus, Ohio
ALICE MIEL, New York, New York
VIOLA THEMAN, Evanston, Illinois
PAULINE HILLIARD, Gainesville, Florida
LAURA HOOPER, Riverside, California
ALBERTA L. MEYER, Washington, D. C.
HELEN HEFFERNAN, Sacramento, California
WANDA ROBERTSON, Salt Lake City, Utah
AGNES SNYDER, Wilmington, Delaware

Core Committee

MARY HARBAGE, Brookline, Massachusetts
FLORINE HARDING, Oakland, California
LELAND B. JACOBS, New York, New York
LOIS JOHNSON, Lincoln, Nebraska
LUCILE LINDBERG, New York, New York
CONSTANCE MCCUTCHEON,* Eagle Grove, Iowa
WANDA ROBERTSON, Salt Lake City, Utah
LUCILLE SESSIONS, Decatur, Georgia
MARTHA E. STINSON, Evansville, Indiana

Acknowledgments to section coordinators who also wrote introductions

AGNES SNYDER, Wilmington, Delaware
MARY HARBAGE, Brookline, Massachusetts
LELAND B. JACOBS, New York, New York
LUCILE LINDBERG, New York, New York
DOROTHY E. WILLY, Evanston, Illinois
BERNICE BAXTER, Piedmont, California

*Former editor

CONTENTS

Page

Dedication to Mary E. Leeper v
Dedication to William Heard Kilpatrick vi
Foreword, *D. Keith Osborn* vii
Acknowledgments ix

SECTION I — This We Believe

This We Believe—*Agnes Snyder* 1
Declaration of Faith—*Erna Christensen, Jennie Wahlert, Laura Zirbes* 2
Democracy Grows Individuals—*Howard Lane* 4
Continuity in Learning—*L. Thomas Hopkins* 8
Excellence Is Relative—*Louis E. Raths* 13
To Wonder and To Ponder—*James S. Tippett* 17
A Good Beginning Has No End—*Lawrence K. Frank* 21
Significance of Kindergarten Education—*Helen Heffernan* 23
Adults Look at Children's Values—*Bernice Milburn Moore* 30
Assumptions Underlying Mechanized Learning—*Alice V. Keliher* 35
The Myth of Competition—*Arthur W. Combs* 40
Values Are Fundamental—*Louis E. Raths* 47

SECTION II — The Child

The Child—*Mary Harbage* 51

THE EARLY YEARS

The Role of Love in Preschool Education—*Daniel A. Prescott* 52
The Importance of Preprimary Education—*James L. Hymes, Jr.* 63
The Five to Eights and How They Grow—*Barbara Biber* 69
Children Come By Meanings—*Marie I. Rasey* 80
Children Want To Know—*Kenneth D. Wann* 83
Except for Michael—*Helen E. Buckley* 89

A WIDER SPAN

From Infancy to Adulthood—*Jean Walker Macfarlane* 94
Emotions and How They Grow—*Virginia M. Axline* 101
Permissiveness Re-examined—*D. Keith Osborn* 108
Guiding Learning—*L. Thomas Hopkins* 113
What Are Children Learning?—*Earl C. Kelley* 118
Time To Grow—*Jean Adamson* 123

SECTION III — The Teacher

The Teacher—*Leland B. Jacobs* 129
Teacher, Know Thyself—*Ralph Witherspoon* 130
The Kind of Teacher Makes the Difference—*Norma R. Law* 134
What Creative Teaching Means—*Laura Zirbes* 138
When Teachers Teach—*Marie M. Hughes* 142
Understanding Others Through Facing Ourselves—*Arthur T. Jersild* 147
Conditions for Creative Learning—*E. Paul Torrance* 151
Brainwashing, Perception and the Task of the Teacher—*Ira J. Gordon* 155
How Adults Influence Children—*Hilda Taba* 158
The Teacher Is a Citizen—*Sam McLaughlin* 162
That Silent One—*Lucy Nulton* 166
Firmer Boundaries for Greater Freedom—*Ina K. Dillon* 169
The Poor Scholar's Soliloquy—*Stephen M. Corey* 175
The Teacher Asked of the Child—*Leland B. Jacobs* 178

SECTION IV — The Classroom

The Classroom—*Lucile Lindberg* 181
What Should We Know About Learning?—*Laura Zirbes* 182
Adventuring in Creativity—*E. Paul Torrance* 187
Research in Creativity: Some Findings and Conceptions—
                                          Elliot W. Eisner 197
The Knowledge Explosion—*Gerald S. Craig* 204
Four Hickory Nuts and a Catbird's Nest—*Glenn O. Blough* 209
Readiness Is Being—*Ethelouise Carpenter* 215
Dramatic Play—*Esther B. Starks* 218
Language in Childhood—*Joseph Church* 223
"Deep as a Giant"—*Claudia Lewis* 227
How Children Learn Their Language—*Ruth G. Strickland* 230
More Than Words—*Leland B. Jacobs* 233
Beyond the Verbal Façade—*Millie Almy* 236
To Write or Not To Write—*Neith Headley* 241
Hoppity—Skippity—Serendipity—*Mauree Applegate* 245
Here's to Success in Reading—*Marian Jenkins* 250
Children and the Arts—*Edward L. Mattil* 260
Hurrying To Rest—*Helen E. Buckley* 265

SECTION V — Inspirations from the Past

Inspirations from the Past—*Dorothy E. Willy* 271
Friedrich Froebel—Apostle of Childhood Education—
                                                        Caroline D. Aborn 272
Ideas and Ideals—*Lucy Wheelock* 278
Beginnings of Education—*A. H. Hughey* 284
The Age Factor—*Arnold Gesell* 288
The Place of Creating in the Educative Process—*William H. Kilpatrick* 290
What About Progressive Education?—*Alice V. Keliher* 295
Toward a More Democratic Citizenship—*James S. Tippett* 304
Growth in Social Living Through the Tools of Learning—*Alice Miel* 309
Preparing Children for a World Society—*Margaret Mead* 313

SECTION VI — Today's Child — Tomorrow's World

Today's Child—Tomorrow's World—*Bernice Baxter* 321
Moving Forward—*Mary Esther Leeper* 322
Today's Children and Tomorrow's World—*Robert J. Havighurst* 326
What Is the Image of Man Tomorrow?—*Edgar Dale* 332
Today's World Is Different—*Beatrice Hurley* 336
Role of Education in Contemporary Life—*Harold Taylor* 342
Unreasonable Expectations—*Boyd McCandless* 347
Hurry! Hurry! Hurry! Why?—*Annie L. Butler* 352
Play Is Education—*N. V. Scarfe* 356
What Price Pressures?—*Gladys Gardner Jenkins* 361
Pressures To Learn Can Be Blocks to Learning—*John I. Goodlad* ... 366
Do We Push Children?—*Alice V. Keliher* 370
With Life So Long, Why Shorten Childhood?—*Winifred E. Bain* 377
Who? What? When? Where? How? Why?—*Agnes Snyder* 381
How Valid Are the Criticisms?—*Afton Dill Nance* 389
Anthropology—an Integrating Science for an Integrated World—
                                                        Ethel J. Alpenfels 393
The United Nations and the Real World—*Chester Bowles* 398
The Teacher as a World Citizen—*Marion Edman* 407
The World's Bounty—*Stewart Udall* 410
For All Children the Teachers Speak—*Agnes Snyder* 413

Section I

This We Believe

This We Believe

This we believe!" Sometimes, as insight suddenly clarifies obscurity, these simple words are spoken spontaneously. At other times, after logical thought has led gradually to a satisfying conclusion, their utterance is more deliberate. But whether spontaneous or deliberate, when thoughtfully spoken, they express deep reflection on experience combined with feeling so strong as to compel action. This is *believing*. This, too, is the element essential in raising the status of teaching from craft to profession. We may be ever so skillful in methodology, ever so ingenious in organization—we may even love our pupils—but unless beneath these is passionate belief in the significance of what we are doing and profound understanding of the "why" behind it, we can lay little claim to having a profession.

Intelligent belief is not easy to achieve. Its two-fold basis in thinking and feeling makes this so. Thinking is a complicated process challenging the best minds with problems at every step along the road to mastery of its skills. The education of the feelings is an equally stern discipline in its requirement of both freedom and control in their expression.

Moreover, there have always been forces within and outside the individual that set up powerful barriers against thinking; and the more complex civilization becomes, the more destructively effective are the barriers. With the passing of each century, tradition increasingly tends to mold our thinking into patterns more set; mass media of communication, increasing in sophistication, exercise subtler persuasive powers; increase in technological knowledge with its standardization of material products leads to comparable standardization of thinking in conformity with the fashion of the moment; and the person, under the pressure of these forces, finds his thinking colored by his own self-interest, interest in his own survival.

What is true of thinking is similarly true of feeling. The more complex the culture, the more difficult is it to develop healthy emotional living. The idols of indolent thinking tend to inhibit real thinking and natural feeling. Early in childhood we take over the loves and hatreds of our social environment. Later, demagoguery rouses our sympathies for this or that; in order not to be alienated from our kind we accept the thinking popular at the moment; surrounded by suffering and violence we stifle our emotions with a protective coating of callousness and refuse to become involved.

Teachers today are in a particularly vulnerable position to withstand the assaults of the idols. Pulled in all directions by parents fearful that their children will not succeed in a fiercely competitive world, teachers find it hard to remain consistently true to their own beliefs. Confronted by criticism from "authoritative sources" and urged by them to adopt systems and methods by which learning will be quicker, easier and earlier, it is only natural that teachers should at times doubt their own judgment. Teachers, of course, find the temptation sometimes too strong to resist attractively packaged gadgets, persuasively offered, that will save time and effort in preparation. Only teachers who have lived through the struggle and the discipline essential to the achievement of genuine beliefs and, in addition, have never ceased in their efforts to modify, to broaden, and to deepen these beliefs are able to conquer the idols.

This does not mean that there is any one body of *right* belief. Teachers are human and, therefore, their beliefs will inevitably vary in kind, quality and quantity. This is good. There is strength in variety, and progress is largely dependent on the clash of honestly held ideas. But unless there is intelligent belief underlying school procedures, education is never convincing and is, for the most part, futile. Teachers meet their responsibility to humanity best—and no group has greater—when with the mighty voice of courage they dare affirm: "This we *know!* This we *believe!* Therefore, this we *do!*"—*By* AGNES SNYDER, *Professor Emeritus,* Adelphi College, Garden City, Long Island, N. Y.

Declaration of Faith

By ERNA CHRISTENSEN, *teacher, Public Schools, Bronxville, New York;* JENNIE WAHLERT, *director, Nursery School, and teacher, Department of Education, Washington University, St. Louis, Missouri;* LAURA ZIRBES, *professor of education emeritus, The Ohio State University, Columbus.*

WE WHO ARE CONCERNED WITH THE DEVELOPMENTAL GUIDANCE AND education of children have *faith*—

in them and their potentialities
in ourselves and in each other

in human values and human hopes
in active and interactive learning
which moves forward, guided by evidences of
- children's needs
- their aspirations and creative urges
- blocks removed and values internalized
- increasing self-reliance and self-direction
- interpersonal competence and social maturity.

Our faith projected and tested in our evaluations is
- validated and extended in our value judgments as we think and plan and act and interact
- renewed and vindicated by the intrinsic satisfactions of our own creative endeavors.

Our faith neither blind nor rigid nor walled in
- shines forth in our communications with children and with those who entrust us with them
- raises our morale, lifts our aspirations, sustains our efforts.

As adults concerned with children we have a high commitment.

We believe the adult, through understanding child growth and development, can plan for a continuous program to meet the individual child's needs—one which provides opportunities for the individual child to carry out his creative drives, revealing his individual differences in knowledge, impressions, feelings, appreciations, skills, methods of work.

We believe the adult, in providing for different learning experiences and giving the individual child creative outlets in all areas, has the responsibility to see that each child discovers himself, his needs, his on-going interests, and at the same time builds respect for self and others.

We believe the adult realizes that the individual child needs freedom to carry out his creative drives—but at the same time needs direction to learn to build responsibility.

We believe the adult values the importance of the individual child's rhythm of work, play and rest and channels the child's energies in the direction sound for him.

We believe adults concerned with today's children need to reaffirm in confident and strong terms the importance of how children feel:
- Unless children are regarded with consideration and understanding and with respect for their human worth, there is grave danger that they may become pawns of an uncertain and confused society.
- Unless pressures "to achieve" which are inflicted on children from many sources are relieved, serious blocks to learning may result and serious damage may be done to their personalities.

We believe the adult of today (in the face of big, sudden and unpredictable changes) must foster the spirit of cooperative inquiry in children.

Children need to know:
- What are the current circumstances?
- How did they come to be?
- Where will they lead us?
- How can they be changed?

We believe the adult should help children acquire the skills with which to ferret out basic issues and deal with them.

We believe the adult working with children needs to share with community groups the knowledge gained through experiences—in developmental guidance and in the findings of research.

We believe the adult has an obligation to children to work with community groups for legislative action in the best interests of children.

The world and all its people and life in all its manifestations provide the content for education. To the degree that understanding adults set the stage and assume responsibility for their guidance, children will grow into mature beings, stable within themselves, effective in their social relations, resourceful and self-disciplined in identifying and solving problems.

Democracy Grows Individuals
BY HOWARD LANE

"We teachers are the professionals in the growing of people. We must so build, arrange and operate our communities, schools and schoolrooms that every child lives well every day regardless of his IQ, skill in the 3 R's, parentage, race," says Howard Lane, professor of education, New York University.

BOY, OH, BOY! ARE WE GOING TO HAVE FUN TOMORROW!" A SECOND-grader exclaimed to her puzzled father. He inquired, "How's that?" "Our wild-life group is going to cooperate with the third-grade zoology group," said the child. Father pressed a bit. "What are you going to do with them?" "Oh, I don't know. We're just going to cooperate." This joyful feeling arose likely in anticipation of doing something different with some different people rather than from the promise of greater abundance through group endeavor.

When this father had started to school somewhat more than three decades earlier his classroom group was joined together only by the confinement of four walls and a firm teacher. Communication among classmates was forbidden; few sins transcended giving or receiving help with assigned lessons. Group enterprise was neither educational method nor goal.

It was then near-blasphemy to question the dogma that the pupils in a school group should be as nearly alike as could be arranged. Uniqueness (we then used the term *individual differences*) among pupils in a group was lamented as a serious problem requiring resolution. Graduate students and their professors worked out schemes for neutralizing differences: demotion, acceleration, multiple tracks, early identification as academic and nonacademic, enrichment, remedial work, special classes, special schools. When God, at long last, revealed to man the natural phenomenon of the IQ, the problem of forming groups of like ability was solved. This led merrily into the concretion of the abstraction *levels,* which has become the great eliminator of all uniqueness other than rate of growth.

Automation Age

As long as man alone did all the work required to keep himself and his dependents fed and clothed, he toiled from dawn to dusk for bare necessities. He had no time to create or admire beauty, to chat pleasantly with friends, to play, to contemplate the meaning of life. Gentlemen and ladies were people who did no useful work, produced no goods, rendered no satisfactions—they had subjects to do it for them. We shall not here recount man's slow development to the harnessing of energies other than man's muscles. We enter now upon the age of automation which, we are told, enables us to pour appropriate raw materials into one end of a factory and wait at the other end for an automobile, a watch or whatever we have devised our machines to produce. We have lately learned how to release and control energies which abound everywhere. Man can now contemplate as his principal productive work the designing of machines and processes and keeping them in order. (The foregoing is obviously oversimplified.)

Industrialization has demanded increased amounts and kinds of cooperation. Individuals have become highly specialized. Today few shoe manufacturers can make a shoe. Who knows anyone who could shear a sheep and from the wool fashion a dress to wear to the ACEI conference? We appear well dressed even on our salaries as the result of the cooperative labor of many people, all specialists, none of whom could carry out all the operations of making a garment. No man alone can make one nylon thread.

Utilizing Unique Abilities

A cooperative—division of labor—enterprise utilizes unique talents and abilities of many people. In the pioneer culture handicapped persons perished or were burdens to their relatives. Modern methods of production can find use in specialized tasks for amputees, the blind, the dull-witted, the crippled.

Working together in planned, organized procedures with ready sources of energy and specialized tools, a man today produces many times more goods than could his grandfather, regardless of his grandfather's talents and zeal. Modern cooperative endeavor frees the individual from arduous toil and provides him with much time and purchasing power to spend in accord with his preferences for a nearly infinite variety and amount of goods and services. Those who render personal services are no longer subjects scrambling for crumbs from the master's table; they are workers carrying out their specialties while living in human dignity.

Man still has far to go in using his new freedom for the enhancement of his own life. The transition from "living to work" to "working to live" has been slow. Too many of our people continue to live in competitive acquisitiveness, seeking to buy a vast variety of escapes. Perhaps the school has used too much the motive, "Study hard, be good, thwart present impulses and desires. When you grow up you'll make a lot of money and can buy a good life." Grownups must see that childhood is a sizeable portion of a life. The quality of day-by-day living is even more crucial to a child than to an adult. The groups of childhood must extend and deepen genuine gratifications in friendships, creativeness, self-respect, value and appreciation, hearty enjoyment. We teachers profess to be professionals in the growing of fine people. *We must then make sure that all our children live gratifying, productive, zestful lives.* An eight-year-old informed me, "Daddy! I'm not waiting to grow up."

Fundamentals Today

Development of the values, concerns and skills required for cooperative living is the basic fundamental of the school today. As this is written, the ether trembles with excitement over the problem of identifying the scientist in the crib and nurturing him (never her) to occupy Mars and Jupiter. As Grandma put it, "People are getting too smart for their britches." Our know-how has raced beyond our characters. Two heads are more than twice as good as one, but *only* when they seek common purposes. In contention, two heads are worse than either. Two people know more than one. No person today can know all the facts or call to awareness all the aspects of any important social or technical problem. One man can know so little of what mankind knows. Thus it is plainly silly for schools to attempt to group together persons who are alike in talent and knowledge. If all have the same characteristics, they are more weighty, not more wise or competent. Members of a group must be valuable to each other; hence they must differ from each other.

Democracy is voluntary cooperation. Since modern living demands cooperation, persons in power are constantly tempted to demand it. Hitler made a very cohesive, efficient group of the Germans. We once heard a small boy explain his low mark in cooperation with, "Ah! that's how well you obey." On another occasion he told his sister, "Social science is how good you stand in line to go to the bathroom." We suspect that the term *cooperation* on rating scales for teachers indicates acquiescence more often than skill in group endeavor. Totalitarianism is imposed cooperation in whatever form it appears!

The most radical statement in history is, "Man was not made for the Sabbath; the Sabbath was made for man." Its meaning: human arrangements, human institutions are made to enhance the quality of living of individual personalities. The author of this idea was executed by the good people of his time. The prime difference between democracy and totalitarianism is found in the interrelationship between the individual and his group. Does the group function for the benefit of the individual, or is the individual the servant of the group?

Appreciation and effective use of unique individual talents are crucial to effective group enterprise. Some of us can write beautiful songs but cannot sing them. One can plan a bridge but cannot weld a rivet. Among us are individuals who can spell out profound ideas while our efforts to communicate them to groups induce peaceful slumber. "Know thyself" is the most significant advice man has received.

Abandon Evaluation by Comparison

Democracy must learn to value and use special talents and abilities without relating them to degree of right to live a significant and gratifying life. Our current procedure of evaluating by comparison must be abandoned. Symbolic marking, special awards, prizes devaluate special abilities in the eyes of fellow group members. The powerful popularity of the term *egg-head* frightens me more than does *Sputnik*. Teachers must learn to value children as they value each other. We do not hasten the development of a frog by snipping off a tadpole's tail. Sensing that their own values are respected, youngsters will not need to restrict the changing and maturing of their own. The small fry are not committed to neatness and punctuality, although most of them seek acceptable compromises.

Among children, as among their elders, groups form and function for many purposes: to play, to enjoy a common interest, to plan work and determine individual roles in carrying it through, to add to all the knowledge and skills of one or a few, to whet minds on each other, to make decisions when forks are encountered in the road and all must go a single way. (A democratic group seldom votes. It reaches decisions by consensus seeking a balance, not merely of numbers, but of the weight of preferences and concerns of each individual in the group.)

Frequently we encounter a group—family, classroom, faculty, legislature which seems worse than anybody in it. The causes of group illness are rather clear. Among them are: lack of defined purposes and devotion to them; individuals or cliques seeking to prevail, or seeking to get the credit; special privilege, recognition and honor for those in the role of leadershp (in democracy, leadership is a job, not an honor); giving attention to "Who is right?" rather than "What is right?"; contests among individuals or subgroups.

Groups persist and flourish as long as they extend and deepen the quality of living of the individual as he perceives and lives it. We teachers are the professionals in the growing of people. We must so build, arrange and operate our communities, schools and schoolrooms that every child lives well every day without regard to his IQ, skill in the three R's, parentage, race. Much of his life is social, lived in groups. He finds life's changing meaning for himself by himself. Let us provide and respect time and circumstances for reflection and repose.

Vol. XXXI—p. 214 (Jan. 1955)

Continuity in Learning
BY L. THOMAS HOPKINS

Continuity is the relating of what goes on within the child with what goes on about him. Here is a thought-provoking presentation to help adults understand their role in raising self-selection to conscious deliberative action. L. Thomas Hopkins is professor of education emeritus, Teachers College, Columbia University, New York.

To THE INDIVIDUAL WHO DOES THE LEARNING OR LIVING THERE IS NO problem of continuity in growing or learning in education or in life. The difficulty arises when other persons, parents or educators want him to accept without change their continuity as they organize it to meet their needs.

The parent has an order or succession of behaviors which he expects the child to learn. The school administrator has a scope and sequence of subject matter which has been selected for the child to study in the schools. The college professor has prepared in advance a syllabus for the student to follow in his subject. The university demands a series of particular courses for the various degrees. I shall not discuss these externally prepared orders of experiences for learners at any age. Rather I shall deal with the normal developmental concept of continuity as inherent in all living and without which the life itself will cease to exist.

All children are born with some capacity to learn. Since they begin life with different genes patterns, they do not have the same potential ability. They cannot learn the same things to the same degree at the same time and under the same external environmental conditions.

All children are born with the same process of learning. This is an upward and outward extension of the normal growth process by which each developed himself from the fertilized egg to a normal baby.

While all children, without regard to their inherited capacity, are born with and hold in common throughout life the same normal way of learning, they must be expected to differ in learned behaviors within it. The transition from their internally controlled prenatal continuity to the externally controlled cultural systems is to them a serious upheaval and is sometimes a ruthless shock.

All children are in continuous interaction with their environment as they interpret it. This ongoing relationship is called experience. It never ceases, whether the child be asleep or awake at home or in school, by himself or with others.

Every child learns through his own experience. Under normal conditions he broadens, deepens and enriches it by his growth process. But a child never carries on *all* his experiences, for he is not the sum of these experiences. Rather he is a qualitative, purposeful evaluator and integrator of them. In relation to his needs as he perceives them, he rejects all aspects of low quality. He picks up to carry on the parts which he believes are usable now and will have increasing value in the future. He cannot prevent this purposeful evaluation of his past and present experiences, as it is as much an integral part of his life as breathing.

Each child self-selects the learnings which he picks up from one experience to carry on to subsequent experience. His selections are based upon his perception of his present needs or internal disturbances, his understanding of his external environment, his concept of himself as a person, and his interpretation of his growth or learning process. Since people are the most important external influence in his life, he invariably carries on his interpretation of how to get along with them and especially what to expect from them. These human traces affect his behavior long after the original experiences are forgotten and cannot even be identified in the ongoing movement of life. His continuity lies in his interpretation of these human factors. This is shaped by how well he and others understand and use their normal growth process. So the quality of *his* self-selections as well as those for *him* are contingent upon the quality of the interaction operating among them.

The learnings which a child self-selects and accepts unconsciously or deliberately become a part of himself and operate continuously in his life experiences. His early unconscious learnings, such as a feeling of rejection by his parents, are more difficult for him to evaluate to improve subsequent experience than are his later thoughtful selections. Self-selection with acceptance goes on whether outside persons approve or disapprove of the process or of the specific behaviors. The child cannot stop it of his own volition; neither can he eliminate it at the request of or under the pressure of parents or teachers. Adults can set the external conditions within which the child's learning process operates and his selections are made. But what he accepts emotionally or thoughtfully under these circumstances becomes himself.

Each child is born a unified whole and acts as a whole in every experience. He self-selects those learnings which he believes will maintain and enrich his wholeness as he perceives the life situations which he faces. This has to be so, for his biological drive to maintain his unity as an operating organism persists in spite of external influences to undermine it. His meaning of his unity varies with his age, variety of experiences, maturity of self, the quality of the external conditions, and his accumulated ability to analyze all factors in their relationship in his life situations. His selections are always directed toward improving his self-integrity and enhancement, even though observers of his behavior may disagree with his judgments.

Each child tries to improve his selections as he grows older, but he is seriously handicapped by his lack of understanding of his growth and learning process. He is the center of his experiences. To improve them he must understand better who he is to himself, how he acts toward others, why they behave as they do toward others, why they behave as they do toward him, the nature of the upsets or situations which such interaction develops, and how he with the others may, through better situational analysis, modify their behavior to the higher development of all. To help him gain this insight and practice within his own experiences is one of the great opportunities of home and school.

Problem of Better Continuity

The problem of better continuity can now be simply stated. Adults must work with the child by his normal growth process so that they—

- recognize the child's right to self-select his learnings
- promote an atmosphere in which he willingly indicates what he is *really* selecting
- help him understand when, why and how he makes his choices
- assist him in interpreting how he reconstructs past experience in and through present life situations
- aid him in improving his present selections which he will carry on to subsequent experience.

This leaves the control of the continuity with the child where it always has been, is now, and ever shall be, *but* it provides the environment in which he can learn how to raise his early autonomic selections to the level of conscious deliberative action. Thus he can go on developing his inherited capacity to levels of self-maturity which the older education denied to present adults.

No adult can give continuity to a child, for he already has it inherent in his life process, in his wholeness, in the integrity of his experiences, and in the development of himself. Others may try to obstruct it or to manipulate it their way, but they do so at the risk of limiting the release of the child's potential creativeness and of arresting his development. Adults can enrich the environment to make it easy for the child to select learnings which enable him to become an independent mature self, or they can restrict it so that he becomes a dependent immature self. In either case the child has within his ongoing experiences a continuity of learning which he controls with as high a quality as he can obtain under the existing circumstances.

Every child is born into an external culture ordered and arranged by adults to meet their needs or to give the continuity to their experience which enhances them. In schools this means a curriculum composed of various organizations of subjects containing the results of the experiences of others in nonhuman form, sometimes called the 3 R's or the essentials, which adults wish the child to accept as they have organized it. This is exceedingly difficult for any child, since he lacks the experience to self-select to meet his needs this concentrated residue of the experiences of others.

Yet every child, without regard to inherited capacity to learn, wants to acquire the media of communication or interaction through which he can develop himself. To become a normal, mature self he must acquire these through improving his own experience by his own creative efforts. And here the difference becomes acute.

Adults assert that continuity resides in the nonhuman materials which they have so carefully organized to satisfy the human unity within themselves. Children know that continuity resides in them, and they are not impressed by these external arrangements. They want the opportunity to create in themselves the scope and sequence of nonhuman materials that help satisfy their needs toward becoming more mature.

Since children are all born unique, no selection and organization of learnings by any outside person can possibly satisfy them. But, since they are all born with the same learning process, they can develop within this common inheritance the media to become their unique selves through interaction with their peers and adults. Thus each child will speak, write, sing, draw, play and read or will learn all outgoing and intaking media of communication in his own way, at his own time, and by his own rate in harmony with his wholeness of growth and development.

The quality of the continuity in learning of any child cannot be guaranteed by any preplanned external scope and sequence in the curriculum whether it be called subjects, units, activities or experiences. Yet preplanning for every experience by every person—child or adult— always operates, since what he has picked up from previous experience to carry on becomes his planned or organized self which acts in present life situations. Therefore, every child has preplanned in his way and every adult has certain tendencies to action which constitute his behavior in the common experiences. To give greatest help to children in improving what they carry on to subsequent experiences, adults plan:

● how to find out more about who they are and how they came to develop their present tendencies to action toward children
● how to change themselves so that they can accept continuity as residing in and developed by the child through his experiences
● how to unfix the existing continuity in subjects, or their variants, which limits the creative development of children.

They should also plan how to extend in schools—

● firsthand common group experiences of children in their environment, as these are the best source for widening and deepening perceptions and therefore for improving self-selections
● group discussions which help children understand how they increase their meanings within these common experiences
● wider use of all media of expression by individuals alone or in groups, helping them locate better what learnings they are trying to communicate to themselves or others and how well these learnings appear in the expressed product
● respect for variability, difference, uniqueness in experience as a normal expectation in learning and as an asset in all group activities when the climate is permissive or releasing and the process is truly interactive.

Children will always have continuity of experience. The issue is whether adults want to help them learn how to improve what they self-select to become themselves or whether adults want children to study and accept an organization of nonhuman materials which they (the adults) believe helped them become the great people they are and therefore should be transmitted by them in their form to children. This issue is always answered by adults through their behavior or through the kind of pre-planning in their lives antecedent to their present action toward children.

If adults can only release themselves enough to trust children, they will find that in a rich, permissive, wholesome environment each child will learn to pick up better selections (including the expanded 3 R's), to increase his meaning of the process through which he makes his selections, and to continue to improve his experiences throughout life. In working together in such schools or homes both the adults and children will achieve that higher living continuity which leads toward more mature selves and higher social action.

Vol. XXXIX—p. 114 (Nov. 1962)

Excellence Is Relative

BY LOUIS E. RATHS

What is excellence? Whom is it for? Who makes criteria for judging it? When is excellence appropriate? Louis E. Raths is distinguished service professor, Newark State College, Union, New Jersey.

WE FREQUENTLY SAY TO CHILDREN: "YOU SHOULD ALWAYS DO YOUR best." Should we? Does the teacher always dress her "best"? Does she always write her best? If we are trying to develop discriminating judgment in children, we foresee a time when they will sense that a situation calls for the very best that is within them to give. It isn't the rigid, compulsive, *ALWAYS BEST* that will give intelligent direction to life. Excellence carries with it the idea of its appropriateness: in time, circumstance and the needs of the situation.

When a child is playing with someone younger who proves to be less competent, should he play his best and overwhelm his playmate? The situation calls for discrimination, for adjustment to the many factors involved. The compulsive "always best" child will meet many situations more complicated than this, and no easy formula can be his best guide.

We sometimes associate the idea of excellence with individuals who win in competitive aspects of life. It is quite easy to get the idea that those who win have indeed exhibited excellence. As teachers, we know that many winners secured their awards through factors other than excellence. It is a difficult task to help children develop their *own* ideas of what constitutes excellence *for them.*

We say to a child, "You can do better than that." Perhaps he can, but it may indeed represent his very best efforts. How do we know so surely that he can do better?

Excellence for Whom?

This raises the question of excellence for whom? If the criteria for excellence lie outside the growing child, he may be at the mercy of a number of adults with greatly varying expectations of excellence. The principal may disagree with the teacher, and both may be at odds with the parents; all three may be far removed from the child's own conception of what constitutes excellence. In a free society we prize variety in individual expression. We prize it more when the child's own ideas become part of the totality of choices from which he may finally decide what is best. We prize it less when these various standards of excellence are absolutes, absolutes in conflict with each other.

In our relations with children, we adults seem to be operating on the assumption that excellence is in hiding and that on demand, threat or coercion we can bring it forth. If we press too hard, ask for too much, expect what is not there at this time and place, we may be inducing fear, shame, guilt and even fear of trying. The very idea of excellence must seem remote to many children: an aspiration, perhaps, but not something to be achieved in this next half hour or tomorrow.

We want children to prize excellence—when it means a great deal; we want children to choose what is excellent—when the choice makes a real difference and when it has significance for them; we want children to get in the habit of wanting and choosing what is excellent—when this habit gives direction to life that is fluid and flexible and takes into consideration the many factors that impinge on their life situations. We want children to have excellence penetrate into their living in such a manner that criteria are often discussed and what is judged to be excellent will be chosen, bought, used, collected, read, until it becomes a part of their very nature.

Best Must Do Honor to Child

How can we best do this?

- A fourth-grade teacher asked all children to submit three drawings from their year's work which they thought were their best. The teacher then made a first choice of the three and entered these drawings in a county-wide art exhibit. One boy's drawing won a high award, and the teacher was proud of her student. He wished that she had chosen a different one. He was explicit and firm in his rejection of this particular drawing as his "best." The teacher was even more pleased with *her* choice when she told him that it had won an award and that he was to go to the art exhibit and get the award in person. She was literally astounded when he said that he would not go, that he thought the picture was not very good and undeserving of a prize.

This boy had developed his own ideas of what constituted excellence. His teacher's ideas may have been superior, but they were not his and he stuck with his own. He could not accept an honor which he deemed unmerited. This picture did not honor him in his view, and when the award came it was not accepted as honoring him. He believed that his teacher's judgment was poor.

• A fifth grade had just had a spelling test, and the children had exchanged papers and corrected them. One child asked the teacher what she thought of his paper. "What do you think of it, Tom?" she asked. He replied, "I don't know how to tell when something is real good." "Well, you got them all right, didn't you, Tom, and that's excellent." "Oh, everybody gets them all right," the boy said.

There was no further questioning about the situation. Tom might have been interpreting excellence as "superior to others in the class." When he was not unique, he was puzzled about the rating of "excellent." He may have been rejecting the idea that the only criterion of excellence was to get them all spelled correctly. He may have been trying to find out the teacher's criteria for excellence in a spelling paper. He found out and didn't feel that they were adequate.

We sometimes say to children that nobody really achieves excellence unless he works hard at his task. Maybe and maybe not. Surely to try hard doesn't achieve excellence by itself. To put it down as a criterion of excellence or a prerequisite to excellence is to oversimplify and perhaps to muddle the situation. We need to help children to identify criteria for excellence. We will not accomplish much with slogans.

The culture which surrounds the growing child is confusing with its many standards of excellence. Is it excellent or a sign of excellence to do something *first?* Or is this act to be judged in terms of a variety of criteria of excellence? If found to be excellent, then and only then will the fact of being first get some added value.

With our centuries-old emphasis upon *bigness,* children sometimes get the idea that bigger houses are better houses, that bigger schools are better schools, that quantity determines quality. Whenever this shows up in class, can we discuss the point? Can we raise questions about what makes something excellent? If we can, we are on the way toward the development of criteria which children may apply to new situations.

Speed is another commonly accepted single indicator of excellence among children. To finish something ahead of everyone else, to get there first, to get things done quickly—this is a goal to be achieved. We should ask about the urgency of the situation. Was speed necessary in this case? Why? What made speed important in this case? And in cases where time is of the essence, let us by all means include it in our criteria for judging the excellence of the work.

Still another single indicator of excellence is *cost* in terms of money. Many children have the idea that those things are excellent which cost the most. While there may be something in this as a general idea, it is useless to apply this generalization to a particular case and judge it to be excellent *because* it is most expensive. Here again we see the need for working with children in the development of criteria for judging excellence. It is a slow process and it has to be repetitive. Wherever choices are possible in the classroom, it is then possible to raise the question of criteria for choosing. In these daily discussions of what makes things excellent, children share their ideas with each other. They learn to reflect before making generalizations about excellence. They come to have ideas of their own about how to judge.

On some occasions we want to say to a child that a particular piece of work is excellent because it is so much better than what he did previously. Is "excellence" associated with progress or is it applied only to the finished product? Judgment of excellence sometimes means excellent for Johnnie at this time and in this place. We see the judgment as a reward for achievement that surpasses previous achievement.

Factors in Judging Excellence

As a child grows into the world in which he lives, he tries to make some order out of it. He learns from his experiences and generalizes from them. He listens and tries to make sense out of what his elders tell him. As he chooses and reflects upon the bases for his choices, as he listens to other people defend their judgments, he comes to have criteria of his own. We need to caution him about the dangers of judging excellence: so many great critics have been wrong in their judgments! We don't really know how to teach him to make judgments: how to weigh the different criteria, how to integrate them, how to give the one or two the central importance due them in a particular situation. Our faith lies in a curriculum where there is rich opportunity to choose, to set forth criteria for choosing, to weigh, to decide, and to share one's thinking with others. We have plumped for the freer society, and only time will tell whether this produces a high order of excellence. We have faith that it does and that it will.

To Wonder and To Ponder

BY JAMES S. TIPPETT

Have you ever stopped to ponder on the variety and multitude of experiences in life today? Have you ever stopped to wonder how children can even begin to undertake the enormous task of seeing relationships in their experiences? James S. Tippett is an educator and poet from Chapel Hill, North Carolina.

IN STATIC SOCIETIES, RANGING FROM PRIMITIVE TO HIGHLY CULTIVATED, children are turned into exact replicas of adults as quickly as possible. Individual differences, creative urges and changing patterns are not tolerated. This was the condition against which Rousseau struggled in France near the end of the eighteenth century. It is the condition that *still* exists—even in the democratic societies Rousseau and other creative minds have helped to advance. Children and society suffer from this condition. They are molded too soon—with no time to find themselves, with no time to fulfill their potentialities of becoming.

These statements do not imply that changing democratic societies have no ideals for their children. On the contrary, their ideals are far reaching and demanding. They lead into realms of intellectual development, physical and spiritual growth, and cultural patterns. Adult leaders in these societies want children to read and enjoy books that *they* have read and enjoyed; to master skills essential in general activities of life; to make progress in fitting themselves for responsible vocational and family life; to act as well-adjusted adults in polite social settings; and, indeed, to become adults with characteristics of the society's heroes.

Leading to Better Growth

The term "democratic society" is currently not in good repute. Its claims are not always justified in the group which applies the term. It cannot rightly be applied to any society which does not respect individuals as personalities or which does not give them full scope for development—the kind which does not harm the growing, self-regulating society. A democratic society looks for future progress to creative possibilities of its individual children and to the already functioning possibilities of adults. If it cramps their full development, it defeats its best chances for improvement through best suggestions for change. "Democratic society" is a good term when it truly means growth leading to constantly better growth of its members and of its total self.

Time and Opportunities

Individual possibilities may never be discovered if the child is plunged at once into set adult patterns. A lawyer wishes his newborn son to become a lawyer. A talented pianist wishes her baby daughter to become another Myra Hess. A successful business community sees financial success as the one desirable goal for its children. Each of these may so arrange educational opportunities and processes as to smother all chances for profit from social workers, pure scientists or poets. Individual possibilities may never be discovered if the environment is limited. Today's world suffers in its social development because of the provincial outlook of a vast majority of people. Small communities are handicapped by even a few narrow-visioned inhabitants. Many individuals have not found themselves because they grew up and are living in gossiping, self-centered and self-satisfied groups. It takes a wealth of opportunities and an abundance of time for the self to discover and develop its true potentials.

A child at birth has only possibilities. It may grow physically, mentally, morally, creatively and spiritually. To grow in any way, time is required; time and opportunities—and inborn possibilities. Discouragements resulting from individual differences in inborn possibilities are frustrating and often tragic. Not every baby girl can become a Cleopatra or a Pavlova. Nor can every baby boy become an Apollo or an Einstein. Some will not be able to talk intelligibly, to sing or to read. Inborn possibilities present a "bugaboo" to educators—in the schoolroom, in the home, in the community. It should not prevent every baby from having opportunities and time to develop his potentialities to the fullest extent for individual and group benefits.

Physical growth is now receiving deserved attention from child care specialists, informed parents, dieticians, physicians, research scientists, and athletic and recreational directors. Child labor was banned in part because of need for time to grow physically. There is *still need for better* local and world-wide distribution of food supplies, for more provisions for recreational facilities and for scientific research in control of disease. However, in *this* area time and opportunities for best physical growth are coming into focus.

Growth in mental, moral, social and spiritual areas especially for children (but also for any adults) is hampered by lack of time, rather than the proper use of time and by failure to use opportunities. It takes time to wonder in placing one's self in proper relation to that self to the social environment and to the huge, changing world. The child in his growth from baby non-consciousness to well-considered beginnings of adult relations must have time to wonder. He must have time to understand what he is and why he is.

The baby is a living thing. That fact he must discover during his process of growth. He is surrounded by a world of other living things and he soon finds that he must try to understand actions of others. He is also in a world of things that are not alive but which can be manipulated either advantageously or the reverse. Behaviors, attitudes and ideas surround him. All these items and many more combine to give him gradual inklings of what he is. A constant occupation of mind and spirit throughout the extent of his life will be to wonder why he is.

Understanding Relationships

No one during a lifetime has yet come to know the world around him in all its details. Knowing the world of the physical—people, light, animals, earth, water, air, plants and space—offers a first and a continuing challenge to wonder. The baby and the young child necessarily slowly develop "an apperceptive mass" of experiences and understandings, beginning with absolutely nothing, but with possibilities for both. Except under most expert guidance many valuable experiences and understandings will be missed. Readiness for further exploration and learning will be curtailed to the extent that backgrounds of experiences are limited. Immediate learning can amount to little if time to place *new* experiences in relationship to similar experiences is not provided. A learning about the natural world—perhaps an experience with light, water or a pet—needs to be enlarged and related to similar experiences. Too often the small child (the adult also) is dragged or pushed rapidly from one experience to another. Confusion results from lack of time to wonder, to place each item of experience in understood relationships to many other items.

The mechanical world also offers its challenges and adds greatly to the quantity of experiences. If these experiences are to be meaningful, they must be placed in relationships. Gadgets that move, lights that turn off and on, or tools that help make work easier can be placed in relation to something that will not move or to a light that will not turn off and on or to tools that make use of other or the same scientific principles—*if* time and opportunities are allowed for manipulation, experimentation and verbal exploration. The mere thought of the diversity and the multiplicity of all a baby has to experience and learn about the natural and mechanical world before he is ready for kindergarten or even for living successfully at four or five makes one pause in wonder that such an enormous task can be accomplished.

The world of ideas about things and behavior becomes still more of a cause for wonder. The natural and mechanical world can generally be relied upon to respond as first experiences with it indicate that it will. Mental and social responses may vary greatly and complicate learning where they are involved. Well-adjusted adults are often puzzled by variations in mental and social attitudes and responses of individuals in relation to defined and understood common experiences. The inexperienced young child is undoubtedly much more bewildered. Snap judgments are likely to be made and faulty patterns of behavior adopted if time is not available for broad, careful and continuous evaluations and re-evaluations of observations, experiments, actions and results in connection with experiences and consequent learnings.

Time is not the only factor which enters into growth in understanding all the diversities presented by any environment. Another important factor is informed and democratic leadership. Under such leadership time is always allowed for full savoring of every experience and for full development of every creative urge, every individual expression and every possibility for growth.

Leaders who accept the following challenge and put it into effect will assure children of time to find out something of the *why* and *wherefore* of themselves and of their environments—of time to wonder and to ponder. They too will have additional opportunities and time to live and learn; time to understand themselves, children and the world to the mutual good of all.

Challenge to Leadership

A child came to me seeking;
He would find himself.

Not mine the task to fashion him,
To mold him in old ways I knew.
So would he be ridiculous,
A little mimic pattern of myself.

Rather my joy to lead him
To fresh pastures,
Succulent from all the rich inheritance
His race had nurtured;
There to help him fit
Each new experience
To the proper niche for his own being
While he made advance
Into some new creative rhapsody,
Some inner freedom
That would make of him
An asset to the social whole,
And equally a self
Harmonious with its own design
As are the flowers and leaves
That help to paint
Some perfect picture of the spring.

—JAMES S. TIPPETT

A Good Beginning Has No End

BY LAWRENCE K. FRANK

Lawrence K. Frank, lecturer-consultant-author, is a former director of the Caroline Zachry Institute of New York.

Growth, development and learning, and the emergence of the human personality are cumulative processes, each step or stage giving rise to the next. Thus later developments may be compromised by deprivation of the early experiences essential to wholesome healthy development and learning.

The great significance of a good beginning for the human child becomes clear when we realize that the infant, as a young mammalian organism, must be transformed by early care and rearing into a personality, capable of living in a symbolic cultural world and participating in our social order. To sustain that transformation, the child needs confidence in the world or basic trust, as Erikson says, especially in people; he also needs courage to cope with the series of life tasks confronting him as he grows older and meets the world outside his home.

If the child is prematurely or too severely curbed in his bodily functioning and his naive impulsive behavior, if he is not adequately nourished and cared for, if he is denied love, comforting and respect for his integrity and his dignity as a helpless child, he may go forward with a heavy burden of "unfinished business" and a chronic feeling of resentment or guilt that will compromise all his later learning.

Thus, in the years before school the child develops his basic orientation to life and learns the fundamental lessons of living in our society and in our culture, always as interpreted and translated to him by his family and as he individually understands and feels what he experiences. Fortunate is the child whose family provides the "psychological vitamins" of love, affection, patient understanding and especially recognition of his unique individuality—neither expecting what he is not capable of nor depriving him of what he individually needs to become a healthy personality.

We can say with ample evidence that the best preparation for tomorrow is to live fully today. The best preparation for the runabout is to let the baby live fully as a baby, to function and behave spontaneously until he individually is ready to give up his infantile activities. The best preparation for a preschool child is to let the runabout be a runabout, to live fully on that level so that he will be ready and eager to go on to the next stage of his development, prepared to cope with new tasks and opportunities awaiting him as a preschooler.

The preschooler's best preparation for school is to be provided with all the opportunities he needs to live and learn as a preschooler, to experience widely and intensely what is relevant and appropriate to that stage. The current pressure by parents to start academic work in nursery school and kindergarten means robbing the child of his childhood, depriving him of learning by direct experience and by spontaneous activity which he needs if he is to cope effectively with requirements of academic programs later.

Most of the difficulties children exhibit when they enter school reflect their preschool experiences—deprivations and coercions that have not only denied them opportunities to live as young children but have often established lifelong feelings of discouragement, timidity, resistance, sometimes chronic hostility toward adults, which they display to teachers and all school learning.

Perhaps we can persuade parents to reformulate their ideas and expectations about early childhood education and school by accepting what John Dewey and Arthur F. Bentley proposed some years ago. In their book, *Knowing and the Known,* they urged that we discard the ancient idea of knowledge as some kind of mysterious substance which has to be acquired or imparted and replace that metaphysical notion with the concept of "knowing" as a dynamic transactional relation which the knower establishes with the known or to be known.

Thus, we can think of the child starting at birth, if not before, beginning to relate himself cognitively to the world and people; progressively learning to establish "knowing" relations by his sensory apparatus, especially through touch, with his mouth, his hands and his feet, then through language and speech, then through concepts and ideas. Each kind of "knowing" provides the basis for the succeeding modes of "knowing" or relating himself to the world, as he learns first to cope with the physical world of space-time, of objects, animals, places and also persons, then begins to relate himself cognitively to symbols through language and concepts which become significant only as he has had actual experiences to make those symbols, especially written words, meaningful to him.

When a child enters first grade he often suffers from a variety of cognitive or conceptual errors. The kindergarten and the nursery school can be of immense help by providing what may be called "cognitive therapy"; that is, helping the child to give up his misconceptions, erroneous assumptions and distorted ideas so that he can replace them with more valid, correct concepts in his "knowing" relations with the world.

Just as the child can play out his fantasies and his feelings, so he can be helped to play out his concepts and to revise them before they become crystallized and difficult to alter, as usually happens in elementary schools.

Many children, unfortunately, do not have good beginnings at home. The nursery school, the kindergarten and the elementary school can, if teachers are alert to this need, provide much help in overcoming these poor beginnings, especially by giving the child renewed self-confidence and courage. They can help in replacing those early patterns that may increasingly become handicaps if not revised while the child is still capable of unlearning.

Significance of Kindergarten Education
BY HELEN HEFFERNAN

This was a talk given to Connecticut teachers in the fall of 1959. The Association for Childhood Education International and many states are working to establish nursery schools as well as kindergartens as children's first school experience. Helen Heffernan, chief, Bureau of Elementary Education, California State Department of Education, Sacramento, is chairman of the Editorial Board of CHILDHOOD EDUCATION.

What Is the Kindergarten?

THE KINDERGARTEN IS THE IMPORTANT BEGINNING OF A CHILD'S SCHOOL experience. Before his first day in kindergarten, the child has lived largely within his family group, with brief excursions into his neighborhood and wider world. He has had little experience in social living. Now he is suddenly confronted with a multitude of new adjustments. He goes forth at a regular time to new exciting experiences. Here his role is changed. Here he must gain acceptance for himself as a participating member of his peer group. For his comfort and security, he must establish satisfying relationships with at least one or two other children. He must adjust to a new adult—his teacher. Her ways may differ considerably from those of his parents.

The child finds himself in a more spacious and less intimate environment than he has previously known. Many new and attractive objects must be shared with others rather than appropriated for his own exclusive use. Many strange and fear-inspiring objects must be judiciously inspected and tentatively tried out to see how well he can control them.

The degree to which the child makes all these adjustments with happiness and confidence depends upon many factors.

How the child adjusts to a new situation depends, for instance, on his social maturity. His behavior shows his teacher how far he has come in learning to get along with others. Is he accustomed to finding himself in a strange situation, or does he withdraw from it and cling to some symbol of security? Does he start right in on an activity by himself, or does he watch what others do? Is his approach to the situation primarily with the other children or with the materials provided?

The kindergarten teacher must answer these—and many more questions—about each child. Each one is a unique personality. To work effectively, the kindergarten teacher must know each child well—his home background, his mother, his father—because education is a joint enterprise of home and school. The better the teacher knows each child, the better can she serve him. The better she knows the child, the more likely is she to start where he is in his development and to have reasonable expectations of the progress he can make.

For how large a group of kindergarten-age children can a thoroughly qualified teacher come to know the needs of each and provide appropriate learning experiences? Probably no specific number is wholly defensible; the number depends on the physical environment, the degree of parent participation, the qualities of the teacher. Experience would lead me to wish not more than twenty to twenty-five children in a single session of three or four hours with adequate time available for frequent conferences with parents and adequate preparation for the children's learning experiences.

Can America afford such an educational program for its young children? America, with 7 per cent of the world's population and between 40 and 50 per cent of the world's wealth, can afford any kind of education we wish for our children. We spend less than 4 per cent of our gross national income on all education; Russia spends twice as much. Little Norway spends over 13 per cent of its national income on education. It is a question of how much we as a people value education and how knowledgeable we are about the strategic importance of these early years of life in determining the future personality, intellectual capacity, and emotional adjustment of the child.

How Important Is the Kindergarten Teacher?

The major factor in how children adjust to the kindergarten is without doubt the teacher. The teacher whom every parent wants to guide his child is a person who understands and loves children and who has had the professional education necessary to carry on a sound program. The teacher has grave responsibility in helping children to become a part of their social world, so she must be a broadly educated person in terms of knowledge and appreciation of our culture. The perceptive teacher knows that the application of science to technology is changing the world in which the child will live at a tremendously accelerated pace. So, the teacher has grave responsibility in helping the child to understand his scientific environment and to expect and accept change.

The teacher knows that all the interests that make life rich and abundant for the child must be nurtured early; so she is interested in art and literature, in music and bodily rhythms. She has learned ways to stimulate children to similar interests.

The teacher knows the importance of the environment the kindergarten provides and how equipment and materials contribute to the child's development.

She knows, too, that despite her years of *professional preparation,* her education as a kindergarten teacher is unending just as the education of a physician, an engineer or a teacher dedicated to any level of human development is unending. Research and the experience of frontier workers are adding to our fund of knowledge about children and how to foster optimum development.

And so the good kindergarten teacher looks forward to a *professional life* in which she never ceases to be a learner. Some of this learning will be through planned formal study in colleges and universities, some in informal study groups with professional colleagues and parents. But above all, the professional growth of the teacher will take place through increasingly insightful observation of the children with whom she works. *Professionally, no teacher's task is more difficult than that of the kindergarten teacher and no service is more socially significant to the future of our nation and our world.*

On the *personal side* of the ledger, living with children of kindergarten age is strenuous business and requires vigorous health, energy galore, buoyant spirits and enjoyment of the outdoors.

To live with kindergarten children three or four hours a day, five days a week for 180 or more days a year, a kindergarten teacher must really *love* four- to six-year-old children. She must enjoy trying to understand them and to work with them. If wriggling, shuffling of feet, an unrestrained yawn or scratching bothers her, if subject matter is more interesting to her than people, she has chosen the wrong niche in life and should seek some more congenial occupation. But, if she really sees each child as a fascinating individual, wants to have some part in helping him realize his potentialities and find his place in the physical and social world about him, she will be rewarded by the personal satisfaction she experiences in the growth and development of children.

Much more could be said about the kindergarten teacher. Although she may not be beautiful by Hollywood standards, she can be the most beautiful woman in the world in the eyes of the fours and fives. They will imitate her manners, acquire her vocabulary and voice quality, accept her ideals and love what she finds admirable. How better could any human being invest a life!

But warm, outgoing and accepting as the good teacher is in her relations with children, *the time has come when she must stand up and be counted on certain issues. The restlessness and anxiety of our times have been expressed in trying to force down in the curriculum learnings for which the child is neither physiologically or psychologically ready and for which he sees no need. We have a mountain of evidence to prove that a perfectly "normal" child—IQ 100—cannot learn to read until he is about six years, six months old. Any attempt to drive him may result in some evidence of reading but at an excessive cost in physiological and psychological damage and at great risk of impairment of his interest in reading. When the time comes he can master it readily.*

What Learning Experiences Should the Kindergarten Provide?

This leads us to ask: What learning experiences should the kindergarten provide? What is a proper curriculum in terms of what is now well known about the characteristics of fours and fives? The answers to these questions engage the attention of well-qualified experts in all parts of our country.

No human being is born with the learnings which enable him adequately to take his place in the world about him. *The modern world is far too complex to hope that the process of growing up will equip the child with the learnings he requires to make a successful adjustment to life.* His quality as a person and his contribution to the social groups of which he is a part are determined by the experiences he has and the opportunities they provide him for learning. The quantity and quality of education are important. *Of great significance are the initial social, intellectual and emotional experiences of early childhood.* In these years, the child meets and, in some manner, solves many of the persistent life situations that command our attention. For example, he must learn to get along with his family and later with other people beyond the family circle; he must learn basic health and safety behaviors in order to survive; he must acquire skills of oral communication sufficient to meet increasingly insistent needs; he must begin to find answers to his questions as his increasing power of locomotion brings him into firsthand contact with his physical and social environment.

The curriculum for the young child is as broad as life itself. The major aim is to help him make the best adjustment to life that is possible for a human being of his potentialities. In situations conducive to learning, the child is encouraged to extend his experience and, in the process, find himself. He is encouraged to use the concrete materials provided so he may deepen his understanding through his sensory impressions. The kindergarten affords the young child an environment in which it is safe for him to be himself, to learn to live with his peers, to interact freely with an environment planned and arranged by professionally well-prepared adults who understand the nature and needs of young children.

The teacher is continually testing the quality of education being provided by asking herself questions like these about the changed behavior of the children:

Are they healthier?
Have they found better ways of relating themselves to other children and adults?
Have they gained power over the skills of communication?
Are they more independent?
Are they able to accept more responsibility for their own care and behavior?
Are they understanding more about their physical world?
Are they understanding more about the world of science?

A good kindergarten program should contribute ten significant things to every child. It should help him:

. . . maintain and develop optimum health
. . . further his physical development
. . . extend his understanding of the social world
. . . enter into his scientific world
. . . grow in understanding of spatial and quantitative relationships
. . . expand his control of language
. . . know and enjoy his literary heritage
. . . express himself esthetically through art media
. . . become acquainted with and learn to enjoy his musical heritage
. . . establish satisfying relationships with children and adults.

If the kindergartens in America achieve these purposes as fully as it is possible in serving each child, we will have no margin of time to "toughen up" the kindergarten program as some unwise but loudly vocal persons demand. People who have devoted their lives to studying young children must not be stampeded into unwise action by superficial and uninformed critics.

What Are the Real Problems?

Improvement *can* be made in kindergarten education. Professional and lay people who wish to bring about constructive change have a clear mandate. We know *now* what changes are needed. We know the real problems of early childhood education.

First, in every community in our country we should take a good look at the physical facilities we are providing for kindergarten education.

Anyone really concerned with improving kindergarten education should take a good straight look at facilities. Nothing the teacher can do will make a seven-year-old of a five-year-old which is in line with the recommendations of some of the critics, but we can do something about improving the conditions of learning so each child may achieve the optimum development for which he is ready.

Second, we should take a good straight look at the provisions for health in our kindergartens. Do we provide medical history and examination before school entrance? Are immunizations provided? Do we provide for daily health inspection? Have we facilities for isolation of a child who shows symptoms of a cold or other illness? Are conditions of ventilation, temperature and sanitation conducive to optimum health? Is a planned nutrition program provided? Are facilities for comfortable rest provided? Is equipment in first-class condition from point of view of safety? Are routine height and weight measurements taken monthly? These are all specific questions we need to ask and answer. We can do something about all of these problems. But somehow the critics show little interest in these down-to-earth questions about which we can do something.

Third, we should take another look at the play equipment and materials we provide in our kindergartens. Have we adequate equipment for active play to promote motor skills—jungle gym, swings, boxes, boards, kegs, wagons, tricycles, wheelbarrows and the like? Have we adequate materials for manipulation and construction—blocks, sand box, clay, wood and tools, puzzles? Have we adequate material to stimulate dramatic play—housekeeping furniture and toys, telephones, locomotive toys, easels and paints, musical instruments, picture books, materials for science experiences?

We can do something about all these things. We can buy them. Mothers and fathers can help us make them. But in some situations where parents are demanding more opportunities for their children in kindergarten, the environmental materials are sparse.

Fourth, as is the teacher, so is the kindergarten. We need to take a good straight look at the problem of personnel.

Obviously, the good kindergarten teacher is a trained professional person. She has a sympathetic understanding of children. She is resourceful in developing environmental factors rich in educational possibilities. She can develop good learning situations. She recognizes individual differences and meets individual needs. She can minimize the tension and strain which inevitably accompany learning. She protects children from danger. She manages routines so they do not take up an inordinate amount of time.

Can we find enough such paragons of all the virtues to staff our kindergartens? We *can*, but there are some things we need to do about it. We need to accept and practice the policy of twenty-five children in a single session as the maximum teacher load. We need to establish preservice professional education programs comparable in length and quality to the professional education of any elementary or secondary teacher. We need to pay salaries sufficient to attract and hold teachers of the highest qualifications. And we need to get over the unproved belief—the myth—that "anyone can teach little children." The competencies required to teach young children are equivalent to those required for successful teaching at any level.

Fifth, we need to improve home-school cooperation. This includes initial conferences with the parents before the child's entrance into school, encouragement of parental observations, informal home visits, individual conferences with parents at least twice a year, group meetings of parents and teachers, provision of a parents' circulating library.

Sixth, we need to be continually concerned about the curriculum. The kindergarten teacher is no "baby sitter" but a thoroughly qualified educator engaged in (1) facilitating learning about (and from) the physical and natural environment; (2) facilitating learning about (and from) people and their activities; (3) facilitating health and habits of self-care; and (4) facilitating esthetic experience and creative activity in industrial and fine arts, music and literature.

As a people, we need to recognize the social significance of the education of young children. No task is more important to the future welfare of our world. We need to put to full use what we know about the growth and development of children, not only in our guidance of the children entrusted to our care but in working with their mothers and fathers. We don't know everything about how human beings learn, but that is not to say we know nothing about how human beings learn. We know a considerable amount about the signs of readiness for learning. We know that learning occurs in sequence; what a child can learn today depends upon what he already knows. We know that children are different one from the other and the rate of learning differs from child to child. We know learning is an active, seeking process. We know that a child must think well of himself in order to learn effectively.

Efforts are being made to deny these facts by uninformed persons in our society. The profession must stand firm on the considerable knowledge we possess and move into innovations only on the basis of pilot studies designed to test hypotheses. Many of the critics applaud the work of the scientist in our modern world but advocate changes in educational content and procedure without regard for the need of a period of careful testing similar to that followed by the scientist. The decade ahead will be one of great progress in early childhood education if we proceed to make improvements in terms of the principles now firmly established about what constitutes a sound kindergarten program.

Adults Look at Children's Values
BY BERNICE MILBURN MOORE

This thought-provoking article will help the adult look at his own values and see his role in helping children develop their values. Bernice Milburn Moore is consultant, Home and Family Life Education, Texas Education Agency and the Hogg Foundation for Mental Hygiene, University of Texas, Austin.

"Play like" is a favorite game of children. Like much of play, the significance is far greater than appears on the surface. Emotional conflict is often detected by close observation; so also does it reveal values a child is beginning to accept.

Values are initially taken over from members of the family, and they reflect in turn the culture from which they come. While values do change from generation to generation, there is a residue handed down from family group to family group. Moreover, the school and the church, as well as other social institutions, add their weight to the value pattern which will be taken over in part by children. Children, therefore, tend to "play like" those whom they want to be like and those actions which they sense as acceptable to important older people.

An indication of developing maturity is the ability to set and work toward long-range goals. Young children find it very difficult to wait patiently to become like older persons whom they admire. They attempt immediate attainment by imitating what they would immediately like to be. "Superman" has the power to escape from the limiting confines of earthly demand. Realistic parents make many down-to-earth demands. The youngster, in his imagination, becomes "Superman" and thereby escapes into the never-never land of effortlessly becoming what he wants to be.

"I want to be like" is a step in development toward maturity. When youth reach this stage, they are indicating their acceptance of the fact that to realize a goal, it is essential to work toward it. If imaginative play is carried over into day-dreaming instead of planning for goal attainment as children develop toward maturity, then there is evidence of maladjustment. Parents and teachers have a real contribution to make in the transition from play to planning by helping young persons establish realistic and attainable goals, by encouraging them and by making clear that the ability to work efficiently and effectively is a worth-while value in itself.

Values as Priorities

Values, as Kimball Young describes them, are a combination of ideas and attitudes which give priority or preference to certain goals. These goals or values take the place of high importance to the personality. Moreover, when values are established, then action and behavior are set into a priority system which is determined by whether or not they lead toward the desired goal.

The values one lives by, then, become needs in the person's life and motivation to work or strive toward meeting these needs. So values tend to control behavior as well as to motivate it.

Values are, therefore, both positive and negative. Each personality holds certain goals as dear and others to be rigorously avoided. Which are held dear and which avoided in large measure depend upon the value pattern of the family. Consistency in positive and negative values indicates their incorporation into personality and sets the stage for predictable behavior.

Values and the Culture Pattern

Values do vary from family to family. However, these variations are within the wider framework of what is generally accepted by groups within the culture and by the culture as a whole. The culture of the United States is distinctive in the values which are considered basic to its way of life. "The American way of life" is derived by a unique combination of the religious teachings of love, kindliness and cooperation with the frontier values of individualistic achievement, competition and the aggressive pursuit of personal success. How to balance this dichotomy of values so that it does not become the source of conflict in children and youth is one of the complex problems of education in the family and in the schools.

That these value patterns, as different as they are, have been reconciled successfully is indicated by emphasis upon individual differences and at the same time upon effective group functioning. Technological and ideological achievements of this "free enterprise-democratic culture" are evidences of the blending of the contribution of different personalities toward the well-being of all. The cultivation of distinctive personalities, each one different and each one having the right to be different, offers opportunity for imaginative creativity. From this creativity has come group productivity which has made this nation the richest in material goods, but even more important, the richest in its ideal of free men working together for common good.

This says each child should come to value and respect his fellowmen. Each child should be motivated by a feeling of good will and by basic consideration of others. Each child should have opportunity to cultivate his ability to live with, work with, and get along with others. At the same time, his motivation must include the development of his own abilities in order that he may make a real contribution to his world. It must contribute to recognition of his responsibility for his own behavior and his behavior toward others. It must help him to mobilize and use his energy toward the achievement of a feeling of personal worth but always in relation to the worth of others.

Cross-Cultural Likenesses

Cultural anthropologists have discovered that though values and their expression do differ from culture to culture, cross-cultural likenesses do exist: ". . . no culture has made of human suffering an end of or for itself; nowhere is indiscriminate lying or cheating within the group approved . . . 'in all human societies there is a basic view that it is good as a general rule to attempt to preserve human life.' "

"Honor thy father and thy mother" also appears to be near universal at least through pre-adolescence. One may hazard the guess that "honor thy father and thy mother" is broadly adhered to because it is living with honorable and creditable parents that children come to accept this same goodness as a part of their own value pattern. Values have been defined by Whiting and Child *"as a custom* (or customary way of behaving) *whose response attributes goodness or badness to some event."* When the event is considered good, it becomes a goal to be sought. If it is bad, then it is avoided.

Values become group standards and determine social practice. They take on the label good or bad, right or wrong, positive or negative. Learning to make value judgments is an important lesson every person must learn, and the beginning of this learning takes place in childhood.

Imitation as Practice

Imitation is practice in behavior. From imitating adults whom they admire, children gradually come to identify with them and with their values. Values, at first imitated, gradually become integrated into the personality. They then become guides for behavior and motivation toward desired ends.

A series of studies reported in the *Source Book of Social Psychology* indicates a close relationship between value orientation and the impression one has of self and of others. R. Stagner, in a research study on the psychological aspects of industrial conflict, divided a group of students into pro-labor and anti-labor groups. They were asked to check on a list of traits, those which characterized factory workers and executives. They then marked traits which they thought they themselves had. Finally they checked those characteristics which they considered pleasant or unpleasant. The pro-labor students saw in workers many of the same traits they had and described them as pleasant. The anti-labor group gave these same traits to executives and to themselves. This would seem to indicate that values which are important to a person he tends to see in others whom he likes or admires. One remembers that children first imitate values they would like to have and finally emulate them in their own behavior.

Children in many instances tend to see in their teachers those qualities which they like in their parents and which are in process of becoming a part of their own personalities.

Values and Predictable Behavior

Children need direct control from mature adults in their formative years. Discipline at this stage of development cannot be too subtle or evasive. The emotional security in children depends upon having definite boundaries within which they must live. Crossing these boundaries comes to be understood as going from the good and acceptable to the bad and unacceptable. Values become established when parents are consistent and predictable in what they will approve as good and what they immediately react to as bad.* When there is fluctuation in reaction to the same behavior, there is no opportunity for the child to come to recognize what is of negative or positive value.

Predictable behavior depends upon values consistently held and lived by. Children are obliged to accept values set by adults. They do not have the experience out of which to determine whether their behavior is suitable to a given situation. It is only when adults define for the child whether how he has acted is good or bad that the child comes to understand what is expected in a given situation.

Many values are obligatory. Through long experience and practice society has determined values which seem consistently to be necessary for the well-being of its members. However, where obligatory values are preponderant, society is autocratic. On the other hand, every society has certain values which its members must hold, but at the same time has a wide range of permissive goals which each person may choose for himself. The range of permissive goals in a dictatorial society is limited. Permissive goals in a democratic society are in the ascendancy.

Children live by obligatory values set by their parents. As they develop and have wider experiences they are allowed to set more and more of their own values. Maturity itself in a democratic society might be measured by a preponderance of permissive goals with a basic value structure taken over from parents and from the culture as transmitted by them.

---

* "Good" and "bad" as here used imply acceptable or unacceptable and do not necessarily have moral significance.

When the authority of parents fades into the rigid authority of the state in values to be lived by, a dictatorship exists. When the authority of parents gradually gives way as children become able to discriminate and make choices in values, the democratic process is at work. Emotional and social maturity imply the ability to use judgment in choice of values and goals of long or short range.

Many values are transitory. They change from generation to generation, from stage of development to stage of development. These do not have either the importance or tenacity of those values which have come to be understood as destructive or constructive to the ongoing of a culture or society. Sometimes conflicts between adults and youth come about because the adults tend to place a quality that the actual transitory value does not possess. What is conventional becomes confused with what is valuable. An expression of this confusion is most often indicated by the statement, "youth is not what it used to be." Yet when demands are made upon the younger generation to sustain the basic value pattern in which they have been raised, they willingly will die for it in order that others may be privileged to live under these same values.

Permissiveness in nonessential values which are of short duration eases the acceptance of basic values of long duration. Discrimination and consistency in values which are held as obligatory by parents and teachers will go far to entrench these values in the lives of children and youth. When these become cluttered and unclear by confusion with nonessentials, their impact upon children and youth is dimmed.

Values themselves are integrating factors in personality. As the person internalizes the values with which he is identified, they become his conscience. If he disregards his basic values his guilt feeling will be relieved only when his behavior once again becomes reconciled with his priorities. Freud saw externalized values internalized as the super-ego, and the super-ego as the controlling mechanism of the social self. Self-regard, so essential to the mental health of any personality, comes about when behavior reflects socially acceptable and basic values.

Sometimes real values become concealed by the opposite in behavior. A child holds as a value recognition and acceptance by his peers. If the child does not gain these desired ends, very often the values remain stable but the means to the end become boisterous and unattractive behavior. When this occurs, it is the responsibility of the adult to help this young person to get his behavior back on the track toward the values which he holds dear. Self-understanding makes for predictability in behavior.

What a Child Values

What children value, then, is what they are taught to value by either direct or indirect means. Parents and teachers show their values in their behavior. If the behavior is admirable, children tend to imitate to achieve immediately that which they admire. As they practice the expression of values by imitation, they come to identify the admired values as their own. When these admired values become "controls from within," as Fritz Redl describes them, they take their place as motivation toward emotionally mature and socially acceptable ways of living.

Values are taught not only by example but by discussion in order that they may be understood. Why certain standards are held and why others are avoided must be recognized if choice in values is to be wise. Present-day society offers a complex and complicated system of values and conventions, and the necessity of choice is inevitable.

Values to live by need to be clear and with apparent worth if they are to become the controlling conscience of personalities trained for and dedicated to a democratic way of living.

Bibliography

1. KRECH, DAVID and CRUTCHFIELD, RICHARD S. *Theory and Problems of Social Psychology.* New York: McGraw-Hill, 1948. pp. 52-53; 68-69; 414.
2. LANE, HOWARD and BEAUCHAMP, MARY. *Human Relations in Teaching.* New York: Prentice-Hall, 1955. pp. 237-238.
3. LINDSEY, GARDNER. Editor. *Handbook of Social Psychology.* Cambridge, Mass.: Addison-Wesley Pub. Co., 1954. pp. 648; 788-789; 952-953.
4. WHITING, JOHN W. M. and CHILD, IRVIN L. *Child Training and Personality.* New Haven: Yale Univ. Press, 1953. pp. 28-32 and Chap. 11.
5. YOUNG, KIMBALL. *Personality and Problems of Adjustment.* New York: F. S. Crofts and Co., 1941. pp. 181-184; 658-659; 808-809.
6. ——— ———. *Sociology.* New York: American Book Co., 1949. p. 110.

Vol. XXXIX—p. 158 (Dec. 1962)

Assumptions Underlying Mechanized Learning: What We Believe Should Guide Us

BY ALICE V. KELIHER

Alice V. Keliher is distinguished service professor of Jersey City State College, New Jersey.

THE PLOW CANNOT CREATE GOOD EARTH; THE NEWEST AND BEST OF reapers cannot harvest a bumper crop from drought-starved plants.

Without good seed, good soil, water and sunshine, the best of machines cannot harvest a good crop. Nor can the machine produce without man with his ability to plan, to foresee, to initiate, to evaluate action.

Even man's most mechanical monster, a rocket planned for Venus probing, was lost for want of a hyphen in the computer. For such a lack of man-made guidance an eighteen-million-dollar spacecraft had to be destroyed.

Two morals for education are that the machine, however ingeniously devised, cannot replace the fine rich soil of human relationships; and the machine cannot be its own guide. The machine does not possess a human spirit; it does not contain a sense of values. For decades one mechanistic device after another has entered the classroom. The early abacus held in itself no guarantee of mathematical accuracy (nor of honest dealing in the market place). The slate did not know what should be inscribed on it. They were known as tools and used as tools.

When radio came along, rumblings began of "replacing the teacher." Then movies. Then TV. Now all those and teaching machines. Tapes. Various forms of programed learning. Again the thought, "Replace the teacher," perhaps couched in new words—"Let the teacher handle much larger groups of children with the machines" or "Let the richness of the machine-produced material supplant the ignorance of the teacher."

Tools Are Unique for Some Things

When such slogan-like approaches were made with the oncoming of radio, sensible people kept their heads and used the tool for those things it uniquely could do. Instant news, special features, fine music, excellent dramatic productions were and are among the enrichments radio brings to the classroom. In the same way TV has contributions. With the rapid advancement of world-wide communications through Telstar and the like, alert teachers can enrich their classroom offerings in ways hardly dreamed of. Motivations for the study of world geography, history, human relations, government are at our finger tips. But this is true only so long as teachers are "at the switch" literally and figuratively As with the farmer, the teacher must plan, foresee, initiate and evaluate all that goes into the child's day and use widely the array of new tools *as tools* to achieve the underlying goals of education.

Poor Use of Tools

Perhaps this evaluation of tools as tools would be clearer with a few examples of what is *not* meant by the wise use of machines.

1. An auditorium full of children forced into silent listening to a symphony concert by radio, with teachers as monitors.

2. Twenty seven-year-old children, earphones affixed, writing a spelling lesson previously dictated on tape.

3. Seventh-grade boys in a deprived neighborhood watching on TV a lady in garden hat and gloves teaching another lady how to raise roses.

4. Four groups of children, ranging from second to sixth grade, filling a "free" period in a departmentalized program, in the auditorium watching a film on toothbrushing.

5. Eighty-seven fifth- and sixth-grade children listening to a lecture (through a microphone, illustrated with overhead projector) on latitude and longitude.

These are a few examples of things this author has actually observed. They are meant to be illustrative of poor usage of tools. Let's look at them for a moment. What were the assumptions underlying these uses? Was the tool itself in error?

In Number 1, was there the assumption that we can *make* children of all ages and varied stages of readiness *appreciate* fine music by forcing them to listen to it silently?

In Number 2, did the teacher believe that all twenty children needed the same spelling words and should follow the same pace in writing them?

In Number 3, was this a "time killer" with no life-connectedness for these children for whom the TV material was most unreal?

Surely Number 4 was a "time killer," a miserable use of a good tool with no meaningful connection to what had gone before or what was to follow in each of the four classes involved.

And in Number 5 the teacher assumed that eighty-seven children were all ready for the same learning and that the lecture method was suitable for the presentation of what is basically a reasoning subject.

Effective Use with Other Weapons

Yet each of the above could have been used effectively with other purposes. The symphony could have been heard eagerly by a group of children who were studying the composer's life, trying some compositions of their own, or initiating a school orchestra. The earphones could have been used in a language lab where older individual children were hearing tapes designed for their particular stage of learning. The TV could have been used for current news and discussion of world events. The film on toothbrushing could have been useful to a group of children or a committee working on a health project. And a lecture has its place, too, let us say by a person who has been to Japan, India, Africa and, with slides, brings children an experience they could not otherwise have. Every tool, every method, has its usefulness. But each must be guided into its proper place by the goals, the values, the good common sense of the teacher.

Good for All Purposes?

What then is all the fuss about? There are still in our profession those who "fall overboard" or "jump on bandwagons." A film is good for something, so it gets to be good for everything and for all purposes. A tape is fine for one thing—it must be fine for everything. The neighboring school has invested in teaching machines. Our school system must, too. This is surface thinking, hardly to be dignified as *thinking* at all. When this happens we find teaching becoming demonstrating and telling through the tempting microphone; learning is passive, children presumably soaking it in while machines do the telling; content is planned and parceled out in advance so machines can give it back in prearranged sequences. The child cannot question the TV teacher; he cannot share in planning the programed material in the machine; he cannot ask the bomber-studio flying overhead for the TV material he needs to further his studies of a given part of the world. He and his teacher take what is given. He is the passive recipient of materials, the average content which misses the local and regional needs of most, prepared for the mythical average—the average child we know does not exist.

Let Priorities Guide Action

Shall we throw the machines out? No more than the farmer should get rid of his plow and reaper because his crops failed. The machines have their place. Our great problem is to know their place and keep them in it. How shall we do this? I suggest that we give careful study to values and arrive at some priorities to guide our actions. We must take time to study and to think before we go hog-wild over the newest device. Yes, we will be called "reactionary" and "status quo-ers" if we call time to sort out values. But let us not forget that the nation's highest civilian honors were awarded Dr. Frances Kelsey for blocking what could have been hasty adoption of thalidomide. The day may come when parents will appreciate those educators who take time to analyze and study proposals that could in many ways be damaging to their children.

Values We Seek

What values do we seek? What priorities are in order? Space permits analysis of only a few. Each school group needs to think them out for themselves. But surely we are all concerned with

* *learning that lasts:* Evidence from research is rich in proof that passive, "soak it up," rote learning does not last as does learning from problem solving, questing, experimenting, doing, planning, evaluating.

- *readiness of individuals:* Mass teaching of skill or reasoning content by whatever form—microphone, TV, film—does not reach the individual child at his unique stage of readiness.

- *growing awareness of human values:* We are in danger, not only in our schools but in our society at large, of developing a rootless, mechanistic attitude toward each other and toward the expression of feelings. The simple elements of warmth, concern, affection, swift communication of joy and grief are muted or sadly lacking. Here, too, research tells us that, like trees, children grow crookedly without the sunshine of human warmth and the nourishment of good feelings. We have seen young children move from room to room of mechanical gadgets for a large part of their school day. It is not surprising that we find such children eager to talk with us about almost anything so long as they can keep contact.

- *putting first things first:* All of these mechanical tools cost money. Well and good *if* adequate financing is going into teachers' salaries. We need the wisest and best-educated people as teachers today. *They* come first. Then what about libraries? Why buy machines that depend on reading when the materials for good reading are lacking? Only 25 per cent of elementary schools have libraries. My money would go here next. Of course we need small enough classes that teachers may know children and their needs well. We need to think about the quality of human living that our school buildings invite. After all such needs have been met, let's have the machines carefully chosen so that they can be used to further genuine excellence in education.

- *making choices democratically:* Regretfully we say that it is still possible to find school systems where a new system of phonics, a plan of team teaching or some other new method is adopted without consultation with the very teachers who will have to carry it out. This is genuinely immoral. It reduces the teacher to a passive recipient of orders rather than a vital professional partner. In the long run such a school system gets and keeps the passive, conforming personalities as teachers. Our children deserve teachers who have vitality, creativity, a zest for planning and initiating education for each unique child and for the group that will tally with the demands of this exciting, fast-moving, unpredictable universe. Such teachers eschew the mechanistic schemes and they know how to keep machines in their place, subservient to the deep and basic needs of our children!

The Myth of Competition
BY ARTHUR W. COMBS

Arthur W. Combs is professor of education, College of Education, University of Florida, Gainesville.

EVERY AGE HAS BEEN THE VICTIM OF ITS MYTHS. OURS IS NO EXCEPtion. When people believed the world was flat, they stayed away from the "edge" for fear of falling over. When people believed in witches, innocent people were put to death. When it was thought that illness was the result of "bad blood," many a defenseless sick man was "cured" of his malady by being bled to death. Myths can have consequences disastrous to our ability to deal with pressing problems.

Guided by Beliefs

What a man believes is important. If he believes the Democrats have the right answers to government, he votes the Democratic ticket. If he believes the Republicans would do a better job, he votes for the GOP. He can only behave in terms of what seems to him to be so. This will be true whether the beliefs he holds are *really* so or not. As individuals or as nations, our beliefs guide our every act. Myths, false beliefs, have the same effects as true ones.

Horrible as it seems to us today, the snake pit treatment of the insane in the last century seemed sane and sensible to our forefathers who believed in the myth of men possessed of devils. Myths have always seemed right and proper to those who hold them. They still do. We, too, can be prisoners of our misconceptions, dupes of our false beliefs. Among the worst false beliefs in our time is the myth of competition.

Misled by Fables

"Competition," we have told ourselves, "is a powerful motivating force." "We live in a competitive society." "Competition makes us efficient and improves the quality of the product." These are fables with which we delude ourselves in this generation. These are principles we have often chosen to guide us in industry, government, athletics—even in education. If these principles are not true, we run a great risk.

We cannot afford to become victims of our myths any longer than absolutely necessary. Modern myths can be just as frustrating and inaccurate as those of years ago. Confusion in our beliefs leads to confusion in our acts. Beliefs based upon false assumptions lead to behavior that is likewise false and ineffective. It is particularly important in time of world crises that the fundamental assumptions on which we base behavior be as clear and precise as we can make them. Above all, we cannot afford to base our educational system upon fallacies lest we saddle the next generation with our own misperceptions. If our beliefs about competition are myths, we need to re-examine some of our most cherished fundamental assumptions.

Myths are insidious things. They provide us with comfort and lull us to sleep. The great danger of myths is not that they are wrong but that myths are likely to be partly right and there is nothing more dangerous than a half-right idea. A half truth is worse than a falsehood. Falsehood is easy to reject, but half truths have just enough of the genuine to give us a feeling of contentment. They encourage us to go on in the ways we have started in the vain hope that, if we can but do it a little better or try a little harder, surely sooner or later we shall achieve perfection. Sometimes this does happen. But sometimes it is better to give up the old ideas and search for better ones.

Let us examine the three most common beliefs about competition.

MYTH #1. *We live in a competitive society.* THE FACT: *We live in the most cooperative interdependent society the world has ever known.* Two great trends in history have made cooperation an absolute must for our way of life—the ever increasing dependence of people on one another and the tremendous increase of power in the hands of individuals. The world has become a very small place where we live, almost literally, in each other's laps. People of whom we have never heard produce and control our food, clothing and shelter. Thousands of people are involved in the delivery of a quart of milk to our door each morning. Milk would never reach us without the smooth cooperation of all friends on whom we depend for its production, processing and transportation from the cow to our doorstep. Thousands more are or have been engaged in producing machinery for handling crops to feed cows, for pasteurizing and bottling the milk or in building roads and vehicles which make its transportation possible.

We are impressed by the competitive features of our society and like to think of ourselves as essentially a competitive people. Yet we are thoroughly and completely dependent upon the goodwill and cooperation of millions of our fellow men. From the engineer who keeps the electric turbines running through the night to the garbage men who keep our cities livable, each of us must rely on others to carry out the tasks we cannot perform ourselves. Few of us could live for more than a very short time apart from others. Whether we like it or not, we are thoroughly and completely dependent upon the goodwill and cooperation of others at every moment of our lives. In turn, thousands of other people are dependent on us. We are indeed "our brothers' keepers" as never before in history.

The great industrial and scientific advances of the last century have made individual people more important than ever. The net effect of our great technological advances has been to place ever-increasing amounts of power in the hands of ordinary people. Even the least of us has control over the welfare of others. The average man has many units of horsepower at his fingertips in a light switch. When he sits behind the wheel of his car, he has a fearful projectile at his command. He could not drive unless he could count on others to cooperate with him by staying on their side of the road. The welfare and safety of each of us in a cooperative society depends upon the cooperation of each of our fellow citizens. We may live for days without competing with others, but we cooperate from morning to night.

The very history of our country has been one of increasing cooperation. Our nation was founded when a group of separate colonies agreed to join in a cooperative republic. Our great Civil War was fought to assure continued cooperation between North and South. Our legislatures, courts, government bureaus and agencies are institutions for cooperative effort. Who can forget the tremendous cooperative effort carried on by our armed forces in World War II? At the very moment we pat ourselves on the back as a great competitive people, we stand in awe of the release of atomic energy, the greatest cooperative scientific effort of all time.

Even our great industries which we often point out with pride as samples of our competitive way of life turn out, on closer analysis, to be outstanding examples of cooperation. Although they loudly proclaim the virtues of competition, our great industrial organizations are thoroughly dependent upon the smooth integration of thousands of interdependent workers. We are likely to forget that the great contribution of Henry Ford to modern industry was the development of the assembly line—a highly organized method of getting people to work together in the manufacture of a product. Our great "competitive" industries are marvels of cooperative effort.

Despite the fact that we live in the most cooperative, interdependent society the world has ever known, we persist in the fallacy that our way of life is based on competition. Even worse, some would have us teach our children, who must live in a cooperative world, that competition is the way to successful living. This is training children to live in a world that does not exist. Fortunately, children themselves resist this process with great vigor. We are lucky indeed that they never quite fall for this deception. They quickly learn for themselves the value of working together and cooperate just like the grownups they see around them.

MYTH #2. *Competition is a powerful motivating force.* THE FACT: *Only those compete who feel they have a chance of winning. The rest ignore the competition.*

Psychologists, sociologists and educators who have been doing research on competition for several decades tell us that the people who work for prizes—who enter into competition with other people—are only those who feel they have a chance of winning. Competition is of limited value as a means of motivation since it motivates few. We do not work for things we feel we cannot achieve. We work only for things that seem within our grasp. It makes little difference how the situation looks to an outsider. We are motivated by competition only when we feel we have a chance of winning. It may seem to others we have a splendid chance for success; if it doesn't seem so to us it might just as well not be so. No one has yet figured out a way of making people feel what does not seem to them to be so. Our feelings are still our private property.

People who do not see much chance of success cannot be inveigled into making an effort. They ignore the competition whenever they are able. Any teacher knows that children who work for scholastic honors are only the few who feel a possibility of winning. The rest of the children sit back and let the competitors "work like crazy" while the noncompetitors go about more important business of their own choosing. Those who feel they cannot achieve are quite content to let others do it. This is very frustrating in children, but adults behave so too. On any fall Saturday afternoon one can find in any football stadium thousands of adults who need exercise gathered to watch twenty-two men who don't need it get it. Competition exists only among those who feel able. The rest of us sit back as spectators and watch them maul each other. Competition as a means of motivation has been vastly over-rated.

Forcing people to compete may even have serious negative consequences, for *competition is threatening and discouraging to those who feel they cannot compete.* Competition is often used as a means of getting people to extend themselves. Although it is thought to be a means of "challenging" people, it may actually be severely threatening. Whether or not competition is challenging or threatening will depend upon how the situation seems to the competitor, not how it seems to an outsider. The difference between threat and challenge is something inside one. People feel challenged when confronted with a situation they feel able to deal with successfully. They feel threatened and discouraged by situations that seem to them beyond their capacities. What seems like a challenge to an outsider may seem to an individual to be deeply threatening and discouraging. How things seem to people is an internal affair that goes on inside their own skins and is only indirectly open to external manipulation.

Left to themselves people will compete only rarely and then only when they feel a chance of success. Forcing people to compete in spite of themselves can only result in discouragement or rebellion. That is what people are like. When the cards are stacked against us, we give up playing or start a fight with the people responsible for the stacking. Forced to compete against his will, a child may simply "go through the motions" of his job in a dispirited listless manner or break out in some form of opposition to his oppressors. It is only those who have been fairly successful who value competition so highly. *People do not learn to feel able by repeated experience of failure.*

A democratic society is dependent upon our ability to produce people who see themselves as adequate and able. People who feel inadequate to deal with life are, at best, a drag upon society and, at worst, an outright danger. An interdependent way of life like ours requires people who feel adequate and able and who are dependable. One of the great tragedies of our time is that millions of people feel far less able than they really are. What is more, because they feel so they behave so. This in turn leads to a deadly vicious circle. Believing themselves inadequate, people behave inadequately. The rest of us, seeing them behave inadequately judge them to be inadequate, which proves what they thought in the first place. This kind of merry-go-round can be dangerous to our way of life. People without faith in themselves are fair game for the Communist lure of salvation. We cannot afford a threatened and discouraged population. Too much is at stake.

The aim of competition is to win and the temptation is to win at any cost. Although it begins with the laudable aim of encouraging production, competition quickly breaks down to a struggle to win at any price. Competition is a powerful motivating force—for those who think they have a chance of winning. Winning, itself, is a "heady" business which can become an end in itself, trapping the competitor in a net of his own making. Many schools can observe this in their own varsity sports where the game and the players are often lost in the desperate need for victory.

The means we use to achieve our ends are always bought at a price. The price of winning may be more than we want to pay. Price tags must be read not only in dollars and cents; they must be read as well in terms of human values, of broken bodies, broken spirits and disheartened and disillusioned people who do not appear in the winner's circle, on the sports pages or as guests of honor at the testimonial banquet.

Competition encourages lone-wolf endeavors, and lone wolves can be dangerous to a cooperative society. We need to be able to count on other people to seek our best interests along with their own. In the headlong rush to win, competition too easily loses sight of responsibility. It values aggression, hostility and scorn. "Dog eat dog" becomes its philosophy. Too often the degree of glory involved for the victor is only in direct proportion to the abasement and degradation of the loser.

MYTH #3. *Competition is a useful device for controlling and improving quality.* THE FACT: *Competition is inefficient and outmoded as a means for quality production.*

Progress of society is dependent upon success in producing the best possible products at the least possible cost. This is true whether we are talking about things or people. Furthermore, to assure improvement, we need to engage in a continual process of evaluation of our products and ourselves. We need to be forever engaged in a process of quality testing. Quality testing, however, should not be confused with competition.

Through a kind of survival of the fittest, competition has historically served as a rough device for screening out quality. There can be no doubt that contrast is an effective means of emphasizing the respective qualities of objects being compared. There can be no doubt either that this sort of elimination process does not provide us with a kind of quality testing. But at what a price! With all the means of quality testing which modern science has placed at our disposal, must we still be tied to horse-and-buggy methods? While competition may result in better products over a period of time, it is an inefficient and fumbling means of improving quality at best. Like going from New York to Chicago, you can make it on foot if you like, but it takes a lot longer that way.

Although competition may sometimes serve as a primitive approach to quality testing, these two are by no means the same. Those testing for quality seek to discover the facts, to determine quality on the basis of disinterested examination. Competition is not concerned with production of quality, but with winning acceptance. One seeks facts, the other seeks to convince. One seeks the truth as an end in itself, the other uses the truth for its own extrinsic purposes.

Encourages Deception

The aim of competition often becomes one of winning the market rather than producing a better product. The salesman competing for my business is not as much interested in producing a good product as in selling his product regardless of its defects. He does not display its weaknesses; he hides them. Competition seeks to prove superiority, even if competition does not exist. It places the emphasis upon capturing the buyer rather than producing a better product. As a result it encourages deception and places a premium upon dishonesty. In testing, one examines the product and rests its case on quality. Testing for superiority is a scientific approach to the improvement of people or things. Competition as a means of assuring us of quality has been almost entirely supplanted by the much better, more efficient means supplied by modern science. So accurate is much of this testing that with modern methods we can even predict the quality of an airplane wing before it is made!

The major value of competition in our modern industrial structure seems to lie in its control of prices. By placing two products in competition we sometimes encourage producers to cut costs and lower prices. Interestingly enough, even then they can only cut costs by improved cooperation for more efficient production. In recent years businessmen themselves have turned their backs on competition. Fair trade laws are needed, they claim, to prevent their being forced out of business by cut-throat competition.

Competition and Democracy

The kind of interdependent cooperative society we live in requires people upon whom we can depend. Competition destroys feeling of trust in ourselves and other people. By glorifying winning even at the cost of human values, competition produces a fear of other people. This is in direct contradiction to the kind of attitude required for a successful cooperating organization. A cooperative society like ours must be based upon faith in other people. One cannot cooperate effectively with people he fears.

The success of a democracy depends upon the production of independent people of dignity and integrity provided with accurate and realistic information about themselves and their surroundings. What undermines respect for ourselves or other people is dangerous to all of us. Whether we like it or not, we are completely dependent on the goodwill of our fellows at every moment of modern complex existence. What destroys trust in ourselves or others makes communication difficult and cripples cooperative effort.

When our beliefs have been clear and accurate, we have made progress. As each age has succeeded in casting off the shackles of its peculiar myths and misperceptions, it has found new ways to deal with old problems, more effective means of achieving a better life for all. When we gave up thinking that weather was solely the whim of the gods, its prediction became possible. The science of medicine became possible with development of the germ theory of disease.

The greatest problems of our times are problems of human interrelationships. We cannot afford to be guided in these relationships by misconceptions about how these human relations can best be achieved. We cannot afford to base educational practices on ideas of doubtful value. Education cannot be satisfied with part truths. The stakes are too great. Unless we can learn to live together, we may not live at all. The myth of competition has been with us long enough.

Values Are Fundamental

BY LOUIS E. RATHS

Louis E. Raths is professor of Education, New York University, New York.

UNLESS SOME VERY SIGNIFICANT CHANGE TAKES PLACE IN HUMAN nature or in environmental sources which affect and shape human nature, children of today and tomorrow will get their values in much the same way we got ours. This is to say they must get them *all by themselves.* Our values do not come as a gift. And we cannot give our values to our children. Values come through "value-ing"; they grow through prizing, cherishing, holding dear—and no one can do this for us. Values also come through discrimination in the face of choices. To discriminate means to weigh, to size up, to judge. If we are to make our own selections, to share in identifying the choices from which our preference is to be made, then no one can do this for us.

Values come from "value-ing" and from reflection. They are also helped into being by the way we plan our lives. When we have made a choice—one that is prized—we are apt to plan our time in a way which gives this value a chance to be expressed. We plan the expenditure of our money in ways which favor the value. We seek readings and other activities which tend to support the value. We often choose to be among people who share our values. This penetration of our values into our lives is our way of continually testing them. Our values are forever undergoing that change which shared living and reflective thinking never cease to bring about.

Among children who do not develop any strong values we are likely to find indifference and apathy toward school activities. We are likely to find the flighty individual, the one who plays at being someone else because he has no self to express, the extreme over-conformer, the nagging dissenter. Among them are the under-achiever, the hesitant and uncertain child.

If we are to help children in this most difficult of all tasks, the building of a self, we must place greater emphasis on values. We must talk, man to man, with children about their purposes, interests, attitudes, beliefs, aspirations, feelings, activities and ways of thinking. We must ask children intelligent questions for which *only they* have the answers. One or two questions at any one time, involving not more than two or three minutes, would be the maximum. The child's answers would always be accepted with your comment that he has now made it plain and that you understand better what he said. He leaves this brief encounter in a thoughtful mood.

If this process of serious interchange can be carried on frequently, the child is faced with the deeper questions of what he prizes, what he should prize and what the alternatives are. Why is this one good? To what does this lead? Do I really want it?

Available evidence suggests that this method leads to reconstruction of behavior as a voluntary act on the part of children. This seems the more appropriate procedure if we are to honor and respect human beings. We cannot legislate values—we have found that out. We cannot indoctrinate values—we have found that out. We cannot coerce children into values through fear or through systematic institutional rules and regulations. Let us turn once again to a serious concern about each child's life: the alternatives he sees in terms of activities, purposes, interests and all the others. As we listen to him, as we reflect about him and as we help him come to decisions which he values, more and more order will come into the situations which are now confused with alternatives and unthought-of consequences.

We used to think that an environment rich in alternatives was rich in potential for child growth. But choices can be overwhelming. Choices are good, but they need clarification. The growing child wants to be somebody, a person, a self. He too realizes that the acquisition of values makes a self. Who will listen to him? Who will talk to him, man to man, about his life? Without this intelligent interaction an abundance of choices may be self-defeating. With this concern about what is important to him, choices become ordered, life is comprehensible, an awareness of self starts to grow. This awareness is a most important element in the growth of healthy personality.

Section II

The Child

The Child

THE FIRST TIME A RESPONSIVE TEACHER
- feels a small warm hand, slightly grubby or shiny clean, slide confidently into his,
- catches an adoring look as it shyly slides toward him,
- finds that he is obviously being imitated as to walk, mannerisms or patterns of speech,
- watches someone who has been called a "reluctant reader" lost to all the world within the pages of a book,
- is simply bowled over with the insights and understandings, the knowledge and maturity of the 4's, 6's, 8's, 10's or 12's,

HE SHOULD WATCH OUT!

That teacher is almost captured by the children, and once captured he is theirs for all time.

Why do we have teacher-training institutions and child study centers; why teachers, principals, directors, and superintendents; budgets and buildings; research and professional publications; school committees and textbook publishing houses? All these exist for just one purpose, one that can be almost lost in the welter of "busyness" with which we surround ourselves—the child and his fulfillment as an individual.

True, we know many things about boys and girls: many patterns of physical growth, some of their greatest needs, their responses in varied educational settings. We are also aware of the "satiable curiosities" of young children; and all too often we watch them slip later into boredom. We are beginning to understand the kind of guidance to which children respond. We have advanced many theories about how learning takes place, how concepts are formed. And each time we are ready to sigh with relief and say, "At last we know," along comes a Jean or a Michael who upsets part of the latest theory—and we start the search again.

Educators think and wonder about children. They read about and discuss them. They observe, test and try. And suddenly different aspects of the search come together and a new insight is gained. But before anyone can cry, "Eureka, I have found it!," he realizes that this new bit of understanding presents new problems, implies more study, and the search goes on.

Children, in all their infinite variety, with all their wondrous capabilities, are the "texts" which teachers study each day. And it is the most rewarding study anyone can engage in—for those who seek to know The Child also know laughter and fun, tears and heartache, success and failure, excitement and adventure, friendship and love—the essence of life itself.—*By* MARY HARBAGE, *Director of Language Arts, Brookline Public Schools, Massachusetts.*

The Role of Love in Preschool Education
BY DANIEL A. PRESCOTT

> *Daniel A. Prescott, director emeritus, Institute for Child Study, University of Maryland, College Park, delivered this address at the World Congress of Organisation Mondiale pour l'Education Prescolaire (OMEP) in Athens, Greece, 1956. Since this topic bears directly on the theme of this issue, we are happy to have been granted permission to publish it. In 1961 OMEP began making reference to "preprimary" children rather than to "preschool" children.*

IT OFTEN HAPPENS IN HUMAN AFFAIRS THAT SCIENTISTS GAIN THEIR first insights by studying illnesses and mishaps. When things go wrong, causes which produce undesirable happenings are sought. As these negative factors are understood, an initial and partial vision is gained into more important positive forces that govern phenomena being investigated. It was so with love.

During the past three decades students of the health and growth of young children arduously have been tracing physical, social, economic and psychological factors underlying disturbances in physical growth which are responsible for emotional maladjustment or for malformation of character in the early years of life. Over and over again they have discovered a deficiency factor, the absence of something needed, to be primary in the causation of these undesirable happenings. An inadequate expression of love seems to have been indicated repeatedly as one of the major causations of these distortions of development.

Only a few of these revealing studies will be cited because I wish to consider in more detail what love really is, what its positive role in human development may be. It is little use to state that maladjustments and limitations of development ensue from absence of love unless one is able to describe positively the nature of the force which must be created to alleviate the maladjustment and to bring about the conditions necessary to the full realization of human potentialities.

Some Evidences of Needed Love

In the United States during the past thirty years the custom has developed of having babies born in hospitals rather than in the home. This has come about so that the mother and the child could receive better medical attention and more hygienic care. Maternal and infant mortality rates have been reduced greatly by this practice. However, the procedure developed of taking the child from the mother in the delivery room and of keeping him most of the time for some days in a nursery with other infants rather than placing him in the bed or even in the room with his mother. His needs were cared for by specially trained nurses, except that at certain intervals he was taken to his mother for feeding and then returned to his bassinet in the nursery.

Under these conditions many children developed nutritional difficulties, and in some a special illness, called "marasmus" (which means wasting away) was identified. This was described by Bakwin in 1942. Subsequently, Dr. Margaret Ribble of New York published several books and articles about this phenomenon. As early as 1937 Dr. David Levy, a psychiatrist, published an article in the *American Journal of Psychiatry* called "Primary Affect Hunger." He made it clear that infants and young children cannot thrive on food and physical hygiene alone but must have the added nurture of love, fondling and contact with their mothers' bodies if they are to grow physically healthy and emotionally adjusted. Bevan Brown has written extensively on the importance of breast feeding for later physical and mental health. The absence of love and nurturing patterns which are the natural expressions of love seems to be an important factor in causing nutritional illnesses in infants.

There is a *second* evidence pointing to the important role of love in the development of children. War and its aftermath disturbed the home life of millions of children and orphaned countless thousands. Institutions have had to be developed in many countries to care for these children separated from their parents. The physical, mental and emotional development of these institutionalized children has been the object of much study by scientists, because under institutional conditions they did not flourish as well as children at home.

Dorothy Burlingham and Anna Freud in their book, *Infants Without Families;* William Goldfarb in a series of articles in the *American Journal of Orthopsychiatry;* John Bowlby in a *World Health Organization Monograph* in 1951 and in an article in the *Journal of Mental Science* in 1953; Rene Spitz in a telling series of research studies as well as Beres and Obers—all have shown that young children separated from the love of their parents languish and fail to achieve their best growth both physically and intellectually. They also develop unwholesome emotional reactions under usual institutional conditions. But happily this has not been true in those institutions where they have had regular, extensive, intimate and continuing person-to-person contacts through time with one particular adult who valued them highly. Again the accumulated evidence points strongly to the fact that a child must have more than adequate nourishment, good physical care and systematic instruction if he is to achieve the full development of his potentials. A person-to-person relationship which can only be called "love," together with the day-to-day interactions implied by this love relationship, is necessary to provide the emotional climate essential to wholesome development.

Anthropologists who have studied family and child-rearing customs of many cultures supply a *third evidence* in the vital role of love in the development of the preschool child. Wayne Dennis in *The Hopi Child,* Margaret Mead in *From the South Seas* and Ashley Montagu in *The Direction of Human Development,* to mention only three among many, have supplied detailed descriptions of child-rearing practices in different cultures and of the psychological aftermaths of these customs in the human personalities produced by them. Ashley Montagu generalized on these findings of cultural anthropologists as follows:

We know from the observation and study of many peoples that the well-integrated, cooperative, adult personality is largely the product of frustration. We also know the obverse to be true, that the disintegrated, non-cooperative adult personality is largely a product of a childhood which has suffered a maximum of frustration and a minimum of satisfaction.[1]

Montagu goes on to indicate that it is primarily love which can insure a maximum of satisfactions to young children and that the absence of love nearly always builds up a disturbing number of frustrations.

These three evidences from scientific research all show that love is vital to optimum growth and to wholesome personality development in infants and young children.

What is the nature of this person-to-person relationship which infants and young children must experience to achieve a healthy becoming and which I have chosen to call "love"? The validity of the term "love" also must be tested against available scientific evidence, and its essential qualities must be carefully defined.

(1) Is love a reality or only a delusive romantic construct of our culture?
(2) If love is a reality, what are its essential qualities?
(3) If love is a reality, what is its role in human development?

I have examined many books on human development, educational psychology, cultural anthropology, sociology, psychiatry and biography. In the majority of the books on human development and educational psychology the word "love" does not occur. When it does occur it is used without definition for the most part. If love is a reality, we need seriously and scientifically to study its influence on human lives and to learn what conditions are favorable to its enhancement and fulfillment. If it is not a reality, we shall need to study the reasons for the emergence of so strong a myth, so frustrating an aspiration, so delusive a pretention.

[1] Ashley Montagu, *The Direction of Human Development* (New York: Harper & Bros., 1955). Reprinted by permission of publisher.

There is a remarkably small amount of scientific material now available about the nature of love.

A brief review of ideas found in some of the books examined comes first. Breckenridge and Vincent, Strang and Barker, Kounin and Wright all mention love as a reality. The general idea expressed is that love markedly influences behavior, development and adjustment. One notes a vagueness about the nature of love as a positive force and finds much more specificity about the negative effects of lack of love and of inappropriate use of love relationships. Kluckhohn and Murray give a great amount of material about sexual behavior and about family processes but no discussion of love as such.

James Plant clearly regards love as a reality but does not define it. In his view love affords children a basic security, a sure feeling of belonging. Insecure, unloved children show anxious, panicky symptoms that contrast with the aggressive overcompensation of inadequate children. Confusion about their security often arises in children as they try to meet the learning and behavioral demands set for them by the authority of their parents and of society and also as they struggle for independence.

Harry Stack Sullivan defines love:

When the satisfaction or the security of another person becomes as significant to one as one's own security, then the state of love exists.[2]

He goes on to say that when one loves "one begins to appreciate the common humanity of people."

Overstreet says:

The love of a person implies not the possession of that person but the affirmation of that person. It means granting him gladly the full right to his unique humanhood. One does not truly love a person and yet seek to enslave him—by law, or by bonds of dependence and possessiveness. Whenever we experience a genuine love we are moved by the transforming experience toward a capacity for good will.[3]

Fromm coins the term "productive love" because the word "love" as popularly used is so ambiguous. He contends the essence of love is the same whether it is the mother's love for a child, our love for man, or the erotic love between two individuals. Certain basic elements are characteristic of all forms of productive love. They are *care, responsibility, respect* and *knowledge*. He says:

Care and responsibility denote that love is an activity, not a passion . . . the essence of love is to labor for something to make something grow . . . Without respect for and knowledge of the beloved person love deteriorates into domination and possessiveness. Respect and uniqueness. . . . Love is

---

[2] Harry Stack Sullivan, *Conception of Modern Psychiatry* (New York: W. W. Norton & Co., Inc., 1953). Reprinted by permission of publisher.

[3] H. A. Overstreet, *The Mature Mind* (New York: W. W. Norton & Co., Inc., 1949). Reprinted by permission of publisher.

the expression of intimacy between two human beings under the condition of the preservation of each other's integrity . . . To love one person productively means to be related to his human core, to him as representing mankind.[4]

Fromm also contends that love of others and love of ourselves are not alternatives:

> The affirmation of one's own life, happiness, growth and freedom is rooted in one's capacity to love . . . If an individual is able to love productively he loves himself too . . . Selfishness and self-love, far from being identical are actually opposites . . The selfish person does not love himself too much but too little, in fact he hates himself . . . He is necessarily unhappy and anxiously concerned to snatch from life the satisfactions which block himself from attaining . . .[5]

The recurring mention in the literature of the relatedness of love for self (self-respect), love for other individuals and love for mankind led me to examine biographies and writings of three men who have lived lives of great devotion to mankind: Kagawa, Gandhi and Schweitzer.

Kagawa says:

> Love awakens all that it touches . . . creation is the art of life pursued for love . . Love is the true nature of God . . . In social life human beings meet and love one another through a material medium. . . . Love spins garments for itself out of matter . . . through love economic life appears as the content of the spiritual . . . Real construction of society can be accomplished only through the operation of education through love. . . Love is identical with activity . . . It means creating existence where there has been none . . . If we view economics so, the study of it changes into a science of love . . . Art must create externally beautiful objects and internally it is itself love.[6]

The practical social and political application of love has worked several miracles in India during our times. Gandhi said:

> To be truly non-violent I must love my adversary and pray for him even when he hits me . . . We may attack measures and systems. We may not, we must not attack men. Imperfect ourselves, we must tender toward others . . . forgiveness is more manly than punishment.[7]

Gandhi told landowners:

> Landlords should cease to be mere rent collectors. They should become trustees and trusted friends of their tenants. They should give peasants finity of tenure, take a lively interest in their welfare, provide well-managed schools for their children, night school for adults, hospitals and dispensaries for the sick, look after the sanitation and in a variety of ways make them feel that they, the landlords, are their friends.[8]

---

[4] Erich Fromm, *The Art of Love* (New York: Harper & Bros., 1956). Reprinted by permission of publisher.

[5] Erich Fromm, *Man for Himself* (New York: Holt, Rinehart & Winston, Inc., 1947). Reprinted by permission of publisher.

[6] T. Kagawa, *Meditations* (New York: Harper & Bros., 1950). Reprinted by permission of publisher.

[7] Louis Fischer, *The Life of Mahatma Gandhi* (New York: Harper & Bros., 1950). Reprinted by permission of publisher.

[8] *Ibid.* Reprinted by permission of publisher.

Gandhi contended that God is love and can be known only through action.

Faith does not permit of telling. It has to be lived and then it is self-propagating.[9]

Albert Schweitzer is another extraordinary international figure who has accomplished the apparently impossible during the past fifty years. He has tremendous reverence for life and respect for the dignity of all human beings, and he believes that love is the great force of the universe.

He says:

By the spirit of the age the man today is forced into skepticism about his own thinking in order to make him receptive to truth which comes to him from authority . . . (but) it is only by confidence in our ability to reach truth by our own individual thinking that we are capable of accepting truth from outside . . . Man must bring himself into a spiritual relation to the world and become one with it . . . Beginning to think about life and the world leads a man directly and almost irresistibly to reverence for life . . . the idea of love is the spiritual beam of light which reaches us from the Infinite . . . in God, the great first cause, the will-to-create and the will-to-love are one . . . In knowledge of spiritual existence in God through Love he (man) possesses the one thing needful.[10]

These three men, all men of action, accomplished the seemingly impossible during their lifetimes in the first half of this century. Each affirmed that love was a central dynamic in his accomplishment —love of other individuals, love of mankind and love of God. Theirs certainly was "productive love." We may therefore regard our first question as answered in the affirmative. Love does exist. It is a potent reality. It has been validated by men of science as well as by three extraordinary men of action.

Nature of Love

Now what about the nature of love? On the basis of my research I have developed a number of theses about love. They will be presented with brief mention of the degree to which they seem to be supported by the ideas found in the material already cited.

1. Love involves more or less empathy with the loved one. A person who loves actually feels with and so shares intimately the experiences of the loved one and the effects of experiences upon the loved one. Sullivan indicates something of how this comes about:

If another person matters as much to you as you do yourself, it is quite possible to talk to this person as you have never talked to anyone before. The freedom which comes . . . permits nuances of meaning, permits investigation without fear of rebuff which greatly augments the consensual validation of all sorts of things.[11]

---

[9] *Ibid.* Reprinted by permission of publisher.

[10] Albert Schweitzer, *Out of My Life and Thought* (New York: Holt, Rinehart & Winston, Inc., 1949). Reprinted by permission of publisher.

[11] Sullivan, *op. cit.* Reprinted by permission of publisher.

2. One who loves is deeply concerned for the welfare, happiness and development of the loved one. This concern is so deep as to become one of the major values in the organized personality of "self-structure" of the loving person. All sources studied seem to agree on this proposition. It is especially validated by the lives of Kagawa, Gandhi and Schweitzer. Each of them has shown by his actions through the years that he values the human beings whom he serves not only as much as he values himself but even more.

3. One who loves finds pleasure in making his resources available to the loved one—to be used by the latter to enhance his welfare, happiness and development. Strength, time, money, mind—indeed all resources—are happily proffered for the use of the loved one. This implies that a loving person acts with and on behalf of the loved one whenever his resources permit and the action is desired by the loved one. The loving person is not merely deeply concerned about the welfare, happiness and development of the beloved; he does something to enhance them whenever possible. All sources seem to agree on this proposition, too.

4. On the one hand, the loving person seeks a maximum of participation in the activities that contribute to the welfare, happiness and development of the loved one; on the other hand, the loving one accepts fully the uniqueness and individuality of the loved one and accords him freedom to experience, to act and to become what he desires. This thesis is agreed to by nearly all of the sources consulted.

5. Love is most readily and usually achieved within the family circle but can be extended to include many other individuals, or categories of people, or all of humanity. In the case of Schweitzer it also includes all living things and the Creative Force of the universe—God. In the same way a person can advantageously experience love from a limitless number of other human beings and living things. Of course, genuine full love is hard to achieve even with a few persons, as several of our sources pointed out. But this is not proof that with greater scientific understanding of its processes we cannot create conditions that will favor its broadening.

6. The good effects of love are not limited to the loved one but promote the happiness and further development of the loving one as well. Love is not altruistic, self-sacrificing, and limiting for the one who loves. On the contrary, it is a reciprocal dynamic which greatly enriches the lives of both. This idea is not too clearly stated in a number of our sources but seems implied where not stated in nearly all.

7. Love is not rooted primarily in sexual dynamics or hormonal drives, although it may well have large erotic components whether between parents and children, between children or between adults. Fromm

seems to support this position when he says that the essence of productive love is the same no matter who is concerned.

8. Love affords many individuals fundamental insights into and basic relationships to humanity and to the forces that organize and guide the universe. It gives many persons a basic orientation to the universe and among mankind. It can become the basis for faith in God. I was surprised to find support for this thesis from all sources. For example, Plant affirms that

> from early adolescence on the Church gives a great many children a sense of belongingness which has greater continuity and certainty for the individual than anything provided by his parents.[12]

Each of the other sources also intimates that love is a great aid in the developmental tasks of orienting the self toward the rest of mankind and within the universe toward God.

These eight theses, I hope, may be of some aid in analyzing the nature of love and the processes by which it develops. Admittedly they represent only a first and faltering attempt. If they are sufficient to focus more scientific attention and research on love, the purpose of this article will have been accomplished.

Role of Love in Human Development

Since love does exist, it potentially can become a reality in the life of every human being. If our theses regarding the nature of love are true, what roles can love play in human development? This question will be answered during the next decade, I hope, by a whole series of researches. The findings should fill many monographs and some books. In the meantime I should like to propose a series of hypotheses as to the probable findings of these researches, in the hope of suggesting profitable research leads.

The *first* hypothesis is that *being loved can afford any human being a much needed basic security.* To feel that one is deeply valued because one *is,* rather than because of the way one behaves or looks, is to feel fundamentally at home whenever one can be with the person who loves one so. From earliest infancy to most advanced age this feeling of being deeply valued is an important precondition to meeting life's challenges and expectations, to doing one's best without unhealthy stress.

The *second* hypothesis is that *being loved makes it possible to learn to love oneself and others.* The capacity of infants for empathy, before language development makes more explicit communication possible, permits the feeling of the nature of love very early in life. The closeness of mutual understanding among preadolescent peers makes its joyous expansion natural. The hormonal creation of unrest in the presence of peers of the opposite sex pushes its further development until it is stilled

[12] James Plant, *The Envelope* (The Commonwealth Fund, 1950).

by intimate sharing of vivid life in marriage. The mystery and the creative fulfillment that come with the first baby begin a cycle of nurturance and guidance of a rapidly developing new personality that brings tremendous fulfillment through the years. But this wonderful growth and enrichment of life by love seem possible only to those who first were loved by others. Indeed we suspect that a person who has never been loved cannot fully respect and love himself but must always restlessly be reassuring himself as to his fundamental worth.

Our *third* hypothesis is that *being loved and loving others facilitate the winning of belonging in groups.* Of course, winning roles in group activities requires that the individual have knowledge and skills that are valuable in carrying on the activities of the group; for example, being able to act in conformity to group customs and codes. Being loved contributes to none of these skills, but being secure through love and being able to give love favor personality characteristics that are easy and attractive in group situations. Such a child or youth has no reason to lord it over others, to be aggressive and hostile or to be shy and withdrawing. Such children do not need constantly to climb in status by calling attention to the failures and inadequacies of others.

A *fourth* hypothesis is that *being loved and loving in return facilitate identification with parents, relatives, teachers and peers by which the culture is internalized more readily and organizing attitudes and values are established easily.* When one feels loved and loves in return it is easy to learn that which is expected, it is easy to believe that which one's objects of love believe, and it is easy to aspire in the directions encouraged by one's object of identification. The unloved child feels so much insecurity that he scarcely dares to try his wings in learning. Or he is so full of hostility that he tends to reject what he is told and to refuse to meet the expectancies that face him as a way of demonstrating his power to himself. Obviously the readiness of loving persons to provide meaningful experiences and to aid him in the learning process are further facilitations that give great advantages to loved children.

Our *fifth* hypothesis is that *being loved and loving facilitate adjustment to situations that involve strong unpleasant emotions.* When a loved child fails at something, the failure does not cut so deep as to make him doubt his basic worth because he is still secure in that love relationship. Consequently he is more easily reassured and encouraged to try again and again. In contrast the unloved child who fails is in double jeopardy. To his insecurity is added the feeling of inadequacy, and the world looks blacker and blacker. When a loved child is frightened, he can literally or figuratively take the hand of the person who loves him, approach and examine the terrifying situation, learn its true dimensions and more readily find the courage to face it. But terror to the unloved child is unfaceable and overwhelming. Fearful things must be avoided at all costs, and if they enter and remain in the child's field they may result in physical illness or emotional breakdown. Punishments, penalties and demands of authority are bearable for loved children because they do not imply rejection or fundamental lack of worth. Consequently they are analyzable by the loved child, who more easily can perceive their meaning and take them in stride. But to the unloved child these things may be taken as indicators of personal rejection or of unfavorable status. Resentment, rebellion against authority, hostility against peers who seem more favored elicit doubt of one's own worth.

Implications

The implications for the education of preschool children I think must be quite clear. Here are a few briefly stated:

1. Children from homes where they are surrounded by a climate that is rich in love—between their parents, between their parents and themselves and among siblings—do not need to find love awaiting them at the nursery school or kindergarten, though it will do them no harm to find it there, too.

2. Children from homes where love is absent or ill expressed do need to find a personal relationship based on love in the nursery school and in the kindergarten. In fact the finding of such a relationship is their main hope of avoiding later maladjustment and failure to achieve satisfactory love relationships as adults.

3. It is necessary that nursery school and kindergarten teachers have a full knowledge of the quality of the interpersonal relationships which exist in the home of each of their pupils, because this information is necessary to a real understanding of the behavior of each child and of his needs. In turn, this understanding is prerequisite to the making of wise decisions when interacting with the child and guiding his actions.

4. The gathering of this information about the emotional climate in which each child lives must be done carefully. It requires considerable training. It must be recorded objectively and the records guarded with the greatest care, the implication being that a strong code of professional ethics governs all who have access to this information.

5. Only persons who have achieved the security of knowing that they are loved should be employed as nursery school teachers, because persons who lack this security will be unable to build the kinds of relationships needed by certain children.

6. The nursery school and the kindergarten must be administered in such a way that relationships between the director and the teachers, between supervisors and teachers and among the teachers themselves will be warm, mutually valuing and mutually assisting each other in

all daily matters. The spirit in which the school is administered does much to create the climate in which the pupils live.

It is my firm hope that more and more children will be nurtured in a climate of warm love and deep respect for them as human beings. I am sure that love gives the feeling of security to the human individual, that security gives rise to respect and acceptance of other people, and that this permits action in cooperative endeavors for the common good. As we learn to work together for the common good, peace will be established among nations as the only sane and reasonable basis of human relationship because we mutually love and value each other's self-realization as much as our own.

Bibliography

AINSWORTH, MARY D. and J. BOWLBY. "Research Strategy in the Study of Mother-Child Separation," *Courier of the International Children's Centre.*

ANGYAL, ANDRAS. "A Theoretical Model for Personality Studies." *The Self* (Clark Moustakas, Ed.). New York: Harper & Bros., 1956.

BARKER, KOUNIN and WRIGHT. *Child Behavior and Development.* New York: McGraw-Hill Book Co., 1943.

BOSSARD, JAMES H. *Parent and Child.* Philadelphia: University of Pennsylvania Press, 1953.

BOWLBY, JOHN. "Maternal Care and Mental Health," *WHO Technical Monograph.* Geneva: WHO, 1951.

———. "Some Pathological Processes Set in Training by Early Mother-Child Separation," *Journal of Mental Science,* Vol. 159, 1953, pp. 265-72.

BRECKENRIDGE and VINCENT. *Child Development.* Philadelphia: W. B. Saunders Co., 1943.

BRUNET, O. and I. LEZINE, "Le Developpement Psychologique de la Premiere Enfance," *P.U.F.* Paris; 1951.

BURLINGHAM, DOROTHY and ANNA FREUD. *Infants Without Families.* London: Allen and Unwin, 1943.

DENNIS, WAYNE. *The Hopi Child.* New York: Appleton-Century-Crofts, Inc., 1940.

ERIKSON, EVE. *Childhood and Society.* London: Imago Publishing Co., 1951.

FISCHER, LOUIS. *The Life of Mahatma Gandhi.* New York: Harper & Bros., 1950.

FROMM, ERICH. *Man for Himself.* New York: Holt, Rinehart & Winston, Inc., 1947.

———. *The Art of Love.* New York: Harper & Bros., 1956.

GOLDFARB, WILLIAM. "The Effects of Early Institutional Care on Adolescent Personality," *Journal of Orthopsychiatry,* Vol. 15, 1945, pp. 247-55.

———. "Psychological Privation in Infancy and Subsequent Adjustment," *American Journal of Orthopsychiatry,* Vol. 15, 1945, pp. 247-55

———. "Effects of Psychological Privation in Infancy and Subsequent Stimulation," *American Journal of Psychiatry,* Vol. 102, 1945, pp. 18-33.

KAGAWA, T. *Meditations.* New York: Harper & Bros., 1950.

KLUCKHOHN and MURRAY. *Personality in Nature, Society and Culture.* New York: Alfred A. Knopf, Inc., 1948.

LEVY, DAVID. "Primary Affect Hunger," *American Journal of Psychiatry,* Vol. 94, 1937, pp. 643-52.

LORENZ, K. *King Solomon's Ring,* London: Methuen, 1952.

MEAD, MARGARET. *From the South Seas.* New York: William Morrow & Co., Inc., 1939.

MONTAGU, ASHLEY (Ed.). *The Meaning of Love.* New York: Julian Press, 1953.

———. *The Direction of Human Development,* New York: Harper & Bros., 1955.

OVERSTREET, H. A. *The Mature Mind.* New York: W. W. Norton & Co., Inc., 1949.

PESTALOZZI, HEINRICH. *Aphorisms.* New York: Philosophical Library, 1947.
PLANT, JAMES. *The Envelope.* The Commonwealth Fund, 1950.
PRESCOTT, DANIEL A. "The Role of Love in Human Development," *Journal of Home Economics,* Vol. 44, 1952, pp. 173-76.
RIBBLE, MARGARET, *The Rights of Infants.* New York: Columbia University Press, 1943.
SCHWEITZER, ALBERT. *Out of My Life and Thought.* New York: Holt, Rinehart & Winston, Inc., 1949.
SOLOVYEV, VLADIMAR. *The Meaning of Love.* New York: Julian Press, 1943.
SOROKIN, P. A. *Altruistic Love.* Boston: Beacon Press, 1950.
SPITZ, RENE A. "Hospitalism—A Follow-up Report," *The Psychoanalytic Study of the Child,* Vol. 2. New York: International Press, 1947, pp. 113-17.
―――. "The Role of Ecological Factors in Emotional Development," *Child Development,* Vol. 20, 1949, pp. 145-55.
―――. "The Influence of Mother-Child Relationships and Its Disturbances," *Mental Health and Infant Development* (Kenneth Soddy, Ed.). New York: Basic Books, Inc., 1956.
STRANG, RUTH. *Introduction to Child Study.* New York: Macmillan Co., 1951.
SULLIVAN, HARRY STACK. *Conception of Modern Psychiatry.* New York: W. W. Norton & Co., Inc., 1953.
SUTTIE, I. D. *The Origins of Love and Hate.* New York: Julian Press, 1943.

Vol. XXXIX—p. 5 (Sept. 1962)

The Importance of Pre-Primary Education

BY JAMES L. HYMES, JR.

This talk, by James L. Hymes, Jr., professor of education and chairman of early childhood education, University of Maryland, was given at ACEI's 1962 Spring Conference in Indianapolis.

THE GREATEST GAIN THAT FIVE-YEAR-OLDS MAKE, IF THEY HAVE THE chance to attend a good kindergarten, can be stated dogmatically without the slighest fear of contradiction. It is almost a universal gain, experienced practically without exception by every lucky Five. It is an obvious gain—clear cut, out in the open, available for all to see. Fives who go to a good kindergarten live the fifth year of their lives with more vigor. They work harder. They see more. They do more. They are happier. They get more from life, and they give more of themselves.

Four-year-olds who have a good school geared to their age make exactly this same kind of gain: They become more fully alive—using more of themselves and with greater contentment, taking more from the world around them. This kind of gain is utterly apparent even with three-year-olds, and even with three-year-olds it tends to be a universal gain.

The importance of pre-primary education is that it enables all children in these years—but fours and fives in particular, without the slightest doubt—to be more glad that they are alive—and to be more alive!

You can say why good schools for this age are so important in four words: *The children are ready.* You can say it in three words: They are popping. They are bursting. They are eager. They have reached a new time in their lives, a time when stimulation, adventure, ideas, challenge, companionship have begun to be of prime importance.

If you do not know children this age, you may feel, "But they are so young." *Young* is a relative word, however. Middle age is young to some. Adolescents are young. Eight-year-olds are young. Fours and fives are young, but fours and fives are also old. These children have lived through infancy. They have long put behind them the time in their lives when security and closeness to Mother were the only things that mattered to them. They have long put behind them their toddlerhood, when they were first getting their feet on the ground. Fours and fives are young, yes. But they are no longer babies.

Every study in child development and the experience of nursery schools and kindergartens (put together, more than one hundred and fifty years of experience!) prove the case. The children come eagerly. They love their parents. They love their homes. But with the fullness of their whole bodies they seek friends their own age, activity, experience. These children are not tied to their mothers' apron strings. They are busy workers, hard thinkers and delightfully social.

They are ready for experiences in more independence. They are eager for companionship, for seeing and talking with and working side-by-side with their own age. They are popping to use their bodies: to test their strength, to climb new heights, to achieve a tingle-y fitness. They are thirsty for ideas, for new words and new sounds and new sights, for new skills and accomplishments and achievements. *And* they are full of ideas of their own. Ideas to say, if someone will listen. Ideas to paint out and act out. Ideas to build with, if they have the tools, materials, time and space.

Nursery School, Kindergarten Supplement the Home

They are only four and five, in the early springtime of their lives. But this is the time—more than any time they will ever again know—when they are reaching out, peeking and curious, thirsty for the new, ready to soak up the sensations and stimulation that a school of richness can bring them. You cannot miss this full-blown readiness as you watch fours and fives in school. Parents at home, whose children are not lucky enough to have a school to go to, cannot miss it either.

Overwhelmingly, from parents who care, the report is: "He needs companionship," "He needs more to do," "He is at loose ends; we are at our wit's end."

These are reports from good homes, not homes trying to shirk their responsibilities or to shed their children. These homes make a basic contribution to fours and fives. They will continue to contribute, during the elementary school years, during adolescence, and even when their young people are away at college. But they know that home alone, even the best home—with its space, its resources, its time—does not satisfy and fulfill older children. *And it no longer meets all the needs of fours and fives.* Perceptive parents reach out to supplement what they can do: to college at one age, to high school and elementary school at another, to camp and library and museum and park . . . to nursery school and kindergarten when children are four and five.

Their children respond. They have no sense of being ignored or rejected. Fours and fives complain on Saturdays and school holidays. Not uncommonly, some even cry when school must be closed. These are our most eager scholars. They don't tolerate school. They beg for it. They come without the slightest reluctance.

"Unemployed" Fours and Fives Need Good Schools

But this is the age we do not serve. The kindergarten idea in America is more than one hundred years old. Yet only about 40 per cent of our five-year-olds have a public school kindergarten to go to. The idea of nursery schools is almost half a century old in America. For all practical purposes you can say that zero per cent of our four-year-olds go to public groups. The actual number is so infinitesimally small.

We have been very slow in responding to the needs of these children. Our response has been almost un-American. The most clearcut evidence of the good that schools could do has not impressed us. Instead we have asked for a negative kind of proof. The persistent demand has been: What's the harm? What's so wrong with their just staying home? We have asked the kind of question a constricting, dying economy might ask. We have sounded more like a frightened and worried society than like an eager, expanding nation glad to encompass more and more of its people. With this age we seem to say that we will act only if forced into action as a last-ditch emergency measure.

Yet there is harm if good schools do not exist for fours and fives. The greatest harm, like the greatest value, is out in the open for anyone to see. And it is almost universal. What is this harm? Without pre-primary education fours and fives are idle. They are unemployed.

They live lives of drabness and monotony. They do the same things over and over, far too often. And what they do has little "guts" and content, little meat for body and brain to feed on. Anyone can see them on the streets—they sit on curbstones and steps. Anyone can see them in backyards—they stand and look. And they are in living rooms too—sitting, staring at TV.

Without good schools fours and fives are isolated from the world of their friends. They are isolated from ideas that could make sense to them. They idly bang around on the fringe of a busy adult world of stores and streets and homes not geared to them.

The greatest harm is that these youngsters are fiddling—fooling around. They are aimlessly, pointlessly waiting.

The harm is obvious, yet it does not move us. Idle preadolescents, idle adolescents—unused, unchallenged, drifting—would soon be in our hair. They would hurt us. They would do damage to us. Fours and fives coasting—not thinking as much as they could, not doing as much, not talking as much, not hearing as much, not working as much—hurt themselves. They twiddle away two years of their lives. This doesn't impress us. We don't seem to care. We know how galling an empty life can be for us, but we have trouble feeling for what it is like when idleness hits these other human beings.

We ask persistently for another kind of proof, too. We keep insisting on evidence of some kind of immediate cash payoff. Will pre-primary education help children in first grade? We want our pound of flesh—a moneyback guarantee. Again, this is the question of a frightened economy. With this age we seem to prefer to stand still, to do nothing, unless we are assured in writing that we will get our money back.

This narrow, special kind of promissory note for the future cannot be written. There can be only one kind of 100 per cent guarantee: Give fours and fives good schools and they will live their fourth and fifth years with a sense of happy exhaustion, having given all they have to give and taken from a rich life all they could absorb. Keep them school-less and they will be hurt. The days of their fourth and fifth years will drag; they will limp through these days waiting for them to end. But their sixth year is another year. Good nursery schools and good kindergartens cannot promise in blood how that year will work out.

Learned Lessons from Their Work

Without the shadow of a doubt some contributions will be made. Some lasting good is bound to result from the enriched past children bring with them. As fours and fives these children have pounded at workbenches, diligently planning ships and planes and cars. They have been engrossed at easels. Fearlessly they have climbed high on jungle gyms. With care and precision and detail they have planned masterful structures of blocks. They have milked cows, sat in the cockpits of planes, ridden on tractors, climbed on fire engines, sat in police cars. They have heard stories galore, sung songs, danced and created music of their own. They have cooked, dug gardens, mixed cement for their own stone wall. They have fed hamsters, watched chicken eggs hatch. They have sped on their tricycles, tugged at their wheelbarrows. Earnestly, seriously, with complete identification, they have played doctor and digger, policeman and conductor, shopper and storekeeper, Mother and Father. Children in nursery school and kindergarten have *worked* for one year and two. The lessons of their work cannot be completely lost.

Lifetime Learnings Have Fruitful Beginnings

First-grade teachers say they can always spot the children who have been to nursery school or kindergarten. But no one can promise-without-fail that any one specific gain will show up always in every child. Children don't "learn" to cooperate in kindergarten. This can't be taught in kindergarten—this is a lifetime learning. All that fours and fives can do is to make a fruitful beginning. Children don't learn self-confidence in kindergarten—this is a life's task, not a grade's task. But they *do* make a beginning. They make a beginning—a four- and five-year-old beginning—in science, in arithmetic, in social studies, in health, in art, in music, in industrial art, in philosophy, in psychology . . . yes, in reading and writing too! But pre-primary education can only do *its* job, whatever its fours and fives are ready for. It cannot guarantee that every child will be ready to read next year when he is six. Or be disciplined next year when he is six.

Prep School?

When a concern for the future sours into anxiety, fours and fives can be hurt. We give them nursery school and kindergarten but not because they are four and five and ready. Because they will be six! We give them nursery school and kindergarten to *make* them ready. We give them nursery school and kindergarten in name only—the form but not the substance. We give them prep schools for first grade.

Pre-primary education does fours and fives no favor when children must line up, when they must tiptoe, when they must whisper. It does its children no favor when it uses workbooks or fusses with phonics or with strange artificial exercises and drills that allegedly "build" readiness. It does children no favor when it makes them color within the lines or sit ad infinitum or go through the exercises that may be appropriate three or four years in the future. Four and five are the springtime of life but not spring training for a tough, hard season to come. *The job of pre-primary education is to help fours and fives flourish, not to reform them.*

The effort is harmful. The effort is wasteful. Even if the goals were worthy, even if the sixth year of life were in fact so much more important than the fifth or fourth, no one could promise with 100 per cent accuracy the future payoff. Even when pre-primary education is completely distorted into boot-training, some will succeed in first grade and some will not. Year Six is Year Six, and too many factors enter into it. A good or bad fourth year and fifth cannot completely control the results. But this does not mean that these years do not exist with value in themselves and with their part to play in the total life of a child.

Potential for Parent Education

There are two future contributions pre-primary education can make which do not distort children's living in these years. Pre-primary education offers an unusual opportunity for parent education. Much more so than later, parents do not simply "send" their fours and fives to school. They come along with them, often physically and always psychologically. *Good school programs during these years have a unique chance to help parents understand their children, how they grow and how they learn and why they behave as they do.* Only free schools, right for fours and fives, can take advantage of this chance. Parents can learn nothing when children are sitting, dominated by adults, not acting their age or being themselves. A good program for children is a good program for parents, too. Just as with the children, no one can guarantee that every lesson will be learned or that any will be learned once and for all or that parents will be transformed into model human beings who from this point on act perfectly. There will be successes and failures, but the special importance of pre-primary education for parent education is a valid point.

Spot Special Needs in Time

Without hurting its fours and fives, good pre-primary education can help the whole school system, too, and the whole of our communities. Good programs in these years are the best devices we now know for spotting children who need special help. They are our DEW line, the only effective *Distant Early Warning* system that we have. They can alert us. They can let us know *in time*. We have no other machinery for uncovering stress and strain that can do costly damage later. Once children start to sit, problems tend to be covered over until the expensive eruptions of preadolescence and adolescence remind us of their presence. When they are in a good group for fours and fives, children have their last chance to reveal to us their need for special help.

Pre-primary education can be a school's and a community's first line of defense in the battle for mental health. It can be the time and place for building strength. It can be the time and place for the prevention of illness. This is a legitimate service to the future which does not deny the present.

There are contributions to the future that pre-primary education makes, some more significant than others, some achieved with less hazard than others, some more easily identified than others. But the inescapable fact remains: the surest, clearest, most incontrovertible payoff is *now*. Now when these children are four and five. This is the only guarantee: give these children good groups and they will be more glad they are alive. The fundamental appeal has to be to our conscience and to the depth of our sense of caring. If the quality of living in these years seems important, then pre-primary education has pressing importance. But if we don't care we won't act.

If we will only take those steps that the coolest calculation of immediate profit and loss forces us into, woe to our fours and fives! Woe ultimately, too, to our sick, our aging, the infirm, to all who cannot yet produce and who must depend on the goodness of the rest of us. Woe to our museums. To the dance and to art. To philosophy. To parks and playgrounds and picnic spots. Woe to music, to literature, to flowers, if a payoff becomes the sole test of importance!

Vol. XVIII—p. 67 (Oct. 1941)

The Five to Eights and How They Grow
BY BARBARA BIBER

Barbara Biber, who is research psychologist at Bank Street College of Education, New York City, has chosen arbitrarily the years between five and eight as the general limits of a period of transition between early childhood and middle childhood. She discusses some of the outstanding trends of this period and shows how the particular social situation in which children mature is reflected in the emerging values and goals of children.

W E ARE WELL ACCUSTOMED THESE DAYS TO THE IDEA THAT EARLY childhood experience leaves lasting effects. The overambitious adult may have been the youngest of a family of seven, who found it difficult to establish a real sense of his own worth and importance during childhood. The vindictive, moralizing adult may have been the child whose early mischievousness was nipped in the bud and who became a premature model of good deportment at the age of three.

We are even accustomed, nowadays, to the notion that the nature of early childhood experience may have far-reaching social significance. Presumably, if the natural hostilities of children's early years could be dealt with less punitively, if they could be controlled and channelled off without involving excessive feelings of guilt, we would have reason to look forward to generations of freer adults.

By this line of reasoning, a portion of the adult aggression and tension in our own times is the outcome of the burden of deeply repressed hostility which our present adult generation represents. The study of adult personality leads one to give credence to this idea even though many people will be unwilling, justifiably, to accept such an oversimplified, single-track explanation of a world in strife. Actually, if we examine each successive period of child development in detail, we find equally challenging and arresting relations between the psychology of individual development and the social structure of which the individuals become a member. The years between five and eight, which can be taken arbitrarily as the general limits of a period of transition between early childhood and middle childhood, are an interesting area for this kind of study. What follows on these pages refers to a particular social group—children of lower middle-class families, living in the city, attending a progressive school, whose needs and problems are a matter of more than ordinary interest and concern to their parents.[1] For these children, these transitional years represent active growth in many different areas, but we shall concern ourselves here with only two aspects—*first,* the changing drift of dependence and independence and *second,* the changing relation to the world of objective reality.

The nursery years which precede this period of transition can be characterized as the period of the child's deepest dependence on adults. Yet, by the time the child has lived through these years, he has accumulated, gradually, an impressive measure of independence which he gains on a dozen psychological fronts simultaneously. The utter physical helplessness of the infant is transformed into the physical adequacy of the five-year-old who can climb to the top rung of the jungle gym, run up the steps two at a time, carry a cupful of liquid without spilling it and pack a real wallop in self-defense. The baby who can only cry and whimper if the milk comes through the nipple too slowly has become

---

[1] Material in this paper is drawn from an extensive research study to be reported in a forthcoming book, *Children in School: A Study of a Seven-Year-Old Group.*

the five-year-old who can speedily clear a lunch plate of its lamb chop, potatoes and spinach, and efficiently, despite the handicap of a fork and a spoon. The infant who could do nothing about feeling cold and wet until his mother remembered that the window was open too wide on a cold winter night has become the five-year-old who can manage the intricacies of a two-piece snowsuit with great dispatch especially if he wants to get out into the snow before it has been trampled. The baby whose mother had to interpret whether his one and only cry meant hunger or pain has become the five-year-old who can tell his nursery school teacher that he wants the next turn at the easel and that he will need red, blue and yellow paint for his picture. The baby who only occasionally deviated from his chronic compliance by turning his head away from the bottle or setting up a wail for a few minutes when put down to sleep has become the five-year-old who can and does express his resistance to adult authority by hitting, calling names, deliberately overturning his cup of milk, refusing to take his bath, disturbing the rest hour in a nursery school and running away from his nurse on the street.

This array of accomplishments in the direction of growing independence represents a genuine psychological yield to the child in terms of feelings of gratifying self-assertion, powerfulness, freedom from control. Yet in these years he cannot live by these alone. Happiness, or in another terminology, security, is not in proportion to the degree of independence. Instead, in these early years, the child's emotional equilibrium is much more clearly a function of the willingness of the adults in his life to care for him, to do for him, since these are the signs by which he reassures himself that they love him beyond question. His independence has come to him almost incidentally as a by-product of learning to talk, to walk, to control his eyes and his muscles. The degree to which he resists adults is a sort of testing of his individual prowess motivated by the ambivalence of his feeling toward these grownups who, in the child's reality, fluctuate between foreseeing and granting his deepest wishes, on the one hand, and stopping him in the tracks of his own impulses, on the other.

In contrast, the two or three years which follow early childhood represent a period in which the child much more directly and actively establishes his independence of adults—their authority, their codes, their omnipotence. His resistance is likely to be expressed not only in the particular form of refusing to do what he is told, but in the more general form of accusing the adult of being too bossy or too strict or just not fair. He may take a special delight in repudiating the adult's code for overt behavior by using unacceptable language, coming to the table with hands unwashed, preferring his most tattered sweater to his newest one.

More significant than this tendency to stand off from the adult, evaluate him and criticize him is the trend during these years to replace an individual kind of rebelliousness with more socialized forms of protest. In the home situation there develops the special kind of communion of feeling that is implicit in the phrase, "us kids." A sit-down strike by a group of seven-year-olds in protest against the length of the rest hour represents the kind of socialized resistance which will occur in a school situation where the natural trends of childhood are permitted freedom of expression. It is important to be aware of the weight of feeling which the child must have associated with this daring adventure of setting himself off, apart from the adults whose protection he still wants and needs and who have just recently been almost the symbols of all life for him. Life remains bearable to children during this period only because as they cast off the relation of dependence to adults on the one hand, they embrace an almost equally strong relation of dependence on the child group.

In the same school group in which the incident of the sit-down strike took place, it was possible to observe a variety of mechanisms by means of which the child group establishes itself as an important social organism. Other groups of children might find other particular mechanisms by means of which to establish a feeling of power and strength among the children themselves. In this group, the children used the technique of voting as a kind of primitive way of establishing their togetherness. It took a thousand forms—putting hands up, putting hands down, voting about whether ice cream was better than cake, which child in the group was most loved and most hated, and so on. Through this technique they reinforced their group feeling by establishing certain common enemies, most notable among them being Hitler. Secrets and secret activities was another common way of keeping something going among the children that actively excluded adults—a symbolic gesture by means of which to say, "We have a world of our own and you, dear grownup, cannot have a place in it." It was noted, too, that during the free art periods these children were very active and free in mutually criticizing, in both positive and negative terms, each other's work so that the situation impressed one directly with its active social interrelationships among the children. In contrast, one need only recall the nursery-school child's perennial appeal not to another child but to a teacher to "Look what I made."

Another interesting trend that seems to lead in the same direction is a marked tendency on the part of these children to be violent in negative criticism of their own performances either in crayons and paints or with pencils and paper. This kind of self-negation, to those of us engaged in the study of this group, seems to belong with the other tendency mentioned above—a consolidation of group feeling among the children. By negating and rejecting oneself as an individual, one is helped to enlarge the feeling of belonging to a whole group of children so much stronger, so much more powerful than one's own small self. Thus we see in this period of transition that the child's growing impulse to become independent of adults goes hand in hand with a developing dependence upon belonging to the child group. His happiness or his security at this stage of development involves the need for real acceptance by the children, for genuine identification with children as a group, for freedom to repudiate much of the adult's code with respect to behavior.

In order to supply the child with the kind of psychological support which he needs, it is necessary that adults take his drive for independence for what it is really—the first steps in the difficult job of constructing one's own individual personality. The child still needs, together with his freedom to grow away from grownups, the confidence that they will stand by.

The Changing Relation to the World of Objective Reality

It is this question of the course by which the child gradually attains his adequacy in relation to the real world that we turn to now as one of special interest in connection with the years of transition that follow early childhood. In his earliest years, the child's reality is primarily one of deep feeling. His greatest needs, his most urgent problems are generated within the family. In accepting himself as a child, as a boy or a girl, as a sister or a brother, he lives through a basic experience that normally involves him in considerable conflict and ambivalence of feeling. Yet, during these same years, there is gradually emerging a degree of understanding and control with respect to the world of things, ideas, relations, causes in which he moves. This control and understanding is not anything that we can teach him like so many nursery rhymes. It is rather something that he accomplishes by himself with ways of learning that are peculiarly his own. Given half a chance, he experiments freely with physical reality and teaches himself a long lesson about how hard one has to pull to dislodge a wagon stuck round the curb, about where one has to sit in order to make the seesaw go up and down, about how to pump oneself on a swing, about how to make a building of blocks that is both tall and steady.

As soon as words become symbolic of experience for him, he sets out on the tremendous task of threading his experience into chains of ideas. Mothers not only are mothers but have mothers, and an aunt may be the sister of one's own mother. Lamb chops and spinach come together at lunch on a single plate, but Millie the cook had to go to the butcher shop for one and the vegetable store for the other. When it's in the air, it's snow; on the street it gets wet like rain; when we bring it into the house it's water; when we put it in the cube trays in the refrigerator it becomes ice. Before he has outgrown the years of early childhood, even his notion of time has elaborated sufficiently so that he enjoys looking back to the distant past when he was only three. Thus, through his sensitive observation, he becomes conversant with the world of objective reality in terms not only of physical relations but of process, change and cause as well.

The free dramatic play of children during these early years serves as an extraordinarily effective mechanism by which they find release from emotional pressures at the same time that they clarify experience in the world. An hour of free play by a group of five-year-olds, during which a fire engine made of packing boxes, boards, ropes, buckets goes through a series of imaginary rescues, has interwoven within it the strands of projection, phantasy and analysis. The child who in the role of the fire chief insists that it is his privilege to decide who may be permitted the roles of firemen may be the child who feels overridden in his complicated home situation that includes not only a mother and father but a set of grandparents and a maiden aunt. Their play may take a pattern of dramatic rescues, a living through imminent danger averted miraculously and thus may be a phantasied expression of the children's feelings of dangers and threats from which they too can only be saved miraculously. In the same play, they may go through a complicated dramatic business about pipes and a hydrant and a pump on the engine to send the water up that is really a way of studying out in simple terms the basic problem of fire apparatus. Thus we see that during this period the child's understanding of the real world cannot be functionally separated from his deep and urgent feelings concerning his own intimate emotional experience.

In the years that come after the nursery years, the child elaborates his understanding of the world by continued experimentation and observation and analysis. But there is added now to this trend an especially powerful drive to master the adult's special ways of understanding the world. He is no longer satisfied with his own child-like reconstructions of reality. He prefers now to adjust and conform to the objective standards of performance implicit in the adult world. Thus it is at this period that we find a fairly universal interest in learning to read and write and figure, to acquire these basic tools by means of which adult experience is organized.

We note, too, that he enjoys his own creative work most when he can make it conform to his notion of the way things "really are." He is patronizingly amused by a Matisse picture because the cup and saucer look as though they are going to slide off the table. He becomes interested in problems of perspective and proportion. He develops an admiration for accuracy—a song sung in correct pitch, a ball pitched effectively, a well-finished boat, a successfully rhymed poem. This general trend toward realism and objectivity shows itself in his thinking especially when we take note of his spontaneous questions and conversations. He is most interested in facts—how big is the biggest ocean liner, how is maple sugar made out of the sap of a tree, how long does it take the Clipper to cross the ocean. He has outlived the stage where a little factual information could be embroidered fantastically and satisfy him completely, but he has not yet reached the stage of interest in attitude or opinions. His devotion is rather to the yes-no, is-it or isn't-it aspect of experience, and he continues to ask, "Is there really a God?" no matter how many times you may have said, "Some people think there is, and some people think there isn't."

This drive toward understanding the world by the ways that adults seem to have for the job involves the child in what might be called a gradual process of de-personalization. Heretofore, he has lived predominantly in terms of his own experience—his feelings of love and hate, his encounters with physical obstacles, his ideas about things and people which he himself has seen or known. Now he turns from this dependence upon his own experience to vicarious experiences, to interest in places he has only heard about in long past times that even adults themselves have only "heard" about. This he does gradually during these years, in a forward-backward pattern, continuously relating the remote experience to some personal content of his own, preferably dramatic in nature, in order to lend it reality. Thus we are not surprised to observe that his ideas have a highly emotional tone and are absolutistic in structure.

His intellectual development during this period shows signs of another influence which accounts as well for the quality of intensity that surrounds his ideas. This influence comes to him by direct descent from the period of early childhood, as mentioned above, in which he managed some of his deepest feelings of resentment and conflict by projecting them onto other children, people, things, in his immediate environment. Now we find many instances of what seems to be a similar projective mechanism attaching itself to more remote personalities and phenomena. The seven-year-old group previously referred to spoke with venom and fury about Hitler with a depth of feeling that could not possibly have arisen in a clear objective understanding of the effects of German Fascism. Their hatred seemed to be in good part a projection of feelings derived from their own experience against an enemy common to the group yet remote from their own lives.

I think it is fair to say that this trend has educational significance of major importance. Children take on as their enemies those figureheads or symbols that are also enemies to the adults whom they trust and aim to emulate. Thus, it becomes obvious at once that at the primitive stage of developing values and attitudes which these transitional years represent, the children are deeply affected by the values and attitudes, not only of their parents but of their teachers. Because so much of the ideational content of this period of development has an emotional quality derived from the child's own deep emotional experience, it may well be that this is the period when many an adult prejudice is given its deepest roots.

Outstanding Trends of the Transitional Period

In general, we can say that after a child has outgrown the period of early childhood, he usually displays in the next few years an active need to free himself from his babyish dependence upon adults, an inclination to fulfill this need by means of attaching himself with another kind of dependence to a strongly socialized child group, an active concern for becoming conversant with the world of adult reality, a tendency to accept the standards of realism and accuracy as the most important ones, an orientation toward factual information and a relative disinterest in attitudes and opinions, a great extension of his intellectual development to include vicarious experience remote in time and space, a tendency to accept vicarious experience as real in the degree to which he can keep on relating it to personal experience, a quality of fervor and almost passionate approval and disapproval in relation to ideas that seem to spring from the continued impulse to project his feelings but now in areas that are further and further removed from the intimacies of home and companions. Beneath all these tendencies there is a fundamental drive to be able to do the things that grownups can do, to understand the world as they do without depending upon them. In short, to develop one's own individual adequacy in relation to as much of the world as one can envisage.

What becomes of the trends of this period depends upon the particular social circumstances of the child's environment. The group of children who were studied in detail with respect to these factors were attending a progressive school, so that we must take into account that their life experience at this level was different in many fundamental ways from that of the children who meet our culture in a more unmitigated form in the public schools of a large city. Nevertheless, it was plain to see how fundamentally they too, were affected by the basic values of our own culture.

Although they were certainly not being pressed to live up to any fixed standards of performance, their behavior showed clearly the many ways in which standards influence the basic organization of experience for every growing child in our society. No one can escape the sense in which our lives are organized around the concept not of what we can or cannot do but rather of how well or how poorly we do what we do. Thus, within the child group itself, we could see growing-up values that have to do with how well one could read, who was the best painter, who had the best ideas for the play, who was the poorest pitcher. Here, in a school atmosphere, where the adults were certainly not supporting the competitive impulses of the children, we noted innumerable ways in which prowess and mastery were fundamental needs and goals.

They reacted to unusual problem situations such as an intelligence test with an eye always as to whether it was hard or easy. Some of their self-criticism, some of their inclination to alibi for their own performances were further signs that they were substituting high standards of their own for the arbitrary standards which they might have been compelled to meet in another school. They are clearly aware of the value which our society sets upon precocity. The Sevens envy the Eights' abilities on the one hand and look patronizingly on the Sixes' infantilism. This cannot be without its effect upon individual personalities who develop their security around feelings that at Seven they are at least as good as some Eights if not better than others. Thus already at this period of development, our children are becoming part of the fundamental fabric of the world in which they live. The social importance of competitiveness, individual prowess, status by means of achievement affects them in ways that not even a conscious school philosophy can undo.

There are other social influences at least as important, such as the cleavage between the boy and girl groups, that are not so pertinent to the two questions which we have set ourselves for discussion. We should note here again, however, that in addition to being affected at this period by the psychological foundations of our society, they are also deeply affected by the attitudes and viewpoints of the adults who act almost as the agents for the vicarious experience of the child. His impulse to project his own hostile feelings further and further away from himself can be channelled into becoming a hatred of Jews, as indeed it has in many countries and, I dare say, in many communities in our own country. In other social settings where the adults have other values and ideals, the child's hostility will attach itself in totally different directions.

These are days when we are concerned not only in the academic pursuit of how society affects children at different stages of their development but in the much more important practical question of how those of us who are influencing children's lives may hope to contribute to changing the nature of society itself. In beginning this discussion, we referred to the notion that less deeply repressed hostility in early childhood might yield as a smaller portion of aggression in adult life. Now we are ready to suggest how our treatment of what seem to be the natural trends and impulses of the child in the transitional years between early childhood and middle childhood may affect not only the children themselves but the kind of social structure they will create in their adult years.

As the Twigs Are Bent, So Grows the Forest

It is not enough to say that a democratically organized classroom will develop more democratic personalities and therefore be a real contribution to the preservation of democracy. My own feeling is that the problem deserves and needs much more detailed analysis, much clearer definition of the aspects of our democracy which we wish to see preserved and the weaknesses in democracy as we know it which need to be remedied.

By not reinforcing in our schoolrooms and in our relations with our children the competitive striving which we breathe in with the oxygen of our country, we are hoping to make of our children personalities less devoted and less dependent upon the ideals of rugged individualism. We try, therefore, to set up schoolroom situations which value most highly the direct gratification that a human being young or old can get from any kind of useful and creative work. Basically, thus, we are trying to develop people who can enjoy what they can do and what they have for those abilities and possessions themselves rather than for the relative status and superiority that they gain from having them. We are seeking to educate a less individualized human being whose happiness and security can come more from his relations to other people and less from the advantages, intellectual or material, that he can gain over other people. When we find children coming to a stage in their development when they naturally seem to seek an identification with a social group at their own level, we do everything we can to nurture this impulse and do not allow our own adult needs to hold the reins over them to interfere with a wholesome community feeling among the children themselves.

If as teachers we can be flexible enough to stand occasional rejection by the children and not be overwhelmed by their criticism of us; if we can be understanding of their needs partly to repudiate us in order to strengthen themselves and at the same time accept our full responsibility as adults to lead and support them and control them when necessary, we will have presented to them a positive ideal for what authority can be in any life situation. Thus we try to give them experience at this level, when they are going through such deep alterations of their feelings toward us, that will make it possible for them to accept leadership and authority in later years without cringing before it or to be leaders or authorities without needing to be despots.

One more point remains to be made. Our democracy needs more widespread responsibility, less feeling that laws are Congressmen's business. This remoteness from the affairs of government, accompanied as it is by an excessive readiness to let government become artificially representative, may be not only a product of our large and complicated country but a by-product of educational techniques. It is in this connection that the distinct characteristics of intellectual development in the transitional years has significance.

If we capitalized the child's impulse to tie up all the first ideas that he gets vicariously with his own firmly rooted personal experience, we might make for a greater devotion to ideas and understanding and diminished feeling that "all that stuff" about history and geography was all right in school but has really nothing to do with me as a person. Perhaps in this connection, too, we can use as an asset the child's tendency to express his unconscious feelings in his ideas, and thus allow his developing understanding to share his deepest feelings. It may be very important that a seven-year-old who doesn't know anything about the election campaign issues should feel free to take sides, to express himself vigorously about what side he is on and only later be expected to take an attitude of deliberation and careful judgment with respect to the intricacies of the problems.

The plea in this connection is really that we shall do for a child's intellectual development what we have begun to accept as good procedure for his emotional development—namely, to recognize that a period of fairly aggressive, freely expressed, unreasoned behavior may be essential to the development of a healthy temperance later on. In other words, we are probably trying to make our children reasonable too soon, just as we once tried to make them socialized too early. The hope is that such educational experience might turn out adults with interests more deeply imbedded in social problems and with greater capacity to cherish and enjoy social gains.

Children Come By Meanings

BY MARIE I. RASEY

> *Even as the child enters school he brings his past experiences with him. What has happened to him before makes a difference in the meanings he absorbs from school experiences. Through this understanding approach to two children we can understand others better. Marie I. Rasey is on leave of absence from Wayne University, Detroit, Michigan. She is working with the U.S. Foundation for Education in India, New Delhi.*

It was a warm September day with the best of summer and a hint of autumn in the air. Miss Wilson, the kindergarten teacher, was admitting the beginners. Mrs. Waters stood in the door near the desk and said: "Miss Wilson, this is William Waters, who is beginning school. He has a brother in the fourth grade who will pick him up at noon. Goodby, William," and she was gone. Any kindergarten teacher knows that this was not the first time Mrs. Waters had brought a child to start school. Parents who leave children for the first time often linger.

William looked about the lovely room. His eyes widened. Never had he seen so much that he coveted—with no larger child attached. He started down the first side of the room picking up, like an oversize magpie, everything he could carry. The next wall and the next, until there remained only one unharvested wall. His arms were full. His small chin was pointed skyward to help hold the loot. With an audible sigh, William deposited his collection in the corner, and found, as does every hoarder, that the only behavior left to him was to sit down cross-legged and guard his treasure.

It is wholly possible that small William could not have put into words the meanings under which he operated. His teacher can, and so can we. He sees the items of his desiring arrayed before him. He judges that nothing lies between him and his desire except that spending of himself to make them his. He acts as if he believed: "Before me lies the end of every man's desire. I will get, while the getting is thus good. If I keep what I have, I will have to sit on it."

William might not have been able to phrase these meanings, but he would have no difficulty understanding them, acquiesing to them, acting upon them.

With the first closing of the small hand around the desired object the feel of achievement, the sense of "I canness," raises his ability to a higher moment—raises it to an Nth power. His unique individual experience is, so far, successful, and carries with it the power associated with success-crowned doing. But it is multiplied many times by the inheritance laid down in his tissues. He is the direct descendant of the good grabbers, since man began, and perhaps since certain of his tissues were differentiated in some less complex organism. We can be wholly sure that William has this inheritance for his existence proves it. The poor grabbers starved to death and left no heritage.

This situation poses a difficult task for the teachers of the Williams. It is not one of education alone. It is, even at this early stage, a question of re-education with all that is involved. William belonged to a well-to-do family. His mother would have said that the house was full of crayons and paper, small toys, scissors and all the rest which William had so exerted himself to collect. He was the youngest of Mrs. Waters' four boys. In the midst of plenty, so far as parents had noticed, there was not only sufficiency but affluence. When three older and more able brothers have had their lion's share, even affluence may resemble poverty for the last-comer.

Each Child Brings His Experience

While we have been looking inside William, many other children have come in, each has brought his family with him, who sit with him on the little red chair, invisible to the naked eye, looming large in the vision of the practiced seer. They constitute the child's initial equipment which he brings to school. From the welter of his externality he selects those items which his experiencing has taught him to recognize and bind to himself with affect-laden bonds.

Each child brings his individual meanings which make a wide scope of meanings within the group. We cannot pause to assess each meaning with which the teacher will be concerned. As each moves through time, toward maturity, he expresses what he already is. The teacher will find it a difficult, but rewarding, exercise of his insight and skill to serve as a facilitator of the process. It will drive the teacher mad who conceives it his duty to replace the child's meanings with those which he "thinks" people ought to have and he coerces the child into behaviors which he thinks will habituate that child to those meanings.

Learning To Be a Tyrant

Jenny's mother brought her in with a death-grip on her scrawny hand. The yellow tinge to her skin bespoke an overrich diet rather than the result of the sun's warm rays. Her hair was nondescript, too. She wore a brown-and-white check dress with elegant but unobstrusive hand embroidery.

"This is Jenny Brown," said the mother in a tone which gave the impression that she was hurrying somewhere. "Jenny is a very nervous child. She won't let me out of her sight. I'll have to stay until she gets used to things. I used to be a teacher and I know." Poor teacher, but also, poor child! Somewhat later Miss Wilson found that Jenny's mother had indeed been a teacher, and a good one. She had married late and Jenny was, as her mother often said, with more truth than insight, "All she had."

Mrs. Brown seated herself in a small chair beside her daughter. Now we could understand her vague hurriedness. Jenny was to fulfill Mrs. Brown's own unsatisfied desire to be "the smartest, the best, the first," in all things that stood for scholarship. It would be a long task at which Jennie might fail or even rebel, for Jennie will likely come to have dreams of her own.

Time and again the next hour the clever teacher almost got Jenny's undivided attention. The small child almost obeyed her strong impulse to slide off the chair and join as an equal with the activities of the other children. But a glance at the mother forestalled the impulse.

Each time Jenny appeared to be joining the children, with her attention at least, Mrs. Brown rose with a show of being meticulously quiet. Jenny watched her from the corner of her eye. Her timing was perfect. As Mrs. Brown grasped the doorknob, Jenny opened her mouth to emit a soul-searing scream—no cry of terror—just the commanding bellow of any tyrant who sees the possibility that his whim might be ignored or not fulfilled. Mrs. Brown scurried back to her chair again. For an hour and a half that child cat-moused her mother, and her long-suffering teacher put up with it. Finally the teacher said with some conviction: "If you will just get out of sight and stay out, I'm sure Jenny will be all right." Mrs. Brown did go and stay. Jenny yelled one more yell. It brought no scurrying mother. She gave herself to the activities of the children, as she really wished to do all the time.

All of us lead our lives or are led by them, in terms of the meanings our experiencing has so far given us. When the valence is heavy on the side of the nurturer, the meanings with which that nurturer sees and interprets furnishes the learner with all the meanings he has. This continues until time has provided the learner with the facilities for his own experiencing with which to correct or modify, or replace the concepts he has acquired by immediate or remote social inheritance. *Thus the teacher's meanings, expressed in what he does and what he is, may prove more important than the things he knows in an academic sense.*

We Behave Our Meanings

Human beings behave themselves in direct exemplification of the meanings they hold. Until they come by different meanings, they cannot come by different behaviors. The meanings they acquire when they are compelled by someone else (against their own meanings) do not hold for long. This furnishes no basis for habit other than those a slave requires. We cannot educate for slavery and produce free men.

And what of the Williams and Jennys and the many others? How will they know life and live it in terms of the meaning they now possess? Will William become a bigger and better hoarder, collector of memberships and chairmanships of all the corporations which conserve? Will he become the watchdog of the bank or the treasury or the guardian of all that has been? Will he speak always of the past and look skeptically or fearfully on the future? Or will skillful teachers help him to new meanings in which he shall ultimately value the worth of things shared above those possessed?

Can Jenny be re-educated to prefer the milk of human kindness to the heady wine of tyranny?

In the teacher's hands rests the responsibility of arraying the facilities round children, particularly in their early years so that their experience can yield them the hierarchy of meanings which releases them into life, that they may lead it, rather than be led by it. As specimens of humankind, and as species, they learn to relate themselves to humanity in total or to its individual components. The relatedness which they have been able to make and to maintain between themselves and their kind is one measure of the degree of humanity they attain.

Children Want To Know
BY KENNETH D. WANN

This study on young children's concepts by Kenneth D. Wann, professor of education, Teachers College, Columbia University, New York, brings out the need for school programs based on this fact.

THREE-YEAR-OLD DANNY, BUSILY OCCUPIED AT THE EASEL, HAS JUST finished a picture of a round ball with a ring around it. Presenting the picture to the teacher he says, "It's a planet." To the teacher's question, "What is a planet?" he replies, "It's up in the sky." Danny, like millions of other children, is a product of the space age. He has had rather direct contact with a wider world than has ever been available to children of past generations. He knows about faraway people and places. He is concerned with the problems of space travel. He wonders about many things he has seen in his travels with his family or viewed on television.

Danny and all the other children like him today probably know more at an earlier age than has ever before been possible. Certainly many more opportunities for experiencing and knowing are available to young children today. Continual flow of ideas through mass media of communication and rapid means of travel have removed the ceiling on what children can know.

While we recognize the impact of our technological age on children's learning, the need is for a more precise understanding of what children are gaining from their experiences and the ways by which they organize and use the great array of unorganized ideas with which they are bombarded. To satisfy our own need in this respect the author and a small group of teachers undertook a study of the concept development of young children. The teachers represented schools in communities of widely differing socio-economic levels. The range was from a low economic level to a high level. They studied three-, four- and five-year-old children in their own classrooms over a period of five years.

Children's Information Is Extensive

We were not prepared for what we found. Casual observation had convinced us that the children knew and understood a surprising lot about many things, but the extent and depth of their information and understanding were sources of amazement to many of us. *A topical analysis of the data collected revealed concern with information about hundreds of topics ranging from dinosaurs to rockets and from people and places to weather and electricity. It was clear that the interests of young children were global, even universal, in scope. Their interests were not confined to any one period of time or to any one locality.*

The range of children's information is illustrated by these anecdotes drawn from hundreds of similar ones collected by the teachers.

- Four-year-old Maggie during morning snack time was breaking her crackers into tiny little bits. The teacher said, "Maggie, what on earth are you doing?"

Maggie responded, "I'm making an infinity of crackers."

The teacher somewhat surprised and not at all sure that Maggie knew what she was saying asked, "What is an infinity, Maggie?"

"Oh, you know, it just goes on, and on, and on," responded Maggie.

- There was Gary, four years old, who said at snack time, "I'm going to fill my cup just like this—one half full. Then I'm going to fill it one half way again and do you know what I'll have? I'll have a full cup."

- Beth and Jimmy, five years old, were looking at a book about the sky. Beth said, "Water comes from the clouds."

"Yeah, but you know air ends up in the sky at the beginning of space," responded Jimmy. "There's no water or air up there, and you can't live there. They're trying to get through, but they can't."

- A group of three-year-old boys spent some time dressing up. They donned ties, bats, gloves, glasses and jackets. They secured brooms and some long-handled brushes and said, "We are going hunting in the jungle and we won't have any sitter."

Children Seek Information

It was apparent early in our study that these children were on a continuous quest for more and more information. We have evidence to indicate that concept development was a conscious process to these children. This is not to say that the children themselves identified their efforts to learn as such. *It was evident, however, that the children repeatedly sought more and more information about a given topic and that they consciously tried to relate and test one bit of information against another.*

Having information and being able to use it in appropriate ways was a source of great satisfaction to the children in this study. Evidence for this conclusion comes from numerous recordings of occasions when children expressed pleasure at having gained information or at the prospect of learning. The five-year-old's remark, "Oh boy, dinosaurs," after the teacher had been persuaded to read another book about their favorite topic is a case in point. The great frequency with which children made a game out of testing one's own or another's information is further evidence of satisfaction derived from having certain knowledge.

The spontaneous conversations between children and their readiness to contribute information to any group discussion were additional indications of the satisfaction children derive from the possession and use of knowledge. Three-year-old Jan's contribution to his group illustrates this point. He and his teacher together had read the book, *How Big Is Big?* and had discussed skyscrapers at length. One morning he spied the teacher and other children looking at the book. He quickly put aside what he was doing and came across the room and volunteered his valuable information. With a big smile he said, "I know what a skyscraper is. A skyscraper is a very tall building that goes up to the sky so far it looks like it reaches the sky."

Children Seek To Organize Information

We were deeply impressed with the struggles of young children to understand, to interpret and to put together into a comprehensible pattern the pieces of the complex puzzle that is their world. This is not easy, and children were found developing misconceptions as often as they were developing accurate concepts. Excerpts from children's conversations will illustrate this struggle.

- A four-year-old saw a great machine excavating for a big skyscraper and asked, "What kind of machine made the world?"

- Other children were confused when they found two large cans of ashes waiting for the trash collector. These city children had never seen a fire make ashes.

"What's in the can?"
"Ashes."
"Where do they come from?"
"Cigarettes, you dope."

- Another group was struggling with their concepts of fish.

"Why do fishes always have to stay in water?"

- When the water in the aquarium was low one said, "See, the fish have been drinking the water."

Even the simplest words can be confusing. When the teacher discussed a class trip, one child asked, "What is a trip? Is it a fall?"

- "Is 'stupid' a bad word?" another child asked.

"No," replied his friend. "It means crazy, but I don't know if it's bad."

In their efforts to put together related information and ideas into some kind of conceptual framework that had meaning for them the children employed all of the processes involved in thinking and reasoning. There is ample evidence that these children were associating ideas, attempting to discover cause and effect relationships, and discriminating and generalizing about those things which they see, hear and feel in their environment. These are the essential elements of the process of conceptualization at any level.

The children's attempts to establish relationships among ideas ranged from the simplest kind of associative thinking to a more advanced attempt to set a classification of ideas. Sandra's discussion of birthdays represents the latter type of thinking.

- One morning four-year-old Sandra approached the teacher with the question, "Whose birthday is today?" After thinking a moment the teacher responded, "I don't know. Whose is it?"

"Teacher, you don't know? Well, guess," chuckled Sandra.
"Is it Judy's or Carmen's?"
"No, teacher. It is Abraham Lincoln's birthday."
"That is right. Do you know who Abraham Lincoln was?"
"Yes," replied Sandra. "He was a president. Both of them are dead now."
That is right, but Abraham Lincoln is just one man."
"I know," replied Sandra, "but I am talking about George Washington, too. Both of them were presidents."

There were numerous cases recorded in which children were generalizing. In many cases the generalizations were accurate and well based. In other cases the generalizations were premature and inaccurate. Since this is an essential element in concept formation, it is significant that children frequently attempt to use the process. Inaccuracies and too hasty generalizations simply indicated a need for help which adults can supply. The following anecdotes illustrate children's processes.

- As the teacher in a day care center four-year-old group remained late on Fridays, she always arrived later on that day than on others.

Alice: "Today we are going to eat fish."
Maria: "Why?"
Alice: "Because when the teacher comes late we always eat fish."

- Five-year-old Frances was getting dressed to go to the yard when she observed, "The teacher next door is a nurse. I know because she has on white shoes and all nurses wear white shoes."

Essential to the development of understanding and the successful interpretation of environmental data is the ability to see cause and effect relationships, to make inferences, and to reach logical conclusions. Observations in this study brought about a growing respect for young children's ability to employ these processes.

- *Barbara:* "I am going to dress my brother like a small boy four years old so he can go with us on the trip."
Teacher: "Won't he still look too tall?"
Barbara: "No, because when they say 'Why are you so big?' he'll say 'Because my mother and father were giants.'"

- Margaret and Laura were watching the teacher modeling clay.
Margaret: "Are you making this for your mother? Who is your mother?"
Laura: "Her mother is her child's grandmother."

- One group of five-year-olds spent some time trying to understand about foreign languages. The teacher was preparing to read them a story.
Teacher: "This book is written by a Japanese person."
Howie: "Can you read it?"
Teacher: "Yes, it is written in English."
Howie: "If my mother were here, she could read it because she came from England."
Teacher: "She could read it in English. English is the language of England. We speak English in our country because a long time ago English people came here and settled."
Howie: "English belongs to England just like Italian belongs to Italy."
Sue: "If this was a Japanese school and you were a Japanese teacher and we were Japanese children, you would read Japanese stories to us."
Randy: "Japanese people have their own English."

Implication for Schools

The store of information young children have today, their continual quest for knowledge and their struggle to organize information into a meaningful conceptual framework have significant implications for school programs. It is apparent that teachers of young children must support their efforts to acquire information and to organize it. Early childhood has not been viewed as a period of great emphasis on these kinds of activities. Nursery schools and kindergartens have usually been more concerned with developing emotional stability and skills of social adjustment than with contributing intellectual content to children's experiences. They must continue to be concerned with the emotional and social development, but it becomes increasingly urgent that they recognize children's need for help in understanding the ever-widening world that they see and hear about every day.

Kindergarten and nursery-school programs built almost entirely around manipulative materials no longer hold the challenge for young children they formerly did. These materials are more and more finding their way into homes, and children are ready for new and more challenging experiences. Many schools recognizing the need for challenge have begun to move toward an emphasis on formal reading readiness or even reading programs in the kindergarten. This does not seem to be the right response to young children's need for support in their quest for knowledge and understanding. In the first place, what could be less challenging intellectually than coloring in squares or drawing lines from one picture to another in a readiness workbook all according to specific directions from an adult? In the second place, that which will contribute most to reading will be a wealth of understandings which bring meaning to the abstract symbols of reading at a later time. *We must find ways to contribute information to young children that will build these understandings. We must find ways to answer their questions that preserve their great zest for learning. We must find ways to encourage and carefully guide their attempts to put ideas together and generalize about their experiences.*

There are some rather pointed implications of this study of young children for elementary schools also. It is apparent that children bring to school with them a background of firsthand and vicarious experiences which have broadened their horizons far beyond their own immediate environment. Their questions and concerns range widely. One is constrained to ask if these children's potentialities for learning will be challenged by the usual primary grade units on the home, the store and community helpers. The same question can be asked concerning the material we expect children to read in their reading textbooks or other texts. The children's level of sophistication is frequently above that of these materials. This is not to imply that there is nothing remaining for primary-grade children to learn about their own immediate neighborhood or community. There is indeed much they need to learn. *They are ready to explore some deeper meanings and relationships in community life.* The most hackkneyed prototype of community helpers, the policeman, offers many challenging learnings to even the most sophisticated children. We need but recognize their ability to explore the community structure which supports and makes the policeman's job essential—the problems of group living, the origin of the law he enforces, and the principle of taxation which enables a community to offer such services to its people. Recognizing this we also recognize that we cannot confine children's interest to their community. They are challenged to explore widely, and we must support their need to do this.

Essential to our utilization and support of the great potentialties of today's children to learn at any level is our recognition of the importance of preserving the willingness to think, reason and seek logical answers to questions, which was so evident in the young children we studied. More important than any specific information imparted to children are the skills involved in these processes. Teaching methods and materials must support and extend the ability to think, to reason and to conceptualize, or education becomes pointless.

Vol. XXVII—p. 377 (Apr. 1951)

Except for Michael
BY HELEN E. BUCKLEY

If it were not for youngsters like Michael, teachers would know a great deal less about boys and girls, writes Helen E. Buckley of the Campus School, State University of New York, State Teachers College, Oswego, New York. It is the brash, uncooperative child, the one completely lacking in group feeling, who teaches us to understand and accept all children and to discover better ways of working with them.

"EXCEPT FOR MICHAEL," I THOUGHT, STIRRING THE YELLOW PAINT IN preparation for the day ahead, "this group of fives would be such fun! Somehow, I don't feel strong enough for Michael today. Maybe he won't come!"

But my thoughts were interruped just then by a familiar voice behind me. "Teacher," Michael was announcing, "I'm here!" Giving the green paint a final whirl, I took a deep breath and turned round to greet him. The day had begun.

It seems a long time ago now, and my attempts to handle Michael seem almost too clumsy to recall. Yet I know well that "except for Michael" I would not have made the discoveries in the understanding of children which I made that year. The courses I had taken in mental hygiene, play therapy, the psychology of individual differences, might have remained in the notebook phase, and all the lectures and discussion groups that I had attended might have been left on the verbal level—except for Michael.

Michael made the sentences I found in articles come alive. He challenged me to use every bit of knowledge and understanding of children I had or could acquire—and the going was slow. The gap between knowing and applying is so wide! Michael forced me to see the gap and to begin to bridge it.

My First Michael

I remember so well my first Michael, peering up at me that day.

"How are you this morning, Michael?" I said, more cheerfully than I felt.

"I'm good, Teacher. I'm going to play with the blocks now," and Michael dropped his sweater on the floor and made for the block shelf.

I watched him go as I watched him every morning. It was always the same. He would pile the blocks very neatly and painstakingly against the open shelf and then prepare to wage war with anyone who approached. Very often he would pile them so high that they would sway precariously back and forth.

To my hopeful, "You won't let them fall, will you, Michael?" he would invariably reply, "Yes!" and clap his hands joyfully as the blocks toppled over with a resounding crash.

Then he would begin building them up again. If another child attempted to help him, or, even worse, tried to take some from him, up would go Michael's arm—loaded or unloaded with blocks. My usual, "We don't hit, do we, Michael?" brought forth the word the question had invited, "Yes!," and only prompt action on my part deterred him from carrying out his purpose.

Michael had a way of passing from one activity to another without finishing anything or attempting to put any of the materials away. One could follow his trail around the room through a maze of Tinkertoys, crayons, clay, puzzle pieces, and paintbrushes. Sending him back to put things away was of no use. He just grew interested all over again in the activity to which he returned, leaving the current one forgotten in the middle of the floor.

The children attempted to help him, to play with him, but his erratic way of doing things, his quickness to hit, his consistency in going exactly opposite to the group as a whole, tended to alienate him from them.

"Teacher," he would announce as we were settling down to rest, "I'm going to shout now" and without waiting for a reply he would proceed to do so—lustily.

After lunch we would hear an inelegant "Teacher, I'm going to burp now!" Or about 10 o'clock, "Teacher, I'm going home now!"

There was certainly no "groupness" as far as Michael was concerned. He liked music but only when we complied with his wish to "do it all by myself!"

"Look, Teacher, I'm a horse!" he would shout, pushing all the other "horses" out of the way; or, "I want to sing now, Teacher. I want to sing all by myself!" At my attempts to include the group in his activity or song, he would leave the piano stamping his feet and shouting, "No, no, no! All by myself!"

Relations soon became strained between Michael and me. The more I urged "Do it *this* way, Michael" or "No, Michael, we don't do that now," the more frequent became Michael's announcements about shouting and hitting and going home and the less and less often he would come of his own accord to group meetings.

Understanding Comes Gradually

Finally I decided that the time had come to do something about the situation. I began to go back through the notes I had accumulated in my education and psychology courses. Every place I came to the word "child" I substituted the word "Michael": "The child [Michael] must feel acceptance and belongingness," I read. "He must gain in self-respect by feeling that he is respected. . . . He must feel that he is a worthwhile person in his own right before he can become a cooperating member of a group."

Then I began to ask myself, "Does Michael feel worthwhile? Does he feel respected? Do I make him feel accepted as an individual?" The no's to these questions frightened me. In fact it took some weeks even to ask these questions of myself and longer to face the answers.

When I began to ask myself why, I began to see myself as a teacher who was more concerned with establishing a smooth-running group than with the needs of the individuals in that group, a teacher who thought that a group was formed on the basis of being "acceptable" rather than "accepted." I seemed to be so concerned lest the principal or supervisor judge my worth as a teacher on the basis of "non-conformists" —the "Michaels"—that it became a matter of pride to "corral" them!

When Michael was shouting my first thought was not "Why is he doing this—how can I help him?" but rather "Oh dear, what if Miss Allen should walk in! *What* will she think?" But life with my pulling one way and Michael pulling the other was unbearable—even my pride was worth the sacrifice!

I forced myself to recognize the fact that Michael would not and could not become a cooperating member of our group until he felt accepted as an individual; so I looked at Michael as if I had never seen him before.

I looked at him as a *person*—not as a child in or out of a group. I jotted down the things he said. I noted his actions—his relations with the other children. I even wrote out the things *I* said to him, and that in itself was a revelation to me. (In fact, in studying Michael I began to get a pretty good picture of myself as well!)

As my notes on Michael piled up—they were really "anecdotal records," but I didn't think to name them—I began to understand him a little better and to see beyond his outward behavior into his feelings.

"All by myself" and "Look at me, Teacher!" Yes, *look* at you, Michael, I thought. You want us to watch you and to tell you how well you do and how much we like you. Perhaps, when you were small, Michael, no one ever told you that. So now you have to tell yourself and prove it to yourself over and over again and ask others to look too and tell you what you need to know.

I discovered, of course, that understanding and accepting Michael and his feelings did not always mean approval. But even when I had to stop him from hitting or throwing or going home before bus time, I could always let him know that I was trying to understand how he was feeling.

"*I want to hit Billy!*"

Now, when the blocks teetered back and forth and Michael hopped about waiting hopefully for the crash, I said, "You would like them to fall, Michael. You would like to hear them go 'Crash, Bang!'"

"Yes, yes!" Michael would clap his hands, "I *want* them to fall!" and then, surprisingly enough (or it was at first), he took the structure down carefully, block by block, placing each one in its proper place on the shelf.

When his hand raised for a crashing blow upon another child, I learned to say quickly, but calmly, as if I were stating a fact: "You are so angry with Billy that you want to hit him hard—hurt him even."

"Yes!" Michael would agree heartily, "I want to hit Billy!" (*want* to—not *going* to) and the hand came down by his side.

It was not the actual deed itself that seemed to be important—the blocks falling, the hand hitting—but the feelings which prompted it, and the need for someone to recognize these feelings and to understand and accept them, someone who seems to know how you feel better than you do yourself, so that there is no need for showing him.

Rest time became quiet by my saying, "Michael, you would like to shout now and make a lot of noise. You want to show the other children that you don't like to be quiet."

"Yes," Michael would answer, "I could make a lot of noise. I could shout now."

"Yes," I replied in a slightly regretful tone, "it *would* be fun."

"Yes, it would," Michael would agree, lying down and closing his eyes. Someone understood how he felt. Someone even showed him so clearly how he felt that he didn't need to think about it any more.

Of course these changes did not occur as rapidly as it appears when one is recording them. It was a long time before I really felt and meant the words I said to Michael, and it was just as long before Michael could believe that I was concerned with him as he was and not set upon changing him. He would do his own changing—from the inside— just as I had done myself. Slowly, slowly the changes came.

At music time when he said, "All by myself, Teacher, all by myself," instead of replying, "All right, but just *once* now, Michael, and hurry so we can all do it," I said, "You want us to watch you be a horse— all by yourself—so we can see just *you*."

"Yes," Michael said as he galloped off, "I want you to watch me— then *all* the kids can be horses."

Michael came to be a group member so gradually that I wasn't aware of it, probably because his becoming a group member had grown less important than Michael himself.

Being Honest About Feelings

Except for Michael I might not have looked at the other children in that group as individuals either. I might not have learned to recognize and reflect back to them their feelings of fear and frustration and aggressiveness.

For group peace I might have been more inclined to pretend that these feelings did not exist, or worse yet, might have said, in word or attitude, *"Big* boys and girls don't do those things," or ". . . aren't afraid" or ". . . don't cry." All those phrases we use over and over again to get children to deny their real feelings because we either do not want to, or feel we cannot, cope with them.

Thanks to the Michaels I am learning to react to the troublesome times in school and elsewhere differently. Now my goal is not to smooth things over as quickly as possible but rather to help children learn to handle and control their feelings by looking at them honestly.

"You cut your finger, John, and it hurts. It hurts enough to cry about. It's all right to cry when you are hurt." It's still hard not to say, "That's all right, John. Stop crying now. It doesn't hurt much. You're a big boy now!"

When Judy painted black all over her picture, saying, "Thunder, bad black thunder, covering everything up. Everything is afraid of thunder— afraid, afraid. . . ." I tried to show Judy how she was feeling. "Everything is afraid of thunder. Everything gets covered up—thunder even makes *you* afraid."

"Yes, yes—thunder makes *me* afraid," agreed Judy looking at the black paint as if it were the fear itself.

Except for Michael, I think I would have said, thinking of my bulletin board: "Oh Judy, you've gone and spoiled your lovely picture! We can't hang that up. Why don't you throw that away and start another?"

And the quiet child, the one who just sits or stands, how often I have said to him, "Don't just stand there, Danny—*do* something."

(Do *anything*—what if Miss Allen should come in and find you doing absolutely nothing in the middle of the morning?)

But my experience with Michael taught me differently. It taught me to try to help Danny understand himself a little better:

"You don't know what to do this morning, Danny. You want me to tell you what to do." Danny smiles up at me. I'm pretty close, I think. "You can take your time, Danny. Maybe you will get an idea watching the others. It's *hard* to choose sometimes." (No one is trying to rush you, Danny, there's plenty of time. Feel your way into this new experience—watch and look until you are sure.)

And so the group grows, a group of individuals—Michael, John, Judy, and Danny—each one beginning to know himself a little better, each one beginning to know slowly and then more surely that he can let himself go a little because here is a place in which he is loved, accepted and understood.

Here is a place in which his thoughts and feelings and fears are recognized too, and he in turn can look round him and love, accept and understand others because he knows how it feels himself. Then, and only then, is he a real group member!

From Infancy to Adulthood

BY JEAN WALKER MACFARLANE

Jean Walker Macfarlane, professor and research psychologist, emeritus, of Institute of Human Development, University of California, Berkeley, who directed the research project, presents data with significance to teaching.

This article is in response to a request for a summary of our long-time growth research project known as the Guidance Study. It has followed a group of infants through childhood and adolescence to age 18 and has seen them at age 30 when they were facing adult tasks, including guidance of their own infants, children and adolescents toward responsible adulthood.

Purpose of Study

The group was selected from the birth certificate registry to secure a run-of-the-mill group in contrast with the many research studies on "problem" samples. The over-all objectives of the study have been 1) to delineate the fact of physical, mental and personality growth and development in a normal group and to ascertain the variations among and within individuals at different developmental periods over a long time span; 2) to see the relationships of these findings a) to the biological facts (constitutional makeup, sex, health and rate of maturity), b) to environmental facts—physical, socio-economic, intellectual and social, including interpersonal relationships to family members, playmates, classmates, teachers and important others, with their varying personalities and impacts upon individual children; 3) to throw light upon critical combinations of facts whereby some individuals are able to realize their full potentials while others fall far short of such realization; some individuals develop mature and sturdy personalities whereas others rigidly or neurotically cling to immature or ineffectual patterns; some individuals under stress gather new strengths, and others give up the struggle or disintegrate; and 4) to assess how much confidence we should have in the predictive usefulness for the short haul or over the long developmental period of our tools of appraisal of personality characteristics and mental ability of the child.

In a short article we cannot give detail on the methods used; but it is clear that with the above objectives we had to repeat systematically over the years a wide range of measurements covering biological, environmental, familial and behavioral aspects of the growing organism. Direct measures such as developmental x-rays, body-build measures, mental tests and projective tests were used; also interviews furnished materials as seen by parents, teachers, brothers, sisters, the child himself and the professional interviewers (clinical psychologists and physicians). Classmate appraisal was secured by sociometrics and cumulative achievement from yearly school records.

Relevant Findings

Now let us look at some of the things we have learned that are relevant to you as persons and as teachers dealing with children from kindergarten to or into junior high school. Let us look at the predictive usefulness of some of our tools in different developmental aspects.

Physical measures, such as height, were much more predictive over a long age span than were mental test measures which in turn clearly excelled personality measures. Interage correlations, which indicate how stable in group position are its members, showed in respect to height for ages 3 and 18, correlations in the .70's; whereas mental test measures at these two ages were around .40. Even for three-year periods, few of our personality measures reached correlations of .40. Additionally, with increasing age, mental test correlations steadily climbed as Bayley and Sontag also have found; that is, children were becoming more stabilized in mental test performance with age. For three-year periods 3 to 6, 4 to 7, 5 to 8 . . . 9 to 12, mental test interage correlations were .55, .59, .70, .76, .79 and .85, the last (9 to 12) reaching the correlations for height of ages 3 to 6. Not only is a centimeter a cleaner measuring device than a composite IQ or a personality variable, but it is also clear that growth in height precedes in time the other developmental aspects. In our sample of 250 cases, girls on the average reached half of their terminal height by 20 months, boys by 26 months; whereas by 20 and 26 months, respectively, a small proportion of eventual mental capacity had been disclosed and, save for constitutionally determined temperamental variables, very little of the durable patterns of adaptation we call personality characteristics is evident.

The variability of mental test scores is perhaps more meaningfully shown in terms of IQ changes for individuals. For the eight tests given between ages 6 and 18, 15 per cent of our children showed a range of less than 10 IQ points; 58 per cent, almost 3 of 5, showed a spread of 15 IQ points or more; 1 of 3, a spread of 20 IQ points or more; 1 of 10, a range of 30 IQ points or more; and 1 of 20, a 50 or more IQ-point spread. Clearly little reliance can be placed on one test, especially at the earlier years, in spite of the fact that three-fourths of the boys and girls for these eight tests showed an average change of less than 10 IQ points.

When details of the history and the life situation at the time of the test were inspected, it was clear that any given IQ was a functional composite of native ability; the intellectual interests and stimulation in a child's home; the verbal values of his environment; *and* his attitude toward mental achievement and toward the examiner; his confidence or lack of it in his ability; his habits of heightened functioning or letdown under stress; his interpersonal ease or lack of it; the saliency of current emotional problems, both within and outside the mental test situation; the nature of the test.

There is, of course, for the group a definite and significant relationship between tested intelligence and the level of attained education; but *one of the striking findings is the number of men whose poor records* on mental tests and school grades, some even into high school, completely belie the creative intelligence demands of their present positions. An llustration of such will be seen among examples of poor prediction.

How a Person Matures

We have been forced to the conclusion from our long study that the only way one grows up, matures and learns to accept and to be comfortable with oneself and to approach one's potential is by having maturing experiences along the whole life span. Of course, the nature of the problems to be solved, the learning to be acquired, the coping devices to be mastered vary with a person's age, potential ability, physical make-up, temperament and health. They vary with his stage of physical maturity, whether he is in a rapidly growing phase as, for example, in infancy, in preschool years or in adolescent years. Likewise what he learns varies with what the persons in his environment, with their personalities and values—parents, teachers, brothers, sisters, classmates—permit, encourage, demand, reward him for and/or punish him for. Of course, the impact of his trainers upon him varies both with the nature of his trainers and their training procedures as they mesh with his own nature. Pressure that is too heavy for the child's ability or methods too offensive to his temperament may result in great variations in his learned responses. One child is motivated to greater effort; another becomes anxious, brittle and erratic; another defends himself with unmovable stubbornness; another rebels with defiant misbehavior; another ineptly and tonelessly "tries."

Predictions: Inaccurate and Accurate

When we see the varieties of learning tasks with which they were confronted, the many incoherencies in the pressures put upon these differing organisms at different developmental periods, we still are not sure why so many of them turned out to be coherent adults. We were so aware of their uncertainties and dilemmas (and those of their parents and teachers) as they were growing up that seeing them as adults some twelve years later occasioned dramatic shock after shock. Close to 50 per cent have turned out to be more stable and effective adults than any of us with our differing theoretical biases had predicted, some 20 per cent were less substantial than we had predicted, and slightly less than a third turned out as predicted.

Our more accurate predictions were for those who early were overcontrolled, constricted compulsives whose defense patterns were so well entrenched that they became largely autonomous and presented an encapsulated system or a hard shell, which appears to have protected them but, by denying them openness to many kinds of learning experiences, to have impoverished them. In a number of cases they were led to the choice of a mate who reinforces the previous encapsulating patterns. Another group of accurate prediction concerns the mentally retarded; a third group were youngsters who were subjected to variability of family treatment, for example, alternatingly so indulgent one moment and so harshly stripping them of confidence at another moment that stable and integrated patterns have not been learned by age 30. It is among the latter group that the majority of our compulsive adult drinkers are found.

Let us next look at the erroneous predictions (20 per cent) where early records and up to age 18 showed great promise on the basis of high ability or talents—artistic and athletic—and/or easy and successful family and social relationships, followed by later adult appraisals showing failure to live up to potential or strained dissatisfaction with their lives or showing far less depth and substantiality of character than predicted. Some of the major examples here are from among the early highly successful athletes and the early good-looking and socially successful girls. Later life has not brought them the excessive approval poured on them by peers, teachers and parents. Extravagant success came when they were too young to take it with a grain of salt, when too much of their energy went into maintaining their image; and life subsequently had not so indulged them. The measure of success at one age level is frequently not the measure of success at a later age. Too much success, if not really earned, can be a millstone.

Better Than Predicted

Next let us look at the very large group (nearly 50 per cent) for whom, on the basis of persistent and what seemed to us overriding evidences of handicapping personality patterning or disorganization, we predicted crippled or inadequate adult personalities, who turned out better than any of us predicted, and especially the 10 per cent who turned out *far better* than predicted and became mature, effective and understanding adults or exceptionally creative ones. They are the first to admit that they are as surprised as we are and are willing that we give excerpts from their lives.

Without discussing the varieties of factors contributing to early patterns, we give a bare description of some of them early and late. Among this 10 per cent are two who for years persistently spent all their energies in defiance of regulations. Although having high IQ's, both got marginal or failing grades throughout their schooling. After spending a considerable proportion of their school life "in the principal's office," each was finally expelled from public school—the girl at 16, the boy at 15. Both now are wise, steady, understanding parents who perceptively appreciate the complexities of life and have both humor and compassion for the human race. The woman, after getting some specialized training, contributes her time and considerable talents to the physically handicapped while her children are in school. The man is earning a good living for his family with his own business and functions as both mother and father to his motherless children. Each commented that "there must be easier ways" to grow up than having to go through such turmoil and waste of energies for so many years.

Another who defied our predictions at age 30 accurately described himself during the years previous to graduation from high school as "a listless oddball." His average IQ through year 18 was around 100. He was held over three times in elementary school, finally graduated from high school at age 21 without college recommendations. He left the community, made up high school deficiencies and now is a highly talented architect, "living out a normal childhood through my children," is active in his community, and "life is exciting and satisfying." Obviously his tested IQ's up through age 18 were no measure of his true ability, although they corresponded with his grades.

Another marginal grade-getter who was a social isolate and a self-centered, unhappy boy is now the manager of a large construction firm.

Another—a large, awkward, early-maturing girl who labored under the weight of her size and shyness—feeling that she was a great disappointment to her mother—worked hard for her "B" average to win approval and was a pedestrian, uninteresting child and adolescent. She had periods of depression when she could see no point to living. Then, as a junior in college, she got excited over what she was learning (not just in grades to please her mother) and went on to get an advanced degree and to teach in college. Now she has taken time out to have and raise her children. Again we see an understanding, compassionate person, and one full of zest for living, married to an interesting, merry and intelligent man she met in graduate school. "Life is now very good—but it took so very, very long to be comfortable and happy."

Factors Leading to Erroneous Predictions

Why were our predictions wrong? As we look over the individual histories, several contributing factors seem to have led to erroneous predictive judgments.

1. It seems clear that we overweighted the troublesome and the pathogenic aspects and underweighted elements that were maturity-inducing. Since most personality theory has been derived from work with pathological groups, we were oversensitized to these aspects in respect both to overt and covert patterning and inadequately sensitized to the stabilizing and maturity-inducing aspects. Data on these last two

aspects were available, but we failed to give them due weight so preoccupied were we with current dilemmas.

2. We unquestionably overestimated the durability of those well-learned behaviors and attitudes that were characteristic and habitual response patterns over a substantial period of time. It appears that no matter how habitual these patterns were, if they were coping devices or instrumental acts which no longer were effective for desired ends in changed situations and with changing physiologies, by the vast majority they were dropped or modified. This relearning occurred not without some wear and tear nor without anxiety and erratic behavior during a trial and error relearning period. This is very clear both in adolescents and in their parents when previously learned patterns proved inadequate to emerging new needs and adequate new patterns had not as yet become stabilized.

3. Another thing we have learned is that no one becomes mature without living through the pains and confusions of maturing experiences. We have even observed experiences which we regarded as highly traumatic and therefore nonmaturing that our subjects as adults regard as forcing them to come to terms with what it was that they wanted and didn't want out of their lives.

4. Still another thing that is clear is that many of our subjects did not achieve what Erikson (1956) calls "ego identity" until after marriage and parenthood forced them or presented an opportunity to them to fulfill a role that gave them a sense of worth, through responsibility to others, not open to them when they were on the receiving end in interpersonal relations as children and adolescents.

5. We had not sensed that long continuous patterns would be modified or converted into almost the opposite characteristics. For example, it has been interesting to see how many of our overdependents have converted their patterns into nurturant ones, yet not to an overnurturant extreme since they are aware that what they want to foster in their children is confidence, not overdependence. One of our predictions was that our long overdependent boys with energetic dominant mothers would pick wives like their mothers and continue their patterns. For one or two we were right, but nearly all the dependent boys picked for wives girls who were lacking in confidence and thereby giving themselves a role as the proud male protector and giver of support. They thrived under this new non-self-centered change of status with themselves. It does not seem a fortuitous happenstance that three of our four policemen were slow-maturing organisms with older competent siblings and at least one dominating parent, or that a number of our socially inept compensatingly became supersalesmen where social skills were required.

6. Some subjects seem to be "late bloomers" or "slow jellers" who took a long time and a change of situation away from their community and family to work through early confusions or inhibitions and to achieve releases to be themselves. Some subjects did not get consolidated until they had a job that encompassed what earlier had seemed conflicting needs or gave them "at last" a meaningful job they enjoyed.

Bring Out Best

You as teachers have a direct impact upon a child for only around 180 days out of his long developmental years, yet it is surprising how many of our thirty-year-olds remembered all their teachers and how many recalled teachers who were especially important to them as the ones who simultaneously respected their feelings, excited their interests and elicited a maximum performance from them. At any age, of course, we all like people who add to our earned self-esteem and bring out our best. In this current wave of raucous demand for the teaching of "more hard facts," there is often naive ignoring of the fact that it is children with all their differences in interests, abilities, temperaments and degree of internal motivation who are to be incited to learning. And this demands of teachers not only knowledge of subject matter but knowledge and appreciation of individual differences of children and flexibility in approach to teaching so necessary to elicit interest and industry. So I urge those of you who enjoy the process of teaching children not to let yourselves be pushed around by these vocal "viewers with alarm." Of course, if you do not enjoy trying to reach this large variety of individuals euphemistically known as the "school child," you should not make teaching your profession because variety in profusion you will inevitably meet!

Emotions and How They Grow
BY VIRGINIA M. AXLINE

Emotional education may not appear on your school's curriculum, but it is being taught, nevertheless. Everything in a child's environment, beginning with his first day of life and continuing through his years in school, is part of his emotional conditioning. How emotions grow toward maturity is discussed by Virginia M. Axline of the Guidance Department, Teachers College, Columbia University.

THE CHILD IS YOUNG. HE IS STANDING ON THE THRESHOLD OF LIFE. He is in the midst of a complex and baffling civilization where everyone's feeling of security is threatened, where life seems tenuous, where fears and anxieties seem to permeate the air.

This child needs to be fortified with an inner strength that will enable him to meet the challenges of his world with all the resources within him. He needs to be acutely aware of himself and his relationship with others. He needs, desperately, emotional education if he is to achieve social maturity. He needs to reconcile the psychological and cultural forces within his personality.

Insecurity Is Contagious

John is twelve years old. He is in the seventh grade. He has been working for a week on a composition entitled "Civilization." It was a baffling assignment for John but finally he finished it. When he turned it in to the teacher, he attached a note to it.

> Dear Teacher:
> I have made twelve different rough copies of this composition and each time it comes out different. This is the best I can do with Civilization. I am sorry about it. Yours truly,
> JOHN.

This is what John had to say about civilization:

> Civilization is all around us. It is what all of your years on earth add up to and it is mostly wars and fights of one kind or another. If countries aren't doing it people are. Like my mother and father. Last month they finally got a divorce and now I haven't got a father any more. Instead of letting my father club my mother like cavemen did civilization gives them divorces. Civilization is a funny thing and I can't understand it completely. This is all I have to say about civilization except that I think wars and fights are not especially good for all people and the older civilization gets the harder it is to know who to like and who to hate.

The child's personality is the sum total of every experience and relationship that touch his life. It is essential to his existence as a personality that he feel secure and worthwhile. In order to preserve his personality he strives to achieve feelings of security and personal worth in devious ways if the direct satisfaction of these basic values is denied him.

He needs an honest understanding of himself and an awareness of his relationship to others. His fears should be kept out in the open area of conscious awareness; otherwise they may change from fear that has some specific object—such as a threat to the self—into anxiety, defined here as emotion without specific object. He needs to be kept free from the kind of anxiety that has been singled out as a crucial problem of emotional and behavioral disorders. This is no small order in the world today.

We know that insecure parents and teachers communicate this feeling to others. We know that fears, hostility and anxiety in parents and teachers color the relationship of these adults with children. We know that an ounce of prevention is worth a pound of cure. But we also know that prevention and cure are complex and elusive and that attitudes and feelings are not altered at one's bidding.

"You're a Big Boy Now"

Let's take a look at the complexity involved in the evolution of a feeling of anxiety in a five-year-old boy. He was prodded continually by his father "to be a big boy," "not to be afraid," "not to be a sissy," "to be strong and brave."

The pressures to outdistance himself never relaxed. And the child seeking a feeling of security in the relationship tried desperately to live up to his father's standards. But the standards were moved higher and higher with each accomplishment of the child. He was caught forever between the disapproval when he did not measure up and the approval when he did, which served as the whip to keep him seeking this reward.

The child was expected to learn to swim. He was afraid that he would not be able to live up to his father's expectations. He was afraid of the water. He was afraid of the seaweed. Any outcry of his fears brought forth only attacks upon his personality, and the child could not bear to have his feelings of adequacy so belittled. He could not think of himself as a boy who was afraid—a boy who was a sissy, a boy who had no courage.

He repressed his fears. He struggled to push them down out of conscious awareness. And soon he did not express fears. He was tense, insecure, uneasy. He had sudden outburts of hostility against his sister and younger children. The feelings of hostility intensified his feeling of anxiety. He had nightmares. He wet the bed. He bit his nails. But he was the first one to dive into the water. He laughed hilariously. He projected his feelings of hostility on to others and soon felt that he was alone in a hostile world.

When this child was finally referred for play therapy and was able to use the toys to play out some of the things that bothered him, those repressed feelings broke loose at last and the anxiety diminished.

In one of the earlier sessions he played with the toy lion in the sandbox.

"I'm a big lion," he said. "I'll go out and eat up every little boy and girl I can find. I'm not afraid of anybody." The lion went pushing through the sand and knocked over all the other figures there. Then a storm came up and he cried out, "Oh look! You bad and naughty lion! The lightning is going to hit you. And don't you dare be afraid. So the lion goes right out in the rain but WHAM! The lightning hit him and he was dead. So the little boy and girl lions was happy because their daddy was dead now."

The feeling of emotional insecurity comes and goes during the many therapy sessions. Sometimes the lion is "the little boy." Sometimes the lion is "the father." Certainly he plays out conflicting concepts in his emotional expression. His hostility is followed by guilt and then more anxiety and more hostility.

It seems to be a vicious circle, broken only by playroom experiences; in the playroom he gains security because he is free to express those feelings which come to him when there is no threat to his personality.

In session after session he plays out mass destruction and "no one knows who did it or why" he says again and again. Finally the lion "bites the father and kills him and never has to be afraid any more."

One day he tells the therapist that he is afraid, "only there's nothing to be afraid of," and as suddenly says he "hates everybody in all the world and will build a fire and burn them all down."

He dramatizes in his play the feelings that torment him. He picks up the hammer and goes around the room pounding everything with vigor. He yells, "My enemies are every place. I don't know where because I can't see 'em but I'll beat up everything and I'll get 'em that way. I'll hit here and here and here before they kill me first."

One day he plays with the family of dolls and he poisons the father doll. He expresses the hate for the father who threatens his personality. He expresses the fear that his father won't like him if he doesn't do what he says. He pins down his anxiety to specifics and somehow seems to have experienced during the therapy sessions a feeling of psychological independence.

He assumes a different relationship with his father—no longer trying to keep up with the unattainable psychological standards which his father has set. He achieves more differentiation of response. He experiences an expansion of awareness of himself as a person relating to others. In his symbolic play he seems to move *through* the anxiety-creating situation and to learn how to handle the specific feelings that emerge.

In an interview with the therapist, the father said, "I don't want my son to be a sissy. I'm trying to prevent the same thing from happening to him that happened to me when I was a child. My father died when I was a baby and I was a mamma's boy—afraid of everything, clinging to her skirts, being so overly dependent upon her that I couldn't do a thing on my own. And the older I got the worse things were. Because I resented my helplessness and my dependence I hated her for keeping me from being a person and yet I was clinging to her more and more because I was so afraid of my hate. I squashed it down under—and—well, I didn't know *then* that it was hate. I wouldn't admit that I could hate anything let alone my mother. Why, she was my existence. To admit that I wasn't identified with her would have finished me. I didn't have a self of my own. And I was out of college before I worked out of it. It was after she married again and I was suddenly left high and dry—I worked through it, but it's left its scars. I'm determined that won't happen to my boy. But why is he so nervous and so—violent at times?"

The father had not intended to repeat the pattern. His fear that his son would experience the same trauma that had been his lot was a decisive factor in the relationship between the two.

Let Children Have Their Feelings

With young children it is not as important for them to know the *why* of their feelings as it is for them to become aware of what the feeling is—and the object of that feeling.

If a young child suddenly finds that he has been displaced in the home by the arrival of a new baby and he is helped to keep his feelings his own property and to know them for what they are, then he is better able to cope with that situation.

If he says he *hates* the baby—that is his feeling. It seems to be of little value to explain to him that he hates the baby because he is jealous. He perceives the baby as a threat. If he can express that feeling and identify the object to which he attaches the feeling, he will be more able to handle that feeling in a constructive way.

Usually, if a child expresses a negative feeling he has the unfortunate experience of being told that he "shouldn't feel that way," that "it isn't *nice* to feel that way," or that "he must *never* express such a feeling again."

The sum total of such experiences only leads the child into feelings of confusion and guilt and shame. He disowns his feelings or feels guilty because he has them. Then in order to enhance his concept of himself he must repress the feeling or divert it and so erase the lines of definite connections between feelings and object and push the feeling into that undefined, nebulous state called "anxiety."

If the child is to feel accepted as he is, then he must experience acceptance as a feeling person, all his feelings, negative as well as positive.

If the adult wishes to convey understanding and acceptance of the child as he is and respect for him as a person in his own right, then that adult will attempt to be sincere and honest with that child and meet him where he is.

If a child is afraid, recognize his fear. Don't deny it or belittle it or attempt surreptitiously to convert it into something of your own making.

There is the example of the seven-year-old boy who was hospitalized for an operation. The child was afraid and fought for his feeling of security. He became aggressive and hostile while in the hospital and cried out his fears and hatreds with gusto. The parents were embarrassed. The hospital staff was not too skillful in handling the emotional problem.

The child was told how the adults *felt*. They expressed to him their "embarrassment," "how ashamed they were." They knew that he would have to return to the hospital for a second operation in the near future and wanted to "build up his readiness" for the return trip and "to make him more cooperative."

They shamed him and then bribed him. If he had to come back again they "hoped he would behave like a man." When it came time for his return trip he was promised a longed-for bicycle if he would only promise not to scream and fight and "say the awful things you said last time" because "there is nothing to be afraid of."

The child followed their dictates. He repressed his feelings. He got the bicycle. He also got a severe case of asthma. "The tears he could not shed outwardly found a safe way of flowing," his doctor later said.

Until the edges of his sensitivity are blunted, the child has an amazing amount of awareness of himself and the relationships around him. If we would be truly helpful to children, we would educate their feelings with meticulous care. We would give to them complete ownership of the richness of their emotional capacities and ownership of their own ideas.

We would let them bring out into the open an honest statement of themselves and let them explore the dynamics of their feelings—let them express and then recognize feelings of love and hate, courage and fear, pleasure and pain.

We would let them go forth exploring their feeling world and keep it in the objective world as much as possible, so that their emotions could be the constructive force in their experience of complete self-realization.

The following letter to the therapist is from a seventeen-year-old girl who had successfully completed therapy three years before and who had learned to know and own her feelings.

Dear Friend:

I remember you because you were the first person who ever believed in me—who didn't think I was all bad, who didn't think I was silly, who took the time to try to find out how I felt about things. And you never dug into me like I was a person without feelings. You let me have my own world my own way and did not try to snatch it away from me without first making me feel strong enough to go live in another world or to seek a new world for a while until I found a new one.

It was as though you said to me you can hate and you can be sad and you can feel cheated by your mother because that was the way I felt. And so I didn't have to lie to you or feel ashamed because I was me.

I painted pictures all the time because then I could think in peace. And the quietness was around both of us like a clean white shawl giving us warmth but not smothering. I washed myself clean in that silence. I crept back bit by bit into the world of color. It had been all black and grey before. I wasn't being sullen when I was quiet with you. I wasn't being hateful that day when I finally said I felt hate. I remember saying it deep inside myself, with the tips of my fingers scratching on the slippery paper. This is hate I feel. It had been a numbness but it was not really numbness. It was not no-feeling. It was so big I was afraid of it.

But that day I let the word creep outside of me that first time and it scared me. But it didn't scare you. I remember it because it struck me like a bolt of lightning. I am a hater, I thought. This is wicked and bad. Then they separated—the feelings and me. I thought you must know I have good reasons for my hate even though I hadn't told you then.

Another time I mentioned my fear. It was then that I learned that a feeling was a changeable thing because I felt it change—in my heart, in my arms, in my head, in my legs. It came out and twisted and turned and lost its sharp edges. From that day on I was a free person because I could separate my feelings from the people I felt about.

Then I began to look at myself and try and figure myself out. I got so I liked myself better. I got so I liked people. I got so I liked the world. I think this all happened to me because you gave me a chance to believe in me. And then I felt I was worthwhile.

I have grown up since I saw you last. As I think back about it you didn't seem to do a thing but be there. And yet a harbor doesn't do anything either, except to stand there quietly with arms always outstretched waiting for the travelers to come home. I came home to myself through you.

Your friend, MARYELLEN.

And so Maryellen describes her experiences as her feelings reawaken. If all people could learn that "a feeling is a changeable thing" and could experience the escape from anxiety that Maryellen so beautifully describes—"It came out and twisted and turned and lost its sharp edges"—perhaps they could all come home to themselves.

Permissiveness Re-examined
BY D. KEITH OSBORN

D. Keith Osborn is Chairman, Community Services, The Merrill-Palmer Institute, Detroit, Michigan.

DURING A DISCUSSION PERIOD A FEW WEEKS AGO A MOTHER SAID to me: "You people have told us so much about personality development and permissiveness that I'm afraid to do anything to my child lest I injure his personality." At another meeting a mother remarked: "My child hits the TV screen with a wooden mallet. I want to stop him but I don't want to hinder this freedom business." During a conference recently a mother commented: "The books and articles I've been reading about freedom and discipline confuse me. I don't know what to do with my child."

Since all parents do not feel this way, perhaps the foregoing statements are a little too strong; but without a doubt psychologists, teachers, freelance writers and others have unwittingly contributed to the confusion surrounding the term "permissiveness."

Perhaps we can achieve some clarity by defining "permissiveness" and then showing what it is and what it is not.

Permissiveness Defined

Permissiveness might be most easily defined as "freedom with controls." We could also say permissiveness occupies a middle road position somewhere between authoritarianism and indulgence. It is neither, and yet it has the qualities of both. Probably in its purest sense it could be called "democratic living"—freedom of the individual and within this freedom a consideration of others' feelings, rights and property.

From this definition we can see that permissiveness allows for freedom of the individual and yet a respect for the other fellow. When operating on this two-way street, it means simply a feeling of mutual respect.

What It Is Not

In further considering the concept of democratic living let us examine some areas which do not represent permissiveness.

STRICT AUTHORITARIAN: Permissiveness does not mean constant control on the part of the adult. Very early in life the child begins to explore his environment by crawling, walking, hitting and knocking over an ash tray. During these periods of experimentation it is only human nature that the parent begins to exert pressures in the form of control. By pressure I am referring to such verbal expressions as: "Leave that alone," "No, not now," "I'll do that"; or to the physical pressures like a tap on the hand or an old-fashioned spanking. Unfortunately, simple control of behavior is so easy through the techniques of threatening and physical punishment that unless one is careful the child may be surrounded (overpowered may be a better term) by a "Wall of No." (See figure 1.)

Figure 1

In the illustration we see that the child is so tightly controlled that he cannot express his thoughts and feelings outwardly—he must turn them back inward to himself. The child confronted with the "Wall of No" begins to learn: "I don't have to think; they will do it for me." "I can't say what I feel, I'm always wrong anyway." "If I do this, I'll get a spanking." We get a picture of a child who cannot respond freely—a child who doesn't allow himself to have feelings. *Granted, we have a child who is learning; but we have a child who is learning to respond out of fear of punishment rather than out of understanding of the situation.*

Perhaps the best example is a child who runs into the street. Under the strict authoritarian situation you "whale the daylights" out of the child if he ventures into the street. Soon he learns not to go into the street. Why? Because of the fear of a spanking, not because of the inherent dangers of playing in the street. This learning works whenever the authority is present; but when the authority leaves (and the fear of punishment is removed) the child may dart into the street.

We can see that under such conditions healthy personality is held back—free expression and autonomy are not allowed to develop. If the young child is to explore and discover, he must be allowed the chance to respond independently in order to discover his own limitations and learn adequate self-control.

Up to now this sounds very good, but unfortunately the professional person often leaves the laity dangling at this point. With the words of "free expression" ringing in their ears, parents may become immobilized by any act that demands an authoritarian position and then do absolutely nothing. This extreme does not represent permissiveness any more than the strict authoritarian picture just presented. We might call this course of action "sheer indulgence."

SHEER INDULGENCE: (See figure 2) Here the child moves freely in any direction without control and without knowledge of the limitations which society demands of him. This pattern is as unfortunate as the strict authoritarian position—perhaps more so, since the child is never made aware of the realistic limits to which he must eventually adjust. If the parent does not present some limiting situations which can enable the child to recognize the demands being placed on him, the child cannot possibly learn to control his feelings. *Learning is almost impossible, and the adult is inviting the child continually to test the situation in a frantic effort to see if any rules exist.* The child is in for a rude shock whenever he enters situations which demand rules. Unfortunately, those who finally teach this "untutored child of nature" will not do so in the comfortable understanding way of the parent.

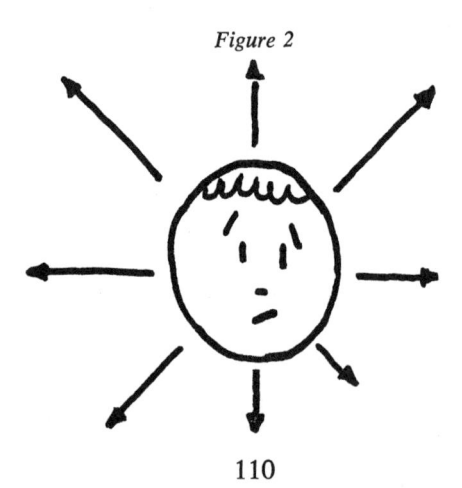

Figure 2

"Do-Nothing" Course of Action:

A third situation which occurs might be called the "do-nothing" course of action—it is the "now you do it, now you don't" sort of thing. The parent in this situation sets very definite limits on Monday, breaks them on Tuesday, sets them again on Wednesday, forgets them on Thursday. Since the same rules are never applied twice it is obviously difficult, if not impossible, for the child to learn what is expected of him. The "do-nothing" attitude on the part of the parent is similar to playing a football game where each player changes the rules to suit himself or the referee changes the rules after each play. Both Mother and Dad can fall into this little do-nothing game. Dad says "Yes"; Mother says "No." *Under these conditions the child does not learn methods of self-control, but he does quickly learn the techniques for manipulating adults.* If the rules are changeable, the adults are too. Here the task is to learn how to get round the adult—then the rules take care of themselves.

What It Is

Having glanced at some things that do not represent permissiveness, let us return and examine what the concept really means. Earlier it was stated that permissiveness is freedom with controls. We might schematize permissiveness in the manner illustrated in figure 3.

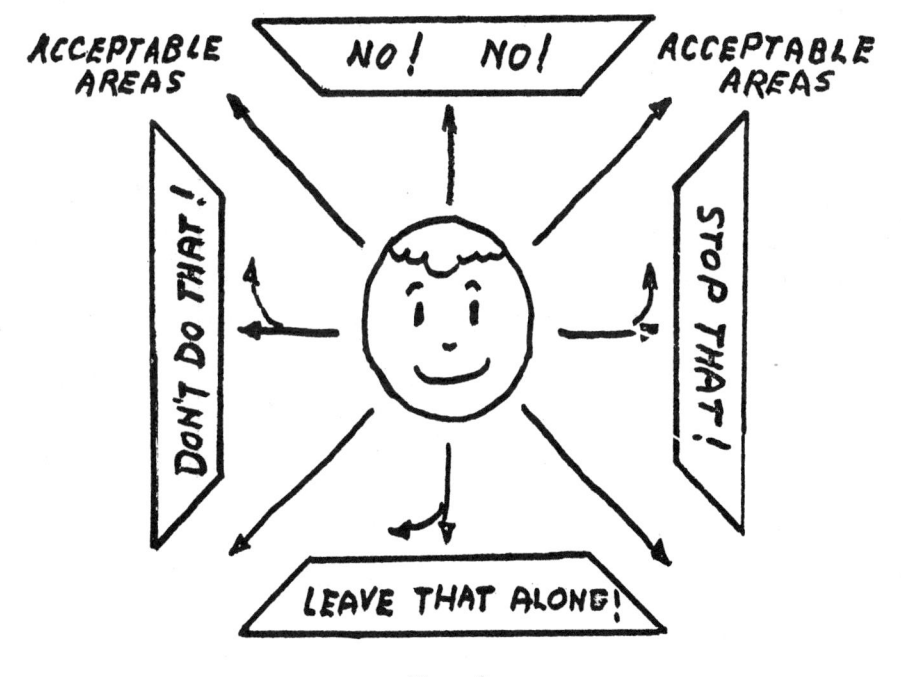

Figure 3

Here we have the original "Wall of No," but now there are openings. In life there are "No's," but in life there are other ways too. There is a "No" to hitting the TV set with a mallet. There is no room for "maybe tomorrow" or "perhaps" or "hit it lightly." TV sets cost too much to allow for the hammer-hitting type of experimentation. However, there are many acceptable areas where a wooden mallet can be used—on a pounding board, an orange crate, an old dishpan.

Ideally, in permissiveness our "Wall of No" remains firm round areas where it must remain firm; but the "Wall" disappears in areas where freedom may be allowed.

Another important aspect of permissiveness is flexibility. Our "Wall of No" is flexible enough to make allowances for unusual situations which may arise. If bedtime is eight o'clock and special company is expected that night, then bedtime may be moved to a later hour. Because special occasions arise, flexibility is demanded.

In accordance with our definition, we might summarize permissiveness in the following manner:

Permissiveness—room for *Yes* and *No;* room for change:

- I like to think of permissiveness as a bank account where we make many deposits of the *Yes* nature and few withdrawals of the *No* nature. When the child moves into situations outside the home and he has a good *Yes* account, he can withstand the buffeting of *No's* which society gives. With many outlets and many acceptable avenues of entry, the child can accept the avenues which are closed.

- Permissiveness implies an understanding of the child's needs and abilities. This means we do not make demands on the child that he is unable to understand. For example, we allow the child of two or three years to explore the feeling of "I-ness" and do not expect the concept of sharing until later, when he is able to understand the feeling of "we-ness." Permissiveness simply implies respect of the child as a person who is learning to cope with this complex world.

- If the home is to operate in a permissive manner it is important for both parents to agree on the basic areas where controls are to be enforced. Agreement on the "rules of the house" helps to make control easier and more consistent; it also avoids confusion for the child. Parents should carefully examine their "rules," keeping them consistent with the over-all goals for the child. Often parents make rules as they go and before long the situation becomes impossible for both parent and child.

- Permissiveness implies learning through understanding rather than learning through fear or learning through confusion. For parents it means

making decisions on the important limits and holding to these, giving freedom in areas where freedom can be freely given. As adults we want to be informed of the rules and laws which affect us. The child too wants to know the rules of his home and society.
- Finally, permissiveness is hard. It requires great understanding and patience. It requires examination of one's own goals and needs; it demands operating the home in a truly democratic spirit. It demands that the child learn to walk down the road of freedom and yet maintain control. But permissiveness gives understanding, stability, freedom with control, a healthy realistic approach to society with an awareness of others and their feelings.

Vol. XXIX—p. 26 (Sept. 1952)

Guiding Learning
BY L. THOMAS HOPKINS

L. Thomas Hopkins, professor of education, Teachers College, Columbia University, New York, presented this material in an address for the Association for Childhood Education International Conference in Philadelphia, April 1952. Because it carries a distinct challenge to all educators we are printing it in response to popular request.

I AM DEEPLY CONCERNED OVER THE *wide gap* BETWEEN WHAT A teacher has tried to teach and what a pupil actually learns of what the teacher has taught.

The problem is not confined to the lower schools, or to public or private. It is also prevalent in liberal arts colleges, vocational, and professional schools including teachers colleges.

This gap between what a teacher teaches and what a pupil learns is not new to educators. Records show that it began in the early schools of this country and has continued to the present. Time, energy and money have been spent by educators both to narrow it and to conceal its existence. Ability grouping, departmentalization, three-track curriculums, nonpromotions, remedial programs, special classes, patented teaching devices organized as budgets or contracts have all been used to no avail.

Vast amounts of money have been spent on instruments to measure more exactly what children do learn and what they should be expected to learn. Essay examinations have been improved. Objectives tests have been developed. The intelligence of the pupils, but generally not of the educators, has been ascertained. Yet on all levels, in all types of schools, the gap between teaching and learning still exists. In some instances, as in cosmopolitan high schools with a heterogeneous student body, it is even wider today than a half century ago when the student body was more homogeneous as to ability, social background and educational purpose.

We as educators have been working only on the fringes of the problem. Since we have not yet found the center, we are unable to deal with the core of the problem. I believe it can be readily solved if we wish to do so. Some of the wider and deeper implications of this dichotomy are in these two questions:

What is the basic problem of teaching and learning in our schools?

What can we do to reduce the gap between teaching and learning?

What Is the Basic Problem?

The basic dichotomy between teaching and learning in our schools arises because we teach children by external authoritarian methods which are the reverse of their internal biological growth and learning process. So the basic problem is one of how to change abnormal teaching methods into a normal learning process.

The child is in a great dilemma. Internally he *has* to grow up by his biological process. Externally people demand that he become educated by authoritarian teaching methods. He has to protect the integrity or unity of himself as a person for without his self he ceases to exist. And the only process he knows organically is the biological growth process.

He protects himself against these reverse external demands by various behaviors designed to remove the pressures before they disrupt his growing self. He usually takes one or the other of two well-defined directions. Either he tries to groove his organic energy into narrow subjects toward externally fixed ends, becoming a good, conforming, complacent child, or he fights against the abnormal controls to become a troublemaker, a problem child or a rebel. In either case he does not discover and release his potential capacity. He uses much of his available energy in overcoming his internal conflict. He arrests his own development at some level acceptable to outside controls. He never reaches the maturity of which he is capable.

Why is this gap between teaching and learning so important to children, educators, and adults who compose our society?

First, all children are born with a capacity to learn. But no two children have the same capacity—for each is tailor-made for him by the combination of genes which formed his early life. So, no two children can be expected to do the same things in the same way at the same time in their lives with the same results. Variability and not uniformity of learning is the biological inheritance.

Second, children must develop their inherited capacity to learn in, through, with, and by the environment in which they are born and reared. This is everything outside of themselves from which they draw the raw materials for their own learnings. When the environment is rich in such nutrients, growth is rapid and sound. When the environment lacks necessary materials, growth is slow and anemic.

Third, children develop only a small part of the capacity with which they are endowed since the environment does not furnish the conditions for or contain nutrients with which they can release and develop their capacity. Adults in the outside environment try to condition every child to the path of social and cultural respectability. The child who tries to wander over the environmental fields better to discover his peculiar tailor-made gene suit is severely frowned upon by his parents and rigidly opposed by the school. So his possibilities are never extended, the depths of his abilities are never plumbed, his creative interactions wither and die in the worn rubble of ancient traditions.

Fourth, there is no known way to improve biological inheritance so that each individual will be born with greater capacity to learn. Therefore, hope for the future lies in educating children so they will release and develop more of such capacity throughout life. This gap is important to children, since the conditions which produce it limit their opportunity to develop their inherited capacity to learn. The gap is important to adults since they create the environment which limits the maximum development of children. The gap is important to all of us since our only hope of a better future for ourselves or a better world for everyone lies in educating children to become adults who can use their capacity in a more intelligent way.

Guiding learning now becomes working with children so that they can discover, release and develop potential capacity by a growth process—a process through which they will want to, and know how to, continue to develop such capacity throughout life.

Obviously schools in America are not, and cannot be, guiding learning, since our standard educational programs are not organized to help individuals discover, release and develop their inherited capacities. Rather they are organized to teach children specific behaviors which are demanded by adults intent upon limiting the capacity of children to learn as theirs was limited for them by their parents and other adults.

No teacher or parent has to give thought to the amount of the capacity which any child inherits, since evidence indicates he has more available ability than he will ever use even under the most favorable conditions which the environment can furnish. The problem becomes one of how to change a limiting and restricting environment to a releasing and developing environment.

What are the characteristics and meaning of biological growth, development, learning? Growth is a *process.* Every individual is a process. All life is a process. But the growth process is *not* just any old process. It has very unique, well-defined characteristics. It is a process by which any living organism selects and takes into itself those materials from its environment which it can make over into new materials for the purpose of (1) differentiating new structure and maintaining old structure, and (2) differentiating new behaviors and reorganizing old behaviors necessary to living in the culture in which it was born. Now every process has a product but the product is the result of the process.

An increase in the height and weight of an infant is a *result* of the process. It merely indicates whether the process is active or inactive, healthy or unhealthy. Changes in behavior are also results of the process. They in turn indicate the activity and quality of such process. And every process has direction. The direction of the growth process is toward maturity of structure and behavior which are together in the self. Direction is toward self-development, self-realization, self-enhancement. For there is no physical or mental individual. There is only one functional operating unity called the self without which there is no existence.

All growth, or development, or learning begins with the organic drive or psychological need of the individual.

● It is *self-selective* in that the organism picks up from the outside environment that which it accepts to satisfy its need as it experiences such need.

● It is *creative* in that the organism cannot use directly for its growth that which it selects. It must change it into some *new* substance, meaning, knowledge or behavior. It uses what it creates out of what it takes in.

● It is *interactive* in that the organism gives back into the environment something different to replace that which is removed. The tree takes in carbon dioxide and gives back oxygen. The child takes in something from what the teacher tries to teach him and gives back a behavior which is always different and frequently startling. So each affects the other.

● The growth process is *differentiative* in that the structure or behavior is produced by the individual. It is never *produced* by anyone on the outside. The farmer never made a tree and parents never produce a child. They only furnish the environment in which the seed or zygote may differentiate toward physical or behavioral maturity.

● It is *cooperative* in that the various organs of the body carry on their specialized activities in a mutual relationship to each other for the preservation and enrichment of the integrity of the whole. In other words, the need of the whole or integration of the self are paramount. For without internal cooperative interaction the individual would cease to exist. It is coeval with life.

● The *quality* in this unique process is the living self, which is the dynamic organization of all learnings accepted to refer to as I, me, or mine which distinguished me from all other selves. Without them there could be no I or no you. But what an individual thinks himself to be may not be accepted by outside persons. And so his troubles in this world begin. But regardless of whether they like or dislike him, they cannot control the process by which he became what he is. And if they understood the process by which they became themselves perhaps they would not make such elaborate attempts to control him.

The drive, energy, or force for growth or learning is in the liv-

ing organism. Genetically it resides within the chromosomes. Physiologically it is associated with hormones, neural impulses and chemical states. Psychologically these forces are called motives, intentions, purposes, values, interests, attitudes, needs, sentiments. All of these are the inner energy drives that regulate, control and precipitate the individual's responses to his external world or produce what outside observers call *learning* or *education.*

Growth then is a self-selective, creative, differentiative process carried on in cooperative interaction with the outside environment in which the direction is toward the improvement of the quality of the self or self-realization and enhancement. And a child born into a new environment biologically expects that such process will be continued. Instead he finds himself facing a reverse process. To outside adults, growth is an externally controlled, conditioned, noncreative process. It is carried on in a competitive environment directed toward the accumulation of specific responses in the amount and quality set by outside authorities.

The child is caught between his normal growth drives or needs and abnormal demands of external adults. He cannot change the conditions, and the outsiders will not alter them. So to preserve himself he develops behaviors not understood by himself and unacceptable to his parents or teachers. He never finds out who he really is, never realeases and focuses directly his organic energy, never understands and uses the process of his own growth and development. He never really grows up as a person, since the environment arrests his development at some favorable spot.

In spite of all of these difficulties, what he really takes into himself to become himself is by the biological growth process. So the child becomes himself by one process without the benefit of guidance while he is taught fragments of the external culture by another with all the appropriate trimmings. The gap between teaching and learning arises and is perpetuated both in our schools and in our general culture.

How Can the Schools Reduce this Gap?

The direction is clear but the implementation is difficult. But here are some suggestions:

First, remove all forms of external authoritarian control wherever it is found, under whatever guise it may appear, regardless of what pressure group may be sponsoring it. Authoritarians want children to learn their fixed ends or the results of growth of someone else.

Second, operate all schools through a cooperative interactive growth process to the end that every pupil who completes compulsory education will understand, accept and use such process in his daily living.

Third, help each other as professional educators revive and nurture in ourselves whatever remains of the biological creativeness not destroyed by the pressures of authoritarian education and their symbols called degrees.

Fourth, help other adults to see that such authoritarian teaching denies the very results which they expect of their children or prevents them from becoming the kinds of normal, unique, creative selves which they and the public in general desire.

This gap can be reduced only as authoritarian methods of teaching become the biological process of learning. Only people can produce such change. And no person can guide the learning of another by the biological process unless he has experienced such process in himself. Our first responsibility as professional educators is to remake ourselves as persons and catch the warm glow, organic energy release, internal confidence and security which such a process begets. For then, and only then, will we be able to achieve the new professional competence of guiding children to become the maturing persons who will by cooperative action bring a better future to a troubled world.

Vol. XXXI—p. 9 (Sept. 1954)

What Are Children Learning?
BY EARL C. KELLEY

How do we know we have learned? What conditions must be present before learning occurs? What is the nature of knowledge? A most thought-provoking challenge to our ways of working by Earl C. Kelley, professor of secondary education, Wayne University, Detroit, Michigan.

THE PURPOSE OF SENDING A CHILD TO SCHOOL IS SO THAT HE MAY learn more broadly and constructively than he would have if he had stayed at home. The child cannot be kept from learning something, no matter where he spends his time, so the value of a school depends upon the quality of the learning experience which it provides.

The schools are presently under attack by several different kinds of people. Some of these people do not believe in democracy and fear the power of an educated populace. Others see the reduction of school budgets as a means of saving money. Still others seek sensational stories as a means of selling their publications, reckless of social outcomes.

The vast majority of the people who are leading or supporting these attacks, however, are earnest, honest American citizens who cherish their schools but who feel that the schools are not doing a good job. These people are comparing the present school with the one they attended—before we had scientific knowledge of the nature of the human organism and of the learning process. They hold a concept of the nature of knowledge which is no longer tenable. It is as though a manufacturer were to say that the factory he started working in did not use this new-fangled electricity.

If we could get the American people to understand and accept what is now known from research about the nature of learning and of knowledge, they would be attacking us for being so far behind the times, rather than because we have in some degree abandoned some of the practices for which one can find no rational support in scientific data. *Our response to attack has been to do harder that which we have been doing wrong.* We have in many cases, like Galileo, recanted the facts. In defense of Galileo it must be said that we become frightened and recant much more readily than he did.

What Is Learning?

Learning is modification of the organism through experience, so that it will behave differently—under the proper circumstances—because of having had the experience. If there is no modification of behavior there has been no learning. As William Heard Kilpatrick puts it, "learning is the tendency of any part or phase of what one has lived so to remain with the learner as to come back pertinently into further experience." (*Philosophy of Education,* Macmillan, 1951, p. 239.) Thus the pay-off is on behavior—or "coming back pertinently into further experience."

Learning is a significance attained from having lived. The quality of the learning depends upon the quality of the living. When we say that the purpose of the school is to improve the quality of living of the children, we mean the quality of learning, because the learning comes from the living. It is the *quality* that is significant, because some kind of learning takes place when the child does not attend school.

Conditions for Learning

There are some important conditions to learning which need to be known by those who would bring about learning in others. If these conditions are not taken into account, desired learning will not occur. I say *desired* learning because of course some learning will take place. The child may learn, for example, that school is a poor place to be.

One of the conditions to learning (present at the start of the planned learning experience) is that the child needs to have previous experience in some degree related to the new experience. If he never heard of anything remotely related to the new experience, he will have nothing with which to interpret it. The new experience will be interpreted in the light of the old one.

Another condition to learning has to do with the learner's purposes.[1] Each child is uniquely purposive, that is, some activities are in line with his unique purpose and some are not. This is another way of saying that we learn what we live and accept, and we learn it in the degree that we live and accept it. We "accept" in keeping with our purposes, which often lie deep below the level of consciousness.

The new learning experience will thus be received and interpreted uniquely. The child was born unique and when he makes his own interpretations of unique experiences he becomes more and more different. This uniqueness is the one quality which we should cherish most highly because it is being different from others that enables the individual to make contributions unlike those of anyone else. The learning process builds the uniqueness of the individual.

This means that learning makes people different from others instead of like them. The more learning, the more unlike others one becomes. This is true because of the unique nature of what the individual brings to the learning, the peculiar experiential background he brings to the new experience, and the learner's own special interpretation.

This shows the fallacy of our efforts to achieve similarity in our learners. We have felt that if we sorted them on some basis of similarity (for example, that modern contribution to mythology, the IQ) and then did the same things *to* them, they would all turn out to be alike. We seem to hold that this would be good, else we would not try so hard for it. All the while, however, if learning has been going on, our children have been growing more and more *different* rather than more alike. Nature will have her way, and she cherishes difference rather than likeness. We try valiantly to repeal uniqueness, but the cards are stacked against us by the very nature of the organism which we seek to improve. If we strive for likeness in our learners, the better we succeed in getting them to learn the more we fail to achieve our aim.

The Nature of Knowledge

Most teachers also hold a mistaken notion of the nature of knowledge, which causes them to do many things which are inconsistent with presently known scientific fact. The philosophers have baffled and confused us on this topic by their penchant for making simple ideas complex. Through the efforts of researchers we can see that knowledge is simply what we know after we have learned. Knowledge, then, is the product of learning and comes after learning. Since learning is unique, dependent upon unique conditions, knowledge must therefore also be unique and uniquely held by each learner. Knowledge (what

---

[1] An explanation of the nature of purpose may be found in Chapter VI of *Education and the Nature of Man* by Earl C. Kelley and Marie I. Rasey, Harper, 1952.

we know) comes after learning and is not a precondition to learning. It does not exist before learning begins.

Teachers and parents generally consider knowledge to be something which has existed in its own right for a long time and that the learner needs only to reach out and acquire it. If all of a certain class reach out and acquire the same knowledge, they will all know the same things. This notion has of course governed our ways of operation, our school buildings, our textbooks and more important, our attitudes toward our children. Since knowledge is assumed to exist in its own right before learning begins, anybody who is willing can reach out and acquire it. Those who do not do so are therefore perverse. Since perverseness of the learner is all that stands between us and success, we seek to coerce the learner. A whole pattern of authoritarian coercion is set up by this line of reasoning.

Since we now know that children cannot learn that for which they lack experience and purpose (or, if you like, readiness), some of them simply cannot learn some of the items which we set out for them. Perverseness has nothing to do with it, although the child, when put in a position of being required to do that which he cannot, may look and act as though he is perverse.

It is easy to demonstrate that knowledge is the private unique possession of each individual. What kind of person was Abraham Lincoln? It all depends on whom you ask. Lincoln only exists as a concept held by individuals who have interpreted what they have learned about him in their own way—in the light of their own experience, purpose and culture. If you want more varied and emotional answers, ask "What is a Negro? A New Englander? A Texan? A Catholic? A Baptist? A Jew?" What are these? It all depends!

What Is Actually Learned?

Earlier it was stated that the child learns, whether he goes to school or not, whether the school is a good one or not. He may not, however, learn what the teacher intends but something quite different. Kilpatrick has told us, and retold lest we miss it, that a child learns what he lives and accepts and in the degree that he accepts it. Suppose we apply this to the child who has been kept after school and required to write "I have gone" one hundred times, so that he will no longer say, "I have went." Does he live and accept "I have gone"? He does not. He probably lives and accepts the idea that although he has been told he should be proud of his school, it is a bad place because a continuation of it after quitting time has been used as a punishment. The teacher is an evil one because she keeps him away from his companions and coerces him to do something that makes no sense to him. Grammar is a meaningless nuisance to be avoided when possible. Society, the most ubiquitous institution, has its hand raised against him, and he must find some way of returning aggression so that he can again see himself as a person worthy of respect.

These real learnings are often referred to as concomitant learnings. I do not see anything concomitant about them except from the teacher's point of view. They are "side" learnings to the teacher because they are not what the teacher intended. These learnings are central to the learner, and if he learns anything about grammar, which is most unlikely, that learning is secondary or concomitant to him.

What We Need To Do

We need to put learning on an experiential basis, where there is a maximum of doing which involves the total organism, not just the eyes and the finger which follow the line on the page. Some elementary schools have gone a long way with this (especially with younger children), but most of them have not.

We need to learn to cherish uniqueness as nature does and stop trying to make people alike against the very structure of the organism we would educate. This means freedom for children to do different things than do their companions in a class.

We need, with the help of the children, to devise better experience than the child would have encountered if he had played in the alley. This is our effort to improve the quality of living for the child while he is in school, so that it may profit him to learn what he lives and accepts.

We need to learn to care more about the child than we care about what he learns. This will relieve us of the necessity for being punitive, compulsive and rejecting. We only need to do these things when we care more about something else (ourselves, maybe?) than we do for the child.

Space does not permit the expansion of this discussion of method or the citing of scientific data to support what has been said. It will take a book or several books to do this. We will not, I believe, be able to cope with those who attack us until we know sound reasons for doing what we are doing and can quote them chapter and verse. We get nowhere when we pit opinion against opinion, superstition against superstition, emotion against emotion. We must begin to operate sturdily in keeping with the known facts about the nature of the organism which we seek to educate. Then we will have something more than a contrary opinion with which to meet our critics. Having sound basis for what we do will not save us from those who have ulterior motives for their opposition to our schools, but it will help most people who are honestly puzzled about what they see in our schools.

With regard to the use of known facts, we are about where the medical profession was one hundred years ago. We would not think much of a doctor who gave us medicine simply because it had always been used. We *expect* him to be scientifically up to date. We demand the newest antibiotic. When George Washington became ill with pneumonia the doctors, I am told, bled him because bleeding was held to be good for the sick. What he needed was more blood instead of less. So he died. If the doctors had not bled him, however, they might have been indicted for criminal negligence. Some of us who are teachers are "bleeding" our children on public demand.

The difference between the attitude of the public toward doctors and teachers shows that it matters a great deal which part of the unitary man one ministers to. If you work on the physical, visible part of man you are expected to use the latest scientific data. If you minister to the psychological, invisible, attitudinal, then superstition, tradition, and emotion are good enough.

The moral of the story is that we need to become well informed about the part of the unitary man to which we minister, and use this information not only in our teaching but in our public relations. Also, if we have the fortitude, we must not recant.

Vol. XXXIII—p. 352 (Apr. 1957)

T-I-M-E
To Grow

BY JEAN ADAMSON

Jean Adamson is ACEI 1956-57 Fellow from Canberra, Australia. She is studying part time at University of Maryland, College Park, under a scholarship from the Australian Preschool Association.

CHILDHOOD IS A GROWING TIME. GROWTH IN THE EARLY YEARS IS SO spectacular that we are apt to overlook the importance of childhood as a living time with value for its own sake.

Life is an accumulation of experiences—not just as a result of what happened before, not just for the sake of what comes after, but with meaning for the moment. Admittedly, each experience will be a resource for the future; nothing is unrelated to the rest of experience. But let us think of the importance of childhood as here-and-now living—living that needs time for the accumulation of a rich variety of experiences that matter *at the moment* for the sake of developing a personality *now*.

Geared to the Future

This is "the age of the child" and "the child-centered home." [1] However, there tends to be concentration on the child in terms of a plan for his future. The importance tends to lie in how he will develop and what he will become rather than what he is now. Always in our concentration on the child there is pressure toward his growing up.

We plan our sons' careers when we enroll them at school at five years of age; we visualize our daughters' weddings when we take them shopping to buy clothes at two years of age; we enroll them at a preschool center to prepare them for school. Fathers nominate their infant sons for membership in the Cricket Club; an excited new aunt presents her first nephew with a football at the tender age of three days.

Always looking ahead, we deny the present. "He looks so happy in the sun there; but if he doesn't have his rest now, it will make lunch so late." "Yes, it's an old bike with one wheel off; but look, we're coming to the station now where all the trains are!" "Oh, you're painting beautiful letters! Soon you will be able to write your name."

Let us look at each childhood experience not only in relation to its value for later living but in its here-and-now context. This is the time for gettting the most from life during years that can never be relived.

Importance of Here-and-Now

Look back to your own childhood. Think how your childhood experiences have influenced and become a part of the person you are now. The vivid pictures are usually of brief experiences or long time-filled activities: picking dandelions in the vacant lot on the walk home from school; gathering tiny patterned shells at the sea's edge until your pockets bulge; collecting thin sticks and breaking them into equal lengths to hold in tight-clenched bundles; letting cold water run from the tap over hot hands on a summery day; listening to your father's voice as he reads stories at bedtime.

Looking back, there may be pictures of an uncle stopping the car at dusk after a family picnic and waiting while each of three little girls was lifted over the paddock fence to see, close up, a newborn lamb with its mother; of a patient mother standing by while a little preschool sister made cakes in the busy kitchen and of the fun of family feasting afterwards; of a tiny child lifted from bed to the veranda on a wakeful

[1] Green, Arnold W. *Sociology* (New York: McGraw-Hill Book Co., Inc., 1956), p. 375.

summer night to experience something new—to see the dark sky pinpointed with stars.

Would today's heavy traffic permit a stop on the highway while three little girls looked at a lamb? Would the authorities in "baby books" permit stargazing to interrupt the night? Does it matter anyway the way you first learn about sheep, stars and do-it-yourself cooking?

Soak up Daily Happenings

Children need time to soak up slowly the things that are happening every day. If the little things are to become part of growing and living, the pace must be the children's—not ours. They need time to watch, listen, smell and say what they are doing; to touch things; to tell long stories; to run in circles in seeming purposelessness; to dawdle, dream and repeat all of these activities for the hundredth time. The doing and the saying and the idleness and the not saying are the purpose in themselves.

As parents in a busy, culture-conforming, crowded household, how can we *find* time to see that our young children *get* time to grow in this way?

As teachers of preschool groups, anxious to offer everything we have as a wealth of experience for all, how can we be sure that each one really needs all that we offer? How can we be sure that each one really finds time to live the way he *needs* to live—the way he enjoys growing most? One of the most impressive directions ever given to me in my student days was "Never say 'Hurry' to a two-year-old." My favorite cartoon is of a four-year-old digging vigorously in the sandpit alone in the playground, while his teacher stands at the nursery door, exasperated but controlled. She is calling to him, "Sheldon, didn't you hear me say it's time to come in?" He is replying, as he digs deeper into the sand, "Yeah, I heard you. Didn't you hear me say I'm busy?"

Be Aware of Growing Times

We need to be aware of all kinds of times and incidents as busy, valuable, growing times. We need to recognize that certain opportunities and materials encourage activities that can be filled with rich growing experiences: a sandpit in the garden, a paint brush and a can of water for "painting" the fence or the bike or the back steps, a swing or some blocks, a bus trip to town instead of the usual seat in the car, an hour or even a half-hour of exploration in a city park.

When we have become conscious of the opportunities we must see that there is time for their fulfillment. We must see that there is time for each child to achieve a degree of individual ease in routines such as dressing, eating, eliminating and sleeping—remembering that winter clothes take so much longer and that wielding a spoon is fun and growing in itself. We must see that there is time for each to play out his fantasies in his own way and at his own pace. We must see that there are opportunities for long periods of play uninterrupted by a trip to the food store or perhaps an unnecessary insistence upon going to the bathroom or a teacher-planned music session which must be fitted into the program.

Enjoy Growing Times

Somehow or other, we must try to find time for ourselves so that we can confidently (not guiltily) sit down sometimes and enjoy the child's growing time with him. Remember that his telling needs to be listened to often or his fantasy cup of tea shared. It isn't easy. Getting up an hour earlier or staying up an hour later can help but doesn't usually provide the solution. I think it is an attitude rather than a practical achievement after planning. An attitude that time is needed for growing even at twenty-three or thirty-three or forty-three years will bring an attitude that time is needed for growing at three. Growing means gaining something from every little incident and experience along the way.

In little things, vivid brief experiences, fleeting moments of perfection we must often find fulfillment.

Let's see that childhood has the time it needs for itself, not just the time it needs to learn the steps toward stage two. Let's not deny the present to our children. It will not come again.

Section III

The Teacher

The Teacher

JUST WHAT IS A TEACHER? A PERSON AND A PERSONALITY, FIRST AND foremost, and then much more: worker with children, learner, manager, appraiser, observer, guide, listener, participator, counselor, decision maker, interpreter, disciplinarian, confidante, adviser, collector, storyteller, explorer, expert, to mention but some of the roles the teacher assumes in the course of a day's activities.

This teacher-person does work that shows. It shows in the classroom environment: in the appearance, stimulation and decoration of the room; in the intellectual atmosphere and the confrontations with content provided; in the emotional climate that prevails; in social relations and social structures. It shows in the way time, space and materials are used.

The work of this teacher-person shows in teaching strategies employed and in style of teaching and craftsmanship which undergird the teaching strategies. It shows in the content selected, in what is done with content, in the ways of knowing which are encouraged, in the amount of tolerance for unusual responses, for divergent thinking, for innovation and invention. It shows in the participation of the children, in their involvement in the day's work, in their freedom to think, to create, to be themselves. It shows in the processes and the products of the learners.

And yet, although the work of this teacher-person shows, what he does—called teaching—is much like an iceberg. What shows is but a portion of what an iceberg really is. What is under the water, that is the iceberg too. So also with teaching. What one sees in the teaching act is but the observable part of its totality. What makes possible the observable (the values, the self-knowledge, the backgrounds in content and culture, the dedication, the understandings about educational practices) is the teaching mind of a particular teacher-person. This teacher mind makes happen what occurs in the classroom. To think like a teacher is to harmonize the many roles, the many components, into a unified approach and order in working with children.

What, then, is a teacher? A teacher is a maker—a maker of teaching.
—*By* LELAND B. JACOBS, *Professor of Education, Teachers College, Columbia University.*

Teacher, Know Thyself
BY RALPH L. WITHERSPOON

Ralph L. Witherspoon is director, Child Development Institute, and professor of psychology, Florida State University, Tallahassee.

Has there ever been a teacher of young children who did not get a glimpse of himself when he came upon a group of children from his class "playing school"? The surprise may have been pleasant, for research shows that children reflect quite accurately the personality, habits and characteristics of the adults they become in their play. On the other hand, the surprise may have been a shock, for who would want to be a teacher like the one played by Mary? Mary was standing in front of her classmates clapping her hands, stamping her feet and screaming, "I won't have it! I won't have it! Go to your seats and act like ladies and gentlemen." Of course, the children were acting like ladies and gentlemen for their respective ages; but Mary, like her teacher, was reflecting her own insecurity.

Jersild and others stress the importance to teachers of understanding the development of self-concept in children. The teacher, and what he himself is, plays a significant role in the self-concept developed by those he teaches. Since children are sensitive to every characteristic of the teacher—strengths as well as weaknesses—it behooves each and every one of us to ask some rather soul-searching questions about ourselves. Further, when the answers become clear, do we have what it takes to accept them, to look objectively at our misgivings, our doubts, the negative aspects of our personalities? If not, perhaps we should not be teaching young children. However, while it may not always be pleasant to face up to our own shortcomings, almost everyone with enough intelligence and willingness to do the work necessary to become a teacher can and will accept himself. What is more, *he will be able to change when change is needed.* After many years of working with teachers of children of all ages, it is the writer's opinion that, in general, teachers of young children have the healthiest outlook on life. They are the most interested in the welfare of those they teach. A thoughtful consideration of the following questions can help in understanding the role played by teachers.

Do I see children as they really are? Or, are my concepts clouded by my own experiences as a child?

Of course, even if you tried it would be impossible to keep your own childhood experiences from entering into the way you see the world. It has been shown that each person's way of looking at anything can come only from his personal experiences. The mature self is capable of self-evaluation and can accept other selves for what they are rather than what the adult self would like them to be. Such understanding on the part of the teacher has helped many a child to feel needed, wanted and loved.

Can I show kindness and affection toward others?
Or, do I feel that this is unnecessary?

Children, even more than adults, must have many continuous experiences which convey the fact that others really care about them. The child who receives little love and few kindnesses at home seeks reassurances of being wanted from other adults, usually from his teachers. Unless his teacher can fill this need, it will be hard for him to learn desirable human qualities of love, kindness and affection. It is sometimes hard to show affection to the child who is dirty. However, due to home circumstances there is no other way he can be. It is sometimes hard to show affection to the child who is mean and uses vulgar language. However, he has only experienced meanness and derogatory language. Adults who themselves have not experienced a long well-established relationship of affection may find it difficult to maintain a genuinely warm, accepting climate for children.

Do my actions and deeds reflect confidence and integrity?
Or, are they merely an attempt to "save face" in
order to protect me from myself?

Studies show that teachers who are not sure of themselves when decisions have to be made transfer this lack of confidence to children. The teacher who goes to great pains to explain a mistake he has made is not fooling anyone but himself. The children respect him less for it. Children develop desirable characteristics only when adults radiate honesty, sincerity, integrity and confidence in everything they say and do.

Do I feel confident that those I teach feel I am a good teacher
and love and respect me? Or, do I feel that they merely
tolerate me because I am their teacher?

Every child deserves a good teacher. When he has a good teacher he feels good about himself and about school. To him, his teacher is about the finest person in the world. He goes to school, not because he has to, but because the teacher makes it a place where he is respected and wanted. The teacher makes it a place where it is seriously important to learn. The teacher makes it a place where he feels the thrill of personal achievement and where he works hard because he is challenged. He does his best in terms of his own maturation and abilities. Somehow he knows that all this happens because of what the teacher helps him experience, and he loves and respects him for it. School is no longer something for the child to get away from—rather a place where you cannot keep him from.

Recognizing that how I feel about my life and my environment is the only frame of reference that enables me to evaluate my actions, am I happy with my lot in life? Or, do I feel that this life has been unkind to me?

Children learn to enjoy life and their place in it when they are around adults who seem to find happiness in almost everything that takes place. Imagine what it means to Johnny when his teacher opens his neatly packaged gift and finds a smelly, ugly looking, half-dead toad and the teacher acts as though it were the most wonderful present in the world! Or, imagine what it means to Johnny when teacher's every word, gesture or smile spells gloom.

Do I view my preparation to be a teacher as a beginning step in my education? Or, am I tired of study and consider that I know enough to get by?

Nature made human beings curious. It gave them the ability to satisfy that curiosity. This we call learning and, normally, the more we learn the more we want to learn. Formal education was designed to prepare one to be able to fulfill this need. When the teacher stops learning, so do the children.

Do I view myself as physically healthy, ambitious and enthusiastic? Or, do I see myself as tired all the time even though I am healthy in the physical sense?

One of the most exciting characteristics of life is the fact that most human beings possess almost limitless energy for the tasks which are important to each of them. Not even ill health or physical handicaps hinder those whose enthusiasm goes beyond their personal feelings. Consider the life of Helen Keller or the almost superhuman readjustment and achievements of many whose lives have earlier been marred by accident or illness. Not only contagious diseases are communicable, as exemplified by the child who greeted his teacher with "I found me a headache this morning so I could be like you."

Do I usually finish each day with a feeling of pride of accomplishment? Or, do I go home merely feeling that I have done my duty whether anything was accomplished or not?

In a sense, the development of children proceeds at an amazing pace but, since learning and achievement are continuous, it is sometimes discouraging to reflect on the observable changes in children during any one day. The understanding teacher knows this and views learning and achievement in its proper perspective of time. He is keenly aware of cues indicating what will be possible next and thrills at the prospects when planning for the days ahead. This sensation is unknown to the teacher who plans only in terms of the next logical step in the subject matter being taught.

Is working with young children what I most like to do? Or, do I see teaching as a job?

Unless an individual has employment which challenges his best talents and interests, life can become pretty monotonous and boring. When a teacher finds this true, his profession becomes merely a job. It is natural to react with defense mechanisms which make life just as unhappy and unrewarding for the children. The goal for every teacher should be to feel like the one who recently said to the writer, "It is criticism such as the schools are now receiving that makes me feel that I have never been prouder of anything in my life than the fact that I am a teacher."

Am I sure that others think of me as their friend? Or, do I feel that I am not quite sure whether I have any friends at all?

It has been said that human beings cannot long survive without friends. Friends are a result of deeds, of thoughtfulness to others, of willingness to share one's talents. It is easy to become so engrossed in one's personal affairs that others are neglected. Never before in the history of mankind have relationships between people and nations played as important a role as they do now. Children need the security of warm, friendly, accepting social situations as insurance for their future relationships with their fellow men.

Do I face crises calmly and confidently so that I can face reality whatever it may be? Or, do serious "accidents" always happen to me?

Things do go wrong—sometimes seriously wrong—and everything that happens could happen to anyone else. Recognition of this fact can often prevent disaster and the unrewarding after-effects of a situation poorly handled. There have been many reported observations of the courage and heroic activities of children when placed in emergency situations in the presence of adults who behave in such a way that the children sense that "everything is going to be all right if we take it easy and apply our best efforts."

Do I recognize the time when I need help? Or, am I afraid of what others will think of me if I seek assistance?

Sad is the lot of the person who lives in fear that his achievements will not be recognized by others. The truly strong person knows when his acts are worthy and proceeds, not with the hope of getting recognition, but as if it were something that is important to do. Interestingly enough, those who possess this philosophy receive the acclaim of others.

If you can answer "yes" to the first part of these questions, the children in your room have a teacher who will help develop their best talents. The children will become the confident, alert, imaginative adults so necessary in today's world. If you truthfully have to answer "yes" to some (or all) of the last parts of these questions, evaluate yourself carefully and resolve to do something about it. Your self-concept is as important as that of each and every child you teach.

Teacher, know thyself!

The Kind of Teacher Makes the Difference
BY NORMA R. LAW

A teacher's wisdom in working with children and adults can only be as deep as his wisdom in looking inward upon himself. If the kind of teacher makes the difference, what do you see when you look at yourself?

Norma R. Law is associate professor of elementary education, Wayne State University, Detroit, Michigan.

WHEN YOU LOOK AT A TEACHER WHAT DO YOU SEE? THERE ARE several ready responses. Some people see a boss keeping order and exercising power, albeit "for the children's own good." Others see a saint loving little children and helping to build a better world. Others see an example, a symbol to which young people may give admiration and society may give status or at least respect. Several see a public servant somewhat restricted in his personal life but relatively safe from unemployment and ruthless competition. Still others see a scholar well informed in his specific field and devoted to intellectual pursuits.

To you who are actively engaged in teaching, these various perceptions held by the general public are important. They undoubtedly had some influence upon your choosing teaching as a career in the first place. As one ten-year-old put it, "When I grow up, I want to be a teacher so I can wear my best clothes every day, answer the door and say, 'Do these problems.'"

Experience

Time modifies our understandings. Just as the ten-year-old was a product of the experiences she had had to date with teachers and teaching, so you are the product of all the personal and professional experiences which have come to you. When you try to assess your own potential, your own strengths and weaknesses, you are face to face with the quality of your preservice and inservice experiences. How these experiences have influenced you and your teaching depends upon how deeply you have committed yourself to them. Books have been read, observations of children made, reports prepared, meetings attended, day-by-day teaching done, interrelationships of subject matter seen and more than one job undertaken. *But only those experiences you have screened through the prism of yourself have become uniquely yours.* You have selected, consciously or unconsciously, only those activities and ideas you have felt were valid. When you ask, "What kind of teacher am I? What can I do for children?", you take not only your experiences into account but your feelings about these experiences. *Whatever you felt, and still feel, you have learned to act upon.*

For example, Florence J. somewhere caught on to the realities of sequential growth, and they will not let her be. Every decision she makes is influenced by this knowledge and her deep feelings about its importance. The equipment used in her classroom teaching is geared to all that she can find out about children, the age with which she is working—their interests, their capabilities, where they have been and where they are going.

George G. in his work with migrant children and their families two years ago became alert to the environmental influences that play upon youngsters and what they learn every day. He never fails to give close attention to home visits, to family information and to interpreting the work of the school to parents. When he plans learning experiences for children he takes careful note of what they know and how it may be applied to new learning.

Margaret A. last summer was a member of a teachers' workshop in creative expression. Her experience there and her feelings about it are quickly apparent in her classroom where children are encouraged to try themselves out with many materials and are unhampered by models of predetermined standards.

Individuality

Just as a teacher's perceptions of what he can do for children depend to some extent upon what he has learned from his past experiences and his feelings about those experiences, so a teacher's perceptions of what kind of person he is will reflect his sense of integrity and self-worth.

Each teacher is unique. This basic truth means accepting yourself for what you are and where you are in your growth. It means being responsible for the quality of your own living. It means liking yourself well enough to face up to problems and choices and to custom-tailor plans for "next steps" in professional growth.

Each teacher is not only unique, but social. Your individual uniqueness needs your respect and loving care because other people need it just as you need theirs to live richly in your personal and professional life. Good teachers are constantly asking and giving help, extending themselves to learn better. When Rita H. asked in faculty meeting if anyone else were interested in working with her on the possibilities of outdoor education and overnight camping, she was expressing her faith in human differences and the value of several heads rather than one.

Teaching and Learning

Some months ago a group composed of student teachers and "old hands" undertook to air their perceptions of themselves in their roles as teachers working with young children. The talk session had been preceded by almost a month of uneasy observing and listening, doing successfully or doing unsuccessfully, being charmed and being bewildered by young children in the relatively unstructured setting of a laboratory nursery school.

"Talking about individual differences is a lot easier than knowing what to do about them" was the touch-off. Because young children verbalize so little and behave so obviously, the teaching team had decided early to keep careful and anecdotal records so as not to miss clues to individual behavior they needed for planning and guidance. It was no accident that sensitivity to individual differences became the first yardstick of effective teaching.

Some ideas were explored more fully than others. All were reinforced with specific examples from classroom and playground that indicated how closely the teacher's ability to free himself from self-concerns is related to what he can do for children. Watching continuously for signs of growth in children, each person had seen the teaching job as helping children grow in health, in their relationships with other children, in independence, and in working with materials that were increasingly complex.

These co-workers felt that the nursery-school atmosphere had gradually become less "charged" and tried to figure out why. What had steadied the atmosphere? Several statements bordering on confession were made. They noted that voices were being pitched lower. Quieter ways of getting attention had been found. Calmness in a crisis was apparent. Better timing of transitions and more flexible planning had been worked out. Children's creative use of materials gave genuine pleasure to their teachers. The need for setting limits had been apparent from the start, but knowing which limits were reasonable and how to help children substitute activities when necessary had been big problems. As one teacher put it, "I've decided that instead of concentrating on limits I'd do better to concentrate on what Jerry's after. If I can help him get it, O.K. If he can't have it for some legitimate reason, then I'll have to help him get what he wants and needs some other way that is acceptable to him and to us."

Helping children develop understandings and readiness for later learnings was seen as every teacher's responsibility. Boys and girls need many opportunities to try themselves out and to engage in firsthand experiences with things, animals and people. They investigate. They build. They role-play. They ask.

These teachers in the nursery school respected what they heard and saw as a guide to their teaching. "Molly and John are all mixed up about what makes the rabbit wiggle his nose. . . . Susie knows exactly how to level a teaspoon and why. . . . Dick's mother may have a clue as to why he is playing doctor day in and day out."

They realized that because nursery schools live close to families and are in partnership with parents, the importance of a child's twenty-four-hour day cannot be ignored. "Working closely with parents is not enough, however. There are other people with whom children have regular contact. Teachers ought to know about brothers and sisters, grandparents and playmates, Sunday school and babysitters."

Teaching as a member of a team had had its hazards, such as keeping informed about everyone's plans, knowing when and how to disagree, and accepting responsibility for independent as well as cooperative action. Team-teaching had paid dividends, too, in underscoring the necessity for several resources in order to assure learning in its varied and unique dimensions.

Professional Maturity

One test of maturity lies in the ability to get along with other people—giving and receiving, teaching and learning, working and playing together. Another test lies in the ability to get along with oneself, to become increasingly intelligent in handling one's own affairs and feelings. Actually the tests are inseparable. A teacher's wisdom in working with children and adults can only be as deep as his wisdom in looking inward upon himself.

No one believes that knowledge of self is something that is acquired once and for all. Rather, it deepens with seeking. And the seeking is self-initiated. If the kind of teacher makes the difference, what lies ahead this September? When you look at yourself, what do you see?

What Creative Teaching Means

BY LAURA ZIRBES

"The bread my mother bakes is not like this," observed a child while munching on bread. A creative teacher saw possibilities and made something fine out of a series of expanding experiences initiated by this child's discriminative and comparative observation. Meanings grew and deepened for all learners involved. Laura Zirbes is professor of education emeritus, The Ohio State University, Columbus.

It would not be a creative approach to begin an article on creative teaching with a definition. Meanings can be developed creatively, formatively, from contexts, from illustrative examples, from discriminative comparison, from shared experiences, and from a combination of some of these with other "makings." Meanings can also be enriched, reconstructed, and expanded by reworking them. These are, in fact, ways in which creative teaching proceeds, sometimes coming out with tentative formulations that are purposely left open for further development or test or extension and for use.

Bread can be defined, but even the clear grasp of Webster's definition cannot match the meanings which creative teaching built into it for a second grade.

At lunch one day a child said, "The bread my mother bakes is not like this." That started comparisons and discussions that led to a decision to visit a farm where wheat was growing and almost ready for the reaper. Two bundles of stalks were brought back. Pictures of sheaves of wheat were put on the bulletin board with a poem, and the poet's reference to the waving fields of growing grain led to a discussion of other grains used in making flour and bread. The machinery used for harvesting and threshing wheat today was compared with old-fashioned methods. Brueghel's picture, "The Harvesters," was compared with views of modern farm implements, a threshing machine and a modern combine at work in a great wheat field in Kansas. Of course there was a great deal of discussion, and in the course of it questions arose which led to a visit to a mill. Here children watched the process and got as dusty as the proverbial miller. Afterward one of them said:

> "We watched the great sieves sifting;
> They looked like huge drums dancing."

They threshed the wheat they had brought from the farm and tried in vain to grind it and get it as fine as the flour they had brought from the mill, but they found that it made good muffins. Muffins brought the talk around to other things made of flour, and to different grains and different kinds of bread, and to bread in other lands. Finally, after visiting a big bakery where hundreds of loaves were baked and wrapped for delivery, one of the mothers helped the children make bread, and they relived the whole sequence of experiences in creative rhythms while waiting for their bread to bake. Then they bowed their heads after the bread was passed before eating, and said:

"For this bread we give thanks."

Creative Teaching—What does it mean? It means the development of opportunities for such life-related learnings, for such understandings. It means guidance which catches a child's question about some phase of his experience and makes something of it—something significant in his further development and in the development of his associates.

Creative teaching took the words *colonial* and *heritage,* which came up in a broadcast, and made them mean more than any history text could convey.

The children in an intermediate grade took a walk with their teacher. They found colonial doorways, colonial windows, colonial architecture in two churches and several homes. They went into two homes by invitation later, and found colonial heirlooms—furniture, silver, and pewter. They found that they were themselves, in fact, heirs, and that these things were all parts of that colonial heritage, as was the Declaration of Independence, the town meeting, the lore and literature of pre-Revolutionary days, the heroism and statesmanship of the settlers and the founding fathers.

Creative teaching makes something fine out of learning situations, whatever they are, and in so doing develops the creative potentialities of learners.

Out of a sudden flood, creative teaching made an occasion for inquiry into what water does and how man has learned to use it and control it, to cross it on bridges, fly over it in planes, or tunnel under it. Something of man's resourcefulness challenged the creative potentialities of those children because creative teaching was resourceful enough to make a situational adjustment by a timely use of what had befallen a community.

Where teaching is not creative, such vital leads would be missed, and the creative potentialities of children would miss the challenge to fulfillment!

Teachers need the challenge to the fulfillment of *their* creative potentialities, too! Every teacher can catch the challenge and do things to foster creativity; to cultivate active curiosity, initiative, openmindedness, resourcefulness, and originality in children. Personalities are in the making in childhood, and the qualities which creative teaching encourages are developed as children respond to guidance which awakens their aspirations and involves their wholehearted endeavor. Striving to develop these qualities in children is a creative experience which transforms the tasks and routines of teaching into creative opportunities in human development. This does not sanction an escape from teaching responsibilities, but proposes a higher level of intelligent concern about them and a formative forward adjustment in approaches and procedures to a fuller concern for creative values. It calls for an abandonment of reliance on stereotyped ways of conceiving teaching-learning situations.

The teacher who guided her children toward a more flexible functional approach in spelling saw spelling as something very different from a list of words a day, to be assigned, studied, pronounced, marked, and reviewed or forgotten. She saw it as an integral part of all written expression, and as a matter contingent on the cumulative outcomes of clear perception—auditory and visual—and of diagnostic guidance in which misspellings and causal factors in misspelling were systematically considered. Her children kept two files, one for the alphabetized list of words which they used in their writing, each clearly marked as mastered or as still in need of mastery because new or because of error or uncertainty, the other for an expanded list. In this one children entered words they thought they might like to use in their writing, words derived from words they had mastered and words for which they had looked up synonyms or syllabication or other information in dictionaries. They offered to proofread each other's papers, and worked in teams on their expanded lists. It was therefore not surprising to find that this creative teaching had raised the standard of spelling performance far above the usual expectations in that group. Furthermore, the level of writing and the attitudes toward written work were involved in creative ways.

There are challenges to creative teaching in other phases of school experience.

A teacher whose children developed a collection of implements used in measuring made the approach to denominate numbers a creative adventure in which meanings were enriched and arithmetic took on social significance.

There is no field of learning or curricular concern in which creative teaching cannot raise the level of attention, insight, achievement, and aspiration.

Assuming that what has gone before in this article serves to challenge many readers to a more creative approach in their own teaching, the following suggestions for self-directed inservice growth are given.

• An unsolved problem or a matter in which you cannot fall back on habits or skills acquired by training or long experience is a challenge to exploratory learning in which you try out two or more ways of proceeding, seeking to "learn by doing."

• By discovering one or more points in one's practice which are examples of stereotyped, habit-bound teaching performance, anyone can project at least one alternative on the way to less rigid, more flexible teaching, and less dependence on routines which get in the way of creative forward adjustments.

• By getting rid of the accumulated stock of devices on which one has come to depend in a more or less mechanical way, one can open one's mind to the creative possibilities of a more resourceful use of recurrent phases of one's teaching, instead of succumbing to the temptation to go stale.

• By involving children in the cooperative planning and projection of certain phases of school living and learning, one can gradually outgrow the tendency to get them to adjust and conform to a pre-planned, teacher-directed regimen in which their initiative and creative potentialities are not valued or developed.

- One must sometimes give one's self the advantage of a new situation, a change of work, new leadership, or new associations to throw off the inhibitions and fixities that block one's creative aspirations, and lull one into stultifying complacency or fill one with anxious resistance to new ideas.

One can actually face up to what creative teaching means, and proceed on one's own initiative or with one's professional associates to project aspirations to creativity into action. Leadership can do much to provide impetus to such efforts and to develop the conditions in which creative potentialities are challenged and realized. This process of facing up to *what creative teaching means* implies a willingness to *act* on the meanings—an involvement in the kinds of formative forward adjustment that contribute to creativity and to creative teaching—an evaluative concern in the whole process and its impacts on personalities and human relations, aspirations, and outcomes.

If, for example, creativity is discouraged when spontaneity is inhibited, and conformity is valued above initiative and originality, it becomes clear that *creative teaching means* a departure from regimented routines such as following directions for drawing, using patterns, stencils to be "colored in," or models to be imitated. It also means provision for spontaneity of movement and expression, as contrasted with imposed restraints that hold expression and voluntary action in check in compliance with repressive demands that stifle creative impulses.

If creativity is developed by freedom to explore and experiment with new ideas, new materials, or resources, then *creative teaching means* fuller provision for such opportunities.

If creative forward adjustments are safeguards against habit-bound rigidity—that complicates human advance—*creative teaching means* an acceptance of the social challenge of forward adjustments in education, and that calls for guidance in adaptive, insightful living and learning, particularly in *childhood education.*

"In interpersonal relations it (creativity) is the ability to invent or improvise new roles or alternative lines of action in problematic situations, and to involve such behavior in others. Among other things, it seems to involve curiosity, self-confidence, something of the venturesome and risk-taking tendencies of the explorer, a flexible mind with the kind of freedom which permits the orientation of spontaneous play."

(From *Identity and Interpersonal Competence* by Nelson N. Foote and Leonard S. Cottrell. University of Chicago Press, 1955).

When Teachers *Teach*

BY MARIE M. HUGHES

How teaching "goes over" can be ascertained from children's reactions to classroom situations.
Marie M. Hughes, Department of Education, University of Utah, Salt Lake City, reports some areas of research on this topic.

How do you think of a classroom? Do you see blondes, brunettes, ponytails, braids, crew cuts, curly hair, stringy hair? Or do you see starched pinafores, blue jeans, sensible jumpers, corduroys, leotards, slacks? Do you sense energy about to burst? Do you sense enthusisam or boredom? Do you sense frankness and openness on the part of your children; or do you see them as timid and withholding or plotting against school, at work only when made to do so?

It is safe to say that no two teachers know a group of children in the same way, since each teacher carries his own expectations of what children are like, what they need and how they behave—more particularly how they *should* behave. Teachers have their perceptions of the classroom; children have their varying perceptions. It is the children's perceptions of which we speak here. If teachers are to be of more influence and aid to children in their learning, it is necessary to acquire skill in ascertaining the reality under which each child is operating. Such understanding is a "tall order" in a one-to-one relationship; for example, mother and child. When the teacher-child relationships are contemplated, the task seems insurmountable; and yet this kind of knowing is the essence of the ability to communicate with the child or group, and this knowing becomes the source of teacher influence.

Interpreting Children's Reactions

Teacher competence may be said to rest upon knowledge of differences in the ways the children are viewing the situation. Such knowledge is gained through skill in noting and interpreting the reactions of children. This skill includes that of listening to children's requests, expressed wants and of exploring questions. Such listening requires an open mind used with undivided attention. Does it seem absurd to mention undivided attention in a classroom of thirty?

There is no mysticism about undivided attention. It is an attitude of mind, a caring about the viewpoints of the children. Again, the caring is not a sentimental notion that children ought to be happy always or do what they want to do all the time. It is a sincere caring about children as human beings. The caring is based on understanding and knowledge of the inherent loneliness and uniqueness of each human being. It is based on the knowledge that the act of communication is complex and fraught with "noise" or "static" as it is filtered through the inner reality of the receiver; therefore, the responses of the children constitute the feedback that permits correction on the part of the teacher. Without a recognition of his feedback, the teacher easily "loses" the child or class. Any time a child "can't hear" the teacher or is hearing something too different from what the teacher intended, teacher influence and aid in learning are at a minimum or are nonexistent.

Children Appraise Situations

As a part of our research project on teaching,[1] we have studied children's perceptions of recurring classroom situations. Children have been interviewed or have responded to the situations presented in paper and pencil tests. The latter have been responded to by 1,400 fifth- and sixth-graders in three states.[2,3]

One common teaching situation is that in which the teacher's intent is to challenge and stimulate children by indicating that the work to come is really hard. The episode we used pertained to arithmetic. After the long division assignment the teacher said, "Let me warn you that in your work on page 38 there will be some that may trip you. I'm sure that you can do them." About 40 per cent of the children responded to the situation with literal appraisal of the situation; that is, they took the warning at face value. Examples of statements of this kind were:

Warning them about problems.
Telling them problems are hard.
Trying to get them to work and be careful.
Trying to tell them they would have to work hard as problems were hard.
"They're going to be hard, but we'll do them."

About 20 per cent replied with positive expressions that might suggest that the part of the teacher's statement they heard was, "I know you can do it." Examples of such statements were:

Teacher gives class confidence.
Boosts them up.
Teacher felt they could do the problems.
They felt happy they were being warned.

[1] Marie M. Hughes and Associates, *Assessment of the Quality of Teaching in the Elementary School,* Cooperative Research Project, U. S. Office of Education, No. 353 (Washington, D. C. 1958).

[2] Arthur Carin, "Children's Perceptions of Selected Classroom Situations" (Unpublished Doctor's Dissertation, University of Utah, June 1959).

[3] Eleña DeVaney, "Perceptions Among Teachers and Students of Varying Cultural Backgrounds" (Unpublished Doctor's Dissertation, University of Utah, October 1961).

Reassured.
Eager to do them.
Felt smart.
Confidence in themselves and the teacher.
The teacher was trying to give the children a helping hand.

Another 20 per cent of the children expressed worry, anxiety and in some cases hostility toward the teacher. Examples of such statements were:

Scared because I won't get 100 per cent.
Afraid I'll miss some.
Not sure I could do them.
I'm going to have trouble.
I feel sort of stupid.
Confused.
I'd feel tense.
I'm afraid.
I'd feel up in the air.
Gosh, I would be nervous.
Shaky inside.
Feel childish for not knowing them.
Very unhappy.

We might expect some children to feel anxiety when presented with school assignments, but few of us would expect children to view the teacher's actions as they did:

Felt he was trying to be mean.
Felt he didn't want to help us.
The teacher is trying to trick us.
Teacher is trying to bribe the class.
The teacher will keep them after school if they don't do well.
The teacher thinks people can't do the work.
She's a tricky one.
Teacher knows we can't do it.
Teacher is purposely giving hard work to make us dumb.

With this simple illustration of a type of teacher behavior designed primarily to arouse motivation, we have four patterns of children's reaction, with only one child in five reacting in the desired manner — that is, being challenged by the teacher's remarks. What does this mean? Are there cues that could be "read" by the teacher if she were looking for them? Are the anxious children in the arithmetic situation also anxious in other learning situations? Sarasen appears to think so.[4] Are the children who wrote, "I feel sort of stupid," and "childish for not knowing them," always children without confiidence in themselves? Do they see themselves as generally unworthy?

It does not seem too farfetched to hold that answers to such questions can be sought by each teacher. There must be signs and other cues children give us if we become sensitive to them. There must be ways

[4] Seymour B. Sarasen, *Anxiety in Elementary School Children: A Report of Research* (New York: John B. Wiley & Co., 1960).

to build up in every classroom the general notion that the teacher is going to help children learn, that there is no external punishment for not knowing. Also, there must be ways to reduce the anxiety exhibited by many children.

Another illustration may prove of interest. The situation was a fifth-grade class selecting library books. Robert, who has difficulty reading, asks the teacher for six words on the first page of the book he selected and then says, "I think I'll get a book I can read; this one is too hard." Whereupon the teacher replies, "I think that's a good idea. You'll enjoy reading if you get an easier book." To the question, "What did the teacher do?" some 60 per cent of 600 children replied that the teacher helped him. Examples of responses were:

Helped him find a good book.
Helped him find one he could understand.
Helped him with words.
Saved him hard work.
Did a favor for Robert.

It is, of course, gratifying that so many children moved immediately to the perception that the teacher helped Robert. It was interesting to note that a negligible percentage of the students saw the situation literally; that is, that the teacher accepted Robert's appraisal of the situation, "agreed he could get an easier book," "told him he had a good idea."

It may be useful to ponder the meaning of responses of 36 per cent of the 600 children to the question, "What did the teacher do?", the 36 per cent who held that it was the teacher's idea that he get an easier book. They completely ignored the fact that Robert made the original statement. Perhaps this indicates something about our pressure toward use of easier books. It may be that our chief criterion for choice has appeared to children to be ease or difficulty of reading. What might be the result if we talked about the *content* of different books instead of their ease or difficulty?

Feelings About Themselves

When we turn to the responses of the children to the question, "How did Robert feel?", some insight may be gained regarding the range and intensity of children's feelings about themselves in relation to the reading situation. Some 60 per cent of the children attributed feelings of inadequacy to Robert. Note how some of the children used the pronoun "I" in an expression of personal identification with the situation:

He felt very far behind the rest of the class.
Like he was a bad reader.
He mustn't get so much help on a page.
He felt like he didn't want to read anyway.
He probably couldn't read an easier book.
Teacher thought he wasn't capable of reading like the rest of the class.

> I'm a pretty stupid reader.
> He gave up.
> Discouraged.
> I'm disgusted with myself.
> I bet he felt sad that he couldn't read the book he wanted.
> Mad at himself because he couldn't read the book.
> I'd better get an easier book *or else*.
> Ashamed.
> He didn't know how to read.
> Felt he had poor judgment.
> I think he felt she wouldn't help him.
> He felt like he didn't want to read.

Interestingly enough a few children blamed Robert:

> He should have practiced reading.
> It's all his fault for not trying to read better.
> I'd better study so I can read what I'm supposed to.

Some responded toward the teacher in positive and negative terms rather than how Robert felt. Some positive expressions:

> Teacher is on Robert's side.
> Teacher was not mad at him.
> Teacher acts like she was interested in my enjoyment.
> Teacher helped me.

Some negative expressions:

> I can tell the teacher is getting tired of telling the words to Robert.
> Teacher spoiled reading for Robert.
> Teacher was impatient with Robert.
> Teacher was mad at Robert.
> A person should be allowed to pick his own books even if they are a little hard.

The last statement is of particular interest since the teacher had not interfered, only agreed, with Robert.

Two categories of children's response are of special interest in this episode; one, the children's perception of the teacher as the initiator of the "get an easier book" statement. Some implications of this perception have already been discussed. The other perception of special interest is the expression of the teacher's feelings toward Robert. If we conclude that the children's responses are based more on previous experiences than on the stimulus of the specific episode, then we can suggest that the helping relationship — "teacher wants to and will aid me in my learning" — has not been established for some children.

The analysis of data such as that presented enables us to sense and understand more clearly the great range of responses with which we are confronted when we teach. From our data, we would have to conclude that the most ordinary classroom episode does not occur without emotional accompaniments for some children. We can begin to appreciate the anxiety experienced by many children. We can begin to sense the number of children who have grave doubts about themselves.

As teachers, then, we learn the importance of reading the cues children's reactions give us. Such feedback becomes the signal by which we monitor our own behavior. Perhaps as our competence to monitor and control our behavior develops, our influence on and aid to children in their learning may become greater.

Vol. XXX—p. 411 (May 1954)

Understanding Others Through Facing Ourselves

BY ARTHUR T. JERSILD

To help a child to grow, a teacher must know the child as a person. This means that the teacher must strive to know himself. Understanding of others and understanding of self are closely interwoven. Self-understanding is especially important to a teacher who would help the child in his efforts to find himself. Arthur T. Jersild is professor of education, Teachers College, Columbia University, New York City.

IN THE SCHOOL THERE ARE COUNTLESS OPPORTUNITIES FOR HELPING the child in his search to find himself. In school the child can discover his aptitudes and abilities. He can be helped to face some of his inner difficulties and to realize that there are limits to what he can do. His attitudes regarding his worth as a person may be affected in important ways since life at school is heavily invested with praise and blame, pride and shame, acceptance and rejection, success and failure.

Everything that enters into the relationship between a teacher and the child has or might have a significant bearing on what a child thinks about himself and how he feels about himself. Everything that transpires in a teacher's dealings with a child might also help the teacher to learn something about himself, for his functioning as teacher is to a large extent a projection of what he is.

In order to have insight into the child's striving and the problems and issues he is coping with, the teacher must strive to face the same issues within his own life. These issues are largely emotional in nature, and the endeavor to understand oneself and others has a deep emotional meaning. It calls for more than intellectual cleverness and academic competence.

To appreciate another's feelings one must seek to recognize and understand one's own. To be able to sympathize with the child who is hostile (and all children are, more or less) the teacher must face his own hostile tendencies and try to accept the implication of his anger as it occurs say, in his annoyance with his pupils, his impatience with himself, his feuds with other teachers, his complaints against parents or school authorities or others on whom he fixes his ire.

He must be prepared to examine and seek to realize the significance of his feelings of being abused, his devices for avoiding responsibility for himself by blaming others. The more a person can face some of the ramifications of his own anger and make some allowance for his tendency to become angry, the more sensitive he can be to the hurts, frustrations and anxieties involved in another person's anger.

Similarly, to realize the turmoil another is undergoing a person must try to examine his own fears and anxieties. To do so may be more painful and threatening at the moment than to keep pretending they don't exist, but unless he can seek to fathom his fears as these appear in his phobias, squeamishness, fear of misfortune, timidity, uncertainties, fear of making mistakes, and fear of what others may think of him, his ability to perceive that others are frightened will be quite limited.

Unless a person is prepared to take at least a little note of his own anxieties he is likely to be uncomprehending when children helplessly express theirs. He may even be harsh when children's anxieties break through in such signs as inability to learn, unwillingness to try for fear of making mistakes, impertinence, inattentiveness, restlessness, irritability, unreasonableness and countless other symptoms which indicate that a child is uneasy and at odds with himself.

To perceive the significance of problems in the lives of others one must be able, at least to some degree, to recognize and face the implications of corresponding problems in one's own life:

- One must undertake to face, for example, one's irrational attitudes toward authority as they might appear in a tendency to be servile or rebellious toward people who have power or higher rank.
- One must face the possibility that unresolved conflicts regarding sex might make one appear to be unconcerned or unduly fearful or prudish or harsh in one's attitudes regarding the sexual behavior of others.
- One needs also to examine the possibility that one's demands upon others are tied to impossible requirements of goodness, brilliance, and perfection which one places upon oneself.
- It is possible that one's complacent attitude regarding the damage competitiveness inflicts on some children may be linked to a tendency within oneself to seek competitive triumph over others. Again, one may have a tendency to pity oneself, to feel sorry for bearing so hard a lot, and being so little appreciated by others and thus have trouble in

perceiving how desperately someone else might wish to be understood and appreciated.

A person's wisdom as he looks outward upon others can only be as deep as the wisdom he possesses as he looks inward upon himself. The further a teacher goes in understanding himself and others the more deeply he can realize the common humanity he shares with others, even with those whom he dislikes. The more genuinely he is involved in his own struggle to understand and to face the problems of life the more he can realize this kinship with others whether they be younger or older, or like him or unlike him in education, wealth, race, religion, social status, or professional rank.

Can It Be a Part of Education?

How does one achieve understanding of self? This is a crucial question in the preparation of teachers. It cannot be answered by the usual courses of study, methods, and lesson plans in our teacher education programs. These may be valuable for other purposes, but knowledge of self requires a different kind of personal involvement than the usual academic course encourages or demands.

One broad principle is this: *To gain in knowledge of self one must have the courage to seek it and the humility to accept what one may find.* If one has such courage and humility one can draw upon many sources in everyday life.

One can learn from experience of life's joys and tragedies. One can profit from self-inquiry into what it might mean that one was so elated or impressed or prejudiced or angry or frightened or depressed after this or that happening. One can learn from seeing a motion picture portrayal of people with emotional tendencies that hold up a mirror to oneself. One can learn from asking why one is inclined to gloat or to inflict pain or to resist so strongly or to yield so meekly. Even to hear a recording of one's voice at a time when one has been expressing grievances, worries or self-reproach may be a revelation.

A valuable help in self-examination which may be mainly intellectual but might also strike at a deep emotional level is the reading of books written by compassionate people who have made some progress in their own painful struggle to know themselves.

The method of "participant observation" offers a promising means of taking a look at oneself. One records what one hears and sees and what one's feelings are as one listens in on a discussion or visits a class and then, preferably with help and through comparison with records kept by other observers, examines this record. The examination may show that what one notices and fails to notice is determined by habits of thought one usually takes for granted, and that the emotional effect of what one witnesses tells a great deal about one's prejudices. What one perceives "objectively" may be, to a large degree, a projection of one's own subjective state and thus tell more about oneself than about the people whom one observes.

This broad principle also holds: Just as it is within an interpersonal setting that one acquires most of the attitudes involved in one's view of oneself so it is likely that *it is only in an interpersonal setting that a person can be helped to come to grips with some of the meanings of these attitudes.*

A relationship that can promote knowledge of self prevails when one seeks private therapy or joins with others in a group therapy situation. It exists also, to some degree, whenever one enters into any situation with people, in any walk of life, who can help one to gain perspective on oneself.

In a group setting a person may be helped to hear an echo of his anger or to catch a glimpse of the impressions his fears make on others. The way others express themselves or respond to him may help him to face in a new and self-revealing light some of the evidences of shame, self-effacement, anxiety, vindictiveness, and other outcroppings of deep-seated attitudes of which ordinarily he is not aware. Likewise, to witness a mimicking of his conduct by a child or by a role-playing peer may throw a little gleam of light on unrecognized conflicts.

It is in a setting of joint and common work and airing of self with other people that some of the richest possibilities for self-examination can be found. In the teaching profession we have hardly begun to explore and tap the resources for growth in knowledge of self which people might gain from one another. The committee meetings, staff meetings, seminars, discussion groups, panels, and other enterprises teachers take part in may serve many good purposes, but usually they do not serve this purpose. Indeed, they often proceed as though they were intended to defeat the purpose of self-discovery, for even when the participants are dominated by emotion they usually make a pretense of dealing with the issue in a reasonable way. When acrimony and anxiety creep in, as often happens, the appearance of being involved in a logical discussion is usually maintained.

Feelings might be aired in a revealing and growth-producing way if people could help one another to learn to be free to come out from behind the curtain that commonly conceals their emotions from others and from themselves. The writer believes that future developments of vast importance in education will come from plowing this fertile field. Some work in this area already is going on through role playing and group dynamics. These activities can be revealing and show the way to further possibilities even when they deal with relatively surface material, as often they do.

A couple of summers ago a workshop attended by teachers from schools in many sections of the United States dealt with the school's responsibility for promoting self-understanding. The members recommended that experiences designed to promote knowledge of self should be a part of every teacher-education program. Experience equivalent to what a person might obtain from group therapy under the leadership of a professionally trained psychotherapist was recommended as an example of what each prospective teacher should have. Such a recommendation is really not far-fetched when viewed in the light of the budget of time and money now invested in the training of teachers.

The exact recommendation is less important than the issue raised. The courage to face this issue is the important thing, and it must be faced if teachers are to realize their potentialities for finding themselves in their profession and for helping others in their search. Knowledge of self can be gained through many avenues, and it is not something that is acquired once and for all, like mastery of the multiplication table. Even those who are quite blind to themselves have a little of it and a capacity to acquire more. One of the outstanding marks of those who have achieved the deepest knowledge is that they still are seeking. No one procedure alone will give the answer since the search for selfhood, when genuine, is pursued through all channels of experience as long as a person lives.

Vol. XXXIX—p. 367 (Apr. 1963)

Conditions for *Creative* Learning
BY E. PAUL TORRANCE

E. Paul Torrance, director, Bureau of Educational Research, University of Minnesota, Minneapolis, presents the difference between learning creatively and learning by authority. He suggests what teachers can do to bring about creative learning.

FUNDAMENTALLY, MAN PREFERS TO LEARN CREATIVELY—BY EXploring, manipulating, questioning, experimenting, risking, testing and modifying ideas. Learning creatively is the natural way of learning; yet we have almost always insisted that people learn by authority. We have maintained that it is more efficient and economical. Some research, however, suggests quite strongly that many things can be learned more effectively and economically if they are learned creatively rather than by authority. It also appears that some individuals have a strong preference for learning creatively, learn a great deal if permitted to use their creative thinking abilities and make little progress when we insist that they learn by authority. Such ideas open exciting possibilities for better ways of individualizing instruction and for educating some individuals who do not respond favorably to present educational programs.

How Is Creative Learning Different?

Burkhart [1] has differentiated creative learning and learning by authority by use of the terms "spontaneous and deliberate ways of learning." On several occasions I have differentiated these two ways of learning by likening creative learning to the cat's preferred way of learning and learning by authority to the dog's preferred way of learning.

Creative learning takes place in the process of sensing problems or gaps in information, making guesses or hypotheses about these deficiencies, testing these guesses, revising and retesting them, and communicating the results. Strong human needs are involved in each stage of this process. If we sense something is missing or untrue tension is aroused. We are uncomfortable and want to do something to relieve the tension. This makes us want to ask questions, make guesses or otherwise inquire. Uncertain as to whether our guesses are correct, we are uncomfortable. Thus we are driven to test our guesses, correct our errors and modify our hypothesis. Once we find out something, we want to tell somebody about it. This is why it is so natural for man to learn creatively.

We learn by authority when we are told what we should learn and accept something as true because some authority says that it is. The authority may be a teacher, a parent, a textbook, a newspaper or a reference book. Frequently it is majority opinion, the consensus of the peer group. In our democratic culture, some teachers emphasize so strongly the importance of voting and the rightness of the majority that children seek to determine the truth by voting. For example, one group of children decided to determine the sex of their baby rabbits by voting. Less conforming and more creative children, however, rebel at this authoritarian approach to determining the truth. The mother of one highly creative boy recently wrote me as follows:

"My second boy has a rigid, peer-oriented person for a teacher, and she never encourages her class to deviate from the accepted, standard way of doing things. . . . What the *group* thinks is important to her, and they vote on everything. My son says he hates to vote and will be glad when he grows up and won't have to vote. What an attitude to develop in second-graders!"

---

[1] R. C. Burkhart, *Spontaneous and Deliberate Ways of Learning* (International Textbook Co., 1962).

From the foregoing differentiation, we might infer that learning by authority brings into play such abilities as perception, memory, logical reasoning and the like—the abilities most frequently assessed by traditional intelligence tests. In contrast, creative learning brings into play such abilities as evaluation (especially the ability to sense problems and missing elements), divergent production (fluency, flexibility, originality and elaboration) and redefinition (seeing something in a way different from the usual, established or intended way or use).

The well-known studies of Getzels and Jackson [2] and those of the author [3] indicate that the creative thinking abilities can indeed be important in educational achievement. These abilities are far less useful, however, in classes and in schools where teachers insist that children learn almost entirely by authority.

What Can Teachers Do?

At an early age some children appear to develop a preference for learning by authority. The human needs which make creative learning a natural process, however, appear to be sufficiently universal to make this way of learning a powerful one for all children. (There will, of course, still be many things which must be learned by authority.) What, then, can teachers do to provide the conditions in which the creative thinking abilities have a predominant role?

One of the most obvious ways of creating conditions for creative learning is to provide a curriculum with many opportunities for creative achievement. This can be done in many ways. It can be done by making assignments which call for original work, self-initiated learning, experimentation and the like. It can be done daily by the kinds of questions teachers ask in class and by the kinds of problems used for discussion. One study showed that 90 per cent of the questions asked by teachers of junior high school social studies courses called only for recall. Few questions called for any kind of thinking.

Educational research has repeatedly indicated that people tend to learn along whatever lines they find rewarding. If we want children to think creatively, we must reward creative behavior. We reward children through the kinds of personal characteristics we encourage or discourage and by the way we treat curiosity needs. *We need to be respectful of the unusual questions children ask.* Nothing is more rewarding to the curious child than to find the answer to his questions. *We need to be respectful of the unusual ideas of children.* Children who learn creatively will see many relationships that their teachers miss. *We need to show children that their ideas have value.* This is done

[2] J. W. Getzels and P. W. Jackson, *Creativity and Intelligence* (New York: John Wiley & Sons, 1962).

[3] E. P. Torrance, *Guiding Creative Talent* (Englewood Cliffs, N. J.: Prentice-Hall, 1962).

by listening to their ideas, considering them, testing them, communicating them to others and giving them credit for their ideas. *We need to provide opportunities and give credit for self-initiated learning.* Overly detailed supervision, too much reliance upon prescribed curricula, failure to appraise learning resulting from the child's own initiative and attempts to "cover" too much material with no opportunity for thinking seriously interfere with such efforts. *We also need to provide chances for children to learn and discover without threats of immediate evaluation.* Constant evaluation, especially during practice, makes children afraid to learn creatively.

Provide for Continuity of Creative Development

For years students of creative development have observed that fourth-graders become greatly concerned about conformity to peer pressures and give up many of their creative pursuits; that the beginning junior highs show a new kind of concern for conformity and their thinking becomes more obvious, commonplace and safe. Through the use of creative thinking tests, we have documented these discontinuities in the development of creative thinking abilities, especially those which occur at about the fourth and seventh grades. On the basis of comparative studies in cultures outside the United States, we have concluded that these discontinuities in creative development are man-made and due primarily to discontinuities in our culture and in our educational program.[4]

For healthy creative development, the creative imagination must be energized and guided from birth. If it is stifled early, as in Western Samoa and in some of the sub-cultures of India, it will become imitative, if it survives at all. It is true that a vigorous creative imagination can survive early stifling; but if it learns only to act vigorously without direction, it is likely to become dangerous.

All efforts to establish conditions for creative learning may fail unless teachers are able to establish creative relationships with children. I like to call the kind of relationship I have in mind a "creative relationship," because it takes place in much the same way as does creative thinking. The creative relationship requires a willingness to permit one thing to lead to another, to embark with the child on an unknown pathway. It is also like the creative thinking process in that the teacher may work hard to establish this kind of relationship and fervently want it and still fail. Then suddenly it happens. The teacher has to be ready to accept it when it does happen, just as the inventor or the scientific discoverer has to do when great discoveries occur.

[4] E. P. Torrance, "Cultural Discontinuities and the Development of Originality of Thinking," *Exceptional Children,* 1962, 29, 2-13.

Brainwashing, Perception and the Task of the Teacher

BY IRA J. GORDON

What can we learn from the techniques of brainwashing? Are these of practical use to the teacher?
Ira J. Gordon is associate professor in the College of Education, University of Florida, Gainesville.

TEACHERS ARE OFTEN CONCERNED WITH THE NEWER IDEAS IN EDUCAtional psychology and human development about perception and selfconcept. They say, in effect, if each child sees the world in his own fashion, how can I teach? They also ask, "If each child sees things in his own way because it meets his basic needs to enhance and defend himself, how can I possibly influence him to change? Suppose a child in my room sees himself as inadequate and I am told he will continue to see himself this way because it serves a purpose for him, what can I do to help? Am I forced to just sit back and say, 'Well, if that's the way he sees it....'?"

While it is certainly true that perception is an individual matter and that we see things in a certain way because of our values, needs and background of experience, it is also true *what* we see is influenced by *what there is to see*. The child in the room sees himself as inadequate because his experience has taught him to evaluate himself this way. But, what has been shaped by experience can be changed by more and different experiences.

Strange as it seems, we can learn something about modifying perceptions, the way we look at and give meanings to ourselves and the world, through the research being done on "brainwashing."

We're all aware of the communist technique to force people to say things quite different from the truth. We now know that this is not done primarily through physical brutality or the medieval torturechamber approach, but through psychological means. People changed their perceptions under concentrated psychological attack.

Perhaps children in our classrooms, too, can change negative perceptions through concentrated psychological attack. Of course, our goals are quite different from those of brainwashing; we want to enable the child to grow and develop to his own potential; we want to remove from his path his own perceptual barriers.

Perceptual Isolation

Just how was brainwashing done, and what exactly can we learn from it for practical use by the teacher?

Canadians (3, 4) and Americans (6) experimented with the technique of perceptual isolation. Subjects were placed in situations of minimal stimulation; that is, experiences with sight, sound and touch were drastically reduced. College students at McGill University were the subjects in the Canadian research; Princeton students were the subjects in the American research. In each study, the subjects were cut off for a period of several days from their normal environment. They wore goggles and other equipment which reduced sensory stimulation to a minimum. At McGill the subjects had light while eating; at Princeton, more visual isolation.

What were the conclusions? Isolation from the normal perceptual environment produced radical disturbances in the perception of one's own body, self-identity and capacity for critical thinking. The students all experienced the breakdown of their orientations in space; they felt themselves to be drifting. The effects resembled those induced by drugs. All experienced hallucinations of varying degrees, although the Princeton subjects did not have as many hallucinations as the McGill students. Normal, healthy college students thus became befuddled and disoriented when deprived of normal perceptual environments. Their selves could not withstand the onslaught of such a sterile environment.

Enabling people to change is also a major goal of psychotherapists. Of course, the therapeutic situation does not resemble the brainwashing one, except that for the individual it is a perceptual environment quite different from what he normally experiences. In psychotherapy, in place of the barren perceptual field of brainwashing, people experience an accepting, warm, understanding situation. In this situation, research indicates they change their views of themselves. (1, 2, 5, 7)

What can we say to the teacher? There *are* some common elements in perception. The perceptual environment, including interpersonal relationships, does influence the person's view of himself. Although each of us is unique, we share many common experiences. The school is one such common situation. While each child makes a personal interpretation of the school, the school itself contributes heavily to his perceptions.

Teachers Set the Tone

Teachers have much control of the classroom environment. Indeed, they set the tone. For example, a kindergarten teacher may set limits by calling a child to her to say quietly, "You know we don't play that way with the planes," in such a way that although the child knows the limit has been set, he still feels accepted as a person. Another teacher may correct a child's error by saying "Joe, what did I just ask you to do?" and "You just don't listen to anything, do you?" in such a manner that the child feels that not only is his behavior unacceptable but also *he* is not acceptable as a person to the teacher. Thus teachers, by words, gestures, posture, tone of voice and other nonverbal communications, set the climate of feeling in their classrooms. If they wish to enable the child to change his perceptions so that he sees himself as more adequate, acceptable and worth while, teachers can do it by instituting environmental changes. *First,* they can make the classroom perceptual environment radically different from what the child has previously experienced.

Through observation of the youngster's behavior, teachers can develop notions and inferences about how he perceives himself, them, his peers, school in general. Suppose a group of teachers arrive at the tentative conclusion that a boy perceives himself as inadequate and his teachers as adults whom he cannot trust. Through staff planning, they can design experiences for him which may so alter his perceptual environment as to make it possible for him to develop new perceptions of self and them. Of course, this requires careful planning and careful follow-up of the results. It requires that the teachers examine their *own* behavior as a part of the child's perceptual environment.

Second, they can make this new environment open, accepting, warm and understanding. What do acceptance and understanding require of teachers? They require that teachers develop sensitivities to the behavior of youngsters and to the meanings of the behavior to the youngster. It means that teachers ask, "I wonder how he must feel to behave in this way? How must he perceive?" In addition to behavior, teachers can get clues from autobiographies, role-playing, drawings and a variety of sources. All these need to be used so that teachers can come to *see with* and *feel with* the youngster; can show him, by their behavior, that they see what he sees.

Third, they can make the classroom rich in stimuli—visual, auditory, tactual, kinesthetic—so that the child can establish new orientations. The lack of stimuli is a crucial factor in the success of brainwashing. People lose contact with reality, lose the ability to think critically when the perceptual environment is lacking in stimulation. If teachers provide youngsers with extensive opportunities to experience; manipulate objects; interact with each other; solve problems; express themselves through art, music, drama, creative writing; experiment with numbers, words, equipment and tools, the chances are increased that children will develop new perceptions of themselves and their world. In this process, individual pupils will be able to develop at their own rate, teachers will be better able to assist those of different abilities to perceive and accept themselves and others more realistically.

Through these processes as well as many others, classroom teachers can influence the self-concepts and perceptions of children. Through these ways, children can be aided to develop concepts of self and world, realistic perceptions of their strengths and weaknesses, concepts of themselves as worth-while persons with value and dignity. These processes do not dictate the end result of what will be the content of any child's self-concept. They merely set in motion, through situational means, opportunities for children to develop adequate personalities.

References

1. BILLS, R. E. "Personality Changes During Student Centered Teaching," *Journal of Educational Research*. 1956, 60:121-126.
2. CARTWRIGHT, D. "Effects of Psychotherapy on Self-Consistency," *Journal of Counseling Psychology*. 1957, 4:15-22.
3. HEBB, O. "The Motivating Effects of Exteroceptive Stimulation," *American Psychologist*. 1958, 13:109-13.
4. HERON, W., DOAN, B. K. and SCOTT, T H. "Visual Disturbances After Prolonged Perceptual Isolation," *Canadian Journal of Psychology*. 1958, 10:13-18.
5. ROGERS, C., and DYMOND, R. (Editors). *Psychotherapy and Personality Change*. Chicago: University of Chicago, 1954.
6. VERNON, J., MCGILL E., and SCHIFFMAN, H. "Visual Hallucinations During Perceptual Isolation," *Canadian Journal of Psychology*. 1958, 12:31-34.
7. ZIMET, C. N., and FINE, J. "Personality Changes with a Group Therapeutic Experience in a Human Relations Seminar," *Journal of Abnormal and Social Psychology*. 1955, 51:68-73.

Vol. XXXVI—p. 200 (Jan. 1960)

How Adults Influence Children
BY HILDA TABA

A great deal of what children learn is a product, not a conscious plan for teaching, but an absorption of the meaning of casual gestures, remarks and expressions of feeling. Children learn from inference what is their style of life. These attitudes become foundations for mature attitudes in intergroup and international relations. Hilda Taba is professor of education at San Francisco State College, California.

THAT ADULTS INFLUENCE CHILDREN IS A SIMPLE FACT OF SOCIAL learning. A great deal of what we call *personality* is learned by imitating adults, as is the case with language; by absorbing adult interpretations, as is the case with attitudes toward policemen and Jews; by adopting the approved behavior and eliminating the disapproved ones—those which are punished in one way or another. While the source of social learning is not generally limited to adults, for young children adults (parents, teachers) are the dominant models of and the chief initiators of their social learning.

The main characteristic of social learning is that for the most part it occurs, not as planned learning and teaching, but as an incidental by-product of plain living. A great deal of what children learn is a product, not of a conscious plan for teaching, but an absorption of the meaning of casual gestures, remarks, expressions of feelings and of what is generally referred to as the *style of life* or the *climate of their environment*. Furthermore, the learning of attitudes and orientation toward people do not always begin directly but are shaped as part and parcel of general attitudes toward self, differences and change. Psychologists have demonstrated that attitudes, such as prejudice toward foreigners or persons of different race and religion, are not necessarily learned directly but are formed in the seed-bed of fear of differences, lack of self-assurance and security, and fear of change or of the strange. If we think of the ways that adults influence children's attitudes toward people, the formation of these general orientations also needs to be taken into account.

Weight of Casual Remarks

Whether they know it or not, adults influence the orientation of children in many ways. Teachers as well as parents express their feelings and value judgments in casual remarks which have more weight than they realize. A class was discussing inventions. One story had to do with how the scooter had been invented. A little boy had thought of putting wheels under a box and letting it run downhill on the pavement. A toy manufacturer saw it and asked the boy to "sell" him the invention. The boy was so glad someone cared about his toy that he gave it to the manufacturer. The teacher then asked the class to tell what they would have done had they been in the boy's place. One would have "surely asked for a few dollars." Another said that he would have "found out what worth the toy had for the man and then asked for that price." A third one said he would have just given it to the man. To the latter, her voice full of disdain, the teacher said: "You will be a teacher." This class had begun to learn that hard-headed people who can make a dollar where they can are superior to those who give and that teachers belong to that unsuccessful and inferior category.

A father who spouts angrily about the possibility of trusting "Dagoes" has sown a seed of suspicion toward people with Italian names. This sort of thing takes root especially in children who for reasons of insecurity need to have a scapegoat and to derogate, as did one first-grader described by Wanda Robertson.[1] After the class had spent a few days with a charming Swedish exchange teacher, the regular teacher was surprised to overhear the following comment in conversation: "Do you like Swedes? Well, I don't. They aren't nice. And they are mean! Did you know that Miss . . . was a Swede? My mother said she is. And wasn't she mean? Do you remember how she picked on us and made us sit in the hall?"

Inflection of Voice

Sometimes no more than a ripple in the voice betrays a feeling. In one first grade with children from lower-class agricultural worker families, the teacher was conducting a group interview about what happened at breakfast. She hoped to learn something about the style of their family life before launching the unit on home. She had been warned not to betray any judgment about what the children said so as not to influence the information they gave. The interview was tape recorded, and one could hear the teacher continuing in a steady, matter-of-fact tone: "Yes, you had biscuits and gravy for breakfast, and what else happened?". . . ."Yes, your mother had breakfast with you, and who else was there?" Suddenly, when one boy said he had coffee for breakfast, the teacher's voice went up: "Coffee?" This inflection did not escape the class, although it did not intimidate them, as would have happened in a classroom with less rapport. The opposite happened. All the boys who followed insisted that they had coffee for breakfast. One asked the teacher whether she would like to know why. When the teacher said, "Yes," he replied: "Doctor's orders. One cup a day." The class had learned that coffee was unacceptable for breakfast and that some justification for having it was necessary.

Illogical Behavior

What teachers do or fail to do about cleavage situations teaches a lot about such things as respect for personality, understanding of deviations, and methods for dealing with problems and conflicts in human relations. In one third-grade class an extremely difficult boy became a focus for such learning because of teacher wisdom in handling the case. A boy who had been "thrown out" of several classrooms because no one knew how to deal with him joined the class.

Miss K. decided to try to help the class as well as the boy. First she found out that his "tantrums" occurred whenever anyone touched him on the shoulder, because his drunkard father often grabbed him by his shoulder and beat him. Mike could not help but react frantically to

---

[1] From *Childcraft*, 1954, "Children Learn About Other People," by Wanda Robertson, page 115. Reproduced with permission by Field Enterprises Educational Corporation. All rights reserved.

any such gesture, no matter what the source. After Mike had hit another boy with roller skates, the children discussed what to do with him. They were inclined to throw Mike out as other classes had done. He had had so many chances and still had not learned to "live by our rules." Miss K. pursued the discussion until one little girl said, ". . .but Mike has not learned how to be kind yet; how could he live by our rules?" This was the start of a plan to teach Mike how to be kind. *First,* the class agreed not to touch Mike on the shoulder—to give him a reprieve, because he could not help fighting when anyone touched him.

Second, there were many informal sessions on what caused behavior and how people sometimes did not behave logically: they felt one way inside but behaved in a way that conveyed another impression, such as tripping the other fellow to say hello or punching when they wanted attention. Persons with such illogical behavior receive something back they did not look for.

The class also considered many ways in which one could express kindness, even though the kindness was not "earned," and then watched for the results. Here was a living lesson in consideration—a lesson in understanding a person who is difficult to understand, in receiving hostility without returning in kind. A pattern was established for causal reasoning about human behavior and for the idea that human reactions are circular. "If you are mean, others are mean back to you"—a lesson which Mike himself learned thoroughly enough to use it in justifying giving heart to another child two years later.

Different Styles of Life

Some influences come from failure to understand the intentions of behavior because teachers are unfamiliar with the meaning of behavior fostered in a style of life different from their own.

Miss G., who considered her students to be moral and intellectual imbeciles, had a good deal of trouble in controlling her class. One day when she had a particularly hard time, one boy came to her and said that he could beat up the class. Miss G. naturally rejected the offer and reprimanded the boy to boot. Only later as she thought about her students and her own feeling toward them did it occur to her what the meaning of the offer might have been. In effect the boy was saying: "Miss G., you have trouble with this class and I should like to help you—to cooperate with you." His concept of control was that of beating up, for only that kind of control had prevailed with him and it was the only control which he could recognize. Miss G's reaction put a further distance between the teacher, the school and the class and probably added its mite toward the growing hostility of this ethnic group toward the "Yankee community" in which they lived.

Finally, some attitudes are "in the air"—a part of a climate or a culture that prevails either in the classroom, at home or in the community. In one wealthy suburb all children in a third grade could not realize there would be any town or village that would have poor people in it. They found it difficult to understand what it meant to be poor. When Miss B. read them a story about a family that had to save pennies to buy their son a pair of shoes, these children said that the story could not be true. They felt that clothes, houses, food and other necessities came free, like air and water, for everyone to enjoy. Persuaded finally that it could be, they started wondering what was the matter with the father of that family. Something must be wrong with him if he did not have money to buy shoes. There was nothing in their experience and hence nothing in their social learning to give meaning to poverty: if it existed, it did so through someone's fault. This class needed supplementary reality experiences to make it possible for them to "see" what it means to be poor, to lack necessities or to be hungry.

The above incidents may seem far removed from intergroup or international attitudes. Yet, dealing as they do with differences of various sorts, they represent the foundation stones for the more mature attitudes in intergroup or international relations. These illustrations show also that non-verbal and situational learning in many ways is more potent than organized teaching.

Vol. XXXIX—p. 227 (Jan. 1963)

The Teacher Is a Citizen
BY SAM McLAUGHLIN

Since social and economic conditions impinge on children, teachers must become involved in action programs to improve community life. Sam McLaughlin was head of the Department of Education, University of Utah, Salt Lake City. [We regret to report that Dr. McLaughlin passed away on November 18, 1962, shortly after writing this article.]

WE SO OFTEN TALK ABOUT CHANGING THE PATTERNS OF LIVING OF children as if it could be done by merely focusing on children themselves, unrelated to their culture and the society in which they live. Obviously, with a little intelligent observation we should know better. Children are the products of their culture and develop the values prominent in that culture. If we want them to develop more intelligent democratic behavior patterns, we must progressively change the culture in line with more democratic goals.

Children who live in a community or state or nation where unethical political maneuvering is rampant—where the prominent are always favored, where a few so-called "leaders" run the entire show, where bigotry and intolerance characterize living, where hypocrisy is a pattern, where material things are the measuring stick of life, where education is an afterthought—will not develop into democratic citizens with great generosity of spirit and lofty value patterns.

Changing the trends in the culture or the society cannot be accomplished within the four walls of a classroom or school. In America changes in social, economic, civic and political conditions come about by political means and political actions. It is unintelligent to try to develop democratic values in children without attacking the discrepancies in the culture and the society in which they live. We, the teachers and educators, must fight hard for a better deal for children. We cannot leave their future to chance. To accomplish democratic goals for children, educators must engage actively, energetically and intelligently in political affairs.

When children live in communities or neighborhoods where housing and facilities are an outrage to democracy and to personal health and development, where sanitary conditions and health situations are deplorable, where recreational and play facilities are a void, where unemployment is rampant and substandard wages are the rule, where racial discrimination pervades the area and where other equally unwholesome conditions prevail, teachers and educators who see the results firsthand must lead the fight to change the picture through political means. To accomplish this objective, teachers must become significant factors in political party machinery and in action groups in the community. Pious talk, mere discussions of citizenship and the urging of others to carry the ball accomplish little if anything.

Builders of Tomorrow's Citizens

For generations politicians and community leaders have considered teachers a sort of third sex, neuter gender, fifth-class citizens, almost indentured servants, conscientious about the unimportant and perfectly harmless. Generally, they have been paid accordingly. Several years ago, at an important educational meeting in Baltimore, a feature writer for *The Baltimore Sun,* having listened to the deliberations for a few days, wrote an article in which among other things he stated, "Teachers are scared rabbits. I don't know whether they are in the profession because they are scared or are scared because they are in it." The birthright of all human beings is freedom to shape their own destiny. Without that freedom, man loses his personal integrity and his basic purpose. One of our fundamental problems is how to retain individuality, integrity and creativity in ourselves and in our children in an age of conformity and hypocrisy.

In many ways the teacher has a greater responsibility than Mr. Average Citizen; for teachers could, if they wished and were prepared, be molders of tomorrow's society, having full access to tomorrow's citizens. They could determine to a large degree the shape of things to come in this brave new world. Teachers have to decide whether they shall be propagators of trivia or builders of tomorrow. Our citizens have to be acquainted thoroughly with all angles of all basic problems of our communities and of our society; they have to be motivated to act. Most of this has to come from the programs of our schools. It will not result from schools if teachers are ignorant, timid, cowardly or inactive politically. They cannot be mice. The problem is a terrific one and means much to the future of democratic life in this world.

To be an effective example to children, a teacher must be aware, informed and active in civic affairs. His responsibility is to help develop citizens who themselves will be aware, informed, active citizens. This can be done only as the school, classroom and community become a laboratory where all angles of crucial problems of the community and the larger society are thoroughly considered. The child as a citizen has to learn how and where he can get valid facts on all phases of serious problems. He has to acquire a background for intelligent judgment. Otherwise he becomes the stupid victim of mass media of communication and may be led to believe anything those in control of mass media may desire.

Involvement in Action Programs

The behavior of teachers is obviously the product of their past experiences and the values and motivations resulting from those experiences. Motivation to civic behavior occurs on the part of a few because of civic interest and activity within the home. However, as far as the majority of teachers are concerned, the awareness, motivation and understandings required for intelligent civic action must come as a result of a well-conceived general and professional education program. Prospective teachers as citizens must have an opportunity to become involved in the solution of the important, baffling social-economic-political problems and issues of their day and engage in political action efforts to accomplish results. Only by participation does one learn the strategy involved in securing community betterment. Only by involvement does he learn to overcome the obstacles to progress and how to make himself a significant factor in political effort. Colleges must provide for these experiences in the curriculum to give prospective teachers motivation for personal action and to provide the educational background and interest for them to include such experiences in the school curriculum. Some colleges and universities, including the University of Utah, have developed such action programs for both prospective teachers and teachers in service. Because of curricular implications, this area of social foundations seems to serve best when it is a part of the professional pattern.

It appears that civic interest and civic action become a part of a person's behavior more readily and lastingly if the learning experiences stem from a real problem, condition or situation which needs solution and betterment and involves a program of action. Involvement in programs of action provides an opportunity for the unity of the scientific method and emotional drive.

Conditions Impinge on Children

In any community or state are numerous serious social and economic problems which can be solved only through educational and political action. Since such situations have serious impact on children and their families, they must be of basic concern to all teachers, and they must unite with those citizens and groups which are trying to improve conditions. It is not enough to vote in a primary or general election; a teacher should participate in the process by which competent candidates get on the ballot. Otherwise the choice in an election may be confined to a choice between candidates who are equal obstacles to social and economic progress.

Since concern, awareness and motivation to action are products of past experience on the basis of maturity, children and youth need to participate in social-political action programs under the direction of teachers. Children are interested in reality, in mature ideas and causes. They see conditions about them. While one should guard against exploiting them, children's natural awareness and concern must be used and enhanced toward the development of citizens for a free democratic society. The problems and situations of an area which impinge constantly on the lives of children and youth need to be made significant aspects of a living curriculum.

Information Needed for Action

Among the most thrilling experiences prospective teachers may have is participation in the solution of important community, state and national problems. To work with the chairman of a legislative committee on a minimum wage law, to be associated with the chairman of the civil rights committee in the establishment of policies and laws concerning minority groups, to develop a state day care program for nursery schools, to assist in the establishment of legislation involving urban renewal or sanitary legislation or slum clearance are among the activities which may occur in a good teacher education program designed to develop awareness and action on the part of a new crop of teachers. A professor in such a course should not attempt to develop a particular point of view. His task is to help identify acute problems which hamper democratic living and provide thought-provoking materials on all angles of the problems. This process provides an opportunity for critical thinking and the weighing of values as well as the enhancing of civic awareness and civic consciousness. The collection of the facts on a problem by student surveys often helps acquaint citizens of a city with information they need for intelligent action.

Teachers are first-class citizens. As the heralded champions of children's welfare, they must be in the vanguard of intelligent political activity for a better deal for their charges.

Vol. XXIX—p. 168 (Dec. 1952)

What should I do about him?

That Silent One
BY LUCY NULTON

How does a teacher vary procedures to meet the differences of children? It must be a very personal approach, as Lucy Nulton, College of Education, University of Florida, Gainesville, so beautifully explains.

FIRST OF ALL, I SHOULD TRY TO BE VERY SLOW WITH THIS CHILD—VERY slow and very gentle with this child who never talks.

I should tell him "Good morning" when he comes, taking his hand softly or touching him lightly (not on top of his head so that I tower over him, but upon his shoulder or his arm, as man to man), smiling, looking straight into his eyes, and for that moment living all alone with him, giving him my whole attention. I should be careful to be casual and happy-hearted.

Then I should let him alone, this closed-tight little child, and not pry at him or pick at him or prod him to make him react outwardly.

But before that, even before the first day, I'd have been getting ready for him—knowing he would come, there is always one—by having a place of beauty ready for him to come into; by providing within the room some little retiring nooks and corners into which he could withdraw when the need was upon him, "far from the madding crowd"; by having many colorful things to do (knowing that life and health and growth require doing—together); by having places and times and things planned and prepared for relaxing and just being— without comment, without pumping, without *anybody* talking. For there are times when silence speaks beautifully.

And there should be beauty and wonder from the out-of-doors to speak to him without talking. Moreover, he might sit in full freedom and stroke the ivory-smooth petal of the magnolia or hold the cocoon pulsing and vibrating in his hand. He might lick the three-sided prism to see if it tasted. And never, never, should I say to him, "Johnny, tell us about it. Johnny, what have you found there?" For who, after all, can explain the growing life in a cocoon or can truly talk except in relatively guttural grunts of this mystic and fairylike band of vividness which flashes through a clear piece of glass?

He might be like that, this closed little boy; sensitively silent before the wonder of the world; quiet in profoundness or newness. That might be his temperament—to meet the world and people without much talk. He has a right to his silences. The world needs his silences.

But he might be afraid. Fears, the fears of the nighttime and the fears of the daytime, can only be talked out when he is ready—ready and sure that no one will laugh. Sometimes fears can only be worked out or pounded out with hammer and nails or kicked out against some inanimate kicking post which can take it without being hurt and won't kick back. There should be all these things—without words. Words, after all, are fragile, shattering things. Words are not all we need for healing!

Should this child be a stranger in a strange land (and who of us is not?)? I should watch sensitively for him, seeking the first outgoing sign from some other child toward him. Then I should try, unobtrusively, delicately, so to arrange things that those two were together on the playground, in a reading nook, dabbling in paint, feeding the live pet, staying after school to help get the room ready for the next day. Almost always there is one such child who can do more for the little silent, needy one than any adult can and do it more sensitively.

I should walk home with him after school, being careful to have arranged it beforehand so as not to embarrass Mother by letting teacher catch her doing laundry; or arrange not to arrive on one of Mother's club afternoons when teacher would be embarrassed; or avoid coming unexpectedly upon Mother and Father quarreling or drunken when Johnny would be embarrassed. If we could not walk I should take him home in my car, being careful to let *him* tell me the way, perhaps stopping en route for a little treat of candy, fruit or a drink. Once there,

I would talk pleasantly about interesting things in the world, steadfastly refusing to talk about Johnny over his head and in his presence. If Johnny were mentioned I would say the good things about Johnny, the happy things about school, and steer the subject on to the nicest or most beautiful thing "not-Johnny" about the place.

I'd make a friendly appointment for Mother to come to school one time (the first of many, I'd hope) to be with Johnny and us to do things with us, and one time when Mother and teacher could talk. "What does Johnny like best? What do you all do together? How was Johnny born? When did Johnny begin to make sounds? What did he say first? Did you think he was slow talking?"

I might talk to his grandmother or his doctor. I should ask his father to help us make something at school and his mother to come cook with us or sing to us, had she a mother-singing voice (not necessarily a trained voice), or to help take us on a trip.

Never, never would I compare! Johnny Blank is Johnny Blank, the one and only Johnny Blank. The best Johnny Blank there is (now).

I should read to them all and sometimes just to Johnny alone. I'd quote poems, ask riddles, tell tales, and lead them to tell and share and quote and "make believe." We'd play games and play make-believe and play school and house and doctor. We'd have music to sing, to experiment with, to listen to.

Johnny might join us or he might not. He should know that it is his right to choose when he would speak and when he would keep silent.

And we would listen. We would all listen. Teacher, most especially, would listen—to the bird outside our window, to the kitten's purr, to the chick inside the egg, to the playing record, to the one-fingered tunes picked out on the piano, to the others talking, to Johnny talking—very quietly, not too noisily listen to Johnny talking. Teacher, most especially, should listen.

I should watch—watch closely, keenly sensitive—for the first flicker from Johnny. When did his posture change? What was it made his eyes move? Was there a little extra light in them just then? My, but I'm glad he hit Mary! What brought that about? Until presently I'd find that something which Johnny can do well—better, perhaps, than the rest of us. I'd use that! But I'd be quiet about it, not yammer, yammer, yammer, "Johnny's so good at this. Johnny made this and this. Don't you want to tell us about it, Johnny?" Of course, he doesn't! But he will expand when he knows I think it good (if it *is* truly, sincerely good). He will stretch a little and relax if he happens to overhear me say to another, "Go over and look at Johnny's horse. It is so nice!" He will move a bit more surely when he is chosen for a special task or a coveted privilege because "Johnny's so good at that." And the group will talk. Strong talk. Talk that nourishes sureness and destroys fears. They will like Johnny too, though he is quiet or because he is quiet.

Then words will come—to Johnny. And they will be sure words, big words for Johnny and our group, because they have had time to grow; they will have cast out fears; they will speak peace; though they may only say, "Aw, fellows, let *me* try it!"

Vol. XXXI—p. 264 (Feb. 1955)

Firmer Boundaries for Greater Freedom
BY INA K. DILLON

Most of us willingly accept limits to our freedom because without them no one could be safely free. How do we help children grow in this concept of freedom? Ina K. Dillon is a clinical psychologist, Los Angeles, California.

A PERSON WHO LOVES MUSIC WILL PROBABLY FIND HIMSELF AT TIMES in the company of those who produce it or of those who use their means to promote it. I once found myself in a uniquely equipped music room. In it were a harpsichord, a spinet, and a grand piano. There were stringed instruments, wind instruments, and a fairly complete library of music written for all these instruments. On the walls hung pictures of Bach, Brahms, Beethoven and other musicians. My hostess said, "Please make yourself at home. The room is soundproof and you are perfectly free to use anything in the room as much or as long as you wish." So far as she was concerned I was free to use her musical facilities. Still I was not free to do so. I could not produce real music on a single instrument there. Freedom at the keyboard results from long hours of training the eye, the ear, the fingers. Musical freedom is the result of musical discipline. I did not have it.

There was once a group of hardy settlers in a new world bent upon escape from tyranny to freedom. They worked and prayed and fought for the greatest possible freedom for the individual, and for the state, as opposed to a strong federal government. After many years of creative effort and war they settled for enough federal control; enough sacrifice of individual and state freedom to insure its survival. This experiment is in its second hundred years now and the balance between freedom and control has not yet been found. More discipline through experience with democracy will be required.

A ten-year-old only child had been reared in an isolated rural area. Her mother had once been a teacher, and with the help of Calvert had done a wonderful job of the child's education. She had not, however, been able to satisfy the child's need for schools or for play experiences with other children. The child was taken for a time to live with her aunt, who provided many such experiences including a gay party. Fifteen boys and girls her own age were invited. She was a polite little girl, but a shy onlooker at her own party. She could not play the games. Neither could she use the apparatus on the nearby playground where they went to play. She was glad when the party was over and glad to return to her parents on the farm. There she revealed that her visit had not been a very happy experience. She had not stayed long enough to acquire the skills, the disciplines involved.

Gradually and Through Experience

Freedom with people, like freedom with musical instruments or self-government, must be acquired gradually by way of experience. It is an inside job. One needs strength, adequacy and discipline to cope with freedom. It constitutes a real responsibility to the potentially responsible. In the hands of others it is a menace, both personal and social.

Freedom develops best within safe boundaries. These outer boundaries are needed until their firm support has become part and parcel of the self. One needs control from without until he has developed enough inner sturdiness and skill for self-control. Therefore, supportive boundaries and satisfying practice in self-control must be a consistent part of child guidance, not one now and the other then, *but the two consistently together.*

Modern living has produced materials and experiences so rapidly and in such quantities that life for children and for adults alike is weighed down by this abundance of toys, lessons of all kinds, radios, movies, parties, television programs. These come so fast and in such amounts that selectivity, self-confidence, and self-respect are at times unable to grow deep enough and strong enough to support the superstructure. The tree of life may become bent, lopsided, or broken by reason of the abundance of freedom not grown into.

H. E. Fosdick, in *Twelve Tests of Character,** speaks of pitching a tent. He says that if you keep on lengthening the ropes which attach a tent to the earth but neglect to strengthen the stakes which hold it, the tent may achieve liberty but not tenthood. A tent is not a tent when it is liberated from the earth. It is only a canvas flapping in the breeze. Longer ropes demand stronger stakes. Increased freedom calls for firmer boundaries.

* New York: Harper & Bros., 1923.

It is not freedom from musical instruments, or from government, or from civilization, or from the earth, or from winds that we want, but freedom in, with, and among these. When a tent has so much liberty that it is only "canvas flapping in the wind," or a man-child so much that he is lonely, confused, inadequate or rebellious, firm supportive limits are needed. Limits can be extended as he gains in sturdiness and skill.

Basic Needs Are Important

Children cannot achieve sturdy selfhood apart from the fulfillment of certain basic needs. Parents and teachers play a vital service in the lives of growing children in meeting growth-needs within supportive boundaries. The parent and teacher will recognize the child's physical needs for right food, water, sun, rest and exercise in right amounts and provide these for the child while by the gradual processes of habit, knowledge and appreciation he learns to provide them for himself. This, of course, takes time.

The parent and teacher will recognize the child's basic social needs, to be of service to others and to receive appreciative recognition for that service. They will also provide an example of such service for him along with the opportunity to render small but gradually increasing services to those who are near him. As parents and teachers express appreciation of these childlike contributions and give recognition to their children as contributors to the family or group, the children will take increasing satisfaction in belonging to, and in being responsible to, their family, school and society.

Teachers and parents will recognize and satisfy the child's emotional need to be loved for his own sake whether such love is deserved or not, while helping him gradually to *win* a place in the affections of relatives, friends, schoolmates and neighbors by deserving it. In these and other areas of life the child is at first completely dependent; bound by his own inadequacy. He is completely undisciplined, irresponsible, unfree. By a series of progressive approximations, that is to say, by imperfect experiences carefully graded and wisely encouraged, the child moves out from this complete dependence toward adult independence, from infantile lack of control toward self-control, from completely irresponsible dependence to relative competence and freedom.

"If to do were as easy as to know what were good to be done," perhaps there would be in life for us all more joy, success and freedom; or is it in *learning to do* that these are found and developed? Making controlled freedom a reality in the experience of any given individual or group will be a lifelong process and never (in this life at least)

171

is it fully realized. We want and can have more of it for our children and for ourselves than is usually experienced.

How Can We Help the Child?

We recognize complete know-how—complete skill in guiding our children—is a long-range goal never to be fully realized. The endless struggle, either verbal or physical, over who is to be boss has been tried long enough. The most that we can gain from such a struggle is the strength to resist authority. At worst it may be a crushing procedure.

Standing over the developing child to tell him what to do, how to do it and when to do it, will develop dependence, confusion or rebellion depending upon the nature and strength of the child's personality. Who then will direct him when we are gone? Or who will reinstate the rebel?

Protecting the child from the demands of life is also worse than futile. By this method we spare him problems, learning, adequacy, and freedom. We keep him a dependent infant to the extent that we succeed. The worst of all bad methods is the adding of blame to failure in the case of mistakes already made.

Evasion may be a valuable momentary device in situations that can be better left to time and to the child's resources, but it is a very poor long-range method. By continued evasion we abandon our leadership and our responsibility to someone else or to chance. Parents and teachers have, by reason of the very fact that they *are* parents and teachers, a responsibility for guiding their children toward self-controlled responsible freedom.

Nothing can take the place of courage, self-confidence and creative intelligence on the part of those in charge of growing children. It is sometimes thought that we used to be, or at least we once *seemed* to be, more confident than we are today. It was once sufficient to say, "People won't like you if you act like that!" Today's child retorts, "Which people?" He comes close to more people. He sees that individuals differ in their views and practices. We used to be able to say, "That is bad! You mustn't do it." Today's child responds, "The president of the Rotary Club does it" or "Who says it is bad? Mr. ——— lets Bill do it. Uncle Joe says it's OK."

The simple old way of dividing one's life-space into two parts, good or bad with a clear line between them, has been taken away from us. We are aware of grays as well as black and white.

Though it is difficult or even impossible to say what may be right or wrong, it is clear today as in the past that there are some things that we may not do. They are positively forbidden. There are also some matters regarding which we may have fairly complete freedom so long as we are willing to bear the consequences of that freedom. I may *not* kill my neighbor, take his goods, destroy the Federal currency, or betray my country to its enemy. These things and others I may not do and still remain at large.

Most of us willingly accept these limits to our freedom because without them no one could be safely free. Because we accept them, we *are relatively free.* We are firmly bounded by accepted law and law enforcement, and we live quite freely within these boundaries. At the other extreme I am quite free to choose my style of haircut, dress or dinner service; to worship God or not to worship; to eat fruit or to leave it.

Between these two extremes there are many ways in which I may be relatively free and relatively responsible; in which I may experiment with freedom. In American life, as we live it today, fortunately the largest area of an individual's life space lies between these two extremes. This large middle-ground is an area of relative freedom to live and learn and to adjust to others who are living and learning. Here it is that we face alternatives involving choice. In this area we are free to make our choices in terms of personal values, or of group values which are also freely chosen.

Since life is like this, it makes sense that children from the start have experiences that will prepare them for it. These learning experiences in childhood will be largely gained through play and playthings shared with others. Playthings and play experiences not only do much to *prepare* children for life but they can be a means of good creative living here and now.

Every child needs some playthings that are his very own with which he may do exactly as he pleases, and for which doing he will take the consequences. If he cuts the ears off his toy rabbit, he has a rabbit without ears, not a new one, just a rabbit without ears. The consequences should be pointed out to him if he gives enough advance notice of his plan, but it is inadvisable to forbid, nag or soon replace the object. These should be things he could safely deprive himself of by way of their destruction. These are the things with which he learns among other things the meaning of freedom and the fact that freedom is as good as the use we make of it and that it is inevitably related to consequences. It would of course be ridiculous to let a child mutilate his clothes and go in rags. It would be unfair to let him destroy furniture and live in a wreck. It would be more than unfair to let him destroy books and do without them. Therefore, every child should have from the start some things that he is taught to respect and to protect.

Good books, appropriate clothes and a dollar bill are his only to use, to enjoy, care for and share. These things and others belong to the culture as well as to the individual. Parents and teachers also are required by the culture to respect objects in this group. By their example and consistent training they usually succeed in conveying to their children the fact that, regardless of age, there are limits to one's freedom. These limits will vary with the time and the place, but the existence of such limits must be universally recognized.

Area for Learning and Freedom

Between the two extremes of complete freedom and rigid control lies an area for learning, an area of relative freedom. It is the largest area of a child's life space in America and therefore a large proportion of children's possessions and experiences should meet its learning needs. This is the area for trial and error and success, for challenge, creativity, choice.

Paints, clay, wood, homemaking toys and all such items would serve this purpose. Sometimes they will overlap with other areas, meeting other needs as well. Earth, water, kitchen utensils and countless materials for learning would also qualify as creative tools with which one may sometimes be quite free. With these materials children construct and destroy. This destruction is like wiping the problem off a slate so they may try to solve it in a new and better way. They may paint a picture, call it bad and throw it in the basket. They may paint another and pin it on the wall until it too has been outgrown. This is growth. They may build a tower that will fall instead of being surrounded with so much teaching, so much guarding that it seems better not to build at all. They may have need to build one that will topple. The toppling does no harm. It could challenge them to find a way to make one stand, or they may be building just to see a tower topple.

Freedom of imagination and freedom with materials are necessary in this type of experience. Failure to make a success in play—as parents and teachers see success—harms children far less than does the feeling of fear or of disgrace which we build in them through our deep concern and over-teaching. Children will try again and again, learning to do better, and learning perseverance, if that trying is not made disgraceful and corroding by adults who regard the child as somehow falling short because he fails to perform according to some standard within the parent's mind. Healthy children can safely fail and try again, but few human beings at any age can bear to be thought of as failures. If our respect for the creative self within the growing child is deep and sincere we may on occasion give a little help to insure success, but oh, so little. What he needs is support and guidance in relation to materials and people within firm but expanding boundaries.

The inner strength required for wise, enlarging use of freedom develops best in an emotional climate warm enough for survival but cool enough to be invigorating. This too is a relative thing. It is neither all permissive nor all directed, neither all sunshine nor all stormy. Just as the length of the rope will depend upon the strength of the stake in pitching a tent and as the need for a curb on the growing tree will depend upon the depth of its root and the amount of wind and superstructure, so the support and shelter needed in one's emotional climate will depend upon the sturdiness of the child and the stresses to which he is subjected.

Guiding a child toward greater freedom is a task for adults who are themselves reasonably confident and responsibly free. We have said that to be free is to be firmly tied to something or to be firmly bounded, but that something to which one is tied or by which one is bounded must be conducive to growth and to continuous liberation. This is true of the persons who bound one's freedom as well as of the other boundaries of the child's environment.

Vol. XX—p. 219 (Jan. 1944)

The Poor Scholar's Soliloquy
BY STEPHEN M. COREY

"Cue to Curriculum" might be the sub-title for this pithy piece by Mr. Corey, who is principal of the University Elementary School, University of Chicago, and professor of education in the University.

No, I'M NOT VERY GOOD IN SCHOOL. THIS IS MY SECOND YEAR IN THE seventh grade and I'm bigger and taller than the other kids. They like me all right, though, even if I don't say much in the schoolroom, because outside I can tell them how to do a lot of things. They tag me around and that sort of makes up for what goes on in school.

I don't know why the teachers don't like me. They never have very much. Seems like they don't think you know anything unless they can name the book it comes out of. I've got a lot of books in my own room at home—books like *Popular Science Mechanical Encyclopedia,* and the Sears' and Ward's catalogues, but I don't very often just sit down and read them through like they make us do in school. I use my books when I want to find out something, like whenever Mom buys anything secondhand I look it up in Sears' or Ward's first and tell her if she's getting stung or not. I can use the index in a hurry to find the things I want.

In school, though, we've got to learn whatever is in the book and I just can't memorize the stuff. Last year I stayed after school every night for two weeks trying to learn the names of the Presidents. Of course I knew some of them like Washington and Jefferson and Lincoln, but there must have been thirty altogether and I never did get them straight.

I'm not too sorry though because the kids who learned the Presidents had to turn right around and learn all the Vice Presidents. I am taking the seventh grade over but our teacher this year isn't so interested in the names of the Presidents. She has us trying to learn the names of all the great American inventors.

Kids Seemed Interested

I guess I just can't remember names in history. Anyway, this year I've been trying to learn about trucks because my uncle owns three and he says I can drive one when I'm sixteen. I already know the horsepower and number of forward and backward speeds of twenty-six American trucks, some of them Diesels, and I can spot each make a long way off. It's funny how that Diesel works. I started to tell my teacher about it last Wednesday in science class when the pump we were using to make a vacuum in a bell jar got hot, but she said she didn't see what a Diesel engine had to do with our experiment on air pressure so I just kept still. The kids seemed interested though. I took four of them around to my uncle's garage after school and we saw the mechanic Gus tearing a big truck Diesel down. Boy, does he know his stuff!

I'm not very good in geography either. They call it economic geography this year. We've been studying the imports and exports of Chile all week but I couldn't tell you what they are. Maybe the reason is I had to miss school yesterday because my uncle took me and his big trailer truck down state about two hundred miles and we brought almost ten tons of stock to the Chicago market.

He had told me where we were going and I had to figure out the highways to take and also the mileage. He didn't do anything but drive and turn where I told him to. Was that fun! I sat with a map in my lap and told him to turn south or southeast or some other direction. We made seven stops and drove over five hundred miles round trip. I'm figuring now what his oil cost and also the wear and tear on the truck—he calls it depreciation—so we'll know how much we made.

I even write out all the bills and send letters to the farmers about what their pigs and beef cattle brought at the stockyards. I only made three mistakes in seventeen letters last time, my aunt said—all commas. She's been through high school and reads them over. I wish I could write school themes that way. The last one I had to write was on "What a Daffodil Thinks of Spring," and I just couldn't get going.

I don't do very well in school in arithmetic either. Seems I just can't keep my mind on the problems. We had one the other day like this:

If a 57 foot telephone pole falls across a cement highway so that $17\frac{3}{6}$ feet extend from one side and $14\frac{9}{17}$ feet from the other, how wide is the highway?

That seemed to me like an awfully silly way to get the width of a highway. I didn't even try to answer it because it didn't say whether the pole had fallen straight across or not.

Not Getting Any Younger

Even in shop I don't get very good grades. All of us kids made a broom holder and a bookend this term and mine were sloppy. I just couldn't get interested. Mom doesn't use a broom anymore with her new vacuum cleaner and all our books are in a bookcase with glass doors in the parlor. Anyway, I wanted to make an end gate for my uncle's trailer but the shop teacher said that meant using metal and wood both and I'd have to learn how to work with wood first. I didn't see why but I kept still and made a tie rack at school and the tail gate after school at my uncle's garage. He said I saved him $10.

Civics is hard for me, too. I've been staying after school trying to learn the "Articles of Confederation" for almost a week because the teacher said we couldn't be good citizens unless we did. I really tried, because I want to be a good citizen. I did hate to stay after school, though, because a bunch of us boys from the south end of town have been cleaning up the old lot across from Taylor's Machine Shop to make a playground out of it for the little kids from the Methodist home. I made the jungle gym from old pipe and the guys made me Grand Mogul to keep the playground going. We raised enough money collecting scrap this month to build a wire fence clear around the lot.

Dad says I can quit school when I'm fifteen and I'm sort of anxious to because there are a lot of things I want to learn how to do and as my uncle says, I'm not getting any younger.

The Teacher Asked of the Child
BY LELAND B. JACOBS

The teacher asked of the child,
"What would you have of me?"
And the child replied,
"Because you are you, only you
   know some of the things
I would have of you.
But because I am I,
I do know some of what
I would have of you."

The teacher asked again,
"What would you have of me?"
And the child replied,
"I would have of you what
You are and what you know,
I would have you speaking and silent,
Sure and unsure, seeking for surety,
Vibrant and pensive.

"I would have you talking and letting me tell,
Going my way with my wonderings and
   enthusiasms,
And going your way that I may know new
   curiosities,
I would have you leading step by step
Yet letting me step things off in my own
   fashion."

"Teach me," said the child,
"With simplicity and imagination—
Simply that the paraphernalia and the gadgets
Do not get between us;
Imaginatively that I may sense and catch your
   enthusiasm,
And the quickening thrill of never having
   been this way before.

"Too, I would have you watching over me,
   yet not too watchful,
Caring for me, yet not too carefully,
Holding me to you, yet not with bindings,
So when the day comes, as it must,
   that we, each, go our separate ways,
I can go free.
Let me take you with me not because
   I must, but because I would have it so.
Let me take you with me because
   you have become, in me,
Not just today—
Tomorrow!"

Section IV

The Classroom

The Classroom

Two classrooms are side by side. As school opens, they appear to be alike, with the same type of walls, windows, doors; the same equipment and supplies. But here the likeness stops. What happens as boys and girls arrive cannot be the same, for each teacher is a unique human being and neither of them can relate to children in the way the other does.

Yet sometimes one teacher is asked to emulate another. He is told that he should arrange furniture in the same way as does his colleague across the hall, that the same type of planning should be done. Even though he initiates discussion using similar questions, uses the same books, makes identical assignments and marks papers using standards given to him, he cannot reproduce the same opportunities for learning. To a casual observer it may appear that conditions are the same in both settings. A closer examination reveals that though the ways of working have been copied, the second classroom lacks the vitality of the first classroom, where a teacher gives himself fully to initiating and planning activities suited to his philosophy and skills.

If boys and girls are to realize themselves, they need to be in classrooms where they can feel excitement in learning, where they will be challenged to search for meanings. Children delight in their own growth when they are aware that what they are learning is special for each of them.

One classroom should not be exactly like another. Yet reading about the planning done by another may start for a teacher a new trend of thinking. As you read you extract that which has meaning for you and translate it into a classroom which is unique. The articles in this section describe some classrooms with climates conducive to learning. Some areas of curriculum are presented which give basic underlying principles of learning upon which each teacher can build creatively for boys and girls of *his* classroom.—*By* LUCILE LINDBERG, *Professor of Education, Queens College, New York.*

What Should We Know About Learning?

BY LAURA ZIRBES

> Laura Zirbes, professor of education emeritus, The Ohio State University, Columbus, presents "today's considerations essential to learning" in contrast to those in the days of the little red schoolhouse. These considerations of children have been overlooked by many critics of modern education.

THE *we* IN THE TITLE OF THIS ARTICLE REFERS TO "THOSE CONCERNED with children," whoever they may be, and every reader of CHILDHOOD EDUCATION identifies those words with the title of the magazine.

Whatever accrues in the way of new knowledge about learning should be known and used as a basis for intelligent concern and action in behalf of children. It should also be used as a basis for the insightful interpretation of behavior and for the sound evaluation of developmental guidance and curricular practices. Many of the critics of modern education fail to take this into account. They assume that what was approved in the days of little red schoolhouses provides precedents for current practices in today's schools.

Adaptability to Change

Not only do today's children live in quite a different world from that in which their parents and teachers grew up; they also face an unprecedented future, since the rate of social change and its impact on learning and living cannot be left out of account. Furthermore, there are cumulative implications in the recent findings of inquiries into human behavior, human development, human aspirations and human relations. They constitute further challenges to continuing forward adjustment in provisions for child nurture and education. These considerations, coupled with the tensions and pressures which characterize this age of unremitting scientific advance and world-wide industrialization, make *adaptability to change* quite as essential to survival and fulfillment as backgrounds of knowledge and competence.

Instructional procedures which seek to fix ideas and automatize habits and skills without concern for flexibility and adaptivity are anachronistic. Learnings which are open-ended are far better suited to times like ours. Teaching becomes obsolescent and derelict when it fails to take the realities of social and cultural change into consideration.

Children whose play is permeated with the imagery and dynamism of the space age are bound to find little to challenge their potentialities in the dull routines projected by didactic instructional materials. The boys and girls of today have had contacts with the wide world; their vicarious experiences with its people have been vitalized and expanded by advances in communication. They need a new deal if their learnings are to expand their knowledge and kindle their aspirations to significant roles into which their education should lead. Of course, they need acquaintance with their national heritage and a sense of identification with it. They also need to learn about the changes which link the past with current events and with the emergent future. Nothing short of lengthening historical perspectives will expand their outlook on ways of living and extend their conceptions of social origins and processes.

Extrinsic motivation and ground-covering assignments in required history texts may prepare them for formal recitations and periodic tests but will not provide a base for liberal learning—much less for scholarship, citizenship or abiding interest in human affairs. We should know that learning which is lacking in genuine involvement and intrinsic appeal is transient and superficial. Social learnings need to be vitalized by life-relatedness and vivid imagery. They need to be enriched and broadened by identification with history-in-the-making, by challenging contacts with the dynamic ideas that have had notable impacts on human values and social living, and by acquaintance with treasured artifacts of the cultural heritage.

Involvement Gives Meaning

There are far more abundant resources for such enrichment than there were of old and they are much more accessible than they were in the days of yore. We should do much more to make sure that learning is not narrowed and impoverished by adherence to "lesson learning" or by unenlightened conceptions of education and child development. We should know that *early* learnings contribute much more to developing personalities when they tap pertinent experiences and use today's wealth of visual and literary materials to challenge potentialities and raise aspirations. So-called "basic" education which consists of passive submission to instruction in pre-organized subject matter is archaic and inappropriate for the most active, formative years.

Persons who are insightfully concerned with human development and fulfillment know better than to advocate or trust such approaches to learning. They know that direct concrete experiences are the social contexts in which children find meanings that set off thinking, understanding and language development. Actual involvement in social interaction with peers is a spur to communication, visual and auditory discrimination and motor skills. Purposeful effort reduces dependence and makes for autonomy and self-direction. Children who have guided access to vital resources seek, gather, organize and use knowledge to satisfy their own curiosity when it is aroused. They use observations, information and ideas creatively in their dramatic play and project them into other forms of expression, interaction and communication. What they learn in these ways comes alive. It not only registers in their memories—it is assimilated as vicarious experience which quickens their concerns and enlivens further learning. Even the very young child's social learnings use life experiences and observations as bases for roles assumed in play.

Children learn by doing, by attempting to do what challenges them. Their make-do efforts may be crude at first, but they are flexible, adaptive and developmental. Their skills are cumulative *consequences* of their make-do efforts.

Before he can walk the infant attempts to get where he wants to go and achieves his purpose by creeping. He makes do with creeping and attempting to walk. He manages to toddle and then gives up creeping and toddling after achieving increasing steadiness and rhythmic coordination functionally in walking. All this proceeds without formal exercises and without lessons. It is facilitated by well-timed, encouraging guidance and by the satisfactions of increasing measures of success. Similarly, self-feeding starts with sucking, but that leads to sipping and drinking. Skill with the use of utensils for eating develops from awkward, messy efforts which *simultaneously* satisfy hunger and the early do-it-yourself urge. Wise guidance respects that urge. Here, too, learning is functional. Initial use is purposeful and satisfying long before it is skillful; the young child's effort is not skill centered.

Toddlers do not learn to talk in systematic lessons, but they use inflected speech and acquire extensive oral vocabularies in their spontaneous communication and in dramatic play. This developmental base of language learnings readies children for an experience approach to reading and creative writing.

The teacher of young children who assumes that mechanical drill is more efficient than meaningful learning is likely to rely on drill and do too little to compensate for the lack of meaningful associations. Children who have had exceedingly systematic formal instruction in beginning reading and those who have had copious word drills are both less likely to use contextual cues to get meaning when they read. Their responses have been too controlled and stereotyped to allow for initiative, inference and associative thinking. Their instruction has been narrowed at the expense of wider values. When Reading is "taught" as a "subject" its relationship to direct experience and prior language learnings is not capitalized. Its carry-over possibilities to other "subjects" are also reduced.

Functional Arithmetic

Instead of learning number combinations by rote, children can learn to *combine* and *regroup* concrete items and objects flexibly and insightfully, to symbolize groupings and components of combinations, to make and test their own inferences and develop them functionally.

The child who has worked out combinations that can be made with twelve objects comes to know more than "combinations." He comes to see how he can divide or group his twelve objects into two or three or four or six equal arrays. He comes to see how he can combine twos to make fours or sixes; how he can combine threes to make sixes; how he can make eight or nine or ten or twelve. Young learners can "see" that the size of a group of objects can be reduced or increased by actually moving objects. They can come to see how this holds with symbols for objects and then with numerical figures as symbols for quantities.

In these learning experiences they approach the fundamental processes as ways of dealing with number and outgrow the necessity of recourse to concrete groupings or symbols for objects when they "see" that twelve objects can be manipulated in ways which can be symbolized and expressed in figures. They factor long before the word "factor" becomes part of their working vocabulary; they can "see"' the implications for larger numbers when they build them from familiar components of twelve or ten, so that twenty-four is "seen" as the result of putting two twelves or four sixes together. The formal writing of "tables" actually encourages a lower level of learning and a narrower array of learnings. True it is that some of the inferential learnings in the wider array need reinforcement and recurrent situational reference; but this characterizes insightful developmental learning and actually favors cumulative effects—whereas formal repetition is likelier to "fix" what is "drilled in" without contributing to spread, inference or insightful use.

The learner who has actually come to see threes, fours, fives and sixes as configurations which he can manipulate is far less likely to regress to counting by ones when he should add. He is far more likely to think out problems and number relations than he is to guess and apply processes blindly. It is in these ways that the relative values of meaningful learning become evident.

Experimenting and Discovering

The child who learns the *names* of the primary colors by formal association of words with color patches gets "fixed," narrow ideas about color but misses the challenging opportunities for wider associations and direct inferences from diverse firsthand experiences with that color. The kindergarten child who discovered that his red and blue drips made purple when they ran together did not have to wait a year or more for a formal lesson on color. Furthermore, he proceeded forthwith to "invent" other interesting color combinations and to enjoy them.

Three children came to school early several days to "monkey" with saturated solutions to see whether they could make crystals. They learned to watch and wait in the true spirit of inquiry and to limit their tentative conclusions in terms of their own findings. In the same room several others were simultaneously experimenting freely with magnets. They, too, were not only finding things out for themselves but getting an experience background for later science learnings. Instruction is often too formal and precipitate to build background or to foster free inquiry.

Insightful Guidance

Sound, unpressured developmental guidance is integrative and conducive to outgoing, interactive behavior and self-extension. Teachers who value these qualities are not likely to substitute responses to directions for the situational responses of learners.

Instruction which requires children to be submissively conformative reduces their learning to a low level of compliance at the expense of integrative effort and intelligent initiative. This explains the effects on the learning and the behavior of those who are bored and those who cannot keep up. It also explains what happens as a result of lapses in attention, absence, conflicting impulses, poor coordination, misinterpretation of verbal direction, poor hearing or defective vision. Insightful guidance requires continuous responsive concern for all these matters on the part of teachers.

It is easy to illustrate how important this is with beginners. There was Sam, for example, who could not see what the teacher was pointing to on the big chart when she told him to locate it in his book. There was Mary, who took so long to locate it in her book that she missed the teacher's next direction and got so confused that she gave up trying. There was Fred, who got interested in the story and read ahead and was reprimanded for not keeping the place. There was Jane, who wondered why the teacher was saying something about bowels (vowels) right in the middle of the word drill. There was Bill, who had to blow his nose; and there was Jerry, who had to leave the room while the lesson went on.

What are the cumulative results of Sam's poor vision, of Mary's slow coordination and consequent confusion, of Fred's dutiful place-keeping, of Jane's erroneous auditory impressions and of conflicting physical demands on the attention of Bill and Jerry and other children who are subjected to didactic instruction and directive teaching? They are registered in the quality of their school experience, in their learnings and in their devolping personalities. Small chance for initiative, self-direction, self-expression, inquiry, spontaneity, individuality or creativity where expectations of conformity and compliance with directions not only limit the learner's role but stereotype reactions and devitalize learning!

Studies of learning and action research in today's classrooms are more reliable bases for improving the education of children in today's schools than presumptive criticism.

To provide evidences of some of the most significant values which characterize creative teaching and developmental guidance, there is also need of creative advances in evaluation.

Vol. XL—p. 79 (Oct. 1963)

Adventuring in Creativity
BY E. PAUL TORRANCE

E. Paul Torrance, Bureau of Educational Research, University of Minnesota, gave this talk at the Association for Childhood Education Study Conference, April 1963, at Miami Beach, Florida.

RECENT ADVENTURINGS IN CREATIVITY INDICATE THAT MANY ASPECTS of the school program can be learned more effectively in creative ways than when they are taught only by authority. Why am I so excited about our adventurings in creativity? First, it is a part of the great dream of the educational researcher that he might through research help bring about a more humane kind of education—a kind of education which will give every child a better chance to become his potentialities. I believe that through research concerning creativity we are learning more about the human mind and its functioning, the human personality and the spirit of man. I believe we are catching sight of a new vision of what man may become and, most important of all, a new vision of a more humane kind of education which would make it possible for children to become their possibilities. We are catching a new vision of what it means to individualize instruction.

Many things are now becoming possible in education which would have been regarded as daydreams two or three years ago. Many forces have contributed to this state of affairs. Adventurings in creativity have contributed a few of these. Through these adventurings it now seems possible that many things can be learned creatively more economically and effectively than by authority alone. It appears that children *can* be taught in such a way that their creative thinking abilities are useful in acquiring even the traditional educational skills, that these abilities are different from those measured by traditional intelligence and scholastic aptitude tests, and that they are important in mental health and in vocational success, even in some of the more commonplace occupations. Furthermore, it appears that some children who either refuse or are unable to learn when taught by deliberate methods or by authority learn quite successfully when given an opportunity to learn in creative ways by questioning, inquiring, experimenting, exploring, testing and modifying.

Many educational workers are beginning to see in these findings a demand for some truly revolutionary changes in educational objectives, curricula, instruments for assessing mental growth and educational achievement, instructional procedures, counseling and guidance procedures, supervisory and administrative practices, and even school buildings. I believe we are experiencing today many significant moves in the direction of a more humane kind of education. I say this in spite of the hundreds of letters which I have received even during the past year detailing the atrocities, the tragedies—yes, the inhumanities which now exist in education at all levels throughout the world. Most of these inhumanities are being committed by hard-working, well-meaning teachers, counselors, and principals who think that they are "doing the right thing." I make this optimistic statement because I have thousands of letters which show that educators everywhere are catching a new vision, grasping new insights and becoming excited about the adventure of teaching. I believe that it is a vision, an insight and an excitement to enable man to achieve a higher level of humanness than he has heretofore achieved and will make our age truly an age of imagination and inquiry.

What Is Creativity?

Creativity is defined in many ways, ranging from definitions which make every adaptive act a creative act to those extremely rare experiences which result in earth-shaking scientific breakthroughs and great artistic triumphs. It is usually defined as either a process or a product, but it may also be defined as a kind of person or kind of motivating or stimulating environment. It is my own preference to define creativity in terms of the process of sensing problems or gaps in information, forming ideas or hypotheses, testing hypotheses and communicating the results. We can then study the abilities and skills which are involved in the various aspects of this process. We can also study the personality characteristics and motivating conditions necessary and the product which results from the process. Under this definition it is also possible to subsume the major features of most other definitions. The production of something new or original is included in almost all of them. Creativity is sometimes contrasted to conformity. In such cases, creativity is defined as the contribution of original ideas, a different point of view, or a new way of looking at problems; conformity is defined as doing what is expected without disturbing or causing trouble for others. Creativity may also be a successful step into the unknown; getting away from the obvious, the tested and the safe; being open to experience and permitting one thing to lead to another; recombining ideas or seeing new relationships among ideas. Such concepts as curiosity, imagination, discovery, innovation and invention are also prominent in discussions of creativity and sometimes one or the other is equated with creativity. I see them only as different aspects of the complex process of creativity.

When creativity is defined as a product, the results of the process are embodied in an invention, a scientific theory, an improved product, a new product, a literary work, a musical composition or a new design. In the child, it may be the discovery of some new relationship in nature (new to the child), a song, poem, story, some unusual contraption or gadget, or even an invention. At the highest level, it is required that a creative idea must be true, generalizable, and surprising in the light of what was known at the time the idea was produced. The United States Patent Office requires that a patentable device measure up to some standard of inventive level, characterized by a high degree of creative strength, usefulness in the sense of being a stride forward, newness associated with overcoming a difficulty, prior failure to solve the problem, prior skepticism, and novelty of instrumentality.

Many scholars have denied the possibility that young children can think creatively and this has led to an overestimate of the child's receptivity. It has led to an overemphasis upon providing a stimulating environment and an underemphasis on the importance of providing a responsive one. This confusion may have resulted from the fact that each scholar has limited too seriously his observations of the manifestations of creativity. They have failed to recognize that no single area of observation or test taps all the child's resources for creative thinking and that the same test or kinds of observations are not valid or adequate at all age and educational levels. Beginnings of creative thinking may be found in manipulative, exploratory and experimental activity of the infant and the use of facial expressions, efforts to discover and test the meaning of the facial expressions and gestures of others.

Of the many manifestations of creativity during elementary school years, greatest attention has been given to creative writing and art. We are now having a renewed recognition of the value of children's writing and art, but we are also discovering that children can be creative in other important ways. Generally, educators of the past have considered children in the elementary and even in the high school years to be incapable of creative scientific thought. Thus, until recently, the introduction of science into the curriculum has been delayed until high school and even then taught as a body of accumulated knowledge to be transmitted by authority and not as a way of thinking or discovery and inquiry. The picture is now changing. Science has been added to the elementary curriculum and even in such fields as history children are being taught the skills of the historian and given some opportunity to do the things which historians do. Similar developments will be forthcoming in anthropology, geography, psychology and sociology.

Measuring Creative Thinking

During the past eighty years, many procedures have been developed for measuring creative thinking abilities of *preprimary* children. Included are such things as: drawings, scribblings, inkblots, imaginative play, picture tests, verbalizations while painting, and standardized problem situations. There has been little relationship between these measures of creativity and traditional measures of intelligence. Some workers, surprised by such a finding, have sought to explain away this lack of relationship, while a few very early recognized and accepted the genuine difference between the kinds of mental functioning involved in the two kinds of performance.

The variety of tasks used in measuring the creative thinking abilities at the *elementary* level is perhaps broader than at any other. Types of tasks include: perceptions of inkblots; picture construction from dots, circles, squares, parallel lines, incomplete figures, and shapes of colored paper; verbalizations while painting; symbolizations of words by lines; designs from standardized materials; ideas for product improvement (toys, common objects); consequences problems, asking and guessing; guessing sounds or imagining images from sounds. Performances are usually scored for such qualities as fluency, flexibility, originality and elaboration.

Scores derived from measures of creative thinking have little relationship to performance on intelligence tests. Investigators have consistently urged the use of both types of measures in the identification of intellectual talent. Recent studies have shown that if we identify the upper 20 per cent of a population as gifted on the basis of an intelligence test, we would eliminate about 70 per cent of the upper 20 per cent on the measure of creative thinking. Unquestionably, some minimum level of intelligence is required for outstanding success of a creative nature, but this level cannot now be specified. Many workers in the field are convinced on the basis of research evidence that cut-off points on IQ at 135 and above as used in most programs for intellectually talented children are too high. Several estimates place this minimal level at around 115 or 120.

Perhaps one of the most important consequences thus far of the development and research use of measures of creative thinking has been an expanded concept of the human mind and its functioning. For many years, the usual concept of the human mind and its functioning was limited largely by the concepts embodied in intelligence tests. Developers of intelligence tests have not claimed that such tests assess all of a person's intellectual functioning. Yet we have generally behaved as though we believe this. An intelligence test has almost always been used as the sole index of a person's intellectual potential. If his achievement in some area fell below the level which would be expected from his IQ, he was said to be underachieving. If he achieved higher than would be expected from his IQ, he was somehow overachieving. Curricula and methods of teaching have been designed to bring about the kinds of growth or achievement related to the mental abilities involved in intelligence or scholastic aptitude tests. Tests of educational achievement have also been patterned along these same lines. This narrow concept of the human mind and its functioning has produced a far from humane kind of education and one which has failed to give the total human being a chance to become his potentialities.

Current research in programed instruction shows that materials can be programed to bring into play different abilities and different strategies of learning. In some experiments, post-program performance is less related to mental age as derived from an intelligence or scholastic aptitude test than to performance on tests of originality. Many findings suggest that we may be finding some of the clues which will enable us to educate to a higher degree many people whom we have not been very successful in educating—our vast army of dropouts.

Patterns of Creative Abilities

From the best research evidence available and the observations of many investigators, creative imagination during early childhood seems to reach a peak between four and four and a-half years, and is followed by a drop at about age five when the child enters school for the first time. This drop has generally been regarded as an inevitable developmental phenomenon in nature. There are now indications, however, that this drop in five-year-olds is a man-made rather than a natural phenomenon.

Findings concerning the stages of creative development during the elementary years have been fairly consistent, amazingly so considering the variety of measures, samples of subjects, and periods in history involved. In the United States most of the creative thinking abilities as measured by tests show growth from the first through third grades, a sharp drop at about the beginning of the fourth, a rise during the fifth and sixth, and another decline at about the beginning of the seventh grade. The rise in the fifth grade is primarily among girls and in fluency rather than in originality. Some investigators have found that the seventh-grade decline extends into the eighth, but our studies show a rise between the seventh and eighth grades with continued growth until near the end of the high school years, at which time there is a leveling off or a slight decline.

Studies involving deliberate attempts to keep alive creative growth in the fourth grade and studies of the development of the creative abilities in cultures outside the United States all suggest that at least the drop which occurs in the fourth grade is a man-made rather than a natural phenomenon. For one thing, it seems that educational and cultural discontinuities produce discontinuities in creative development and that these can be reduced in a variety of ways.

Non-Test Ways of Identifying Creative Behavior: It will be some time before existing tests of creativity will be in common use. Many schools do not have school psychologists, counselors or others qualified to use such tests. Also, some children are not motivated to perform creatively on tests. Tests almost always have time limits and creativity cannot always be hurried or forced. Some highly creative children have difficulty in communicating them orally. Thus, there is a need to continue to develop non-test ways of identifying creative talent.

Most teachers, however, have to redefine some of their customary concepts and values before they can identify creatively gifted pupils. When asked to evaluate pupils in terms of specific criteria of creativity, teachers generally report that this is the first time they have thought of their pupils in these terms. Much behavior which manifests the presence of creative talent is labeled by parents and teachers as undesirable. One boy was so clever and ingenious in the way he cheated on a test that his teacher recognized his talent and was challenged to modify his teaching methods. The resulting change in the teacher's behavior was accompanied by dramatic changes in the boy's behavior and the development of an outstanding talent.

One study revealed that the most frequently named non-test ways of identifying creative talent by teachers are indicators of curiosity, inquisitiveness, investigativeness and penetrating questioning. One rather well-validated set of indicators of curiosity includes: positive reactions to new, strange, incongruous or mysterious elements in the environment (exploration, manipulation); exhibition of a need or desire to know about one's self and/or his environment; scanning of one's surroundings seeking new experiences; and persistence in examining and exploring stimuli in order to know more about them.

Other frequently listed non-test indicators include: originality in behavior (unusual solutions, unusual answers, unusual approaches to problem solving); independent, individualistic, courageous behavior; imagination (fantasy, storytelling); non-conforming behavior (not bothered by pressures to conformity); unusual perceptiveness of relationships; being full of ideas; experimentation; unusual flexibility in meeting emergencies; unwillingness to give up; constructiveness; daydreaming and preoccupation with an idea or problem; and going beyond assigned tasks.

As teachers gain a better understanding of creative behavior they will be able to redefine many behaviors they have usually labeled undesirable and see in them indication of abilities which give promise of highly desirable talents. The next step would be an acceptance of the challenge to guide individuals who possess such talents to apply their valuable abilities in creative, productive, socially valued achievements.

Creative Learning and Blocks [1]

Learning creatively involves the process which I described in my earlier definition and brings into play such mental abilities as evaluation (especially the ability to sense problems, inconsistencies and missing elements); divergent production (fluency, flexibility, originality and elaboration); and redefinition (seeing something in a way different from the usual, established or intended way or use). In contrast, learning by authority brings into play primarily such abilities as recognition, memory, logical reasoning and the like—the abilities most frequently assessed by traditional tests of intelligence and scholastic aptitude.

At an early age some children appear to develop a preference for learning by authority. The human needs which make learning in creative ways such a natural process, however, appear to be sufficiently universal to make this way of learning a powerful one for all children, though not an exclusive one. Some of the more obvious ways of creating conditions for this kind of learning are by providing opportunities in the school program for creative behavior, developing the skills required for learning in creative ways, rewarding creative achievements, providing for continuity of creative development, and establishing creative relationships with children.

Although a great deal of research remains to be done concerning the inhibitors and facilitators of creative development, a few of them

[1] See E. Paul Torrance's "Conditions for Creative Learning," p. 151.

appear rather clear. Perhaps the biggest task of nurturing creativity during the preprimary years is to keep alive fantasy until the child's intellectual development is such that he can engage in a sound type of creative thinking. The trouble is not that the child is eager to give up his fantasy but that there are pressures upon the child to be realistic and to stop imagining. Since the early 1900's investigators have been rather consistent in their recommendations for nurturing creativity, but there is evidence that the influence of these recommendations has not been widespread.

Investigators have also frequently called attention to the stifling effects of "holding-back operations" to prevent children from learning more than they are "ready" to learn, premature attempts to eliminate fantasy, and overemphasis on sex roles.

Teachers face some difficult problems in coping with blocks to creative development. Social and cultural forces which impinge upon such development are indeed strong. Social expectations of the kinds of behavior which should or should not be permitted are powerful. The traditions of punitive approaches to education also greatly influence teachers. One of the difficulties of the teacher is permitting spontaneity, initiative and creativity while maintaining discipline. Teachers frequently find creative children threatening to their own status and security and disconcerting in other ways. Some promising concepts now undergoing experimental testing which may help teachers resolve some of their dilemmas are: provisions for self-initiated learning and learning on one's own, creating a responsive environment rather than just a stimulating one, revisions of readiness concepts, developing more realistic and favorable self-concepts, recognition of the uniqueness of the individual, and the development of the roles of specialists, such as counselors, psychologists and social workers.

Some social forces most frequently mentioned by investigators as blocks to creative development are: an extremely peer-oriented culture which emphasizes conformity to peer group norms in behavior, sanctions against questioning and exploration, a success-oriented culture which makes errors fatal and makes children afraid to take a chance on trying a new approach, overemphasis or misplaced emphasis on sex role differences, the equation of divergency with abnormality or delinquency, and the work-play dichotomy. Some of the positive approaches which have been proposed for testing are: learning to reward a greater variety of abilities and kinds of achievement, helping children recognize the value of creativity, teaching children research skills, developing a creative acceptance of limitations, helping highly creative children to become less obnoxious, developing school pride in the creative achievements of its pupils, providing sponsors and patrons for highly creative children, and helping highly creative children learn to cope with the fears and anxieties which block their creative functioning.

Goals in Guiding Creativity

The creative imagination is one of the most powerful forces on the earth. It has given us the alphabet, printing, radio, television, computers and space craft. It has given us our great art, architecture, music and literature. It has given us our great advances in scientific discovery and medicine. It has *also* given us war, plunder and atomic destruction.

Understanding, measuring and developing the creative thinking abilities is a part of the educator's great dream of achieving a more humane kind of education in which every child will have a better chance to achieve his potentialities. It is of obvious importance to society that creative talent be identified, developed and utilized. Already, the understandings derived from research concerning the creative thinking abilities have broadened our concepts of "giftedness" from that of the child with the high IQ to include also the highly creative child and perhaps other types. It is becoming increasingly clear that nothing can contribute more to mental health, the general welfare of our nation and the satisfactions of its people than a general raising of the level of creativity. There is little doubt that the stifling of creative thinking cuts at the very roots of satisfaction in living and eventually creates overwhelming tension and breakdown. Research in progress suggests that it is important that creativity be energized and guided from birth. If it is stifled early it will only become imitative, if it survives at all. It is true that a vigorous creative imagination can survive early stifling and opposition, but if it learns only to act vigorously without direction it becomes dangerous to society and perhaps to civilization.

It has already been pointed out that the creative thinking abilities are important in the acquisition of even the traditionally measured kinds of achievement when children are permitted to achieve some of these goals creatively. Their importance in vocational success has also been mentioned. Goals become clearer and more urgent, however, when we look upon the creative thinking abilities as just one part of our expanded and expanding concept of the human mind and its functioning. An acceptance of this broader concept of the human mind opens up many new and tremendously exciting possibilities for teachers, placing a new emphasis upon consideration of what man may become. The broader concept suggests that we can educate to a higher degree many persons whom we might not otherwise have been successful in educating. As we have begun to understand more deeply the creative functioning of the mind, the case for learning creatively rather than just by authority has been strengthened. This may soon enable us to learn what it *really* means to individualize instruction.

No matter how successful research becomes in determining methods whereby creativity can be identified, developed, and encouraged in the child, teachers must never forget that the very life and function of creativity is to go courageously into the darkness of the unknown, which involves ever searching for the truth and living honestly. We shall be handicapped in achieving such a goal as long as we condition children to authority acceptance and dishonesty in the home, school, church and government. The truly creative person, the kind we need so urgently, must be able to make judgments independently and stick to them, even though most others disagree. It must be remembered that every new idea in the beginning almost always makes its originator a minority of one. Being a minority of one is tremendously uncomfortable and is more than most people can tolerate. Thus, creativity takes great courage.

Unfortunately, the results of research are not encouraging when it comes to attitudes about the importance of courage. Teachers and parents in the United States do not give a place of great importance to either independence in judgment or courage, according to what they consider an ideal pupil or an ideal child. In a list of sixty-two characteristics, courage ranks about thirtieth, lower here than in any of the other six countries for which there are data. It appears to be far more important to teachers and parents in the United States for children to be courteous than to be courageous. It is more important that pupils do their work on time, be energetic and visibly industrious, be obedient and popular or well-liked among their peers, be receptive to the ideas of others, be well-rounded, and willing to accept the judgments of authorities than to be courageous. Obviously, such values are more likely to produce a people ripe for brainwashing than a people that can think creatively.

The characteristic rated at the top of the list by both parents and teachers in the United States is "consideration of others," certainly a valuable one. Preoccupation with "consideration of others" or "politeness" has been noted by a number of foreign observers who have lived in the United States. In their judgment, generally, they found this preoccupation caused us to be dishonest in dealings with one another. "Politeness" causes us to promise to do things we have no intention of doing. The characteristics of eminent, creative persons as revealed through research would certainly suggest that anything which conditions children for dishonesty endangers creativity.

Conclusion

I hope I have not conveyed the idea that research has solved all the puzzles about creativity. To do so would be a gross error. There are many more questions that need to be answered before we have adequate scientific base for guiding creativity in the classroom. It is my conviction that we know enough from research to enable us to do a far better job than we apparently do in achieving even the most widely accepted goals of education. No matter how much we learn from research, the individual teacher's ways of teaching must be his own unique invention. He must arrive at this personal invention through his own creative processes in trying to accomplish his teaching goals. As he fails or succeeds in reaching these goals, he becomes aware of his deficiencies, defects in his techniques and strategies and gaps in his knowledge. He draws upon his past experiences. He increases his search for clues and his ongoing experiences. He tries to apply creatively the scientifically developed principles he has learned in his professional education and reading. He sees things of which he has hitherto been unaware. He starts making some hypotheses, testing and modifying them. Through the pain and ecstasy which accompany this process, the teacher's personal invention—his way of teaching—evolves. I hope you find this adventure a truly exciting and rewarding one.

Vol. XXXIX—p. 371 (Apr. 1963)

Research in Creativity:
Some Findings and Conceptions
BY ELLIOT W. EISNER

Elliot W. Eisner, assistant professor of education, University of Chicago, presented the substance of this article to the Rochester (New York) Branch of the Association for Childhood Education International on January 26, 1963.

SEVERAL IMPORTANT ASSUMPTIONS UNDERLIE THE WORK OF PSYCHOLogists who study creativity. For one, creativity like most human characteristics is *not* viewed as a special gift possessed by a limited few but rather is conceived of as a capacity possessed in some degree by all human beings. Second, creativity is *not* considered a mystic or spiritual force that, when left unfettered, bursts into human action but rather is considered a product of both thinking on the part of the creator and judgment on the part of the viewer. That is to say, creativity exists in the transaction or relationship between the characteristics of a product and someone's judgment of it. Children, for example, may function in highly creative ways; but whenever these ways are private they cannot be observed and hence fall outside the domain of human judgment. This means that, while a child may have all sorts of creative experiences, in order for him to be considered creative he must produce some product, some object or idea that meets at least two requirements. First, it must be public; second, it must be judged as novel, tenable, and useful or satisfying to some group at some point in time.[6] A third assumption is that creativity can be elicited through certain test situations and that the responses to these test situations can be measured. Keeping these assumptions in mind—that creativity is a capacity possessed in some degree by everyone, that creativity *for the researcher* must be public and that creativity is measurable—I would like to examine some of the intriguing creativity research of the past twelve years.

Although the Progressive Education Association deserves the deepest bow for fostering interest in creativity, the person who probably has done the most to develop this interest along scientific lines is J. P. Guilford, a psychologist working at the University of Southern California. In 1950 he spoke of the appalling neglect of creativity by psychologists and outlined a research program that he was going to use to investigate it.[3]

Divergent and Convergent Thinking

Subsequently Guilford developed two concepts which have been extremely useful in studying this behavior: divergent and convergent thinking. *Divergent* thinking is the type that most characterizes creativity. It is thinking that is speculative, that "takes off" from information already possessed. *Convergent* thinking, more conservative in character, uses information to converge upon an already existing answer. For example, in teaching about the Civil War, a question that would elicit divergent thinking might be, "What might be different today if the South had won the Civil War?" or "How differently would the South have been treated if Lincoln had not been assassinated?" A question eliciting convergent thinking might be, "How did Sherman enter the city of Atlanta?" or "How was the South divided after the Civil War?" In each subject area it is possible to devise questions which elicit these different types of thinking processes.

Creativity and Intelligence

Concepts of divergent and convergent thinking were then used by Guilford to construct some highly ingenious tests, some of which have proven to be useful in the study of creativity. It was these research tools and others that were used by my colleagues, Jacob Getzels and Philip Jackson, in their important study of creative adolescents.[2]

Their study provided convincing evidence that the highly creative adolescent differed in many significant ways from his highly intelligent but not-so-highly creative peer. Getzels and Jackson found that the highly creative adolescent valued a sense of humor as a personal human trait more deeply than the high IQ student, that he had a much wider range of vocational aspirations, that he had a much richer phantasy life and that he considered his personal values and those of his teachers to be somewhat opposite.

Perhaps the most significant of the Getzels and Jackson findings has to do with the fact that they found that intelligence was far from a reliable predictor of creativity. Being highly intelligent does not insure high creativity and vice versa. As a matter of fact, if scores of tests of intelligence were used to identify creative youngsters, approximately 70 per cent of the most highly creative would be overlooked. Paul Torrance, who has also done much to further our knowledge of creativity, has some interesting findings.

Longitudinal Studies

One of the most interesting of Torrance's findings is derived from his longitudinal studies of creative thinking.[7] If you examine areas like reading, arithmetic or spelling and plot a curve describing achievement in these subjects over a time for a large group of children, what would the curve look like? You would expect that, on the average, achievement would rise as the age level increased. This is exactly what occurs. But what happens to this curve when it is drawn for creative performance? Torrance found that creative behavior increases from first grade through third but around fourth grade and again at seventh grade, creative performance sharply decreases. On the Ask and Guess Test (the student is shown a picture and asked to raise as many questions as he can that cannot be answered by the data in the picture) the number of questions third-grade boys asked was high and the fourth-grade dip was low. It took until the tenth grade for boys to raise as many questions as were raised at the third-grade level. The same general pattern holds for girls.

Torrance suggests that highly creative children who frequently meet pressures to conform tend to suffer greater emotional strain than children who are less creative. Psychopathology may be fostered by the child's struggle to harmonize conflicting internal and external demands.

Conditions Encouraging Creative Thinking

There are some identifiable conditions that seem to encourage creative thinking on the parts of students. *First,* there is some evidence to indicate that highly creative individuals can tolerate a great deal of ambiguity. They do not seem to have a pressing need to obtain immediate closure or immediate answers to problems. They can tolerate hypotheses of a highly speculative sort; it might be more accurate to say they enjoy such ambiguity. In the classroom this suggests that it might be useful to encourage children to deal with alternative solutions to problems, to put off formulating answers until they have explored a range of possibilities.

Second, children seem to need what Carl Rogers [5] has called *psychological safety.* Osborn [4] in his brainstorming technique has a standing rule that when idea sessions take place no one is allowed to evaluate them. At these sessions people are made to feel as comfortable as possible, and criticism is not allowed. His reasons are simple: to remove the threat of embarrassment and to help the members of the group get their ideas out no matter how silly or "way out" they might seem. Providing this psychological safety in the classroom is extremely important if children are to feel free to venture new ideas.

Third, the individual needs to have experience and skill in the subject area itself if he is to be able to function in a highly creative way. In the past it was believed that just leaving the child alone would be sufficient. The energy of the libido left unhampered would rush forth in a splendorous burst of creativity. This is not only ethically irresponsible; it just does not work. For example, a child who has to worry about what color he will get by mixing yellow and blue to use in painting, or a child who has to struggle with spelling and grammar rules in writing, is unlikely to have enough energy left to think in highly creative ways; in addition his attention will be focused elsewhere. This does not mean that spelling and grammar rules should not be taught. It means only that it is difficult to function in highly creative ways if these concerns are really problematic for the child. Those people who are the most highly creative in the disciplines are the ones who have so overlearned the basic tools and techniques that they are no longer problems. It is when they have done this that they can deal with other aspects of the problem. Nursery-school children often produce exquisite pieces of art work precisely because they pay little or no attention to technical precision or representational accuracy. When a child becomes primarily concerned with technique, and *at some point he must,* it often becomes difficult for him to capture the spontaneity that he displayed at a younger age.

Fourth, it follows from what has been said that to the extent that different subject areas make different sorts of demands on the child, to that extent they require different sorts of skills. Creative ability is, to a significant degree, specific to the subject matter. While some general traits such as flexibility and tolerance for ambiguity seem to be conducive to creative thinking, a person must be able to control the syntax and techniques of the discipline within which he is working if he is to be able to use the discipline in a highly creative way.

Fifth, creative behavior, like most other types of behavior, should be appreciated when it occurs. Perhaps one of the fundamental pieces of knowledge in the field of psychology is that behavior that is rewarded tends to persist. If recall is rewarded and divergent thinking unrewarded, creative behavior is not likely to flourish. Torrance has pointed out that not only is highly creative *behavior* unrewarded, but *children* who are highly creative are not always looked upon favorably by their teachers or their peers. In the Getzels-Jackson study when the teachers were given a list of the highly creative and high-IQ students and asked to identify the ones they preferred to have in class, it was the high IQ's rather than the high creatives that they preferred.

Types of Creativity

Up to this point I have been discussing creativity as if it were one kind of behavior. I do not believe this is the case. In my own research I have formulated a conception of types of creativity.[1] When I was teaching art in elementary and secondary schools it occurred to me that children were highly creative in quite different ways. For example, some students were highly creative in the original way they incorporated ideas into their art work. Their drawings and paintings were not always the most esthetic but frequently the most imaginative. I call these youngsters *boundary pushers* because they always seem to want to push the limits of ideas or objects. This group is creative because it used ideas or objects in novel ways like the man who first thought of installing electric shaver outlets in automobiles.

Another group of youngsters were quite creative in the way in which they used color, line and form. Their creativity was displayed in the highly esthetic way they organized visual qualities. I call this group *esthetic organizers.* They might never produce any really imaginative ideas but they have a marked sense for esthetic order. Their stories, poems and paintings are beautiful. These children are esthetically creative.

A third group of children who invent new objects by combining materials I call *inventors.* I recall one fifth-grade boy in the Laboratory School who spent a full two weeks of his art class trying to invent a new color for a crayon. He did this by making a plaster mold and by melting down an assortment of different colored crayons. The invention failed as a product—the wax would break when he tried to take it out of the mold—but his behavior was inventively creative just the same.

A fourth type of creativity, *boundary breaking,* is most rare. It rejects the assumptions that everyone else takes for granted and formulates new premises and proceeds to develop a radically new system of thought. Copernicus is one example. Because of him we now believe that the sun is the center of our planetary system. Would it not be revolutionary if someone were to prove that this was all wrong? Our whole conception of the universe would be shattered and we would have a new and perhaps a better one to take its place.

I have found through my own research that children who display one type of creativity in art do not always display another type. Even within the visual arts, children who are highly creative with one medium (like clay) may not be highly creative in another (like painting or drawing). If differences in creative performance exist even within one area, what should we expect about the carry-over of creativity from subject to subject? If we look carefully enough we would find that almost every child is highly creative in one way or another*—if not in some area of the curriculum, at least in some area of life. It is a mistake to look for *the* creative child. A person highly creative in all fields is rare indeed.

Intelligence Which Includes Creativity

One other issue concerning creativity has to do with the relationship between creativity and intelligence.

In previous years the tendency to link creativity to intelligence was quite common. The person thought to be highly creative was the person with the high IQ. The very concept of giftedness itself was most often conceived of in terms of IQ. With the Getzels-Jackson study and with work by other investigators this tendency has been sharply reduced—almost to the point where some conceive of these behaviors as being mutually exclusive. I have discussed creativity and intelligence, but this is mainly because I have followed terms used in the research. However, I reject a distinction between these concepts. If our conception of intelligence were more adequate, if we conceive intelligence not merely as what intelligence tests test but as the efficient and effective utilization of means to achieve desired ends, then the need for a separate concept of creativity disappears. In short, I am suggesting that the reason creativity and intelligence seem to be unrelated is that we have been using in our research a restricted conception and measure of intelligence.

In the adult world, such as in areas of literature or painting, a person

---

* See *All Children Have Gifts* (Washington, D. C.: Association for Childhood Education International, 1958).

is considered creative only after some group of people—usually experts or critics—compare the artist's work to the work of others and make a judgment about the creative quality of the work. The artist's age, country or amount of education are considered irrelevant. The work stands or falls on its merit as compared to others. As we move down the educational ladder we begin to take other considerations into account. For example, works by high school students are compared with works produced by other high school students to compete with adults. These considerations continue to expand until the primary grades, where the first things we want to know before we make any judgment of the creative quality of a child's product are his age and many other things: the experience the child has had with the material, the amount of instruction he has received, his background and so forth. Similarly, in tests of creativity as in tests of intelligence, comparisons to groups are also made. Any individual's responses on a given test are compared with those of his peers. *Instead of comparing a student's product to the context of the group, why not compare his products to the context of his own work?* If it is true that novelty is one of the defining characteristics of creativity when an individual copes with a new problem, when he generates answers or solutions that were *personally novel*—in short, any time he uses his intelligence to create personally new answers to problematic situations—he is functioning creatively in some degree.

It does not seem to me that the only (or necessarily the best) context for creativity is the group, whether it is a group restricted to a particular age level or a group consisting of those over twenty-one. If the hallmark of a problem is a state of affairs for which no adequate response is available and if intelligence is the process through which an adequate response is formulated, then the exercise of intelligence in problematic situations is by its very nature creative. I hold that the distinction between creativity and intelligence is artificial; that the seeming separation between these concepts is due to a too narrowly conceived concept of intelligence. Indeed, without a conception of intelligence that includes "creative" thinking it would be difficult to understand how man could survive.

References

[1] Elliot W. Eisner, "A Typology of Creativity in the Visual Arts," *Studies in Art Education*, 4 (1962).

[2] Jacob Getzels and Philip Jackson, *Creativity and Intelligence: Explorations with Gifted Students* (New York: Wiley, 1962).

[3] J. P. Guildford, "Creativity," *The American Psychologist*, 5 (1950), pp. 444-454.

[4] Alex Osborn, *Applied Imagination* (New York: Scribner's, 1953).

[5] Carl Rogers, *Client Centered Therapy* (Boston: Houghton, Mifflin, 1951).

[6] In this second requirement, I follow Morris I. Stein's lead, who has defined the creative product as: "The creative work is a novel work that is accepted as tenable or useful, or satisfying by a group at some point in time." See Morris I. Stein, "Creativity and Culture," *Journal of Psychology*, 36 (1953), pp. 312-322.

[7] E. Paul Torrance, *Guiding Creative Talent* (Englewood Cliffs, N. J.: Prentice-Hall, Inc., 1962).

The Knowledge Explosion
BY GERALD S. CRAIG

All children must be educated to be responsible and resourceful in a world of uncertainty. Furthermore, they must learn that the world can be made what they desire it to be.

Some have felt that the preservation of the free world depended solely upon the education of the so-called "talented" in science. This could be one way to lose our democracy from within. Science is fundamental in the education of ALL children.

Gerald S. Craig is professor emeritus of Natural Sciences, Teachers College, Columbia University, New York.

MANY HAVE DEEP CONCERNS ABOUT WHAT IS HAPPENING TO CHILDREN in this period of rapid acceleration of knowledge. Is it not a fair assumption that whether this rapid learning of man about himself and his universe benefits or destroys mankind depends in large part upon the kinds of meanings children establish about themselves and the universe about them? This means that we, as classroom teachers, must think wisely about both children and science and continue to rethink the place of science in childhood education.

Evolutionary Nature of Knowledge

In participating in the education of children in science, it is important to keep in mind the nature of science and to relate it to what is known about the ways children tend to interpret the environment.

In practically every area of human knowledge we find that what is considered reliable information one day may have to be revised the next day as a result of new findings. Even then, the revised knowledge is subject to revision. Revision is to be expected in science. Absolute knowledge is unobtainable. Mankind is always in the process of learning new information about the universe.

New information cannot be learned in a real sense by sheer memorization. *New information has to become acceptable to a child if it is to be truly learned.* This may mean that he must reorganize his intellectual structure about the subject. He must discard some items, fit others into what seem to be their rightful places and thus build a new structure or concept. Furthermore, he must recognize that he may have to reconstruct his ideas again and again. This may require time. It is an evolutionary process, and it may at times be revolutionary to children. Education at home and at school should be geared to this evolutionary nature of science learning.

Mankind is learning all the time. A considerable part of the effort of learning by mankind is science, and children have something in common with mankind in that they are learning about their world too. It has always seemed to me that children sensed a common bond between their own efforts and the larger efforts of mankind in learning through science. And, indeed, it is important that this relationship should become real to children.

We are living in an age of vast changes. It seems as if the impossible has become possible. The present generation has had to make many adjustments. Only a few years ago we all found ourselves living in an unreal world. It takes less effort for an individual to cross the continent today than it did to reach the county seat a few decades ago. Traveling from coast to coast in less than a half day left many of us slightly bewildered at the end of the trip. Traveling from the north temperate zone, crossing the tropics and arriving in the south temperate zone in a few hours were equally unreal. Man's new ability to operate with atoms and their parts is even more impressive.

Children Adjust to Change

For many years I taught both children and adults. Children seemed to welcome the vastness of space. Their eyes flashed with the thought of the solar system being only an infinitesimal part of the vastness of a larger system called a "galaxy." At the same time adults frequently admitted to me their feeling of discomfiture in the thought of a universe so generously constructed. *Children make the adjustments to discoveries in science more easily than adults.*

One could follow this comparison into other patterns or designs of the universe. Unless their minds have been closed or warped by superstition or by adult prejudice, children accept readily the ideas that go with the great patterns of the universe such as adaptations and interrelationships of life to survival. The same is true for the patterns such as energy, change, time, balance and unbalance.

One characteristic that aids children in a knowledge explosion is that they are less conscious of status. An adult is fearful of appearing to be ignorant. Children, unless influenced by an adult, are free to start from zero. But in reality one can scarcely say that any child of school age starts from zero. He starts at birth to interpret his universe. Much of a young child's learnings about his environment is received from bodily impressions. His ideas of gravity, balance, equilibrium, speed, inertia and heat may have definite meanings in terms of experiences in the past. As a result, *science learnings uniquely involve both the body and the mind as an integrated unit.* A child begins his space learnings at birth.

Children Construct Hypotheses

It has seemed to me from my earliest experimental teaching of young children that there was a genetic basis for the making of hypotheses in children's behavior. A child seems to push or pull on an object to see what happens. He varies the push or pull later. He repeats this again and again. He may go on to other interests, but he may come back and repeat the same manipulations. He seems to delight in variations of his own efforts. He seems to have an inquiry in mind as he manipulates. It is a kind of hypothesis without words. *A child seems to be examining his environment continuously with his whole being.* He touches, feels, pushes, pulls, holds, smells, tastes again and again. There must be a tremendous learning going on to which he later learns the words as the attentive parent supplies them for him, the words then becoming part of the experience. I have never agreed with those who say a child does not concentrate. He *does* concentrate on learning about his environment with great intensity. Although his interpretations may be fragmentary at first, he is moving toward a unification of interpretations at a fast pace. If he is not helped to make reliable interpretations he will form his own interpretations.

Children's Approach to Discoveries

Teachers are often deceived by children's apparent familiarity with some kinds of new discoveries; for instance, space exploits. Exploits in some cases may be so interesting to children that they will spend considerable periods of time thinking about them or doing some kind of activity associated with the events. Children repeat the words; they tell each other about the event that interests them; they report it to their parents and to their teachers. But an adult may give only brief attention to it while reading the morning paper or listening to a news broadcast.

However, it should be noted that children do not necessarily interest themselves in a balanced diet of new discoveries. Recent accomplishments concerning health, medicine, chemistry and other areas do not have the same appeal as does a trip to the moon. *We as teachers should see that children have a sane balance of interests.*

The television-watching type of education inadvertently may encourage a superficial view of events rather than a basic understanding. This superficial background is not always properly associated with children's own experiential background. In fact, it may be exotic compared with their usual experiences. Their learning may become a series of words learned from news reports.

Children are able to learn from experiences better than an adult, for they tend to repeat fragmentary interpretations and later join these into a larger field picture or unified learning. *Childhood education in science seems to be largely a matter of joining fragmentary interpretations of experiences together into a large interpretation.* A trained observer can even see children testing their interpretations as they proceed in their spontaneous learning.

It is well for a teacher or a parent working with children to learn what it is they know, what they think and why they think it. *We need to give much more attention to children's spontaneous expressions of thought.* It is through such expressions that we can evaluate the quality of their thinking.

Children's learnings about space exploits have a place, but there is much more to science in childhood education than this one particular area. Most, if not all, of our children will need to make an adjustment to Earth. Science is the interpretation of phenomena in the environment, and the environment of a modern child may begin with his skin and go on out to the vastness of space. A child lives within his skin, and he must interpret the here and now as well as have a vision of the future and of distance.

Children need a balanced education in science. They will live in a world of powerful poisons in the form of new killers, such as insecticides and weed killers, in which it will be possible for a generation improperly educated to exterminate many forms of life. The interrelationship of living things in the web of life will be an area in which they must not be ignorant if man is to have Earth as a dwelling place. Man does not live to himself alone but in a web of life in which he is but one of many species.

Children must have an opportunity in the early years for a balanced program of learning concerning living things, conditions necessary to life, health, safety, conservation and the physical forces.

From the point of view of children to be educated for the preservation and promotion of democracy, there is a danger in the feeling that anything is possible. I have detected in some children an attitude that has had the earmarks of gullibility. While we want to encourage children to use their imaginations about matter and energy, time and space—and other small and large ideas—we shall need from time to time to have them check their imaginations against the reality of the present.

How Can We Use New Knowledge More Effectively?

We as teachers may as well expect children to be interested in man's day-to-day accomplishments in conquering the unknown and in man's learning about space and atoms and the forces that operate throughout the universe. We must expect the novel and the unusual to be challenging to children. Landing on the moon, even the preparations for such a landing, orbiting Earth, the equipment with which it is done and the information sought—all this is exciting to children. We should not stop this interest. We as teachers and parents should use it as a challenge to a more thorough study of basic principles. Also, it provides an opportunity to learn more about individual children.

I do not conceive the task of a teacher to be that of answering questions. A teacher's task is to permit the interaction that seems best for the child or children concerned. I have observed good teachers do nothing more at the moment than listen attentively to a child and then look off, reflecting on all the child had said. It was evident that the child felt satisfaction because his hypothesis was plainly being explored by the teacher as he thought about it. *A good teacher respects the inquiries of every child.* Even if he cannot possibly assist the child, he can show respect for the child and that he considers his questions important.

The relativistic nature of modern science, including the necessity for its constant revision, is perhaps the basic element to be taught. It should permeate the entire curriculum in science.

The teaching-learning in science is much more than memorizing facts. In reality the content of science is much more than a mass of facts. Some of the subject matter testing and programming miss the point of the relativism of modern science. Much of the content of elementary science is in the form of hypotheses. Who can say for certain there are only nine planets? Every day there is a revision of content in some area. It isn't that the content of science reverses itself in our modern period, but there is a constant growth in our understanding of phenomena. New findings are made which have a bearing on some aspect of the environment, and hence a revision inevitably follows.

Part of a teacher's task is to encourage children to join their fragmentary experiences into a related whole and to help children understand the basic principles involved.

There is power in the knowledge of science. People living in a democracy should realize this and keep the control of this power in their own hands. This means that science is fundamental in the education of ALL children.

Some have felt that the preservation of the free world depended solely upon the education of the so-called "talented" in science. This could be one way to lose our democracy from within. Power must be in the hands of all the people. Our boys and girls will live in a world of uncertainty—a world demanding an ability to make tentative but important decisions and to revise those decisions in the face of new knowledge.

All boys and girls must be educated to responsibility and resourcefulness in a world of uncertainty. They must learn that our world can be made what they desire it to be. We must teach and learn with boys and girls and have faith in them and their future. *Science must be the property of all mankind. It can become so through childhood education.* As teachers of children we have no difficulty in believing in the capacities of all boys and girls for education to responsibility. Science must belong to all children everywhere.

Vol. XXX—p. 324 (Mar. 1954)

Four Hickory Nuts
and a
Catbird's Nest
BY GLENN O. BLOUGH

Glenn O. Blough is Specialist for Elementary School Science, Elementary Schools Section, U.S. Office of Education, Department of Health, Education and Welfare, Washington, D.C.

FOUR HICKORY NUTS, A DESERTED CATBIRD'S NEST, A HORSESHOE magnet and a piece of petrified wood—these were the subjects for our Monday morning *Show and Tell* session in the third grade. While we were in the midst of discussing these bits of nature lore, Helena raised her hand and said, "I saw a bird yesterday. It was sitting in a tree and it was all yellow and green and blue and it had a long black tail and made a noise like an old rooster." So saying, she surveyed the faces of her classmates, noting with satisfaction the expressions of awe and wonder. This inspired Alex to tell about his observation of airplane skywriting while he was riding in the country. He ended up: "And the smoke came out of the tail a mile a minute." Here, from hickory nuts to skywriting, are glimpses of the modern child's environment. It is in this environment of living things, machines, energies, and forces that today's children live.

Through our teaching we hope to help them learn to enjoy this world of things and movements, to help them understand its complications as much as they can at their early years, to keep their interests in it alive and expanding. Through the study of this environment we hope to change their behavior for the better, make them good problem solvers, and develop an attitude of careful investigation, cautious generalizing and suspended judgment.

The Environment

We are sometimes a little glib and indefinite about what constitutes a child's environment. Actually it's whatever surrounds him, wherever he is. It's what he sees and experiences on Saturdays when he flies kites, "lolligags" in the park and is otherwise free to investigate on his own. It's in his home where he's surrounded with gadgets that use electricity, where the heating system operates on scientific principles, where there are mechanical devices that save work and time and where there are countless other expressions of the scientific mind. It's around him when he loiters on the way home from school, sees his reflection in a mud puddle, tries to step on his shadow or watches pigeons. It's the telephone, television and telescope. It's the sun, stars and smoke. It's sprouting seeds, crickets in a coffee can, and toadstools.

Making Selection

Now how can we use this environment to help children grow and develop and to realize both our own intentions and those of the children? Several problems are involved, none as difficult to solve as is sometimes supposed. For example, out of all of this world's stuff and forces how can we make selections for study? On the basis of children's questions, the observations they make and report, and the stuff that lands on the science table? On the basis of the contents of textbooks, science outlines and courses that are handy? As a teacher, which of these criteria guides your selection? Probably both. And it is generally supposed that this produces the best results. It takes the interests of children into account and supplements with environmental problems that have not occurred to them as possibilities. It takes into account the child but allows for a developmental sequence of science subject matter that helps somewhat to keep sixth-grade children from saying, "Aw, we studied that in the third grade." We have, of course, disposed of this problem of organization with too few words and perhaps not the right ones. There is certainly much more to say about the environmental material that is to be selected and organized, but our chief concern here is its use. So let's get to that.

What We Intend

First, let us be clear about this one thing: A good science program is built on our hopes, aspirations and intentions for children and not on test tubes and deserted birds' nests. Here, as in any other field, we keep both eyes on the objectives and use the material.

Getting back to the four hickory nuts and the catbird's nest: how we use them depends on our intentions. Suppose we hope to stimulate interest and observations on the part of more children in the third grade to use these materials to promote scientific investigation methods and to develop scientific attitudes toward problem solving. Having thus committed ourselves as to purpose, from now on our procedure must be in line with this aim. What does this mean? It means that first of all we must encourage children to bring things to school because we want them to be convinced that school is the place to find out things they want to know. We intend to make the experience as satisfying as possible to all concerned.

Since we wish to promote investigating, we do not intend to give forth all the knowledge we happen to have (if fortunately, we have any). We hope to set up ways to find answers and proceed together on the trail of the information. To do this, teachers need to know how to guide the process of problem solving through finding and using books and other printed material, through experimenting, asking somebody who knows and studying pictures. It means too, that "Who says so?" is as important as "What does it say?" and that "There is still more to know about this" is as important as "Now we know."

How We Proceed

This means then that pupils may first show the materials and tell anything they know about or think they know about them. Frequently, this procedure provokes discussions as, for example, when the pupil who brings the magnet says, "It will pick up metals." He may immediately be challenged by "It won't pick this ring up, and it's metal." And there we're in a dilemma which we get out of only by careful experimenting, some reading and some observations. Other magnets will be brought from the environment, i.e., junk boxes in garages, ten-cent stores, junk yards, and elsewhere; and the teacher provides a place (a table perhaps) where children may use the magnets to discover anything they can, by manipulating and observing. The material is used before school, during free time, at noon and during other spare moments. It is used by individuals and by the whole class. As a result of this experimentation and reading, pupils discover that:

Magnetism can travel through wood, cloth, paper, and glass. Some parts of magnets are stronger than others. Some magnets are stronger than others. Magnets have poles. On some magnets the poles are marked. If a north pole of one magnet touches a south pole of another magnet they pull together. Magnets will attract iron and steel.

These are discoveries made by pupils and teacher together. They have been carefully checked by doing experiments more than once, observing carefully, generalizing only after sufficient evidence. The pupils know that there is still more to learn about magnets, for they have been unable to explain to the satisfaction of some of the more curious pupils *why* like poles of magnets repel and unlike poles attract. Later in grade seven or eight they will learn more about the use of magnets, how magnets are made, and how magnetism and electricity are alike and different.

In this case the teacher knew only a little about magnets. But she was curious about them, knew how to help pupils locate information, knew how to help pupils discover by careful trying out, and above all knew why she wanted to have magnets around.

Starting with a Problem

We have examined briefly how pupils might use a lump or so of their environment which they brought to school. Nothing unusual about the procedure. It's much the same way that might be used with any other material. Now let's start with a problem instead of a *thing* and see where the environment comes in.

It's a rural community in spring. It rains every day. Farmers are worried about getting crops into the ground, and seeds that have been planted are not coming up. So? For one thing pupils watch the rain and hear adult conversation about corn and beans and ask, "What does too much water do to bean seeds when they have been planted?" A discussion of this leads to problems about what seeds and plants need in order to grow. Specific problems are listed. Now comes the use of knowing environment in answering them:

Seeds of various kinds are brought from home to use in planting.

Samples of different kinds of soil are collected for use in experiments with sprouting seeds and growing plants.

Plant pots and other material are collected from homes and elsewhere to use in experimenting.

A father of one of the pupils comes to school to explain how certain farm crops in the community are cared for and how tiles are laid for drainage.

The county agriculture agent shows children how to tell whether soil is acid and helps to answer other questions about soils and crop-raising in their community.

A small plot on the school ground is selected in which to make a garden to put into practice some of the science that has been learned.

At home several pupils have been given a small plot to use in planting vegetables and flowers. They are reporting their progress and problems to the group.

Some pupils are exchanging seeds and plants with each other.

The class visits a greenhouse to find how plants are propagated, to observe experimentation with plants, and to collect some samples.

These environmental activities are selected because they bring real meaning to the learning that is going on. They have been planned and carried on by the class and the teacher together. The teacher thought of some activities; the children thought of others. Evaluation was based on the original intentions for them.

More Than Science

This environmental study involved more than science. There were considerable *reading* and *listening* to find the answers; *writing* to make records and to get information; *speaking* to tell what had been learned or to communicate questions, problems, and requests. The social aspects of earning a living, interdependence of peoples, importance of farming, and conservation practices were considered. Who is to say if the experience was science, social studies, or language arts, and we might add, who cares? When examined on the basis of our intentions for children, this study of an environmental problem stands up better than some of the other ways of spending time in the elementary school. The answers and information made a difference to the girls and boys—a situation to be desired and not always attained.

Taking Excursions

It is generally agreed that children should become better acquainted with their environment through sallying forth into it now and then. Such excursions may be a real part of the school learning situation or they may be useless, depending on the definiteness of the purpose. No one concerned should be in the dark about why the excursion is being made.

For what purposes are excursions made into the environment of the school? To gather material to use in solving a problem (pond animals to see how animals are fitted for water life); to observe happenings (changes that animals are making as the seasons change); to observe to solve a problem (how plants change according to the amount of moisture and light they receive); to enjoy natural beauty and thus to develop appreciation (a woods early in spring); to observe a process (purifying water); to summarize a study (study of machines at work in house construction); to create an interest and to raise some problems (observation of many uses of electricity in and around school). These are some of the important reasons for taking children out of the schoolhouse. No matter what the purposes are, the results will be the more satisfying if:

    Children themselves know why they are going.
    They plan how the objectives are to be accomplished.
    They assume responsibility for specific observations to make, materials to obtain, or questions to ask.

The teacher and a committee of children carefully make preparations for the trip by an advance visit and selection of personnel.

There is careful evaluation after the trip when the material is used, data organized, and experiences discussed.

Many Places, People and Things

As we have said, the environment of children consists of their immediate world. From it come many of the useful materials to make learning live. From the *school building* come: the fire extinguisher, electrical equipment and installations, heating systems, the cafeteria, lighting equipment and machines. From the *school yard* come: the plants and animals (trees, bushes, birds, insects), erosion and its control, kinds of soil, and playground equipment that illustrates scientific equipment. From the *sky above:* clouds, wind and other weather phenomena by day; stars, planets and moon by night. From *home* come: machines and tools, heating and lighting control, uses of plants and animals, and communication instruments. From the *community:* stores that sell products and services that use scientific information (heat, light, sound, communication, pest exterminators), the water supply and sewage disposal, museums and libraries.

There are all the *people* who know things that pupils want to know: an amateur astronomer, a bird watcher, an electrician, a gardener, a high school science teacher, a doctor, a dentist, an agriculture agent, a forester.

And then there are *things*—musical instruments when we are studying sound; animals and plants, machines, insulators and conductors when we study electricity; thermometers when we study heat.

The Teacher

The environment of children is indeed a lush one, provided they are lucky enough to work with teachers whose eyes are open and who have will to explore.

Unfortunately *all* children are not exploring their environment in school. They do it on Saturdays, Sundays, and on vacations. Then they are free to find, examine, ask, tell, show and wonder. But on these days there is often no one to share in the exploration. On these days nobody knows the answers to all their questions, which is to be expected. But children hope that in school there will be someone who is *interested* in the world of science who is not afraid to say he doesn't know but who *knows how* to find out and is *willing* to try.

Teachers who have decided to try more science with their children have made some discoveries by themselves. For the record, here are a few of them:

Science at the elementary school level is not nearly as difficult as I thought it was.

Children usually do not need or want detailed, technical explanations.

It is not necessary to have a room full of complicated apparatus. Children bring some, we make some, we buy a little, and we gradually accumulate a closet full of resources.

Many children like science and will take considerable amount of responsibility when it comes to searching for materials and books, and arranging for people to help us.

I've discovered that teaching science isn't much different from teaching social studies and, as I think of it, I don't know all of the answers to questions that children ask me about the 'Westward Movement' either. We find them together.

Experiencing science with children has made me more interested in things myself. I even started a bird feeding station at home. I can identify seven constellations and last summer on a trip I astounded myself by making a rock collection.

There's a considerable amount of material written on my science level and the more I get acquainted with it, the more confidence I have to teach and learn.

Perhaps from these remarks we can gather that more and more teachers are teaching more and more science—better; that children are learning how to interpret their environment and therefore adapt themselves to the world in which they live. As a part of our living with children, we include science environmental studies to make our living more complete and effective.

Vol. XXXVIII—p. 114 (Nov. 1961)

Readiness Is Being

BY ETHELOUISE CARPENTER

Can readiness be taught and practiced through devices and paper-pencil techniques? Can readiness be measured by a child's ability to cross out a rabbit that doesn't look like other rabbits? Ethelouise Carpenter, assistant professor of early childhood education, Kent State University, Ohio, has some clear-cut reasons for saying "No!"

READINESS FOR ANYTHING IS A STATE OF BEING. IT IS A COMPOSITE of many factors and must be measured in many ways. It is not a thing to be taught. It can neither be purchased in a box nor developed on paper. It is an individual state unresponsive to mass production. It is a part of life. A state of readiness manifests itself in many ways. Sometimes the outer appearances represent only a superficial readiness. Something vital must shine through. Manner, attitude, facial expression and expectancy are good indications of an inner acceptance of what *is* in order to meet what *is to come*. It is a kind of reaching out which is recognizable to the skilled teacher as he works with children at any age level. It is a recognition which goes beyond the limits of testing.

Maturing Process

Children are constantly involved in different degrees of readiness. They are called to meals and they linger; they are put on their feet to walk and they plop down on the floor. There are signs for being ready and for not being ready. The state of readiness has not come about through practice of the things to come but through a maturing process fed by successions of related experiences. A child does not become ready for walking by walking. When all elements are perfectly coordinated he begins to walk and he perfects this skill over a long period of time.

Many people have come to look upon readiness as something that must happen to children during the spring preceding first grade. This readiness appears to be made possible through certain specific devices involving symbols. Visitors to kindergartens say, "When and how do you DO your readiness?" Has reading become so organized a *process* that even readiness for it must be dealt with mechanically, piece by piece? No wonder children in kindergarten think there are two kinds of reading—the kind you do in school and the kind you do for enjoyment! Many areas have instituted summer kindergartens which advertise the teaching of reading readiness.

Competencies Needed NOW

Nursery schools and kindergartens are provided for what a child needs *now* and serve as a preparation for first grade only to the same degree that any experience supports a later one. Readiness evolves from practice with the environment, people and materials which promote the desire to look beyond the commonplace, beyond self-interest; to reach a level of physical maturity, of social competence, of emotional control and of mental alertness. Readiness for reading, as for anything else, is built on such experiences over a long period of time. In nursery school and kindergarten the child is helped to listen to others, to wait his turn, to do critical thinking, to take responsibility to the degree that he needs these competencies right now in order to be a contributing member of his present group. He is not taught to conduct himself in a particular way because "the first-grade teacher expects it." The plan of living in preschool groups makes possible a comfortable evolvement of self and readiness for what is and what will be. It is an environment of exploration, not of heated preparation.

In many schools reading has become such a huge Thing to be dealt with that all else is incidental. It often begins with dull experience charts which have grown out of equally dull and controlled trips. Children are still eager but often frightened, parents panic over grouping, discipline problems inconveniently appear, and everyone wonders what could have been done to *prepare* children better so that reading could move along more smoothly. Then eyes turn back to the kindergarten, and administrators and others think they see the trouble in "too much play." If children are moving around they cannot be learning. They must be sitting, producing on paper and quiet in order to learn and to work! Often the "solution" is the purchase of readiness materials for kindergarten. They can be ordered easily, they are paper, they *teach* readiness to all children alike. Reading is looked upon here as a cold process from which one can isolate the various steps and work on them. There are sheets and charts (many based on readiness tests!) for learning left-to-right eye movement, yet the child goes blithely on looking at life from right to left, up to down, in whatever way he finds best to read his environment. Children labor over marking the largest tree in a row, yet they have no difficulty finding the largest cookie on a plate!

Can a Program Be Purchased?

Unfortunately schools which hire untrained preschool teachers think they can solve their problems of preparation by purchasing a program. Material falls into the hands of people least qualified to evaluate it; often no ones knows how to use it, so it either explodes in their hands or is fed to children too limp with boredom to refuse it. Loud cries of protest are coming from well-trained and creative teachers upon whom this material is often forced. It is not merely a protest at the readiness materials but a protest at the complete disregard for all that has been gained in the child-development field.

During the preschool years children work with many materials and great varieties of ideas. They learn to manipulate their environment and to feel the worth of themselves and others. They find answers to questions by talking, moving freely, feeling, listening, looking. They grow in skills for finding out. They learn that books are sources of wonderful information and pleasure. They can challenge ideas and feel right about being different. They learn many ways of arriving at the same conclusions. They make fresh discoveries and use language which is delightful, colorful, imaginative and highly descriptive. They number and label as they feel the need; their own written symbols are a message to them but may be unintelligible to an adult. They become aware that certain combinations of letters on signs means something to someone, but for them it is enough to know that this is communication. There is time to live in the preschool atmosphere, and wider experiences and opportunities for exploration develop throughout the years. Boredom certainly is no sign of readiness to read but rather a clue to a stagnant program. In a good program children are developing the very skills which make later reading meaningful. These skills are not isolated bits of learning relegated to chopped-up pieces of clock time but are outgrowths of an environment of active participation.

The child whose teacher thinks readiness can be taught and practiced through devices and paper-pencil techniques should openly rebel, and many do! A few professional tears should be shed for the child whose readiness for moving on to the next delightful phase of life is measured by his ability to cross out a rabbit that doesn't look like other rabbits and to take left-hand mice to right-hand holes! *The time for being ready is short, but the time for getting there is long.* Readiness lies somewhere between wanting to and having to. It is the solid substance of growth, personality, imagination, self-realization. Let us work with it, take it out and examine and test it occasionally; but let us stop waving it around aimlessly. Certainly today's children deserve something better from progressively better-qualified teachers.

Vol. XXXVII—p. 163 (Dec. 1960)

Dramatic Play

BY ESTHER B. STARKS

By observing a child during dramatic play, understanding adults can learn about his social and emotional development, interests, concepts and informational background. Values of dramatic play for young and older children are pointed out by Esther B. Starks, assistant professor, College of Education, Ohio University, Athens.

DRAMATIC PLAY IS A "NATURAL" WITH CHILDREN; ACTUALLY THE TWO seem to be synonymous. It is a normal activity of the young—the unrehearsed, spontaneous re-enacting of some experience (real or imaginary) in which a child may be a cat, a train, a mother, a baby, a fireman, a spaceman, an Indian, with the appropriate sounds and with fairly recognizable accompanying actions. Usually the impersonations are closely related to well-known people or things, and the child "becomes" that character for varying lengths of time . . . two minutes, three hours, a week. Although such behavior may be a nuisance to adults in the home or a hindrance to the teacher whose curriculum does not provide for ponies on the day that Tom wants to be one, many important things about the child—social development, emotional development, interests, informational background and concepts—may be learned.

True dramatic play is creative, original and impromptu. *Through this play, children give voice to and enact their feelings, their wishes, their understandings. Through this re-enactment children learn and gain security and confidence in their world.* Sometimes the play indicates a child's confusion or misinterpretation of facts. Sometimes it allows a constructive release of physical energy or of emotional tension. Sometimes it is doubtful whether such release is actually constructive, as it may lead instead to overstimulation or even to physical danger, if not to fixing ideas which may be antisocial or harmful more firmly in the child's mind. Sometimes when these learnings are questionable the guidance of an understanding adult is needed.

For All Ages

Dramatic play can be a valuable part of the school curriculum for all ages—from the preschool children who imitate familiar home and neighborhood activities to the elementary school children whose class projects often start with informal dramatizations of the roles of storekeeper or banker. Children who are filled with research in history frequently pretend that they are pioneers; then through this dramatic play comes the realization that more facts are needed and, with a more mature desire for perfection, they formalize the experiences into a creative dramatic production which is far beyond the realm of the initial informal dramatic play.

• A group of fourth-graders was studying about the life of the early settlers in their Pennsylvania community. As in many other areas, there was a wealth of material recalled by families and relatives as well as tangible objects which were relics of the early days. Although some of the fragile objects were added to a display "not to be handled," others piqued the curiosities of the twentieth-century children. As benches, old books, cradles, iron cooking utensils, pewter plates, wooden bowls and candle molds arrived, the children set up a corner of the room where they could try them out, pretending they lived in the olden days. Facts gathered from research in books and through conversations with older members of the community were incorporated in the dramatic play, and through these experiences the children came to appreciate their heritage. Later the desire to organize and shape these into something to be shared with others led them to write their own dramatic productions to be performed for parents and friends.

Harriet Johnson has said, "Dramatic play is the child's way of organizing experience." [1] Through it he arranges facts and observations into a sequence meaningful to him. If that arrangement seems incorrect to an adult, at least it furnishes concrete evidence of where clarification is needed. Also through observation of children engaged in

---
[1] Harriet Johnson, *School Begins at Two* (New Republic, Inc., 1936), p. 110.

dramatic play the adult can see many things appearing: possible fears and even possible attempts to master these fears (as *being* the big dog and chasing children or other dogs); attempts to organize and comprehend various facets of everyday living (as Daddy's going to work, Mother's role at home, a doctor's protective attendance, firemen and policemen engaged in activities other than chasing "bad men"); relationships with family members (loving care of baby or possible twinges of jealousy toward siblings, cooperative living within the family unit, dependence upon parents). Frequently these and other attitudes are reflected in children's free play.

- At each side of the low square table sat a five-year-old girl. On Kathy's head was laid a small red napkin. In back of Jane stood Bonnie running a small wooden rolling pin (in lieu of comb or brush) up and down over Jane's long hair. Anne came to the table with two cylinders from the block corner inquiring, "Would either of you ladies like a coke to drink while you are waiting for your permanents to get finished?" Jane and Kathy each took one and Jane added, "I'll have a manicure, too, while I wait."

- Donna was busy in the doll corner ironing. Suddenly she stopped, reached for the phone and said, "Hello! Oh, Margie, how nice of you! I'd *love* to come. But I have a *big* ironing to do, the baby's sick, and I have to get dinner for the men. They'll be here any time now." After hanging up the receiver, she went to the doll's bed, carefully tucked in the "baby," felt its head, rushed to the phone and said, "Doctor, doctor! The baby's worse. Come right over!" In no time "Doctor" Bob arrived, looked at the doll, pulled a bottle out of his satchel and said, "She'll be O.K. tomorrow. Give her one of these pills. But to be sure of it, I'll give her a 'noculation too. Hold her still."

Expression: Action and Words

Dramatic play is a means of expression both with and without words. It encourages language skills—in the young child, through social contacts with others who use a similar basic vocabulary of everyday familiar terms as well as a gradual sprinkling of new ones; in the older child, through varied experiences which encourage extension and enrichment of vocabulary as well as the skill of expressing ideas and meanings with clarity. Certainly dramatic play aids social contacts and relationships, due largely to its informal nature. Being another person enables the shy, self-conscious child to shed his own personality and assume other roles. In the same way, the aggressive child may experience being a baby or being one who is told what to do—a role which may help him appreciate another viewpoint as nothing else would. There is a place for the purely imaginative, the fantastic (provided it is known to be just that and is not too confused with reality) and the delightfully individualistic rearrangement of everyday occurrences.

Housekeeping routines, beauty parlor experiences, visits to doctors and illnesses at home, train trips, shopping excursions, vacation fun, firemen, cowboys, puppies and kittens, farm activities, air pilots, spacemen, pioneers, skindivers—the list of dramatic play interests is endless. Why, even breakfast can be composed of chocolate ice cream and pie with no harm to anyone!

- In the out-of-door kindergarten Susan and Millie ran about on tiptoe, waving their arms as wings and calling, "Peep-peep-peep." A few minutes later they were busy piling the grass which had accumulated from a recent mowing into a thick, circular shape under a spreading tree in one corner of the yard. Very soon three large stones were added and Susan promptly "sat on the nest." As other children became interested, Peter brought her "worms" and later Don took a turn on the nest while Susan flew off to climb the jungle-gym. As this play was returned to on successive days, new experiences evolved—a "hawk" frightening the mother bird, various birds driving the hawk away, baby birds hatching (with the nest enlarged to hold two or three children who became babies) and later baby birds being fed and making weak attempts to fly from the nest. Although Susan remained the dominant factor, the dramatic play involved most of the children (at least for short periods of time) and furnished much rich discussion as information about nests and baby birds was added by various individuals.

- Seven-year-old Jock stood in back of a table on which were arranged empty cartons, bottles and boxes. He was busy ringing up sales on a toy cash register he had brought from home. "That'll be 79 cents," he said. Bill objected. "How do you know? That's too much for eggs." "My mom said so!" For several days playing store had gone on in a corner of the classroom, before school and during free periods. Little by little the supplies increased as the children brought empty containers from home. Although Jock was usually the storekeeper (it had been his idea and he had done most of the initial work) the fun was catching, and many others wanted their turns.

"Why don't we build a better store," asked Jock, "and maybe we can sell real stuff—pencils, paper, maybe gum or cokes or apples and things?" Enthusiastically the children and their teacher laid plans for a group activity which started from spontaneous dramatic play and extended it, through careful planning and organization, into a valuable group project. Cooperative endeavors and learnings in arithmetic and economics became real and vital to this second-grade group; in time the roles of manager, storekeeper, delivery man and clerk became serious jobs.

Guidance, Not Interference

Not only does the adult need to be aware of what is emerging and is fully evident—he also needs to gain an understanding of what is happening while it is taking place. Is there development in this play or is it merely a repetitive experience? Although frequently some repetition has value, especially when children's attitudes or emotions are developing, repetition can indicate stagnation, lack of challenge and need for stimulation or information. It is here that the teacher's guidance should further constructive activity through wise leading questions, informative discussions or excursions, or even brief adult participation in order to encourage and express interest. *Adult interest in the child's play can do much to spur its quality and open new channels to enrich and extend it.* But—adults *can* interfere too much and shift the emphasis from child initiative and creativity.

Frequently when dramatic play depends too closely on props and is purely repetitive, imitative action, it deteriorates and lacks any constructive value. An example of this is the racing, "bang-bang" type of play (often with holster and cowboy hat) aping the shoot-'em-up programs—hardly a challenge to the creative abilities of active young minds. *True dramatic play is creative and in it each participant is challenged as he re-creates some impression or experience according to his own interpretation and embroiders it as he goes along—spontaneously, informally, unrehearsed.*

Simple, adaptable props are, however, aids in furthering dramatic play, but these should be merely suggestive. Blocks, for example, can be used in an endless variety of ways—constructions ranging from city offices to farm buildings, from roads to rivers. Low screens which can be moved and rearranged are more challenging than a permanently constructed house or store. Various lengths and types of material or scarfs can be tied around shoulders as capes or around waists as skirts or aprons or party clothes. A few dolls, furniture and dishes for a housekeeping corner, open shelves, planks or large blocks (which children can convert into a store, a post office or a bus station) serve as challenges to originality.

As children become more mature, they can form a puppet stage where stocking or paper-bag puppets perform impromptu plays. Later they can be the rough setting for playing pioneers or for dramatizing the latest satellite launching. Only when the play becomes loaded with obvious attempts to perfect lines, memorize parts, and practice performances—so that the emphasis is on production and staging for the enjoyment of an audience—does it need to cross out of the realm of dramatic play into that of dramatics. Yet many creative productions begin with true dramatic play.

Dramatic play has much to offer in providing opportunities for the rich development of children. It is important for the wise teacher and the intelligent parent to encourage and observe this normal play of children and to use these activities as a key for guiding children into the balanced, mature personalities which they hope will emerge.

References

Association for Childhood Education International, 3615 Wisconsin Avenue, N.W., Washington, D. C. 20016:

"Doll Play and Other Dramatic Play," *Creating with Materials for Work and Play Portfolio,* 1957, 12 leaflets, 75¢.

What Are Good Play Materials? by Rowena M. Shoemaker, CHILDHOOD EDUCATION, March 1960.

The Natural Rhythm of Work, Play and Rest, by Glenn R. Hawkes, CHILDHOOD EDUCATION, March 1960.

Language in Childhood

BY JOSEPH CHURCH

How does the child learn language? What is language learning? What are its effects?
Joseph Church is professor of Child Study, Vassar College, Poughkeepsie, New York.

BECAUSE THE STUDY OF CHILDREN'S LANGUAGE HAS CONNECTIONS with linguistics, philosophy, sociology, anthropology, genetics, animal behavior and development, psychiatry, and the psychology of perceiving, thinking, learning, and personality formation, it is a subject that can easily get out of hand. To keep our discussion manageable, I should like to focus on just three questions: (1) How does the child learn language? (2) What is it that the child learns when he learns language? (3) What difference does it make to the child that he learns language?

Learning Language

There are two distinct phases in learning language: the first, a *passive* period in which the child comes to understand much of what is said to him but still does not use language himself; the second, an *active* stage in which he actually begins to talk. His learning to understand language is easily accounted for as a process of associative conditioning—words and objects coincide in time and the word (or groups of words) becomes the signal for its object. Speaking, by contrast, is not so easily explained. We know, of course, that the words the child speaks are imitations of the words he hears. There are, however, several weaknesses in a simple imitation theory of learning to talk. *First,* we are far from understanding how any imitation takes place, how an external stimulus gets converted into a neuromuscular sequence that reproduces the stimulus. *Second,* the baby imitates only selectively, apparently on the basis of what he finds meaningful. *Next,* imitation may be delayed until hours or weeks after the stimulus has come and gone. *Again,* imitation theory does not tell us how the child transposes things to suit his own viewpoint, as in learning to use pronouns correctly. *Nor does it explain* how the child learns general rules of spoken composition, such as formation of plurals and tenses, correct word order, etc., including misapplied rules and invented flexions. *Finally,* imitation theory does not explain how it is that every normal child says things that he has never heard said, constructing innumerable original—although not necessarily creative—formulations of his own.

The psychologist's theoretical lot would be much easier if children made many mistakes, producing quantities of words or sounds, appropriate and inappropriate, which the people around him could selectively reinforce or extinguish. But the hard fact is that the young child, once past the stage of expressive jargon (which he may omit completely), is remarkably parsimonious and accurate; and his occasional errors almost always have their own logic. For instance, a three-year-old, told by her politician father that he had lost the election, replied, "Don't worry, Daddy, maybe you'll find it again." Similarly, a three-year-old observed of the cars whizzing past, "They're sure not slowpokes—they're fastpokes!" Or again, "Sometimes nobody eats with me, and sometimes lots-of-bodies." It seems obvious that children learn language not mechanically but intelligently, and that they learn more than just words. Which brings us directly to our next topic.

What Is Language Learning?

To read textbooks on the acquisition of language, one might think that vocabulary was the entire substance of language. While it is true that learning names or labels is an important part of a toddler's first linguistic learning, it is by no means the whole of it.

I have already said that the child picks up and begins to apply "rules" of grammar and syntax. It is interesting that people learn the rules of spoken composition without being in the least aware that there are such rules, and often from mentors who themselves do not know about the rules. In addition, the child learns—without being taught—a dazzling variety of supra-linguistic "operations" (some of which have prelinguistic analogues): counting, summing, evaluating, comparing, contradicting, bragging, rhyming, alliterating, teasing, joking, talking nonsense, making believe, hypothesizing, defining words, drawing inferences, finding analogies, describing, narrating, and so forth. Some of these are learned on the model of what he is exposed to, while others arise as byproducts or corollaries of learning.

These learnings are the linguistic tools, but language also has content—it refers to the way things are or might be. By listening to other people talking, the toddler learns language and, *through* language, about the world he lives in. Implicit or explicit in what people say to children —in the form of questions, commands, jokes, reproaches, comments, warnings, explanations or whatever—are notions of things and their attributes, of spatial and temporal relationships, of cause and effect, of quantity and magnitude, of significance and insignificance, of value, of virtue and wickedness, of possible and impossible. Adults and older children provide the child both with models of linguistic operation and with a version of reality, together with notions about their and the child's place in that reality, with powerful implications for the child's sense of identity and competence.

Most generally, the child picks up—contained in the styles of thought of the people around him, in the substance and feeling tone of what people say, and in the way people react to what he says and does—a total cultural outlook that shapes his attitudes and capacities for perceiving, feeling, thinking and learning.

Two things should be noted here. The child cannot grow up to be a sane human being without a culture—he has to learn how to be human. But there are cultures that foster freedom, originality, creativity and even a limited ability to transcend culture; and there are cultures that stultify our humanity, that warp or blunt us as people and conceal or falsify reality.

Effects of Learning Language

We have already said that learning language enables us to learn through language. But in addition to being open to what people tell him, the child also becomes able to formulate his own experience and thus to teach himself. We must not forget that *language is not simply an instrument of communication but also of thinking and feeling.* It is only by virtue of symbolic formulations that we can live in a concrete present set in the perspective of past and future and hypothetical; of esthetically and morally pleasing and repugnant; and of abstract general principles, ethical and practical. A whole series of studies, begun by Vygotskii[1] and carried forward by Luria,[2] demonstrates the essential role of language in self-direction and self-control. It is thanks to language that we can engage in fantasy, spin out elaborate jokes, and delude ourselves about our own characters and motives. I cannot postulate a causal connection, but pictorial representation always comes later in development than speech. It is only with symbols that we can refashion our experience as myth, art, philosophy and science—and, we must not forget, as delusional systems.

Obviously, without language we could not learn to read. We are liable to forget that a huge proportion of our learning must of necessity

---

[1] L. S. Vygotskii, *Thought and Language* (New York: John Wiley & Sons, Inc., 1962).

[2] A. R. Luria, *The Role of Speech in the Regulation of Normal and Abnormal Behavior* (New York: Liveright, 1961).

be vicarious and that much of it comes to us through the printed word. We are even more likely to forget that the printed word is an important source of emotional learning, that through literature we can share in all the vicissitudes and passions and degradations and triumphs of being human. In general, we are inclined to "protect" young people from strong literary meat and drink, just as we protect them in everyday life from the facts of sexuality and old age and death and money and abnormality and violence. It is certainly not the business of parents and teachers to rub children's noses in the earthier realities, but we should probably be grateful for all the corrupting influences of people and literature that fill out our children's education.

Strongly implied in the above is that language enables us to be intelligent, not in the narrow sense of being able to perform well on intelligence tests but in the broad sense of being open to new experience, having deep and variegated feelings, exercising reason and judgment, knowing compassion, maintaining perspective, being capable of serious commitment, respecting evidence, resisting empty verbalisms and verbal magic, and having whatever else distinguishes the superior person from the average. I am here seconding Hunt's [3] and Fowler's [4] ideas that intellectual differences are very largely a product of differences in early experience, as regards both strength of emotional identification and exposure to good models of cognitive operation.

If intelligence develops out of the child's symbolic functioning, parents and teachers must be prepared to nourish it. Because we do not understand how it is possible for a biological organism to be capable of consciousness and self-consciousness, of self-direction and self-control and self-sacrifice, of altruism, of love and hatred, of jealousy, of esthetic enjoyment, of wit and humor, and of creative and imaginative symbolization, we may be inclined to dismiss all these as metaphysical fluff and, in dismissing them, practice the self-fulfilling prophecy. As parents and educators, we must bear in mind the highest reaches of humanity and work for the conditions that will allow great numbers of children to attain them. As scientists of human behavior and development, we must practice humility and tolerate great quantities of ambiguity.

[3] J. McV. Hunt, *Intelligence and Experience* (New York: Ronald Press Co., 1961).
[4] William Fowler, "Cognitive Learning in Infancy and Early Childhood," *Psychological Bulletin*, 1962, Vol. 59, pp. 116-152.

"Deep as a Giant"
An Experiment in Children's Language
BY CLAUDIA LEWIS

Four- and five-year-olds think that water can be as "deep as a giant," that some things are as "slow as you grow up" and others as "quiet as you cut cotton." Delightful, imaginative concepts which give sparkle to living. Claudia Lewis is teacher of the four-year-olds in the Harriet Johnson Nursery School, New York City.

E LIZABETH, FIVE YEARS OLD, STOOD LOOKING AT THE LARGE BOAT SHE had built of boxes and blocks in our school play yard. "The water around my boat is deep as a giant," she said.

This concept of deepness surprised me. I realized that if I had been called upon at that moment to describe the water around her boat, I probably should have said, "Deep as anything."

When we went in from the play yard to our classroom, I told the whole group of children—about eight of them—what Elizabeth had said and suggested that they all think of some other deep things. "We might write the deepest story in the world," I said. "What *is* the deepest thing in the world? Deep as . . ."

"Deep as sand down in the ocean.". . . "Deep as dirt under the ground.". . ."Deep as from the sky down!"

These, and many more, the children poured out, shouted out, with zest and delight. And so began a year-long experiment on my part, a game on the part of the children—a game of playing in this way with our concepts, our speech, for the fun of it.

One day I stopped a child who had just said, "Oh, it's easy as pumpkin pie!" and asked him and the others to think of what was *really* easy. It was hard for me to jot down fast enough the thirty or so easiest things in the world that came tumbling out of their mouths, ranging from "Easy as drinking water," and "Easy as wind blows paper all around the sky," to this epitome of ease: "Easy as when you wash your face in the morning, your cheeks get red."

The next step was to concentrate on the difficult things. First came: "Hard as catching a train when you come up late and it's just leaving." . . ."Hard as to break your hand.". . ."Hard as to cut your hair like a barber." Then these four lines followed inevitably one upon the other:

> Hard as to hear when you're deaf,
> Hard as to see when you're blind,
> Hard as to talk when you're dumb,
> Hard as to walk when you have a broken leg.

Again, we tried to think of what was fast and what was slow. To a five-year-old a wink apparently is not the quickest thing in the world, nor is a snail the slowest! But fire burning paper is fast, and an electric fan is fast, and so is a fireman sliding down a pole. One clear-visioned little girl said simply and casually, "Fast as you see yourself in the mirror."

When we turned to the slow things, we found: "Slow as your new teeth come in.". . ."Slow as clocks.". . ."Slow as you grow up.". . . and this last which is so painfully slow that even I find it hard to conceive of: "Slow as one man building a bridge."

"Flat as fishes," "Flat as a button," and "Flat as a necktie," came as welcome variations of the well-worn pancake.

But what seemed to please us all the most was the Quiet Story. The children recurred to this again and again, spontaneously offering more suggestions from day to day. Not one among them mentioned that a mouse was quiet. Instead, they said: "Quiet as you close your eyes." . . ."Quiet as sunshine comes out.". . ."Quiet as a thermometer goes up." . . ."The sky moves very soft and the whole world.". . ."Quiet as you cut cotton." And it was Elizabeth who startled me again with, "Quiet as a splinter comes in."

I didn't always ask for these more or less abstract concepts. One day during a heavy snowstorm when the flakes were coming down crisscross, as I should say, I asked the children to look out and tell me how the snow was falling. Martin saw his analogy right away: "The snow looks like darning." Another child looked for a while, said, "I feel like *I'm* going around and around in a circle." Cynthia puzzled me for an instant, so unaccustomed were my adult eyes to such fresh ways of seeing: "The snowflakes go like a kitten's tongue."

Another time we were watching our pet white mouse: "His nose looks like a little church, a sharp little church with the point up.". . . "His tail looks like pink linen."

Once when we had turtles in our room, I asked the children to tell me the difference between turtles and people. To help them organize their thoughts I gave them a pattern, a form, beginning: "Turtles have eyes, just like people, only . . ." They carried it on: "Only their eyes are as small as bugs." We went on:

> Turtles have mouths, just like people,
>   Only their mouths are as small as my fingernail.
> Turtles have heads, just like people,
>   Only they have stripes and we don't.
>   They don't have hair.
>   The stripes are their hair!

I have said nothing of another angle of this language game of ours, concerned with the rhythm and sound of words. It seems to be as natural for children this age to coin their own words, especially words representing sounds, as it is for them to see the analogy between the snow and the kitten's tongue. "Hear them shattle, shattle," said Betty, speaking of the familiar clinking of the milkman's bottles in the bottle carrier.

To give the children opportunities for using this talent for hearing has been a part of my experiment. These words of their own coinage seem to come when the things they are talking about are brought vividly before them—when the children are looking, listening, touching, or when they are vividly remembering sights and sounds.

One windy day we wrote a windy story. It was a relief and a joy to all of us to get away finally from an interminable series of "The wind blows this," and "The wind blows that," to "Sometimes the wind goes *bumbling* over like a wave," and "The wind blows papers fruffle, fruffle, fruffle."

As with sounds, so it is with rhythms. When I helped the children recall clearly, with all its noises and motion, the steam shovel we had seen, I found that we could get some of its ponderous swing in our speech:

> My big dipper moves
> Down to the dirt,
> Then swings around,
> Around in a circle.

We could make a word picture of our hungry, nibbling pet mice, a picture that gives the quick little rhythm of their movements:

> Shake, shake and nibble, nibble,
> Wiggle, wiggle tail,
> Wiggle, wiggle nose,
> Wiggle, wiggle ears,
> Down and up and down and up, little feet,
> And all around the cage they go,
> And nibble up again.

To conclude, perhaps I could do no better than to quote Ann's reply, when I asked her how we might bring our train story to an end. Said she abruptly, "Caboose! It's ended!"

How Children Learn Their Language

BY RUTH G. STRICKLAND

Ruth G. Strickland, professor of education, Indiana University, Bloomington, states that a child builds his real and psychological worlds as he builds his language.

ALL OF US LEARNED OUR LANGUAGE SO LONG AGO THAT WE HAVE NO notion of how we learned it nor even any recollection of having learned it at all. The code has become so automatic that we are aware of it only when something goes amiss with it or when the meaning we try to transmit is so abstract or so unfamiliar that we have to give special thought to making it intelligible to others. Linguists and students of child development know some things about how language is learned, but their knowledge is still incomplete.

All language is concerned with meanings, but the language itself is not the meanings. The language is a code of signals by which messages-meanings can be sent from one individual to another. The process of learning to talk, the linguists tell us, is the process of learning a particular code of language signals which correlates with the meanings the child is building up through his experience. The content of the messages the child can send and receive is limited by his own individual range of experience.

The physical apparatus for the production of speech is present when the child is born. The muscles of respiration which will be used to produce the necessary air flow and pressure; the muscles which will control the vocal cords to produce sound; and the muscles of tongue, jaws and lips which will shape the speech sounds are all present and ready for use. Most children begin to "talk" their native language before they are two years old which means that they have learned to coordinate the systems of muscles so that they work in harmony to produce patterns of sound which signal meaning.

Combining Sound Patterns and Experience

A child may recognize elements of a language code long before he uses them. He hears his mother say she is going to the supermarket, and he runs to get his coat so that he can go with her. The patterns of contrasting sound his mother has used have transmitted a message to him even though he cannot yet "talk" those sounds. When he does begin really to use words he is combining sound patterns with elements of experience. He says "Daddy," "Mommy," or "doggie" when the corresponding individual appears. A single word can signal the meaning usually carried by a sentence when the inflection he uses for the word *ball* means "Give me the ball!" or "Is that a ball?" Fragmentary repetitions of sound patterns in situations where the meaning is evident condition the child's own vocal responses.

Often children begin to use jargon at about fifteen months, and some use it predominantly until they are about two years or a little older. Listening to the jargon of a little child makes clear the linguists' contention that the child early learns not only the sound patterns that we call "words" but also the patterns of pitch and stress that help to carry meaning in our sentences. Sometimes the jargon follows so closely the patterns of adult speech that it is difficult to believe that the child is using few or no intelligible words.

Most students of child language agree that the child does not learn to make new sounds wholly by imitation. He makes a great variety of sounds in his early babbling. Adults call attention to the sounds in the child's own repertoire that are close approximations to real words, and they repeat these over and over. A child learns new groups of sounds he already uses spontaneously. Imitative words are favorites for a time with many children, words that imitate the sounds made by animals and objects such as "meow," "tick-tock" and "choo-choo" often used in duplicate form. During this early period children use many words more generally than adults. Any four-legged animal may be a dog or any man may for a time be called "Daddy."

Sounds That Make Word Patterns

Learning a language involves becoming aware of contrastive sounds which signal quite different meanings. "Your pen is on the box" means something quite different from "Your pet is in the box," yet the two statements contain only two differing sounds. Children learn very early to take note of the sounds that make up word patterns. They learn to be aware of differences in word order and intonation as well. "You are coming with me" requires a different response from "Are you coming with me?" Pitch and stress signify meaning in many combinations of words. "Will he be surprised?" means something different in attitude as well as idea from "Will *he* be surprised!" (See Figure below.)

"Will he be surprised!"

"Will he be surprised?"

One can ask five different questions in the words "Are you going tonight?" with meaning depending upon casual asking of the four words or asking them with sharp stress on any separate one of the four words in the cluster.

Children begin very early to learn that meaning is carried not by words alone but by words in patterns of arrangement and by the way one uses his voice in saying the words. Learning to give attention to these signals is fully as important as learning the words themselves since the meaning signaled by the words may be greatly modified by the way they are used. All this is inherent in the learning of the language.

Speech and Thought the Same

The amount of talking a child does increases rapidly as he learns more words and develops language power. By two and a half many children carry on long monologues associated with the activities in which they are engaged. The speech accompanies the action and is in itself satisfying to the child. Speech and thought are one and the same at this level. At three years of age the child is probably using language fluently and with confidence. Many four-year-olds use language almost continuously and can exhaust any adult any day with their persistent flow of questions.

Studies of children's language recently completed at Indiana University indicate that children use all types of sentences at age six. The patterns within the sentences may be handled awkwardly or they may not achieve acceptable levels of grammaticalness, but the child has learned to put together sentence patterns just as the adults around him do. The grammar he has learned is well learned and will not be easily changed.

From this point on, language development involves the adding of vocabulary and meanings through actual and vicarious experiences, refining the structuring of sentences, improving for some children the level of grammatical usage, and for all children many opportunities to use language to express meaning and observe the effect of their expression on others.

Language and Experience Needed To Think

A child builds his real and his psychological worlds as he builds his language. His concepts of things, people and all that make up human interaction are closely intertwined with language. A child can think only in realms in which he has both language and experience to draw upon. His learning of his language is the most amazing feat of learning in which he will ever engage, and the basic task is accomplished in the relatively short span of early childhood.

But the learning does not end there. Experiences with life expand language continuously. A language in itself is inexhaustible in its possibilities. New words are forever being added to the language—most of them like "telstar," "astronaut" and "sulfadiazine" being coined of old parts put together in new ways. Opportunities to know and enjoy literature which are the birthright of every child introduce him to the possibilities inherent in the language for precision, beauty and originality of expression. There is no upward limit to learning unless the school puts a ceiling on learning by limiting the child's experience with good books.

Children love language. The eagerness with which they acquire it, their fondness for playing with new words, with testing their language in endless ways, and the joy they find in listening to stories and poetry all attest to this interest. Our task is to provide the opportunity, encouragement and inspiration which will keep them forever growing.

Vol. XXXVII—p. 160 (Dec. 1960)

More Than Words
BY LELAND B. JACOBS

Leland B. Jacobs is professor of education, Teachers College, Columbia University, New York.

LITERATURE FOR CHILDREN IS MORE THAN WORDS, MORE THAN READing matter, though it is made up of words and becomes reading matter which is unique, original. It is more than language signs and signals, though it uses the common language of a people and it cues the reader, the receiver of the written language, to its intent and content. Literature is a way of coming at life through impression and expression in prose and poetry. It is a special way of focusing experiences and relationships with words, wherein the focusing and form-making of the stuff of experience or of the quality of human relationships is the distinctive, the unique achievement. Literature is a way of querying life, of ordering the components of existence in such a manner that that which might be mundane, ordinary or menial is, instead, illuminating, engrossing and extraordinary. . . . .

A Bond of Two Kindred Spirits

Literature for children is more than words, though words are the tools of both the author and the reader. Words are the sharp tools with which the author fashions and orders the images, moods, events and characters which form his writing. Words are also the trusty tools with which the reader works to find his way into the feeling and form which the writer has written into the images, characters, events and moods which are of his creation.

That the imagination of the writer and the imagination of his young reader are not alike is not necessarily an impairment of the bond between the two. The bond is not formed through the identical but rather through identification. The reader must feel receptive to the author's ordering of life through the imaginative elements in the writing. However, in his response, his identification with the writing, the reader will not duplicate the writer's perceptions. The reader brings his own imagination to bear upon the printed symbols and lives in the enterprise as his own perceptions dictate. The meeting of the writer and the reader, through words, is a meeting on the level of esthetic feeling for what to both of them seems reasonable and fit and beautiful concerning life.

Reasonable and Fit and Beautiful

Literature for children is more than words, though words are the vehicle in which the writer makes his way to his product, to the fulfillment of his dreams and drives. Words give the writer's perceptions of life and living their momentum and melody, their vitality and verisimilitude. Words convey to the reader this movement and cadence and reality and truth-to-life on the printed page. Thus words are the carriers of the message between the author and the reader, but they are not the larger meaning. The larger meaning is more than words. It is written and read between the lines.

Each Must Go Alone

In the literary experience the reader expects the writer to go ahead of him, to prepare the way and to do so so skillfully that he can make his way to where the author has been. Yet each must go alone. The reader cannot—nor does he expect to—make his way through the paragraphs or stanzas in the manner in which the writer did. The reader must make his way through the trails of print which the author has blazed. He knows that, if ever, he will only catch up with the writer at the end of the trail. But throughout the going the reader senses that, in spirit, the writer is with him. The reader expects the writer to guide him in his pursuit of meanings and feelings, which he could not otherwise experience had not the writer set the trail and cleared the path and made the going memorable.

Literature is more than words, for though the words are the pegs upon which the literary production is hung, all the words written by the author cannot be held exactly in the reader's memory. The writer, in order to develop his mood and meaning, necessarily employs many more words than the reader (or the writer for that matter) can immediately recall. What the reader considers the big ideas, the pivotal meanings, constitutes what he keeps in mind as he continues to read. He does not even try to hold onto all the words that the writer has employed. Instead, the reader makes of the words such sequences or series of meanings as seem urgent and sensible for him to move ahead, comprehending meaningfully. He lets the words construct time, place, scene or situation—or whatever it is that the writer is developing—and it is these vivid constructs that the reader clings to that he may go ahead with the author with confidence. To the extent that time, place, siuation, mood or character are made arresting and vivid through words, they can serve to aid the reader. By their precision and fitness, they help the reader to hold in the foreground of his mind the ingredients of the prose or poetry that are essential to the central thought, the total meaning of the author's work. . . . .

More Than Words

Yes, literature for children is more than words, though there would be no prose or poetry without words. Without words—the right words for the right place—the writer is bereft. With the wrong words, the writer flounders. With words that do his bidding, that express feeling, querying of life, ordering of the components of existence which he hopes to express, the writer is satisfied, is fulfilled.

And what does the child reader find beyond the words in his literature? He finds adventure, mystery, nonsense, biography, fancy. He lives in times, places and family patterns he has never known. He perceives moods of nature, moments of love, celebrations of accomplishments which heighten his rejoicing and awareness in living. He walks with kings; he talks with animals. He fights for freedom, takes journeys into outer space, overcomes prejudices and conquers fears. Beyond the words the reader finds magic and make-believe, human enterprises and undertakings, hopes and dreams and foibles and frolics. Here, through literature, the reader responds to the confirmation and extension of his experiences and his relationships; to a natural and a man-made world; to questings and achievements in growing and in growing up.

The child, thus, gains stature as a reader—a sensitive, critical, perceptive reader, a reader appreciative of words and their ways in the literary experience. Such a child develops into a mature reader. Through his many contacts with writers who use words with discrimination and taste, the child becomes a real reader whose early bonds with them prepare him for a lifetime of seeking writers' company in the wisdom and wonder and joy—in and beyond words—of books and of the literary experience.

Beyond the Verbal Façade

BY MILLIE ALMY

Millie Almy, professor of education, Teachers College, Columbia University, reports a research project currently under way in Horace Mann Lincoln Institute for School Experimentation, Teachers College, Columbia University. The major goal is to study meanings young children bring to the explanation of certain natural phenomena.

YOUNG CHILDREN RELISH WORDS AND LEARN NEW ONES RAPIDLY. By first grade, the extent of their vocabularies is often surprising, even to their teachers. "Satellite," "launching pad," "dinosaur," "radioactive," "transistor" are words not listed in the basic vocabulary for first- or second-graders, yet they come readily to the tongues of many of the youngsters.

The easy and rapid acquisition of new vocabulary can be a tremendous asset to the child, but his verbal facility sometimes obscures the difficulties he has in understanding. Adults are prone to mistake the child's ability to imitate or to reproduce what he has heard as evidence that he comprehends what he says. However, when they look beyond the verbal façade to the meanings the child has for the words he uses, they often find confused and erroneous conceptions.

To study the meanings young children bring to the explanation of certain natural phenomena is the major goal of a research project currently under way in the Horace Mann Lincoln Institute for School Experimentation at Teachers College, Columbia University. In the exploratory phases of the project, two groups of kindergarten children were observed in their classrooms and individually interviewed two or three times. Most of the children were also interviewed after they had completed first grade (1). Subsequently, several kindergarten and first-grade teachers conducted similar individual interviews with the children in their classrooms.

Ways of Thinking Revealed

The interviews consisted of demonstrations of such phenomena as the floating or sinking of a group of familiar objects and questions designed to elicit from the child his predictions and explanations regarding movements of the objects. A full explanation was obviously beyond the abilities of children of this age, but their answers did reveal their ways of thinking about the phenomenon. Also included was a demonstration of the conservation of liquid. This was intended to ascertain whether a child had a stable concept regarding a given amount of liquid or whether he tended to think that there was more (or less) liquid when it was placed in a vessel differing in shape though equivalent in volume.

These and several of the other demonstrations used were drawn from the work of Piaget (2). Piaget contends that the thinking of the child to the age of six or seven is qualitatively quite different from that of the older child or adult. The young child to a much greater extent than the older one is caught up by the appearance of things. He finds it difficult to think of more than one aspect of a phenomenon at a time. Thus he may pay attention first to the height of the column of water in a vessel, then to its width. But he cannot deal with these two variables simultaneously. Consequently, he fails to recognize that a given amount or quantity retains its entity despite the manipulations it undergoes. At this stage in his thinking, the young child is untroubled by contradiction. Results of this study have raised a number of questions that are immediately relevant to the classroom.

To the extent that an interview confronts a child with problems similar to those he might encounter in the classroom, it resembles a slow motion picture of his performance there. It differs from the classroom in that neither he nor the interviewer are distracted by the presence of other children. The child's "guesses," his evasions, his misconceptions are often more clearly revealed in the interview than in class.

Few Verbal Children Not Representative of Group

This leads to the first question. How adequately does the typical kindergarten or primary-grade classroom provide opportunities for the teacher to talk with and listen to each child? As a group discusses the seeds and pods they gathered in the fall or how the water gets to their drinking fountain, how many children come to the conclusions the teacher hopes they will? How often is the "good thinking" (thinking that satisfies the teacher's expectations) of three or four verbal children taken to represent the thinking of the group?

This question takes on special significance when the children involved come from homes where parents have little time or inclination for conversation or discussion with their children. A number of youngsters who were keenly attentive during their interviews revealed good observation ability and quite insightful thinking, but their teachers found them rather inadequate in the group, where they did not seem to "pay attention." The interviews suggested that they needed adult help to learn to focus on the relevant aspects of a problem.

Intent on the generalizations they want the children to draw from a particular experience, teachers often overlook the young child's propensity to view things in an extremely personal, individual way. Not until he is able to see the world in the same way as the adult does is he likely to reach similar conclusions. Thus a second important question to ask is, "What does the child think the teacher wants?"

Some Expect Conformity

Some teachers make it abundantly clear to the children that they expect conformity. As one teacher said after studying the questions used in the interviews, "My children will have difficulty with these. They expect me to tell them what to do—color the circle red or cross out the third bunny. They don't expect me to ask them what they think."

But teachers who are concerned with more than the child's ability to go through the motions of learning will also find that children tend to shape their responses to fit their notions of the adult's expectations.

To a considerable extent the children's ways of dealing with the adult's questions in the interviews reflected their customary ways of relating to adults. Children who were ordinarily somewhat apprehensive round adults tended to be restrained and not very expressive. Often it appeared that they regarded "I don't know" as the safest answer. Children who were usually free and expansive with adults seemed much more inclined to venture their opinions in the interviews. Even they, however, clearly looked to the adult for clues to the "right" answer.

Learning To Test Answers

Obviously young children learn a great deal through being told. But the teacher who is interested in helping them to think effectively wants them to learn to test the rightness or wrongness of their answers. This is particularly true in science and in mathematics. Yet it is not easy for a teacher to phrase his questions in a way that takes the child back either to the phenomenon he has observed or to a similar one for verification of his answers. In the conservation of liquid demonstration, for example, some teachers, surprised that a child seemed to think there was more water when it was spread out in a shallow dish, repeated the demonstration. They elicited from the child the assertion that the amount of water in two identical glasses was "the same." Then they poured the water from one glass into the shallow dish, and said, "Now if this was the same as this when it was in the glass, wouldn't it be the same here?" Some children accepted the implication in the question and said, "Yes." Two or three stoutly maintained their original position. Who is to say that those who changed to "yes" had or had not had a genuine flash of insight?

The teacher of the young child as well as the researcher who would investigate his thinking needs to be wary of the leading question. But the question that the child does not understand is equally suspect. Had many of the youngsters been questioned about "floating" or "sinking" they might not have comprehended. They described floating objects as "staying on top" or "swimming," sinking objects as "going down." Half the lower-class group called a plant having no blooms a "flower."

Confused About Meaning of Terms

Just as an inadequate vocabulary or confusion about the meaning of certain terms may hamper the child's expression of insight, a very fluent vocabulary sometimes masks intellectual confusion. For example, several children were quick to offer the explanation, "It needs air (or oxygen) to burn," when they observed a candle go out after a glass jar was placed over it. Nevertheless these same children later revealed confused concepts about air, as did many of the children who could not appropriately phrase it.

Teachers alert to the adequacy of young children's learning look beyond what the child says to the meanings that may lie behind the words. They are concerned with the glib response as well as the inept and with the elusive "I don't know." They ask the important question, "What does the child's comment reveal about his thinking?"

However capricious a youngster's expression may seem, it has significance for him. Responses are not made at random. Even when a child is "just guessing" his answers may reflect his level of development, his previous experiences and his concerns.

Concrete Thinking Is First

Although the nature of children's mental development is not yet fully understood, it is clear that predominant ways of thinking change from one stage of development to another.

Imagination, fantasy and the tendency to view things subjectively so characteristic in the nursery-school years gradually give way to more objective kinds of thinking as the child moves through the elementary school. Other qualitative differences also distinguish much of the thinking of the younger child from that of his older brother. Certain abilities emerge later than others.

Young children think in concrete and specific terms for a considerable period before they develop the ability to handle more abstract classifications. An apple is defined as something to eat and described as round and red and having seeds before it is conceived as a member of a class of objects including oranges, peaches and plums (3).

Similarly, younger children tend to be able to classify objects on the basis of a single variable—for example, color or size or form—before they can handle these simultaneously (4). There is also some evidence to suggest that children may tend to be more preoccupied with certain properties at one age level than another. Many children under the age of five who were questioned about floating and sinking objects tended to concentrate on the size of the objects. Older children rarely referred to size, and almost all of those who were six or older talked about the object's weight. Whatever a child spontaneously pays attention to may provide some clue to the level of his intellectual development.

Experience Affects Thinking

Often, however, it indicates something of the experiences the child has had. For example, children who predicted that a stone put in water would melt or change color may have thought of occasions when something placed in water did change or disintegrate. A youngster may puzzle over a particular phenomenon for a long time, collecting information and eventually testing the validity of his own explanations (5). The tenacity with which some children hold to a particular idea was apparent in the almost identical explanations they gave when they were five and one-half, six and seven years old. One child, for example, always spoke of the material of the objects; another commented on the stone's hardness.

Some comments apparently reflect both experiences and emotional concerns. When a youngster is deeply disturbed about some aspect of his living, he tends to view the world in the light of that problem. A possible instance of this tendency was provided by a little girl, whose explanations relating to aliveness all had to do with loneliness and the loss of "Mommy." Although both researchers and teachers need to exercise caution in making inferences from a child's comments to his deeper concerns, the emotional dimension in young children's thinking cannot be overlooked.

Words come readily to the young child, but the meaning they have for him is not always immediately clear. If the teacher is to help him to build more adequate meanings, meanings that are shared with other people, meanings that help him to understand and cope with his world more effectively, he needs first to understand what lies beyond his words. The teacher needs to grasp the essential characteristics of his thinking, the ways it resembles and the ways it differs from his own. For if the teacher fails to understand the mental development underlying the words and takes them too literally, he may be dealing with "nothing real at all, only façades, make-believes and shams" (6).

References

1. Almy, Millie and Chittenden, E. *Young Children's Thinking About Natural Phenomena.* Interim Report to Horace Mann Lincoln Institute of School Experimentation. New York: Teachers College, Columbia University, 1960.
2. Piaget, J. *The Child's Conception of Physical Causality.* New York: The Humanities Press, Inc., 1951.
———. *The Child's Conception of the World.* London: Routledge & Kegan Paul, Ltd., 1951.
———. *Play, Dreams and Imitation in Childhood.* New York: Norton, 1952.
3. Welch, L. and Long, L. "The Higher Structural Phases of Concept Formation of Children." *Journal of Psychology,* 1940, 9: 59-95.
4. Reichard, Suzanne; Schneider, M., and Rapaport, D. "The Development of Concept Formation in Children." *American Journal of Orthopsychiatry,* 1944, 14: 152-62.
5. Navarra, John. *The Development of Scientific Concepts in a Young Child.* New York: Teachers College, Columbia University, Bureau of Publications, 1955.
6. Isaacs, N. *Piaget's Work and Progressive Education* (bulletin). National Froebel Foundation, 1955.

Vol. XXXVII—p. 260 (Feb. 1961)

To Write or Not To Write
BY NEITH HEADLEY

There are many forerunners to writing which help develop eye-hand coordination in kindergarten, writes Neith Headley, College of Education, University of Minnesota, Minneapolis.

ALL TOO OFTEN PARENTS AND KINDERGARTEN TEACHERS TEND TO take the child's interest in imitating the reading and writing activities of older siblings as an indication that the child is ready to be taught how to read and write. What kindergarten teacher has not been handed a carefully if somewhat grubbily sealed envelope upon which her own name has been laboriously inscribed only to open the envelope to find a sheet of note paper covered over with a strange assortment of smudgy hieroglyphics? The one legible word on the sheet is usually found at the bottom of the page and it may, either easily or with great difficulty, be recognized as the child's own name.

The teacher accepts and recognizes this offering as one of the many signs of the child's awakening awareness of a written language. But heaven forbid that, because of this awakening, she should feel compelled to sit down with the child to "teach" him and his peers precisely how to formulate letters and words. No parent would dream of trying to teach the child who is learning to walk—the child who is taking his first steps—the proper techniques of walking. And yet, in a sense, that is what is often done when a young child shows the slightest interest in trying to write.

At the age of four or five most of the children in our culture exhibit some interest in trying to formulate written numbers and letters. A few with seemingly little effort but much practice, resulting from sheer self-determination, acquire considerable skill in "writing." Those who have not yet developed the necessary fine muscle and eye-hand coordination find printing to be a most taxing undertaking. Have you ever watched a young child in his early attempts to direct lines into letter shapes? He usually grasps his crayon or pencil with cramped fingers and then proceeds to *draw* the letter lines stroke by stroke. Frequently each and every stroke is accompanied by trunk, shoulder, head and even tongue movements. Upon the completion of two or three letters he may shift his body weight or he may even stand up, look at something across the table or perhaps converse with friends before continuing the arduous task of printing MOTHER . . . I LOVE YOU or whatever he is trying to write.

The good kindergarten teacher will recognize the many exhibited degrees of "writing" skill within her group, but she will not isolate the skill as something to be developed through drill and practice. Instead, she will provide many experiences which will further the development of muscle and eye-hand coordination. Through experience-living situations she will provide opportunities for children to pursue their growing interest in "writing"; by way of her own easel and chalkboard recording and the recording of children's stories on the back of their pictures, she will alert children to techniques used in manuscript writing.

Forerunners Help Coordination

The following rundown includes a sample of many kindergarten experiences which, in one way or another, help to develop eye-hand coordination and the muscles which are basic to achieving handwriting skill:

Finger painting; painting with brushes; operating the spring clips which hold the paper on the easel; using chalk or large crayons; manipulating puzzle parts, stringing beads; cutting with scissors; posting pictures; lacing shoes: tying knots and bows; arranging felt or flannel board figures; dressing and undressing dolls; working zippers, snaps, hooks, buckles and buttons on their own clothes or helping friends with their dressing problems; strengthening hand and wrist muscles on climbing apparatus; using tools at the workbench; building with blocks; working with modeling materials; folding paper; applying paste and combining this piece of paper, cloth or what-have-you with that (as in a collage); pouring fruit juice; folding napkins; experimenting with piano keys or chords and strings on the auto harp; washing and drying seeds and later counting out and bagging them; tying peanuts and threading such things as cereal, bread and popcorn for the birds' Christmas tree; planting seeds; weeding in the garden; experimenting with magnets, batteries and wires; winding and setting an alarm clock; arranging leaf, seed, stone and other collections; carefully turning pages or searching through a book, page by page, for specific information. There is just no end to the listing of experiences which might help to develop muscle and eye-hand coordination!

Pictures Are Symbols, Too

Throughout the year many experience-living situations will arise which can be used to feature handwriting as a means of conveying ideas and information. Children can be encouraged to paint or crayon their names, perhaps even dates, on the backs of completed pictures and notes to take home. In addition to adding their names to messages, children can also help to "write" messages. For example, if the group is planning to make applesauce and the children need to remind themselves or ask their mothers about bringing such things as apples, saucepans, spoons and sugar, they can make a picture or printed symbol of the idea to be remembered. A picture or printed symbol made by the child and that symbol pinned on his coat or appended to a typed note will convey the message more effectively than a note typed by a secretary and put into the child's fist at dismissal time. A simple check on acquired printing skill can be arrived at by asking children to place their signatures on a letter which has been dictated by the group. In connection with this recording of signatures, the teacher must remember that a signature is a very personal thing and it may, even in kindergarten, vary all the way from a marked X to an almost Spencerian script imprint.

Left to Right Concept

Through observation of the teacher's printing and the teacher's casual comments about her own printing and the children's printing efforts, the children will see and come to understand (a) that when putting letters together we proceed from left to right and (b) that words follow each other from left to right on a horizontal base. It helps to fix the idea by showing the difference between our way of writing and the ways in which other people write. The Japanese set their characters down, one below the other. In some countries it is the custom to suspend the letters from the horizontal line rather than to set them *on* the horizontal line. If after such a shared experience a child sets the letter of his name down in a right to left sequence, the teacher can point out the fact that she *can* with some difficulty read the name but that it would be much easier to read if he would proceed from left to right as is the custom in writing the English language. Let's not forget that the concept of left to right is not yet well established in the five-year-old's mind!

Letters Seen and Used

It is sometimes suggested that first-grade teachers would prefer that children do no printing before entering the first grade. Such a preference is based on a concern for techniques. There was a time when kindergarten and first-grade teachers were so concerned with techniques of writing that the kindergarten handbook contained a sample of manuscript writing and parents were encouraged to teach the child the proper manuscript technique to be used in printing his name. Now we are asking why this great concern for technique? Children will see and in time need to become acquainted with capitals, lower case and even script letters. But they will not come upon these in any logical sequence. They will come across all three letter forms, as you and I do, in everyday living. As I type this material, I find that the keys on my machine are marked with capital letters and most of the letters appear on the paper as lower-case symbols. At my elbow there is an issue of the *Saturday Review* which carries the title in script; a calendar on my desk uses all three forms of print on a single 4" x 5" area.

The young child will probably select for his use (a) the style of letter which is the largest and therefore the easiest for him to see and (b) the style of letter which is the simplest in design and therefore the easiest for him to make, i.e., the capital letter. The teacher, in developing ideas with the children and in recording these ideas, will use capital and lower-case letters as the situation demands. She will make a real effort to use in her manuscript writing those techniques to which the children will be introduced in first grade. She may even comment aloud on the things she must keep in mind in forming the letters.

Writing Not Drilled

Writing as a drilled skill has no place in the kindergarten, but there will be many opportunities for the children to
- develop muscle and eye-hand coordination
- appreciate the left to right sequence in setting down letters and words
- appreciate the fact that in writing our language the letters are placed on a horizontal base line
- be alerted to the fact that there are several kinds of letter symbols which may be used in writing
- see how manuscript letters are formed.

By way of experience-living situations, there will be many opportunities for the children to experiment with and further pursue their interest in "writing."

Hoppity — Skippity — Serendipity

BY MAUREE APPLEGATE

Mauree Applegate is supervisor of practice, Elementary Division, Wisconsin State College, La Crosse.

Horace Walpole started it—that word "serendipity." He wrote a short story about the princes of Serendip who, on their quest toward one type of goal, found so many unexpected pleasures along the way—little bonuses that turned out to be of greater importance than the goals they were seeking.

"Serendipity" is a lilting, dancing word, not shod in clumsy shoes as is "concomitant," the usual educator's word for the attendant rewards of any learning project. Concomitants of children's creative writing are indeed serendipities, since they are of far more importance than the end product—the writing itself.

The modern viewpoint toward imaginative writing in the classroom is: What does this writing do for this child? What growth does it register concerning him? What does it tell us about the kind of self he is, that we may learn to live with him and he with himself in growing comfort and peace?

Certainly the product a child creates is important—but only as it relates to the development of the child and can communicate to us concerning the state of his inner being, serving at the same time as a satisfaction to him.

A child's creative writing builds a bridge from his inner self to a teacher's heart and mind—a fragile, swinging bridge, easily destroyed by heavy steps.

My weekly radio program over The Wisconsin School of the Air, for grades four to eight, gives me an opportunity to become familiar with the writings of hundreds of children (50,000 children listen). The teachers are often kind enough to write a bit of a note on the side of the paper about the child who did the writing. One week last spring, from a program entitled, "If Dreams Were for Sale, What Would You Buy?" I received this poem from fourth-grade Patrick. The teacher's note explained that the lad was misshapen and short and very, very overweight and clumsy. She said he had a well-balanced personality, withal, and she never dreamed, until he wrote this verse, that he resented his bodily handicaps.

If Dreams Were for Sale

If I got a wish along the line,
I'd wish I wasn't a frankenstein
I'd wish I was short, but not too short,
I'd wish I was good at any sport.
If I had another wish,
I'd like to be a real cute dish.

The teacher reported that she was trying to build up the boy's status at school through his creative writing and extra assignments at which he could excel.

No cry from one human heart to another has ever affected me as this communication from sixth-grade Betty. The child's whole biography of heartbreak is written large here for all to read. It came from a broadcast, "Courage Has a Million Faces."

It Takes Courage

It was my birthday. I had invited everybody. It is first now that I realize what happened.

All of a sudden I was in the world I had always wanted. I was what you might say popular. Everybody who was invited to my party was my friend. I remember it so clearly, even though it has been three years now. The night of the party was excellent to every extreem.

After the party I started to loose all my friends, until I was back to the old routine; That wasn't all.

All my life I had been rather clumsy. I gradually grew worse until my muscles couldn't pull me up the stairs. Then the worst of it came. I was broken the news that I had muscular distrophy.

Every day I have to do exercises to help strengthen my muscles. The exercises seem so easy that even a baby could do them.

What can a teacher do to build status for this child? If nothing more she can show her a dozen times a day that she cares about her. As she passes her desk she can let gentle fingers brush her sleeve; she can often give her a secret understanding smile; she can make her feel important in many little ways. I know one teacher who placed a tiny occasional inexpensive gift in an unpopular child's desk, marked in "cut-out and pasted" newspaper words, "from a secret friend." The child thrived under the therapy. Betty doesn't need pity; she needs friends.

The personal writing of a sensitive child sends an SOS to the teacher, not for probing, not for exploring, but for friendly understanding and thoughtful therapy. And yet, a teacher must not feel that he has the whole story from one single clue on a child's paper. Each contact with the child adds still another clue to the mosaic of his personality.

Not only is the need for status communicated to a teacher through creative writing, but the beginning of mental illness usually shows itself in a child's paper—witness fourth-grade Jean's.

My Toys

I did not like my doll so I wanted to brack her head off. I would of nocked out her eyes, nose, and mounth but I could not. I liked my little doll better so I made a doll house for my little doll. Dolls are bad. Dolls are sad. Dolls are good.
The End

If professional help is not available to Jean, she can often be induced to draw, write out her fierce feelings, play them out in creative play or dramatics or with hand puppets. It seems evident that Jean is transferring her feelings about people to dolls. Maybe her home is more frustrating than she can bear, so she must be given many chances for success at school. I'm sure this teacher must have visited the home after this paper. I don't believe she could possibly *not* have done so.

Children who can learn to explode on paper often are able to keep from screaming at home or at school. On the "Let's Write" program we try to provide the children with one pop-off program each year. The therapy provided thus, say the teachers, has a healing effect. For when our inner hates and fears are subjected to the sun and air of another's reading, they lose their musty odor of morbidity.

Fifth-grade Paul, a "Let's Writer," too, was far more able to treat his sister with respect after this unbrotherly but perfectly normal outburst:

My Sister

My Sister doesn't care if she gets to school ten hours late. She never hurries. She goes as slow as she can. She knows about as much as a mouse. She's what I call a mad sister. Always mad! I would like to give her one so hard she would fly to the moon and never come back.

Never be worried, teacher, about such unbrotherly attacks flattened out on paper. Just be honest with yourself and remember how often you have felt the same about a relative, a fellow teacher, or even about your life mate. Writing out one's feelings is good therapy for adults as well as for children—providing, of course, one destroys the evidence.

Fourth-grade Edward dared not tell his dad his true feelings, but one can easily feel vicariously his release after writing this paragraph!

Me and My Bank

My dad always keeps taking my money. One day I saw him taking some of it. About a week later, I found a mouse trap in the house. Then he put his hand in my bank and got his finger caught in it. Boy and did I get it from him. I could not seat down for 1 or 2 hours that day.

What needs does this story by sixth-grade Terry wig-wag to his teacher?

In Africa

One day I decided to go to Africa and hunt lions. I got there on Monday, November 15, 1948. I went hunting the next day. I was 20 feet from some bushes when a lion charged me, but I wasn't scared. I aimed my gun and shot it in the eyes. An hour later I had six lions, two tigers and one bullet left. What was I going to do? All of sudden two lions charged me, I shot one and then I was out of bullets. I dropped my gun and started to wrestle with it. As the rounds went on I got tired but I was going to stick it out. Gong! The tenth round is ready to start. I picked up a stick and put it in his mouth so he couldn't bite me but he bit my stick in two. I was scared. I started chewing my fingers until they were sharp. Then I dug my hand into him and killed him. I was the champ.

I went home and never went lion hunting again.

Only the meek and the fearful are so desperately brave as to write in this way. Could it not be that an exclusive diet of comic books and horror programs (on television in Jerry's case) needs supplementing with some almost-good books? Be careful, however, teacher, not to change reading diets too fast or too completely lest personality upsets develop.

Creative writing alerts sensitive teachers to other needs of children than friends, understanding and therapy. The need of a child's mind for standing on tiptoe, for being stretched to its utmost, is often communicated through his imaginative writing.

What does eighth-grade Jon's "Just How Does a Wheel Feel?" suggest to a teacher about the need to personalize her teaching of geography and history so that a child feels that he has actually been there? How else can we ready hearts and minds for the gradually coming One World?

Just How Does a Wheel Feel?

I've often wondered just how it would feel to be a wheel zooming down the street supporting a car, a bus or a bike. The wear and tear those poor things take, all the glass and things that lay in the streets these days! I'll bet it really hurts when they get a blowout. I never hear a word but I know I wouldn't like a nail jabbed into me.

They see many things though and travel many places. And they see things from a different view, but I suppose things look pretty mixed up when they're spinning around so fast.

Another thing I wonder about is when I walk by the junkyard and see all those hundreds of tires piled up all over the place. I suppose to them it's a big celebration, a get-together of all the old tires. They probably tell about all the places they've been and all the things they've seen. And I suppose just like humans some of them make their stories just a little exaggerated.

But I don't suppose I'll ever find out these things unless I become a wheel myself.

What need must sixth-grade Neil's teacher provide for the children in her room who long for enriched vocabulary and the taste of ripe words on the tongue?

My Garden

My garden is so gorgeous
With its sun-bloomed roses
Its rain-drenched daffodils,
The hail-hammered violets
Have almost lost their purpleness.
My flowers are like gems to me
My sister thinks they are
    the epitomy(e).

And the Jennifers in her room who so need music and the other arts for their soul's hunger . . . What of the Jennifers, Teacher?

I think I'm playing the music, and in some music I think I'm dancing to it. I feel it in my heart. The swaying of the music. It feels so touching, that I like to play music all the time. I wish every one loved music as I do. I love to dance to music. When I'm alone I make my own music. I love the way the notes go from one to the other. I love to play my records over and over. I sing and dance to the music.

And the Carols in a fifth-grade room who need to touch, see, smell and feel in order to appreciate. What of the Carols, Teacher?

These I Love To Touch

I love the feeling of mother's furs
Of hands that's full of money,
I love the feeling that you get
When sticking clean fingers in honey.

I love the feeling of a nice, warm bath
Clean bedclothes on my bed,
I love the feeling that you get
With "shampooey" hair on my head.

I love to touch new dresses
Especially "netty" ones.
I love to touch the letter for me
Whenever the postman comes.

I love the feeling of soft, clean hair
I love the feeling of flowers
I also love the feeling of books
And to browse around for hours.

I love the feeling of a nice, cool lake
Most always on a "tropical" day,
I love the feeling that I get
When I go to the beach to play.

I love the feeling of lots of shells
And wiggling toes in the sand,
I love the feeling of shopping around
And taking my sister to a band.

All of these I love to touch
And many, many more
There are so many things people love to touch
Ever so many galore!

And the Roberts who are already thinking of their future roads. . . . Do you take plenty of time with them for fine literature, Teacher, or are you spending all your time on what businessmen call the essentials?

There is a little of the Robert in every child. What of the Roberts?

> **Roadways**
> I don't know where my road leads to
> It's an undiscovered trail
> And can only be blazed by myself
> But as I grow older
> I hope to blaze it wide and clean of brush.

Ah, truly, to travel is better than to arrive, as Robert Louis Stevenson pointed out so long ago. At least this is true in the field of children's creative writing. What the children say between the lines is so much more important than the lines themselves.

If we teachers just had more time to listen to those "quiet ditties of no tune". . . But a teacher's days go by . . . Hoppity, Skippity . . . Serendipity . . . But then, so do everybody's.

—Self-Selection Helps

Here's to Success in Reading
COMPILED BY MARIAN JENKINS

> This material was prepared by Helen Brandley, formerly assistant principal, Ranchito School District, Pico; Marian Jenkins, consultant in elementary education, County of Los Angeles Schools; Antoinette McChristy, consultant, Whittier Elementary School District; and Dorothy Soeberg, formerly director of curriculum, Little Lake School District, Santa Fe Springs. The following people (from California schools) contributed generously of their ideas, abilities, and skills:
>
> Little Lake School District, Santa Fe Springs: Dorothy Anderson, Mabel Annabell, Eve Billings, Millie Chichester, Opal Johnson, Marguerite Lewis, Barbara Ott, Marguerite Selvig, Ilah Wilstach.
>
> Los Nietos School District: Mildred McMurray.
>
> Ranchito School District, Pico: Mimi Eshelman, James Harper, Betty Johnson, Margaret Klug, Christina McDonald, Rita Pennington, Bud Richards.
>
> Rosemead School District: Marguerite Swafford.
>
> Whittier Elementary School District: Neal Avery, Jean Bachelder, Robert Barden, Barbara Bast, Thora Carlson, Jacqueline Chadwick, Lillian Culver, Grace Garrettson, Luella Lowell, Ruth Maguire, Ruth Mohler, Gladys Nohara, Melvin Packel, Allen Rice, Louella Risch, Beatrice Stepp, Agnes Tuttle, Irene Whitcomb, Arlene Young, Joyce Young.
>
> Los Angeles County Schools, Office of County Superintendent: Grace Adams.

Hear this from children: "This is a sissy story, may we read the story about the pirate next?" "No, I want to read about covered wagons." "Our group doesn't get as much reading time as the Green Book Group." "My mother says I should be in a higher reading group." (19)

Hear this from teachers: "My class is so large I can't help individual children much." "What can I do when one child is picked on?" asks a teacher about a slow learner in the second grade.

"The idea of 'groups' always disturbed me because I was never sure that every child was given optimum placement. There is a wide range of abilities even within the groups. Children . . . lose interest when stories become lessons. . . . Wandering attention, not 'keeping place,' ineffective oral reading are frequent. Attention under duress isn't attention at all. . . . Somehow children should be taught not only to read, but also to enjoy reading as well." (19)

IN OUR ROUNDS AS CONSULTANTS WE HEARD COMMENTS BY CHILDREN and teachers and observed children who are not making much progress. We were disturbed and sought help. Willard Olson's ideas of "self-selection" in learning intrigued us. (15, 16) In addition, we learned of a study in which a teacher endeavored "To Determine the Reaction of a Fourth Grade to a Program of Self-Selection of Reading Materials." (17) In talking with teachers about children selecting material for their reading, these insights regarding learning were revealed:

Children work hard and long when they choose their own jobs. They move ahead when they have opportunity to set their own goals. They read with greater enjoyment when they choose the material. In self-selection the teacher works with individuals and knows their interests and needs more adequately than when a group works on a single book chosen by the teacher.

Teachers Ask Questions

"If we did try self-selection," said these teachers, "where would we get enough books? How would we know where each child was in his reading?" "When would instruction in reading skills be given?" "What would parents think?" "I can see possibilities with the fast learners but what about the slow?" "Is it safe?" One teacher made suggestions to another, principals and consultants added ideas, and several indicated their desire to try out self-selection. They all felt it essential to understand purposes and possible outcomes, ways of beginning and organizing a class, ways of working with children in individualized reading, of keeping records, and of talking with parents.

We made it clear that there have always been teachers who devised means of individualizing instruction; but that Willard Olson has given the idea a strong new base as a result of his long years of research on child growth and development. Studies reveal "that children try to escape tasks that they perceive to be clearly beyond their ability and tend to persist in working upon those in which they hope to succeed." (14) Olson concludes that "a healthy child seeks from the environment those experiences which are consistent with his maturity and needs. . . . If the appropriate environment does not exist ready made or is inadequate in some major respects, the human being . . . works creatively for the conditions that advance his well-being." (15) This "seeking behavior" is the basis for self-selection. This principle is being applied successfully by parents in the self-regulating or self-demand schedule of meeting needs of infants for sleep, food, and elimination.

When then is the application to reading? "The self-selection principle as applied to . . . reading implies that a teacher will provide help and a suitable environment, but the child himself will be the judge of whether or not and at what time he should be consuming reading materials." (16) "When a teacher or parent has a high regard for seeking-behavior and self-selection the child grows into the reading experience." (15)

The Palmer study states: "Self-selection in reading is a method that gives the child an opportunity to respond to . . . reading in *his own way*. It does not force him into a difficult book before he is confident that he can handle it nor does it require him to read material too simple for his interest and ability." (17)

Just as a child takes from the environment what he is ready for and motivated inwardly to do, so these teachers took the idea of self-selection and used it in a variety of ways, with almost unlimited possibilities of adapting it to individual needs.

● A third-grade teacher first used this technique after Christmas with her "top" group. Two other groups continued "regular" reading and used self-selection as an independent activity. Another third-grade teacher who started in the same way, with one group during the first semester, had all children using self-selection by the second semester and continued it for the remainder of the year for the full reading program.

● In November a first-grade teacher used self-selection for a library period, and in the second semester used it with all the children as regular reading. Another teacher of first grade worked with experience charts for several months. When some of the children seemed ready for preprimers she urged each to choose the one he wished to read. Gradually all of the others chose their reading materials, while charts continued to be used at sharing time and during social studies.

● A fifth-grade teacher started with fifteen minutes at the opening and closing of the day for self-selection in reading. Soon children were selecting their materials for the full reading time, though these "fun reading" periods continued. A teacher said one day to her sixth grade, "It's time for reading groups, children, but today instead of our usual fifteen or twenty minutes around the table together, we'll spend the whole hour reading at our desks. Or you may read with a classmate or two if you wish. You may read anything or any book in the room."

"Really?" "May I read my science book?" "Do we have to give book reports?" "May I read a book I brought from home?" "May we plan a play together?" "Do I have to read?"

The teacher reports, "We took the next fifteen minutes to discuss this change in reading procedure. I told the children that I believed they would learn as much and enjoy their reading more . . . I assured them that I would give them any help they needed. I also told them that I would enjoy having them read to me . . . anytime they wished." (19)

● One group of youngsters who had had self-selection all year in the fifth grade, on going into sixth, badgered the teacher in a nice way until he sought information from his principal. On learning further of the plan he agreed to try it. In several seventh- and eighth-grade classes great enthusiasm was evident on the part of both teachers and students as they adapted the method to their needs.

We urged these teachers to approach this technique in ways that made them feel secure. As consultants we were available to teachers, so we could talk informally with them, encourage them, observe their classes at work, and listen to their enthusiastic responses as they related children's reactions. They showed their own feelings of relaxation and release of tension which came as children were more relaxed and less competitive. They reported changes in attitudes of slow readers when they could go ahead on their own, the spurts that fast readers made when freed from group reading in a single book, and the enjoyment that average youngsters showed in being able to set their own pace.

Organization within a class was a big question. If not "regular three-group" reading and if each child were on his own, how could the teacher manage? A variety of ways of approaching the problem was discovered. No prescriptions were laid down; we listened to teachers' ideas and urged them to try them.

Some teachers, in the middle and upper grades particularly, used all kinds of books and periodicals gathered from school, public and personal libraries. Books were selected for classroom use closely related to children's interests as observed by the teacher or as revealed in interest inventories, conferences and conversations with the children, and in general class discussion. Texts of all kinds furnished at school were easily obtained, and browsing books were also available. In some classrooms shelves were organized according to type—adventure, science, sports, history. Other teachers organized books according to reading level, while some wanting to find out as much as possible about children's choices distributed the books round the room in convenient spots for browsing but without classification.

Some teachers discussed self-selection with their classes ahead of time, its organization as they sensed it, and the responses expected of the children. Others started with the selecting of books and then developed details with the class as it went along. It appeared to the consultants that teachers accustomed to using children's ideas and developing plans with them used the latter method. Those who were more comfortable with plans well developed in advance found the former way more satisfying.

Plans shaped up in about this manner: children were given an agreed-upon amount of time to choose their first books, perhaps two days or a week of reading time. This meant that they could browse and decide in an unhurried way which book was really the one they wished to tackle.

Some children found great difficulty in making choices. They wandered, looked at pictures, tried several books and wandered some more. Teachers observed these children carefully and held off exerting any pressure or even making suggestions, in order to find out all they could about children's ways of approaching a new technique—one in which their own decision, not the teacher's, was the crux of the matter. Teachers felt free to move about among the youngsters and to engage them in informal conversation about titles and about their interests and feelings. This informal exchange gave support to the hesitating and the uneasy wavering ones and showed the teacher's trust and confidence in the ability of the children eventually to come to a decision. Once the choices were made, books read and further choices made, most of the children were equal to the occasion and looked forward to new choices.

Choosing One's Own Reading

Choosing one's own reading is the heart of self-selection. It is a strong motivating factor. Where reading has little drawing power, self-selection is a means of developing strong interest. To observe children's reactions to reading in a situation of relaxation and pleasure is a joy.

A pair in a corner are talking about their books, reading to each other and perhaps making plans for telling others about their choices; individuals are scattered about the room, in the patio or under a tree. Around the teacher has gathered a group whose individual needs are being cared for by a word pronounced, a meaning discussed, phonetic elements clarified, a question about the story answered and by being a willing listener to oral reading. The observer notes that a record of the help given each child is being jotted down in a notebook or on a card. A child may be making additions to the record of pages read or of his plans to share the material.

Children are encouraged to react to their reading in a variety of ways. Their ideas are often most creative. Here is a list that one sixth grade made:

> Write a brief summary on a 3 by 5 card
> Tell the story to the class
> Write a formal book report
> Read a story or excerpts to the class
> Discuss the story or book with the class
> Dramatize the story
> Make puppets to tell the story
> Make a shadow box
> Read the story to the lower grades
> Make a movie sequence to fit our "Lug Box Theater"
> Make a poem about the book
> Draw pictures illustrating the story
> Bring magazine or other commercial pictures to illustrate the story
> Bring phonograph recordings of story

Classes vary in agreements about reading the entire book or, as in the case of a reader or science book, perusing a single section related to individual interests or to finding answers to questions. Some teachers find that enthusiastic children, or those not too eager to read, spend too long on projects.

By discussion, agreements are reached on kinds of stories appropriate for dramatization, a puppet show or flannel board. Talking over a story and reading orally to the teacher are important ways of reacting, and one need not react before the whole class, or even a group, on everything read. Limitations on time to be spent on projects are set, as well as suggestions made that different ways of reacting be tried. The traditional oral and written reports are acceptable, though many other exciting ways are devised. Some teachers who started with formal reports eventually gave them up as boring to both teacher and pupils.

Teacher's Role Is Different

In self-selection, the teacher's role is somewhat different from the traditional one or at least the emphasis changes. Rather than being the one to determine who shall read together, what, when, and how they shall read and what questions they shall answer, the teacher becomes the encourager, the listener, the approver, the recorder, and the appreciator of the child's decision and plan. He may move round the class during the reading time sitting near individuals as they indicate their needs. Or he may move quiety to an individual to listen to him read aloud, to check on words, phrasing, comprehension, or whatever the record shows has been giving him trouble. The teacher and the child fill in the record, indicating when the book was begun and finished, problems in the skills, what has been done about each problem and when, and ways that the child has reacted to the materials.

Often groups come together to work. The reason for grouping varies with the needs, the requests for help and the desire just to talk about reading with friends. On such occasions those of different reading abilities can find many satisfactions in being together. Flexibility is the keynote here, with groups varying from day to day or staying together for a short period of time to work at a common problem.

Teachers find that children are ingenious in devising ways of helping each other. This is one of the most important outcomes. For instance, an able reader may undertake on his own to help one less able, who has a mutual interest in horses. A couple of plodding readers may go off in a corner to labor together over a science book which has answers to their questions about snakes. One enterprising group of girls reading *Little Women* brought dolls and dressed them as the main characters.

It has been a constant source of wonder to teachers, principals, consultants and parents to observe the self-initiated plans, the ingenuity of self-dependent children, and the great progress in reading made by the able and the less able. Even those with dual language, those with deprived home backgrounds, and some of those with emotional difficulties connected with failure in academic learning are finding some modicum of success in reading.

The amazing thing discovered is that as children increase their amount of reading, get pleasure and satisfaction from it, and receive some encouragement and praise from their peers and their teacher, the need for continuous help with some of the minutiae related to the skills is lessened. Children discover for themselves some of the rules that are customarily used for drill. This self-discovery appears to be more potent in producing permanent learning than the traditional teacher-directed study.

A second-grade teacher observed several children in their approach to words ending in "ed" and "ing." Her first thought was to get these children together and help them with the rule and practice such words. Her second thought was, "I'll watch this a bit longer." As she moved among these youngsters and talked with them, she began to realize they had found out independently that every time a word had "ed" on it, it was in the past tense. This led to a similar discovery about "ing." The excitement of this new learning led these children to notice endings on other words, to look at those which were like ones they knew, and to speculate and seek help on unknown ones.

As children grow into the need for more refined skills of comprehension, group work again can be very useful. *The important factor is that the group is gathered for a particular purpose which each member has in common with the others and it will stay together only for the time needed to accomplish its purpose.* Children in any one group may have varying degrees of reading ability and will still be reading books of their own choice.

Some teachers were concerned that in self-selection the informality of the organization and the amount of child initiative needed would be serious problems. They were fearful of "disciplinary" problems. Of course, any change in the routines of group organization and leadership needs time, thought and planning for full flowering. Naturally, some children responded more readily and wholeheartedly than others, but in most classes the children rose to the opportunities offered.

Going over the children's reading records, observing classes, hearing reports from principals and looking over test results all led us to the conclusion that this is a way of teaching and learning that brings enormous stimulation and satisfaction to most of those participating.

A fifth-grade teacher wrote, "Our experiment has proved to those of us who have used it, that comfortable working conditions, adequate individual help, and the realization that each child has a rhythm of his own in learning are more important tools than formal technique." (6)

Some Results

Note some sample test results from a combination class *many of whose members have dual language* and, according to group tests, are certainly among the less able:*

Name	Grade	IQ	Oct. Rdg. Test	June Rdg. Test	Books Read
Stella	5	93	6.0	8.5	13
Lillian	5	94	4.0	5.2	19
Vincent	5	97	4.0	5.0	26
Danny	5	90	3.8	4.5	10
David	5	90	3.8	5.0	22
Dianne	5	79	4.1	5.4	25
Alfred	6	90	4.5	6.0	29
Gilbert	6	90	3.8	5.4	21
Joe	6	85	3.2	4.5	14
Sandra	6	90	4.8	5.8	24
Becky	6	88	5.9	7.0	30
Mary Lou	6	80	3.3	4.1	14
Rose	6	72	3.6	4.8	20

- A school psychologist presents a summary of findings from a third grade using self-selection in reading from October 1954 to March 1955. "This class of 25 children with average IQ of 105 showed an average gain in reading age of seven months as measured by alternate forms of the California Achievement Test in reading. A larger gain—of 8 months—was shown in the average reading comprehension grade placement." **

- Test results show certain kinds of growth while children's verbal reactions show other aspects. Enjoy with us the comments of children as they evaluate self-selection. They said they enjoyed it. One teacher asked, "Why?"

"I can read faster to myself." "We can read anything we want." "We have so many and different good books."

These same children reported reasons why they did not like traditional reading groups.

"Too slow, we lost interest." "Kids lose the place and ruin the story." "We had to read stories whether we like them or not." "We had to leave in the middle of a story every time." "We didn't get to read enough, our turns were too short."

Responses of Parents

- A parent, who had been helping her son at home, ran across his problem with "th" words. In a conference with the teacher she was shown the record card on which the child and the teacher had noted his need to study "th' words and the plans being used to help him. The parent was gratified to see this evidence of individual consideration and help.

- Many parents report their children are asking to be taken or to be allowed to go on their own to the public library. One mother beamed as she said she *had* to take the children to the library now as part of regular trips to the market.

- A parent, who had observed in one class where there was "regular" reading and another where self-selection was under way, remarked on the noticeable difference in attitude. Children using self-selection were more

---

* Los Nietos School District.
** Little Lake School District.

enthusiastic about reading and found it difficult to stop reading, while in the other class when reading time was over, the groups just put books down and went to the next job in a matter of fact way.

Numerous reports indicate new interests in reading, the increased desire to use reference books, the able handling of dictionaries and encyclopedias, and the reading of daily papers and weekly news periodicals. Others parents are overjoyed to find their children getting along better in other subjects and liking school better.

We Move Ahead

From the small group of teachers who first tried self-selection a year or two ago the news has spread in a steady manner. Each month there are others starting on this venture in learning. Teachers who have not tried it, but who have received classes grounded in self-selection, have commented on the children's enthusiasm for reading, their command of the skills, and their ability to plan for their own learning.

As principals and consultants worked with teachers we tried to demonstrate a way of operating that encourages and supports teachers in being flexible and in capitalizing on their ingenuity and imagination in working with their colleagues and with children.

There are many other angles which might be discussed. However, the bibliographical materials will help those who wish to try self-selection. For those who have undertaken it, the materials listed may serve to reassure them and be suggestive of refinements and additional ideas. Palmer's summary indicates several important findings about self-selection in reading:

> Children tended to read something that was difficult and then something that was less difficult, thus establishing a kind of rhythm of effort and relaxation that is impossible to achieve under a three-group system in which the children are immediately presented with a more difficult reader upon completion of the book they were reading. (17)

A report from Marie M. Hughes, former principal of the William Stewart School, University of Utah, states clearly that:

> 1. Children choose to read in a rhythm of easy, hard, easy, hard, quite contrary to the way we take them from one book to the next harder. 2. Children *do read*. 3. The child most sensitive about his reading ability finds ways to protect himself while trying to learn. 4. Children want to grow in reading. If watched carefully you can discover how each one is making that effort.

The teachers who contributed to this article corroborate these findings and indicate that many children are gaining increased satisfaction, not only in reading but in expressing their ideas in writing. Improved sentence structure, more variety in choice of words, longer attention span and energy output are among the outcomes noted. In some classes self-selection in spelling and in mathematics also is being developed.

Many teachers say they feel more relaxed and secure in using a number of teaching techniques new to them.

In addition to the advantages of self-selection to children, teachers are free to be more creative in supporting and guiding the child when he carries his own load of learning in such an active manner. As one teacher said, "The visible progress and interest of each child is exceedingly heartwarming." (6)

Bibliography

1. Bortner, Doyle M. "Pupil Motivation and Its Relationship to the Activity and Social Drives." *Progressive Education,* Vol. 31, No. 1, Oct. 1953. Pp. 5-11.
2. Burrows, Alvina Treut. *Teaching Children in the Middle Grades.* Boston: D. C. Heath, 1952. Chap. 9, "Fostering the Language Arts."
3. Durrell, Donald. *Improvement of Basic Reading Abilities.* Yonkers-on Hudson: World Book Co., 1940. Chap. 4, "Classroom Provision for Individual Differences."
4. Evans, N. Dean. "An Individualized Reading Program for the Elementary School," *Elementary School Journal,* Vol. LIV, No. 3, Nov. 1953, Pp. 157-162.
5. Gans, Roma; Stendler, Celia B.; and Almy, Millie. *Teaching Young Children.* Yonkers-on-Hudson: World Book Co., 1952. Chap. 7, "The Child as a Reader."
6. Garrettson, Grace. "How One School Read the Needs of the Slow Learner." *Claremont Reading Conference,* 19th Yearbook, Calif., Claremont College Reading Laboratory, 1954.
7. Guilfoile, Elizabeth. "Developing the Reading Interests of Children," *Elementary English,* Vol. XX, No. 7, Nov. 1943. Pp. 279-286.
8. Harding, Lowry W. "How Well Are Schools Now Teaching the Basic Skills?" *Progressive Education,* Vol. 29, No. 1, Oct. 1951. Pp. 7-14; 32.
9. Hymes, James L. Jr. *Three to Six: Your Child Starts to School.* Public Affairs Pamphlet #163 (22 E. 38th St., N. Y., 1950). "Learning To Read." Pp. 20-28.
10. Kaar, Harold. "An Experiment with an Individualized Method of Teaching Reading." *The Reading Teacher,* Vol. 7, No. 3, Feb. 1954. Pp. 174-177.
11. Maib, Frances. "Individualized Reading." *Elementary English,* XXIX, Feb. 1952. Pp. 84-98.
12. Mooney, Ross L. "Creation, Parents and Children," *Progressive Education,* Vol. 31, No. 1, Oct. 1953. Pp. 14-17; 25.
13. National Council of Teachers of English. *Language Arts for Today's Children.* The Commission on the English Curriculum, N. Y.: Appleton, 1954. Chap. 6, "Reading."
14. Olson, Willard C. *Child Development.* Boston: D. C. Heath, 1949. Chap. XII, "Concepts of Child Development in Curriculum and Methods."
15. ———. "Seeking, Self-Selection, and Pacing in the Use of Books by Children," *The Packet,* Vol. 7, No. 1, Spring 1952. Boston: D. C. Heath. Pp. 3-10.
16. ———. "Self-Selection as a Principle of Curriculum and Method," *School of Education Bulletin,* Vol. 16, No. 4, Jan. 1945, Ann Arbor, Univ. of Michigan. Pp. 52-55.
17. Palmer, Delores Cooper. *To Determine the Reaction of a Fourth Grade to a Program of Self-Selection of Reading Materials.* Unpublished master's thesis, Salt Lake City, Univ. of Utah, 1953. Director of Research, Marie M. Hughes. Chap. VI, "Theoretical Considerations Underlying a Program of Self-Selection in Reading with Recommendations."
18. Reid, Chandos. "What Are the Skills for Modern Living?" *Progressive Education,* Vol. 29, No. 1, Oct. 1951. Pp. 1-6.
19. Swafford, Marguerite. "A Project in Individualized Reading on the Sixth Grade Level." Unpublished term paper presented at Los Angeles State College, Spring 1955.
20. *Teaching Reading in the Elementary School.* By the staff of the Maury School, Richmond, Va.: Interstate Printers and Publishers, Danville, Ill., 1941.
21. Veatch, Jeanette. "Individualized Reading—for Success in the Classroom," *The Educational Trend,* #654, Arthur C. Croft Publications (100 Garfield Ave., New London, Conn.), 1954.

Children and the Arts

BY EDWARD L. MATTIL

Edward L. Mattil is head of the Department of Art Education, The Pennsylvania State University, University Park, and president of the National Art Education Association.

WHEN I STARTED MY DAILY WALK WITH MY DOGS THIS MORNING, my little neighbor Barbara was waiting to join me, as she regularly does. Barbara has just started nursery school and, of course, has a tremendous amount of information to share with me. Since these walks started a few months ago, I have had an unusual opportunity to engage in a kind of self-renewal that most adults need—especially teaching adults. Oh, like most teachers, I renew myself regularly through the usual means: reading, attending lectures, going to professional meetings. However, I have suddenly come to an understanding of another need—that of reviewing and reflecting on those things we hold as our truths.

Barbara has been a great help, for I am privileged to join her in the marvels of life and the discoveries that only a young child can make. She is four years old and like most four-year-olds sees and listens to everything; she touches, smells and tastes with delight. She asks endless questions as she thinks about what she has perceived and oftentimes has personal feelings about things which she is able to express in a straightforward and uncomplicated way. She may tell me about it with a simple gesture or act it out in great detail. If time permits, she may draw me a picture with her crayons to record her whole idea in tangible form.

World of Reality

Occasionally we have to walk over Sharon's complex drawings made in soft-colored chalks on the sidewalk. It is an interesting world that Sharon portrays and shares so generously with all who pass. Sophisticated adults who wear it away as they walk over it may consider it fantasy. I think it is Sharon's *world of reality*. But fantasy, reality—what does it matter as long as we recognize it as Sharon's world? As I look at these rich chalk drawings, I get strange feelings. All sorts of things come to mind. She must have a tolerant mother to allow the entire sidewalk to be covered with colored chalk. It could get tracked into the house! No, not tolerant—wise. She values one of Sharon's most basic urges, the need to create. She provides her some of the conditions to help her reach her full creative potential. If a child is ever to reach his full creative potential, I ask myself, are the same conditions necessary in the home as in the school? What are those conditions?

Conditions for Expression

First, there must be an environment with opportunity to use materials and tools, a place to work, and encouragement which stimulates the child to try out his potential, which means that at home (as in school) we arrange a work space where a dab of paint or some spilled water does not bring about a crisis. It means an enhancing environment not built on prevention.

Cathy, don't spill the paint!
Don't get any on your clothes!
Don't waste good paper on scribbles! (Wait, I suppose, until you are able to draw before drawing.)
Don't move around! Don't do this, don't do that, don't, don't!

Under such conditions, how long does it take a child to decide that it is safer (and less annoying) to do nothing? This would eliminate the risk of failure or negative criticism. Like a frightened turtle, he pulls himself inside his protective shell, unwilling to emerge to use his many senses to perceive the world around him—the very "stuff" that growth is made of. There he continues to stay until the sensitive teacher draws him out by means of irresistible experiences—the kind he can reach with his own means and absorb. The teacher knows he can't force open the shell and pour it full of ideas or knowledge; the child has to get it for himself.

Potentiality

Every child needs the opportunity to explore his abilities through a wide variety of experiences. He must try these new-found abilities over and over until he becomes the master of them. This means regular time periods for creative activities and a long-term program of activities. For example, no child could be expected to reach his full potential as a musician if his ability were not identified early and if he were not given the opportunity to use this ability regularly during his growing years. This is also true with other creative abilities. Schools should try to identify special abilities early and to provide sustained programs which insure that abilities will develop fully. Every child needs interested parents (or substitute parents) and a skilled, mature teacher for reinforcement and guidance. Watching a child work reveals how much he will do through his own spontaneous exploration and how often materials or personal motivation will cause him to accomplish large amounts of work without adult supervision. But if a child is left only to his own resources, his spontaneous trials and exploration will carry him just so far—often just far enough to develop stereotyped concepts which are difficult to shed. At this point, there is the need for a skilled adult to supply information, to guide, to suggest, and to provide various kinds of stimulation which incite the child with interest and which assist him to higher levels of achievement, richer concepts and more efficient performance.

Developmental Stages

In examining Sharon's drawing carefully, it is easy to see the vast difference between her work and Barbara's. Sharon, the older, has a well-developed schema—a personal system of symbols for almost everything she draws. Barbara is in the later stages of scribbling where some forms are becoming clear and everything that she draws is named or identified. It is amazing how each child begins to develop a highly personal style even at an early age.

Most of the books and articles on art education which deal with developmental stages have appeared in the past two decades.* Lowenfeld gave us the deepest look into this phenomenon. Others before him had beginnings of ideas, and others since have suggested modifications. Some have renamed the stages. *Schematic, symbolic, scribbling, manipulative*—it makes little difference which school of thought teachers use as long as they recognize differences and realize the importance of something happening at every level of development. Knowing about these stages is not enough; good conditions must be provided at every stage of development. It is erroneous to assume that growth is automatic and takes place in spite of what we provide for growth to feed on. If scribbling is a kindergarten phenomenon then preschematic (or presymbolic, depending upon the school of thought) will follow, and that will be closely followed by schematic (or symbolic). Each stage is arrived at with weak or strong concepts, depending upon how fully the conditions of potentiality are met. And as each stage builds upon the preceding one, the weak tend to become weaker and the strong, stronger.

Some scholars have suggested that art experiences are not cumulative and that it is unnecessary to consider activities that are sequential. I cannot accept either of these theories.

Some months ago, a friend who has been working in the Orient for many years showed me a remarkable collection of prints made mostly from woodblocks by Japanese and Korean children. I marveled at the technical quality and the completeness of expression of these art works, in a medium generally considered advanced for young children. The quality of the prints was high enough to have received praise even in a college graphics class. I wondered—are the children of the East more creative than our children? I looked again. No, I concluded, they are expressing themselves as our children do; but their

---

* *Editor's Note:* Those of us who were fortunate in having outstanding art supervisors (kindergarten through eight grades) were cognizant of developmental stages in children's art in the late twenties and early thirties.

statements are more skillful and more complete. Superior results suggest that they have mastered their tools and have learned to work for extended periods of time to achieve their desires. I asked my friend at what age children begin with these tools and how often they use them. They begin, he told me, when very young and use the sharp gouge as frequently as our children use paints and brush. The child works with gouge and woodblocks so often that he has ample opportunity to explore its many possibilities. Furthermore, its use is so natural that the tool becomes an extension of his hand and thinking. When he reaches that point, the medium is no longer the object of his experiments and explorations; it no longer stands in the way of his ideas. There are few technical problems to block his way. The tools become his means of expression rather than ends in themselves.

I recalled how I, like thousands before and after me, learned to make linoleum prints.

It was nearly Christmas and time was of the essence. We were to hurry, to listen carefully. "Don't make any mistakes." "Please be careful not to cut yourself or the desk." "Don't make any miscuts as there are no more lino blocks." "Reverse your lettering." "Bandages are on the desk." "Make a wreath or a candle or something!"

All that effort for a one-time activity which, if we did survive it without calamity, didn't give us a chance to say Merry Christmas in a child's way! It was a process that became all mechanics and no expression.

Several years later, when another brave soul pulled out the lino equipment just before Christmas, all the children moaned in unison, "Oh, not again, we did them in fifth grade!"

What is the point in relating all this? We are expected to provide all kinds of experiences with the widest variety of materials so that children can explore, experiment and discover for themselves, hoping that each child will find the materials and the means for a personal way of expression. Inherent in this broad assault on experimentation and self-discovery is the possibility that children may become so accustomed to something new and different with every lesson that they begin to believe it undesirable to repeat experiences over and over to gain mastery of a material or a process.

Dynamic Teaching

The new-material-new-process-every-day approach has a monotonous rhythm: everything new, everything novel, everything fast, everything shallow, everything acceptable. *Dynamic art teaching does not reveal with any certainty its next direction.* Rather, it sets up a rhythm that is seldom monotonous; it moves fast, then slow; it is broad, then deep; it is calm and orderly, then suddenly exciting; it takes long looks into the past, then projects into the future; it expects exploration but requires perseverance; it expects mistakes but encourages efficient performance; it values creative ideas of children and allows them to be used; it recognizes differences in children but makes no effort to establish conformity. What I have said may sound like heresy to some teachers who have entered the materials exploration race with a passion. These suggestions do not imply any major changes in art education programs; rather, they call only for a greater balance of approaches. When we allow children the joy of a freewheeling finger-painting experience on one day, we must be prepared to go into depth with drawing or painting the next lesson. Only if we select one or two mediums to work with in depth can we expect children to develop the necessary skills and personal techniques that will satisfy their critical awareness as they get older. Only if we allow children to work with one or two mediums in depth can we prevent their abandonment of creative work because it looks too unskilled and immature.

An art lesson is a learning experience for the teacher and the child. Experiences are needed to provide feelings. It is *not* "draw what you want to draw today, children," or "draw what you feel inside" when there have been no experiences provided to make anyone feel anything. *The teacher sows the seeds of interest.* If there are only animals to paint or people to draw, where does the thinking begin? What can the teacher anticipate from a group this age? Can he expect a little more? What will loosen them up, keep them open and flexible? Keep them unafraid and willing to take some risks? What can the teacher find that he can show or talk about that might enrich their present concepts? What deep experiences have the children had to call upon? What will the teacher talk about that will activate their passive knowledge? How can he excite the children's curiosity and stir their imaginations and fantasies? Should the teacher stress some skill or demonstrate a process? Can the teacher relate what the class is doing to our cultural heritage? What art history relates to this topic? Can the teacher offer some new art vocabulary? How do children this age perceive? What might increase their esthetic sensitivity? How does the teacher let children know that he values creative thinking? Can creative thinking be developed? How can children value criticism and weigh the ideas of others? How long should they persevere? Can the teacher extend their span of interest? What will the teacher do to stir renewed interest when it seems to be on the wane?

If a lesson's planning session begins with a multitude of thoughts whirling around in your brain, you have captured the essence of imaginative teaching. Such thinking makes teachers uncomfortable, but being uncomfortable should be comforting, for this is a sure sign that the truth is not in the palm of the hand. It is still being sought. H. L. Mencken put his finger on it when he said, "It is the dull man who is always sure, and the sure man who is always dull."

Hurrying To Rest

BY HELEN E. BUCKLEY

> *A kindergarten teacher asked: "What was all this hurrying? Wasn't it enough that as adults we rush through life, without making children into frenzied copies of ourselves? . . . What was more important . . . to rush through our painting, building, singing, juice-time, rest, story and outdoor play, or to slow down . . . enjoy and savor what we are doing? Helen E Buckley is coordinator of early childhood education, State University, Teachers College, Oswego, New York.*

Juice time was over in the kindergarten. The five-year-olds moved about, throwing away paper cups, sponging off tables, pushing in chairs, putting away leftover crackers and getting out rugs and blankets for rest. We had had our usual busy morning of painting, building, drawing, singing, rhythms and talking together. Now at 10:40 a.m.—already ten minutes behind schedule—we were getting ready for our rest.

"Hurry up," I heard myself saying as I crossed the room to lower the shades: "Hurry with your rugs and blankets so we can have our rest." Hurrying to rest! Suddenly it occurred to me that fifteen minutes before I had stood in that very spot saying, "Hurry up now and get your hands washed for juice-time." I knew that at the close of *this* period I would be saying, "Let's hurry and put our blankets away so we can have our story."

What *was* all this hurrying? Wasn't it enough that as adults we rush through life, without making children into frenzied copies of ourselves?

I switched off the lights and settled myself on a low hassock among the sprawling arms and legs of twenty-five children. I wondered. How much longer would it have taken them to get settled down if I had not hurried them? Did I really believe that children had to be hurried in order to get them to do anything? Or was *I* feeling pressure of too many things to do in too short a time? What would happen if we did not do *everything* every day?

Savor What We Are Doing

Many times the children had asked for two stories or even three in addition to the usual one. Always my answer seemed to be, "There just isn't time—tomorrow maybe." But tomorrow would always be as hurried as today—a day broken up into small pieces of activities. Now what was more important, I asked myself—to rush through our painting, building, singing, juice-time, rest, story and outdoor play, or to slow down and give ourselves time to enjoy and savor what we are doing even if it meant leaving some things out some days? Somehow this "hurrying to rest" did not seem the wisest way to encourage relaxation. Perhaps just slowing down itself would accomplish as much! As I got up to turn on the lights, I decided what I would do.

The next morning, as the juice committee was busily setting the tables and pouring the juice, I said to some of the children who had just come from washing their hands: "The juice committee is not quite ready for us—suppose we go over to the library table and find a good book to read?"

"Could we listen to my new record now?" someone asked.

"Yes," I said, settling myself in a rocker already occupied by two dolls. "All the listeners could go over to the recorder with you, and the readers could stay here with me. The juice committee will let us know when they are ready."

Slowing-Down Campaign

So there we were, launched on a slowing-down campaign, although no one seemed aware of it but I! The committee was left free to work, and the rest of us settled down to catch our breath after a rather strenuous work period. It was not surprising, of course, that the juice committee became somewhat distracted by the new record and wandered over with cups, napkins or crackers in hand to listen more closely. But no one hurried them, and they managed to get their job finished and hear the record too.

When we finally sat down at the table, I noted with a rather grim satisfaction that we were twenty minutes behind schedule. "Good!" I thought and said to the children: "Let's not hurry with our juice today—we had such a relaxed time over our books and records that I do not think we need to take out our rugs and blankets today. We'll just take our time and eat and drink slowly." And so we did. I found myself growing quiet inside, even to the extent of not minding in the least when someone spilled his juice. For who was in such a hurry that he would not have time to sponge it up and pour himself some more?

Once started, I found many ways to lengthen our day so that we would not feel the pressure of time. We did not "leave out" our rest time every day—many a morning found us collapsing quite happily on the floor of our darkened room. On such days we may have shortened our work time, taken our juice "cafeteria style" or forgone our group singing time.

Apropos of the latter, I learned that the day was not necessarily lost if we did not sit down around the piano for singing and rhythms. I found that some of our most valuable music experiences arose by letting them flow naturally into the work period.

Geared to Children—Not Clock

When I was geared more to the clock than to the children, I would say to the child who wanted me to listen to his song or to the group who asked for a record for dancing: "Let's wait until music time for that—this is work time." (*Now* I know that children do not label their activities—they do not box themselves up into tight little schedules.) I began to bring out scarves, records and instruments along with paints, brushes and crayons. In fact, just four of us might go through an entire songbook, crowded cosily on the piano bench with painting and building going on all around us; or some beautifully dressed ladies from the playhouse might take their dolls walking to a favorite lilting record; or someone's new song might be set to music after a small conference at the piano. When there was no need to stop for music, then we would have time for all these things.

But there were mornings when we gave paints and blocks a rest to have a longer time for group songs, rhythms and dramatization. And we got over having guilt feelings because we "didn't do thus and so this morning."

Occasionally I would sit down with myself to evaluate this change in our program. There was little doubt that we were less hurried and that we enjoyed our work and play more. But what about our schedule? I had learned that little children especially needed an organized framework within which to work. They needed to know "what was coming next." Were these days too upset for them—too flexible? Were they having to look constantly to me for direction? My immediate answer to these questions was, "No." True, our schedule was flexible—no two days were exactly alike—but the framework, the organization remained. The difference lay in the fact that some of the cross-pieces of the framework had been removed—the pieces which had been boxing us in, hurrying us. Now we seemed to be taking our cues from our interests and feelings rather than from the clock.

Planning Decreases Hurry

There are those who say that we gain security from a routine way of doing things, and I believe this to be true. Yet all of us have seen adults—and children too—for whom the routine itself seems to become more important than the people following it. This had been happening to us, I believe—or to me. When this occurs, insecurity rather than security seems to be fostered.

We learned to plan each day in the morning. From time to time through the day we did more planning so that we *would* know what was coming next. In this way, we seemed to spend each day for itself—neither pulling it out of yesterday nor pushing it into tomorrow. We had ceased to hurry, and it was good!

Section V

Inspirations from the Past

Inspirations from the Past

IN OUR FAST-CHANGING CULTURE THE ENVIRONMENT OF EACH GENeration is so different from that of all other generations that education has not been able to keep up with social progress.

The thinking of Rousseau, Pestalozzi and Froebel brought the use of "the senses" and "freedom to investigate" into a school dominated by memorization procedures and harsh discipline. Their philosophies centered interest on the child as an individual. In the nineteenth century sixty children, or more, with one teacher was often a school situation in a first grade. What was to be taught was of prime importance—not the child who was the learner. Restraint rather than wise freedom was the general practice. One grandmother of today vividly remembers peering through her teacher's hair to discover the eyes which the teacher as she faced the blackboard said "are in the back of my head."

As our national democracy developed, the seeds of a more democratic citizenship were sown in the school. Interest and research centered on what education is and when it begins. *Hughey* emphasizes this as an adjustment to living which begins at birth. *Tippett* says it "means ability to work together, to share property, to assume responsibility, and to grow at a maximum in all directions consistent with the good of others."

Kilpatrick emphasized the place of creativity in the educational procedure. *Miel* advocates growth in social living through the use of "tools of learning." Many educators have discussed, agreed and disagreed on the place of tools of learning and how and when they should be developed. *Mead* discusses the world itself in its birth pangs of emerging as a more democratic world order and shows its influence on the early elementary school.

These are but a few of the many past leaders in education who have helped shape our educational philosophy. We are grateful for their tremendous contributions and realize that oncoming educators will sift out what seems unwise and add their ideas and that education will continue to be a process so flexible as to meet children's most desirable needs.—*By* DOROTHY E. WILLY, former Chairman, CHILDHOOD EDUCATION Editorial Board, and Editor.

Friedrich Froebel
Apostle of Childhood Education
BY CAROLINE D. ABORN

"The prime purpose throughout is not to impart knowledge to the child, but to lead the child to observe and to think." Perhaps the greatest merit of Froebel's system is that it furnishes a philosophy of education for the teacher and not a code of management for the schoolroom. Miss Aborn, director emeritus of kindergartens, Boston, in this article on Froebel gives us the European beginnings of the kindergarten.

AMONG THE IMPRESSIVE BUILDINGS RECENTLY ERECTED IN WASHington, D. C., is that of the Archives, where are preserved all the important documents of our nation. On each side of the entrance are two life-sized figures. On the base of one are the words, "What Is Past Is Prologue"; on the base of the other an even shorter inscription, "Study the Past."

These significant words are particularly pertinent at this time—the one hundredth anniversary of the establishment of the first kindergarten by Friedrich Froebel in Blankenburg, Germany, in 1837. In order to comprehend and appreciate the value of the kindergarten, of the doors it has opened to a deeper understanding of the needs of young children, and of the evolution throughout the years of wiser, richer and more scientific ways of responding to these needs, we too should study the past. It is to the prologue we must turn to seek the sources, the roots and the beginnings of the emphasis today on the importance of early childhood.

FORERUNNERS OF FROEBEL

Without attempting to mention all the forerunners of Froebel in the field of education, we may well call to mind a few of those most nearly contemporaneous, whose influence, doubtless, helped to form his philosophy. Foremost among these are Comenius, Rousseau, and Pestalozzi, in whose writings are to be found the germinal ideas of the kindergarten and of the entire modern conception of education.

Comenius, born late in the sixteenth century—a student of education from early school years, teacher, minister, and at the same time supervisor of schools—wrote many valuable textbooks for his generation. The *Orbis Pictus,* the first illustrated textbook for children, and his *School of the Mother's Knee* are of most interest to us at this time, since they show a distinct foreshadowing of the kindergarten. The purpose of the latter book is, as the title indicates, to point out to mothers how they could begin at an early age the education of their children.

Rousseau was born in the early eighteenth century and there is nothing in his early life to give promise of his influence later on the development of educational thought. In *Emile*—a treatise on education according to nature—Rousseau sets forth his ideas for the education of youth. "The first education," he writes, "should be negative. It consists, not in teaching the principles of virtue and truth, but in guarding the heart against vice and the mind against error." The child's education was to come from the free development of his own nature, his own powers, his own natural inclinations.

One may note that Rousseau, in his writings, condemns the customary restrictions of swaddling clothes, of other forms of restraint on freedom of body, and advocates plenty of outdoor life. He would not curb the natural inclinations of childhood, for "nature desires that children should be children before they are men."

Rousseau stresses a natural, rather than an artificial, type of education; a development from within, rather than an accretion from without. Strange as it seems, Rousseau, with almost no actual knowledge of child nature, did appreciate that education must come through experience. Thus he became the prophet of the nineteenth century. From his teachings came the new education based on interest.

The theories of Rousseau and of others who followed in France, Germany and England, namely: that children should be treated as children, not as adults; that physical exercises and games should find a place in the child's education; that early training should be connected with motion and noise, since children love these; that instruction should be connected with realities rather than with words—are root ideas which were worked out and made practical to a marked degree by Pestalozzi, Herbart, and Froebel.

Pestalozzi emphasized the new purpose in education and demanded as a natural right education for every child, rich or poor:

"Sound education stands before me symbolized by a tree planted near fertilizing waters. A little seed which contains the design of the tree—its form and properties—is placed in the soil. The whole tree is an uninterrupted chain of organic parts, the plan of which existed in the seed and root. Man is similar to the tree. In the new-born child are hidden those faculties which are to unfold during life. . . . It is not the educator who puts new powers and faculties into man—he only takes care that no untoward influence shall disturb nature's march of development."

How Froebel Became a Schoolmaster

With this glimpse into a period when a new attitude toward childhood was emerging, we turn now to the coming of another, who was to be, indeed, the apostle of childhood and whose crowning work we are honoring this year.

In the little village of Oberweissbach, in the Thuringian Forest, Friedrich Froebel was born in 1782, and in this section of Germany he spent most of his seventy years. His father, a Lutheran clergyman, is described as "learned, resolute and preoccupied." The mother died when Froebel was an infant, and although the youngest of five brothers, he spent a lonely childhood in the gloomy parsonage, handicapped by the lack of mother love and of a father's understanding, of playmates and helpful play. He early turned to nature for companionship and found joy in the clear, bright sky in that hill country, in the stirring breezes and in all growing things in his small world.

His boyhood and early manhood were periods of restlessness and confusion, hard work and earnest endeavor to find his own niche in the world. In his early twenties he met Gruner, a schoolmaster and follower of Pestalozzi. As they conversed together, Gruner said, "My friend, you should not be an architect; you must become a schoolmaster."

For the first time, Froebel saw clearly what he wanted to do with life; but the road was long and difficult before he attained the desire of his heart. At twenty-three years of age, he began his teachings with a class of thirty to forty boys between the ages of nine and eleven. In a letter addressed to his brother, he wrote that he "felt like a fish in water or a bird in air."

After two years he left the school to become a private tutor to three boys whom he took to Yverdun to Pestalozzi's Institute. Here he took up the double duty of teacher and pupil for another two years. His keen desire for educational reform led him to complete his university course which had been sorely interrupted: eighteen months at the University of Jena; one year at Göttingen and six months at Berlin—amounting to three years' work, spread over a period of fourteen years.

Froebel's First School for Boys

In 1816 Froebel established his first school for boys called "The Universal German Educational Institute," which in the following summer was moved to Keilhau and housed in a peasant's cottage. While the cottage was being made ready, Froebel lived on potatoes, bread and water, in order to save money to pay the workmen. Each week he bought two large loaves of rye bread and marked on them with chalk each day's allowance. For fourteen years Frobel was the head of this school which saw some prosperous years. His faithful friends—Middendorf, Langethal and Bishop—were his backers and eager disciples.

In his autobiography Froebel writes, "My life was early brought under the influence of nature, of useful handiwork, and of religious feelings, or, as I prefer to say, the primitive and natural inclinations of every human being were fostered in me." Therefore, we are not surprised to find in the school at Keilhau that "nature became a familiar friend" to the boys. In the story of his life as a pupil at Keilhau, George Ebers writes:

"We took long walks up the mountains or in the forest, the older pupils acting as teachers. We discovered every variety of insect on the bushes and in the moss, the turf, the bark of trees, on the flowers and blades of grass. We listened to the notes of birds; and how many trees we climbed, what steep cliffs we also climbed, through what crevices we squeezed, to add a rare egg to our collection. Our teachers' love for all animate creation had made them impose bounds on our zeal, so we were required always to leave one egg in the nest, and if it contained but one not to molest it."

Froebel's purpose, the story continues, was "the preservation and development of the individuality of the boys entrusted to his care. He sought to rear the boy to unity with himself, with God, with nature and with mankind, and the way led to trust in God through religion; trust in himself by developing strength of mind and body; confidence in mankind by active relations with life, and a loving interest in the past and present destinies of fellow-men. This required an eye and heart open to their surroundings, sociability and a deeper insight into history," and we may add, character training in its richest and most practical form.

"Every boy was to be educated according to his peculiar temperament, with special regard to his disposition, talents and character. Although there were sixty of us, this was actually done in the case of each individual." A record of achievement was kept and sent to the parents, "containing a description of character, a criticism of the work accomplished, partly with reference to the pupil's capacity, partly to the demand of the school.

"Some of these records," continues Ebers, "are little masterpieces of psychological penetration."

In this school of the early nineteenth century, we find the system of student government well established, as the following record indicates:

"We formed one large family, and if any act really worthy of punishment was committed by any pupil, Barop summoned us all, formed us into a court of justice, and we examined into the affair, fixing the penalty ourselves. For dishonorable acts, expulsion from the institution; for grave offenses, confinement to the room—a punishment which pledged even us who imposed it, to avoid all intercourse with the culprit for a certain length of time; for lighter misdemeanors, the offender was confined to house or courtyard. Froebel regarded these meetings as a means of coming into unity with life."

FROEBEL'S PHILOSOPHY OF EDUCATION

There was no provision made at Keilhau for younger children. Not until 1826, when Froebel published the *Education of Man,* did he turn his attention specifically to educational opportunities in the earliest years of childhood. He had, of course, been a close observer of young children and had utilized the spontaneous activities of play to a greater degree than had been previously done. Plato, Fenelon, Locke and others had written on the educational value of play—in fact, a wave of interest in play as a factor in physical development had swept over the country—but with his usual insight, Froebel saw intellectual and moral obligations in play also, and in his educational system play was an important element in the all-round development of children.

One who will take time and some patience to read Froebel's *Education of Man* will find portions of it astonishingly in accord with modern theory and procedure in many respects in spite of its involved style, its obscure and unscientific passages. In the opening paragraph Froebel states the one universal law to which he relates all educational processes—the law of unity. To quote from another:

"He saw relationships and inner connection with marvelous clearness. If he had been fortunate enough to have had the advantage of the scientific development since his death, he would have seen even more clearly the unity of all created things, organic and inorganic, and the universal law working through them."

Recognizing the need of continuity in education, Froebel says:

"The child, the boy, the man should know no other endeavor but *to be at every stage* of development wholly what that stage calls for, for only adequate development at each preceding stage can bring about adequate development at each succeeding stage."

He saw the child a growing organism, developing only through creative activity, and he would have education "passive and following, not prescriptive, categorical, interfering. We grant space and time to young plants and animals," he writes, "because we know that in accordance with laws that live in them they will develop properly and grow well; arbitrary interference with their growth is avoided, but the young human being is looked upon as a piece of wax, a lump of clay, which man can mould as he pleases." [1]

---

[1] It is interesting and enlightening to find in the *Education of Man* and in the *Mother Play* which was written seventeen years later (1843) many allusions to principles and methods held by modern educators today. For example: The emphasis on individual differences (*Education of Man,* Pp. 18, 20, 21); the importance of parental education (*ibid.,* Pp. 19, 62, 64); the significance of the earlier years (*ibid.,* Pp. 24, 56, 68); with suggestions for sleep, fresh air and food (*ibid.,* Pp. 47, 60, 63, 71); on correct sense training (*ibid.,* P. 47) and speech development (Pp. 54, 65-67, 75, 79, 90).

"The child loves all things that enter his small horizon and extend his little world. To him the least thing is a new discovery." These words of Froebel suggest the need of an enriched background and the development of worthwhile interests through experimentation and self-activity. Froebel amplifies this thought by continuing, "Do not, however, tell him in words much more than he could find himself without words. To have found one-fourth the answer to his recurring questions by his own effort is of more value and importance to the child." Again, he says, "To lead children early *to think*—this, I consider, the foremost object of child training."

FROEBEL'S EARLY KINDERGARTENS

In an unpublished manuscript written some years ago by Grace Owen of England, the author has gathered from various sources descriptions of the early kindergartens founded by Froebel or by his disciples during his lifetime. We read that the number of children admitted to a kindergarten was smaller than is the custom today, and that Froebel considered this desirable. In a letter Froebel says, "On Tuesday, the Rodolstadt Kindergarten (one of the first established) was opened from two to four in the afternoon with twenty-four charming children varying from two to five years old, accompanied by their mothers, by some fathers and a few other relatives."

In the Blankenburg Kindergarten, and apparently in others, a considerable part of the children's time was spent in gardening, for Froebel believed that each child should have a small garden of his own, and that there should be two large beds common to all, one for flowers and one for vegetables.

In a small book written by Middendorf in 1848, called *Die Kindergarten,* one chapter describes a typical kindergarten. I abbreviate Miss Owens' translation:

"When all have arrived, the children form a circle, moving lightly and happily, singing a cheerful song. Since gratitude springs naturally out of joy, the children fold their hands and sing a morning hymn of thanksgiving. Then they take their seats at a long table and *look around for some means of playing out the ideas which are filling their minds more or less clearly.* At their request, small boxes of blocks are given them and they begin without delay to play eagerly. One child remembers his breakfast and builds a table with chairs around it, using leaves of some flower he has brought for cups, and flower petals for bread.

"Another child builds a fireplace for he knows his mother is in the kitchen now preparing a meal. Another lad saw a shepherd starting out in the early morning with his flock, so he represents the shepherd prominently and his sheep following. In this manner each child follows his individual interests.

"Luncheon follows, after which the children march out of doors singing a marching song—'Let Us into the Garden Go.' There they dig and weed and plant, water their garden beds, and visit each other, helping and receiving help. In order to give plenty of scope for the love of activity, an inviting and suitable playground is provided close to the garden. The children rush into the playground, jumping and wrestling, then unite to play games; first a game of bees, which they have just seen hovering over their flowers. Bird games follow, and a flight of pigeons over their heads suggests a pigeon game."

As one reads what Froebel has written regarding childhood education and all that is available concerning the practice of the early kindergartens, one feels confident that formality and regimentation had no place in his plan. In his endeavor to create a system of education which would embody his philosophy of life and interpret it in practice, Froebel arranged what he considered a corresponding sequence of materials.

In the one hundred years since that first kindergarten in the little village of Blankenburg, many changes have been made in play materials and their use, but we honor Froebel today for his distinctive contribution to education for the youngest children, and believe that the kindergarten in some form will always be an integral part of our educational system.

Vol. I—p. 6 (Sept. 1924)

Ideas and Ideals
BY LUCY WHEELOCK

Lucy Wheelock is principal of the Wheelock School, Boston, Massachusetts.

AN IDEA IS SOMETHING SEEN. AN IDEAL IS SOMETHING SEEN AND followed. The idea must precede the ideal, therefore the kind of idea that dominates the mind is of importance. Men and women who have shaped the course of events in the world have been possessed of an idea which has become an ideal to pursue constantly and to the end.

Froebel gave his life, his time, his comfort, his few worldly goods to the service of an Idea. He spelled it with a big I. His Idea was so compelling that it enlisted the enthusiasm and devotion of the entire circle of friends who surrounded him and of others who came to see and to believe. These early advocates of a new gospel of education counted not life so dear that they might attain unto a better humanity redeemed from old errors and failings, by giving man a chance "to become himself." They saw that creative beings must have opportunity from the very beginning to gain ideas of the world in which they are to live and to gain power to use and control it.

The pioneers of the kindergarten in this country had the same vision. Through rough paths of opposition and misunderstanding and often of ridicule, they followed the ideal of a New Education. They proclaimed the gospel of Froebel at gatherings of parents and conventions of teachers and school officials, wherever a hearing was possible. They wrote, spoke, taught until "those who came to scoff, remained to pray."

The kindergarten today has so leavened the school system that we often fail to recognize the source of the ideas and ideals which have vivified the old school routine. The story of the pioneer days of the kindergarten has just been published, as a fitting memorial to those who bequeathed to us our educational inheritance.

All biography has a great human interest. It tells us what ideas and ideals have led to the life work of an individual. It tells us of success or failure. Any career may become a guide to those who seek a similar goal. The current wave of interest in biography is wholesome. It indicates a general desire to find out how to live, as well as how to get a living.

Of all recently written accounts of the working out of great ideas by those dedicated to them, I know of none more inspiring than the record of the life and devoted service of our kindergarten pioneers. They illustrate the enthusiasm generated by a fructifying idea, which becomes an ideal to pursue without faltering and without rest. The lesson they teach should not be lost.

In an industrial age like ours there is danger of overemphasis on production and efficiency and too little consideration of the ends most to be desired. A few men have the ideas which make our aeroplanes, motor cars and radios. The great industrial army becomes the hand to carry out these ideas. The hand is now raised in protest against long hours of labor with no chance to enjoy the good things of life.

What are the good things of life?

And how is the power to enjoy gained?

A few thinkers put their ideas and ideals into books, others paint pictures and construct buildings, and others write the songs which cheer a nation's heart.

Many may sing the songs and enjoy the pictures and read the books; but to many more life goes on as if these things did not exist. Added leisure may not bring the capacity for enjoyment. Industrial education alone will not suffice to give this capacity. The subordination of ideas to the industrial arts will not furnish a complete education.

In the old days of the kindergarten, we believed that education should foster the love of the good and the beautiful. We employed the agencies calculated to inspire such appreciation. We hoped that every child might have his chance to enjoy a book, to gaze with admiration upon a fine picture, to find pleasure in rhyme and metre and to sing a song which might become a song of life. We believed it to be the function of education to secure for every individual a store of ideas which should become productive and creative forces in life. We believed that "through admiration, faith, and love, do we ascend in the scale of being," and that one of our tasks was to see that these were "well and wisely fixed." We saw the child go forth every day. We saw him look upon the objects which surrounded him. We believed that we had some responsibility in controlling the environment, so that pity, love and dread might be properly guided. We thought such guidance might make children more intelligent, more loving, more inclined to pleasant ways.

Are we to lose these beliefs and thereby lose the best results of the kindergarten? Is the environment our eyes see and our hands touch the only environment? What is reality? Is the elevated road with its "klingety klangety kling," the subway with its "zippety zimmety zip," the only song for a New York child? The robins sing in the open places of New York. Central Park has dandelions in the grass. Stars shine at night above the subways, the elevated road, and the Woolworth building. Are these not also real? And the ideas they inspire, are they not pleasant to cherish?

The water comes indeed through pipes into a bathtub. The pipes are real. The tub is real and very useful. The water comes in with a "chug-a-chug" and a cheerful splash, very real and very pleasant. But the idea of the water need not stop with the tub. Far away is the beginning in a hidden brook and the brook sings:

> I chatter, chatter as I go
> To join the brimming river,
> For men may come and men may go
> But I go on forever.

Ideas are broadened and enriched when one looks for the beginning as well as the end of things.

A green leaf may be a boat a-floating. That is real. One may see and touch it. But:

> Away down the river
> A hundred miles or more
> Other little children
> Shall bring my boats ashore.

That also is true and real. The little brook like the Entepfuhl road may lead anywhere, even to the end of the world. And these are childlike thoughts and ideas, because a child lives in a world of wonders. It is "a great, wide, wonderful, beautiful world." Why make it only a workshop?

A real house made of boards and big enough to sit in may afford satisfaction. It calls for ingenuity and skill in its construction. Windows and doors must be planned. Ideas are called for in the planning. But it is the real thing and not the miniature. It is a part of actuality which too soon presses upon the growing child. Compare this with the joy of making a playhouse which may be changed in a trice into a two-story mansion by adding a few more blocks. A tower makes it into a church or a school and a few columns transform it into a temple or a state house. The arches found in the building set suggest a gateway, and a park entrance appears. A wall soon surrounds the park. A summer-house is erected. Then a pond is desired and placed appropriately. Boats must be made to float upon its surface. Seats are made in the park for the chance traveller and trees are planted. A play world is made by a playing child.

A child is an architect before he is a carpenter. He plans and transforms and discovers his own patterns. His tools are the simplest things he may choose to represent his ideas. Hammers and saws may serve at times; but they belong to the carpenter stage.

Dollhouses and boxes may be painted. When need requires, jars and jugs may be covered with seemly green for a special use; but when they are once done there is nothing more to add. Our mothers covered jugs with small embossed pictures and placed them on the parlor mantels. They were harmless ornaments; but they did not elevate the artistic sense of the household. The painter is not the artist. The little artist should have material which conforms to his creative bent and admits of changing and improving representation.

Children have delight in dressing up; but a very little dress will do; while fancy supplies the rest. An apron or yard of cloth makes a queen's train; a stick makes a king's sceptre. A May queen is crowned with a wreath of leaves and rules with a rose as a wand. The time for dressmaking is not yet. The old kindergarten sewing did not lead to any practical use of the needle. Let us rejoice in that. It was indeed too prescriptive, too nerve-straining, too difficult; but the pliant line of wool for art purposes, for simple design and picture making is not to be despised.

Oh, little hands so soon to take up the burden of toil, let us not force upon you too soon the tools of the industrial world! Oh, little feet so soon to walk the crowded city streets, wander yet longer in grove and meadow still "apparelled in celestial light!" Little eyes, look not always on skyscrapers; but up at the blue sky and at the stars and wonder what they are! Who is to preserve for you these realities if not the kindergartner?

What ideas are of most worth in a child's life? What materials, what activities give creative ideas? How are ideals which control the stream of thought and the course of life awakened?

Two youths* in Chicago have committed a crime unparalleled for fiendish calculation. Both have superior intellects and excel in scientific interest and knowledge. Their awful crime was planned to give opportunity for scientific examination of a human being in agony. What has been lacking in their environment and education? Did they as children go forth every day to look with pity, love or dread upon the face of Nature? Did they sing songs of the bluebird who tells us that "summer is coming and springtime is here?" Were stories told them of heroes who saved life and helped the weak? Did they know of knights of old who were brave and bold and kind? Did no one ever tell them of the "Line of Light" or of the hero of Haarlem, who saved a city by his own heroic deed? Were there any hymns sung of a God who is great and good and whom we thank? The dominant idea of scientific investigation became the cruel ideal of a human monster who holds nothing sacred, not even human life.

The newspapers tell us daily of the mental condition of these unhappy boys; but the reporters do not tell us what produced them. One plain conclusion may be drawn. Education may not omit the giving of fundamental ideas of human values and of ideals which govern right conduct.

Last of all should these things be omitted from a kindergarten curriculum. Our materials have changed, as they should. Froebel's own emphasis on creative work has often been obscured by a rigid devotion to a logical order of gifts. Our curriculum has changed, as it should. A fixed program does not conform to the needs of a group of children with varying tastes, interests, and skills.

We are in the way of growth. I rejoice in this new freedom. I rejoice that we are putting a premium on individual experiment and discovery of new and better ways. But I deplore a tendency to forsake fundamental ideas and ideals and the time-honored means of securing them.

---

*Editor's note:

The author has reference, undoubtedly, to the infamous Leopold and Loeb case of 1924.

Folk songs and plays are good. They have the stamp of approval of many generations of singers and players. But we inherit many other songs and much melody to make life sweeter. A song may be simple and musical and yet suggest something to think about or to keep in one's heart. The mental image or idea it presents should be considered.

"Knick-knack paddy-whack" is a fine old Welsh counting song. "The old man came rolling home" before Mr. Volstead's time; but probably a four-year-old has no definite picture of the old man which would alarm any foe of the saloon. It is an excellent song for rhythm; but not an entire repertoire.

I hope we may still hear the brown thrush telling us "the world's running over with joy" and may declare in song that we are "as happy as kings" and give thanks for "the pleasant morning light."

And stories! With the whole realm of child literature, why should we limit our storytelling to Black Sambo? And why read Black Sambo, after all the years of training in storytelling and our knowledge of the superior value of the spoken word?

We live in the Here and Now. What is Here? What is Now? *Here* is made up of all the contributions of the past. *Now* is only a point in the current of time. There is no *Here* devoid of a past and no *Now* which is not a moment of eternity. We inherit the mind of the race created by the fairy tale, the legend, myth and song, as well as the struggle with the forces of nature. These tales contain the idea and ideals which have made our civilization. We need the bard, the minstrel and the storyteller today. The soul of music is not dead. It lives in every child's heart and should voice itself in a child's song. The teacher should "lend to the rhyme of the poet, the beauty of her voice," for ideals are stirred into life through the poet's lines, which awaken desire and high thoughts. The story has a nobler mission than ever before, because of our need of ideals, of patriotism, of service and of brotherhood.

The child dreams of a star and sees a pathway of light leading up to the heavens above. The dream of a child is the ideal of a man leading out of darkness into the light.

Oh, little child, dream on!

Beginnings of Education
BY A. H. HUGHEY

A. H. Hughey, City Superintendent of Schools, El Paso, Texas, presented this talk before an evening session of the thirty-fifth annual Convention of International Kindergarten Union at Grand Rapids, Michigan, April 17, 1928. The following is excerpted.

WE MUST SOMEHOW DEFINE EDUCATION IF WE TALK ABOUT THE *Beginnings of Education.* Is education the development of the individual? In passing let us note that the individual in prenatal life passes through the physical forms that are fundamental in the development, not of human life, but of all life. He is born a human being, but is born not so much of his mother as of all life that has preceded him. He is endowed already to the major extent with what he is to be in a general way and we cannot change him fundamentally. We can sustain and help and guide and mould and see wonderful results from our care of him, or we can injure and destroy. But if education is the process of adaptation to environment, as some define it, or the guidance of growth, then the newborn babe is our subject and education begins there.

If we talk about the beginnings of a child's education, we would better attain its successful accomplishment by educating his parents to be ready for him when he makes his appearance. We must see the tremendous importance and need of right care and education of a child from birth to the age of four or five. Are those who attend to that real teachers? They don't ordinarily have a certificate from a state department of education, assuming that certificates ever meant anything anyway. Is it not the greatest need of humanity that the race's parents be ready for parenthood? Will it ever be possible for the young men and young women of our race to learn from competent, correct and careful sources how to start off the next generation?

We must conclude that the problem of beginning the education of a child is mainly the problem of providing for him parents who have a kind of education, not now very common, which fits them to provide the right environment for the child first from birth till the age of four or five. Hence, this reasoning leads us to think of even the kindergarten as a sort of postgraduate course in a child's education, and all education beyond that sinks to the level almost of mere training or creating of proficiency in the details of further adaptation to environment.

But let us narrow the definition of education still further, as being the conscious, organized or planned process of guiding a child's development outside the home.

We must realize that, great as are the results that can still be accomplished, there is but a minor fraction of the child's development as an individual that remains. That fraction looms large in our eyes and in individual cases we seem to cultivate wonderful results, but it should not obscure what has gone before.

James starts to the kindergarten one morning. What is he physically? What has his prior life done to his eyes, his hearing, his teeth, his stomach, his nerves, his heart, his health make-up and habits generally? Will not the answers to these questions reveal that James may have already had his life development largely determined physically? And this physical temple of his mind will have a serious influence on the mind itself. What has his previous life done for his character, his nature, his temperament, his spirit, his soul? Is lying, stealing, cowardice, selfishness, fear, shame, cruelty an ingrained part of his make-up? If they are, will the kindergarten remove them? Sometimes yes, if such scars are not too deep to be offset by good kindergarten training; sometimes no.

We must make allowance here for about 2 per cent of our population who are congenitally defective, constitutionally subnormal, and destined to handicap society to the extent of using up about one-third of the cost of civil government. But the treatment of these cases by human government is among the duties which I urge later in advocating the earlier entrance of social or governmental agencies into the education and care of the very young.

The natural inference then is that every infant should somehow have the opportunity for his best development. We are committed to the kindergarten as a solution of the question of what public agencies can undertake at about the age of five. Parents and voters in this country do not need now to have the benefits of the public kindergarten proved to them.

The greatest treasure which we adults have on earth now is not our capital or our present state of material progress, but it is this unformed multitude of infants and young humans now in the cradles, the nurseries, the kindergartens and the schools. It makes little difference now who their fathers and mothers are. They are the children of our race, of our country, of our community. What shall our public agencies or government do about them or for them? The poverty-stricken kindergarten child now without shoes may some day hold the reins of government and take my property for nonpayment of taxes, or passing me on the street may drop a dime in my hat. Or he may have my life in his hands in the cab of a locomotive or at the end of a revolver. Should I not be vitally interested in him right now, should I not help to give him the best possible opportunities to grow up right?

The children that might have been are not here. Shall the courts and jails and almshouses and hospitals and asylums and charities be our answer for the children of our submerged population? I say let community government take a nurse or worker to the home or hovel of every underprivileged future citizen and at least offer to help in the improvement of home conditions for the child's sake that he may not grow up handicapped by disease, stunted by lack of intelligent feeding and sanitation or misguided into crime and evil ways. He is *here,* and thirty years from now the question of whether he is digging a ditch or running a railroad, burglarizing my home or governing my community is mainly answered by what we do for him now. He is here, whether four years old, three years old, two years old, one year old, six months old, his education has begun, and if it is logical and sensible to give him a year in the kindergarten preceding his other public school education, it is just as logical and sensible and wise to precede the kindergarten with the nursery school, and precede that with the public welfare worker and the public health nurse, and public community service to the underprivileged, the submerged children, homes and communities.

Children come to the kindergarten with natures as varied and interesting as they can be made by the varied and individualistic parents now existing. Some are partly socialized, some lack any trait of socialization, some have initiative, some are completely repressed, some have personalities already interestingly developed, some seem altogether crushed with souls bruised and stunted, some already have wretched habits, all have many habits of one kind or another. One year of a true kindergarten, though coming at a more important stage of life than any later year, will not insure a child's retaining his kindergarten benefits entirely throughout life. The grade schools and higher education can be so mismanaged as to nullify much that the kindergarten has done. Yet the benefits of a real kindergarten can never be entirely lost. The teacher of the first grade readily distinguishes between the children who have had a year in kindergarten and those who have not.

Let us analyze some of the unvoiced, groping, blundering, yet obstinate and powerful impulses and subconscious conclusions of the American public about their schools and the nation's children. A boy commits a horrible crime in California. The attention of all people is focused on that boy in an effort to explain, to understand. And one outstanding fact is seized on for attention. He went to high school in a certain city and finished as what was called a good high school product. Now we know, and on second thought the public says, that this high school is not responsible for that boy's later behavior. We think we are clear on that point, yet are we clear entirely? The average American school patron will say, "Oh, of course, you can't blame the school for the outcome of this boy."

The public school teacher can always retort to the parent, "You brought him into the world, you gave him part of his nature by inheritance and about all the rest of his nature before he entered school and his home life environment after he entered school." The schools are absolutely not connected with responsibility for the kind of human being he is. This teacher may be partly responsible for his knowledge of English, that teacher for his knowledge of arithmetic, the other for his knowledge of history and other subjects, and the principal of the school, say, for the proper socializing environment in his school life with other boys and girls.

What is to be the outcome of all these fundamental differences of opinion or point of view. Will the teachers decide? No. The people, men and women, who pay the taxes and support the schools will decide and will grope along till they have their own way. Then what will be the result for teachers and professors? They will have to go back to the kindergarten or to the beginnings of education for their point of view, their inspiration, their training. They will have to teach life as well as the course of study. Character must somehow be taught or instilled or improved, independence under self control must be developed, self expression under self control must be developed, mankind must be made to grow up with the fullest possible understanding of mankind as well as of things and with the aim to better the world through living in it. Teachers must consciously and persistently guide the development and the habits of character, of life behavior and the socialization of the children in their charge. If such had not been the ideals of the original kindergartens, we would have failed with our kindergartens, just as we are partially failing with other school work.

So the words of one superintendent to others are just these, "I know we have our hands full with administering the teaching of subjects and managing or dealing with teachers and school boards and the public. I know we think we are doing well if we 'get by' with well-organized schools and an increasing number going on into high school

and college, and we applaud the high school graduates and the college graduates—and then forget them. I know that these results are the main ones that show for our work and worry. But if our teachers are not much more than teachers of subjects, if our product is not one that is much more than examples of mental proficiency, we are on the wrong road. All along the line of the pupil's school life there must be more attention to what I shall boldly call the kindergarten side of human development or to the principles of the beginnings of human education. *Kindergarten principles and attitudes must permeate even college teaching because they are sound educational principles and ideals.* . . . ."
(Editor's italics).

Vol. V—p. 134 (Nov. 1928)

The Age Factor
BY ARNOLD GESELL
Yale University

UNLESS THE FUNDAMENTALISTS ARE RIGHT, THE UNIVERSE DID NOT come into existence in a twinkling. Some stars are young; others old; parts of our earth are much more recent than others; the very elements of chemistry differ in "age." Science has steadily built up the concept that the physical world is a product of ordered growth. The biological sciences are extending the same concept to living nature, including the human mind. Among teachers, at least, it is a truism that the mind of the child is subject to the laws of growth.

The truism, however, like many truisms, is so profound that it is readily forgotten and even opposed in actual practice. Narrower concepts of training and rules of discipline come into conflict with the genetic approach at every turn. Particularly in the complex field of character education, it is easy to ignore the factor of immaturity in the growing child.

Susanna Wesley, in a letter to her famous son, John, in 1711, naïvely summed up her philosophy of preschool education in the following striking passage: "In order to inform the minds of children, the first thing is to conquer their will and bring them to an obedient temper. To inform the understanding is a work of time and must with children proceed by slow degrees as they are able to bear it: but the subjecting the will is a thing which must be done at once; and the sooner the better."

Has this distinction between the will and the understanding entirely vanished from our present day attitudes toward young children? Parents are ready enough to grant that children must proceed by slow degrees in the learning of arithmetic, reading and spelling; but in the field of social behavior, in matters of obedience, unselfishness, truthfulness, tidiness, these same parents often assume a rigorous ethical attitude which exacts more than the child mind can meet. There is an absolute theory of morals which takes an unduly gloomy view of certain behavior problems, and conversely places an unduly flattering estimate on conduct which is only superficially "good." The only corrective for an overrigid approach to early behavior problems is a more genuine appreciation of the age and growth factors which condition all behavior whether behavior of "the understanding" or of "the will."

The lying of young children presents a problem in point. This lying reflects at once the immaturity of the child's logic and of his conduct. It clearly illuminates in the influence of the age factor. Piaget in his recent volume on *Judgment and Reasoning* has admirably shown how the egocentrism of the child makes him astigmatic and insensible to contradictions of language and of thought. Up to the age of eight years the child's thinking literally teems with contradictions. For example an intelligent boy of seven and one-half years explained that boats float because they are light; but in the next breath he asserted that big boats float because they are heavy and strong. Being so big and strong they easily support themselves in water, he reasoned! The boy was, of course, blissfully unaware of the contradiction in his statements. In such psychological soil, veracity (in the adult sense) does not always take root.

If the child's failures in logic need tolerance, his limitations of conduct deserve sympathetic interpretation. The goal is not to instill perfection, "the sooner, the better"; but to establish conditions favorable to growth. A just regard for the factor of age and growth alone can prevent our zeal for training from going too far.

The Place of Creating in the Educative Process

BY WILLIAM H. KILPATRICK

William H. Kilpatrick is professor of education, Teachers College, Columbia University, New York City.

> *Do you believe in creative work? For everybody or only for the few? How much creation do your pupils show? Do you think of creation as a dainty accomplishment, the "latest thing" in education or as an essential ingredient in all educative activity? Do you strive in every possible way to increase creation among your pupils? Are you yourself creative? Are you a creative teacher or do you simply follow "The Course of Study"? Do you or do you not enrich your personal life by the creation you put into it? Do you really believe that creation is a worthy essential in the good life?* W. H. K.

CREATING IN EDUCATION IS NOWADAYS MUCH ADVOCATED. BUT IF WE listen closely we hear discordant voices. Some find a place for creation only in such as "art," "music," or "writing." Others would extend it much more broadly. Still others, more "scientifically" minded, tell us that only the few can, in fact, create—possibly one-tenth of one per cent. The rest must be content with "appreciation" and "fellowship." But to this many will immediately object. When, further, we look into the schools we see that traditionally creating has no admitted place. In more modern schools it is advocated, but thinking about it is seldom clear and practice accordingly suffers.

This situation challenges us, both to clear up our thinking and to make our practice conform. If practice is to go forward we must answer, as least tentatively, some insistent questions. What does "create" mean? Is it properly limited to certain kinds of work or does it belong to all of life? Is it limited to the few or do all create more or less? What part does "creation" in fact play in life? Could a different education make it play a more significant part? It is these questions in general, not probably all in detail, that we propose now to consider. Widely different answers suggest that widely different definitions may be at work. So here. The main effort will accordingly be devoted to a consideration of the meaning of the word "create."

Probably the word "create" came into our thinking from the first verse in the Bible and so meant to form out of nothing. Later the term was extended. The great artists and thinkers were said to "create."

Being men, they used material to begin with; but the results were so much above the majority as to seem mysterious if not divine.

Here we have a beginning. The ways of men we can study. What do we find? Is their creation limited to "art," "music" and "literature"? Or do we find it as well in statesmanship, generalship, invention, research? Do we not in fact find it present more or less in every realm where man has concern enough to achieve? And is such creation limited to the very few? Do we find the great ones standing quite apart from the rest of us, doing things the like of which we lesser ones cannot do even in smaller scale? Are they a different kind of being from us, so that they alone create and we can only imitate? Or do we all create, only in different degrees? Does not history in fact show one unbroken stretch ("distribution of creative ability") from Shakespeare or Beethoven or Einstein down to us, with everywhere each one in the line almost as creative as the one next above, no break anywhere to mark off the "creative" ones from the rest?

At this point some not liking the trend of discussion will rise to propose that we admit the distribution of ability in different degrees among men but limit the word "create" to the significant contributions to the world's store. Certain things could be said in favor of such a definition, but the other line developing above seems to promise better for helping education forward. We shall then first consider it further.

It was suggested above that "creating" extends itself more or less among all people and into all aspects of life. This line of thought we now wish to pursue. Possibly from it we shall reach a more satisfactory definition of the word "create," get light on the part creating plays when present, and consequently get guidance for education.

As it is life that concerns us, let us begin with biology and even with a lower animal form. Such an animal living in its natural habitat has its accustomed ways of getting food, etc. Its life seems stereotyped. But let a sufficiently new situation present itself. The animal is stirred to effort. Three results are possibilities. The animal may "get used" to the new stimulus and henceforth ignore it, or he may succumb and die, or he may "master the situation" by responding in a novel fashion. If the latter, the new reaction brings or means a "corresponding structural change" (Haldane). Careful observation seems to corroborate these findings. Even a very low animal form may in the face of a novel situation contrive a (to him) novel response to meet the situation, and this response will abide as a structural change. These facts we may describe in two ways: the animal has "learned" a new response or the animal has "created" a new response. Note here that "create" and "learn" (the latter in at least one of its aspects) are made to mean the same thing. "Learn" thus becomes a more active and creative affair than most seem to think. Create is brought more lowly, if you will, but still means to make something that beforetimes did not (for the learner) exist. Old material may enter constitutively, but the result is something qualitatively new. For the learner (if not for the world) actual creation has taken place. The reader is asked, if he will, to reread this paragraph, and let the word "learn" and "create" assume more adequately (at least to try out) the new meanings here suggested.

Let us now move up the biological scale to human thinking. Life, if we look closely, is a novelly developing flux of events. Any event is in itself unique though within it we recognize familiar elements. We never experienced this event before. We cannot tell far in advance (less than a minute more often than more, my students recently judged) *just* what the next event will be. Some elements of the approaching event, yes. *Just* what in its *entirety,* no. But all the same we have to act, and for this we have to plan. Often our plans work. Often they fail. It is a hazard. The greater the step, marriage for instance, the greater the hazard.

Now thinking (in any full sense) is the effort to grapple with this novelly developing flux of events in terms of what we have learned from the past. We may succeed, we often fail. Thinking is sizing up the moving, shifting situation already here so as best to manage in the light of what is coming. Moreover, I as a fully responsible person (in contrast perhaps with children, slaves or prisoners) have to decide in matters significant to me my own course of action. If I try to shift the decision by seeking advice, I still have to decide whose advice to seek and then whether to follow it. If I decide to imitate my neighbor, it is still the same. The final decision I must make and in terms of my situation as best I can decide. Such a decision then is itself a "creation" in the same sense as the active constructive learning discussed above. I make it. Thinking like learning, in any full sense, is creative. And whether we call it "thinking" or "learning" or "creating," it is the same active constructive grappling with impending fortune to manage it to our ends. And this is life at the highest. It belongs to every person as such, but can be increased in each. Education exists to promote it. Now creating begets creating. As then creating is the essence of living at the best, so also is creating the essence of education.

But "learn" needs further study before we can leave it, especially in relation to imitation. To most people, including many educators, the learning process does not begin until the thing-to-be-learned is set before the learner as a copy to be imitated or a rule to be got or knowledge or skill to be acquired. There is something to be said for such a definition. It seems on the face of it to be the method of acquiring the racial inheritance, admittedly an invaluable endowment from the past. But clearly this conception of "learn" is markedly different from the active constructive creative learning presented above. Can the two be got together? If the answer be no, then we have a dualism in education. Some learning comes passively or imitatively (let us say), while other learning comes "creatively." Dualisms generally give trouble, especially to the weaker (whether in age or ability or social fortune). Let us see if we can reduce this apparent dualism to a difference of degree, a question of more or less.

Begin with a skill, say learning a golf stroke. The professional shows me his swing, even explains it in detail. I try and fail. Mere imitation does not suffice. I have to do some contriving myself. He may show or suggest, but I have to do the contriving. In short, taking my existing stock of habits and skills I "create" a movement new to me (and, believe me, mine is never exactly his). Without his help, however, I had done less well. What I do is thus part "creation," part "imitation." But the same thing is true of Shakespeare. Supreme creator that he was, he profited still by what others showed him. No man can create out of nothing. Always there are things that suggest. It begins to appear that there is a creation-imitation scale. At one end the greatest possible amount of creation in proportion to imitation. At the other end the reverse, the least possible amount of creation in proportion to imitation. With all gradations in between. Even Shakespeare shows greater creation at times than at others. Many of us would be glad to reach his lowest. Somewhere in this scale each act belongs.

Even in learning such things as $7+6=13$, there appears to be some creation present. Some children are mentally too young to "sense" the numbers. Clearly then a learner is not merely passive, he has a part to play requiring a degree of maturity, that is, a degree of effectual intelligence. But intelligence is in general defined practically as the creative grappling with a difficult situation. Certainly an actual "creative" element is present and the same holds of "sensing" the relation between $7+6$ and 13. Again is a certain mental maturity necessary. That is, this relation cannot be really learned without the exercise of something best conceived as "creative ability." Lack of space forbids further argument, but it seems most probable that every learning, however pronounced the imitation, has in it some personal exercise of "creative ability." We seem warranted in giving creation a place in every learning activity.

Well, what of it? What difference does it make? Much, every way. Education takes on a different life and spirit. Some things may be said specifically.

1. We cease in caste-system fashion to divide mankind into two separable groups, those who create and those who do not. All create to some degree. Those who fall below a certain amount are institutional cases. All who properly go around loose have to create every day and much of the time. Crossing a busy street is one very simple instance. I have to make my plan on the spot at the time. Driving a car is another illustration, again of low order to be sure, but still it quite definitely illustrates the need of a continual creating. Higher up is giving a dinner party. To do this successfully requires much of creating. Any conversation worth the name is another instance. Creating is a necessary element in life.

2. Still further, it appears in general true that the more of creation we can put into life (other things being equal) the richer it is in satisfaction, and satisfaction of a kind by best consent called "higher." If this be so, then it becomes our business as educators to try to bring into each person's life as much of creation as possible. Here is where we wish a different aim and content to school and education. Making the home beautiful would be an excellent instance for the new adult education. Making the home happy may perhaps also be accepted as a proper object of creative study.

3. This is to give up the idea that creative work is confined to such as making pictures or composing music or writing. That these are *among* the supreme instances no one would deny, but wherever there is a difficult and complex situation to be met significant to man, there is also opportunity for worthy creative work. So far as concerns school, everything proper to go on there has its possibility of the creative in it. This is not to say that we expect a different multiplication table, but that multiplication will be learned creatively and put to use creatively in many pupil enterprises. Nor need this outlook deny a proper place to "drill" (or better, practice) after creative work has brought the need. But creation we shall seek in season and out. We shall measure our success largely by the amount of creativeness that emerges in all that is done. Along with creativeness we shall seek the integration of personality. These two stand together helping each other and quite opposed to the ordinary subject-matter achievements. To stress subject matter in and of itself, especially as measured by centrally administered standardized tests, is often, perhaps generally miseducative, hurtful both to creativeness and to the integration of personality.

4. And we shall cease to think of "appreciation" as confined to "art." Only after we have extended the latter term can we accept the unique connection. Appreciation does attend each successful attempt at creating, and this is life, the life good to live. If we think of art

as the honest and sincere effort both to face meaningfully each of life's situations and to contrive (create) the best possible answer to its demands, then with this larger conception of "art" we shall say appreciation should attend it and we shall hope to bring it as an enrichment of life more and more into all we do.

Vol. XI—p. 243 (Mar. 1935)

What About Progressive Education?
BY ALICE V. KELIHER

Alice V. Keliher is supervisor of Elementary Education, Hartford, Connecticut.

THERE ARE TWO GROUPS WHO MAKE IT DIFFICULT FOR THE INQUIRING individual to get an adequate picture of progressive education. The more dangerous group consists of those who call themselves progressive and who attempt to "put over" progressive education in the form of an activity program. They take inordinately rapid strides; they countenance, and perhaps even boast of, an utter lack of discipline; and they disregard the skills and controls so necessary for effective self-direction. The other group consists of those reactionary critics who use such extreme practices as the target for their witticisms and damaging statements. This is characteristic of the prevailing tendency to establish the extreme as the norm—always unfair and confusing. The great majority of really progressive developments have crept in and have been accepted as part of a slower growth process which moves in closer harmony with the nature of man. The critics conscientiously avoid mention of these developments, and the pseudo-progressives reject the slower but psychologically sound methods which are essential for growth. We must, therefore, dismiss the confusions that have been created by these two groups and attempt to clarify some major questions which have been asked by earnest public school educators.

Is a change in public school education necessary? Changes in public school education are not only necessary but inevitable. One need only touch his finger against the pulse of events to realize that the content and form of education must move on with the times. The trite example of the shifting map of Europe is still one of the best proofs that what is here today may not be tomorrow's fact. Years ago, medicine in its crude stages was considered a boon to humanity. Now when we penetrate the fastnesses of cloistered areas to find voodoo doctors creating charms to cure diseases which we now know are germ carried and fatal, we realize what strides modern medicine has made. We realize, further, that with the progress in intercommunication, voodoo doctors will probably have few successors of their kind. In the same light, by looking back over a very brief period of time, we realize how rapidly and how readily new findings of science and new modes of living have been accepted. Thoughtful educators, realizing this, are beginning to penetrate the thickly wooded courses of study, the impenetrable stereotypes of inherited facts, to find voodoo equivalents in the education of children. Maps are not accurate; facts long disproved remain in textbooks; beliefs, bigotries and superstitions long discarded by the intelligent public are still given access in our schools. Of more importance, those learnings least effective for creative and critical thought are still given precedence. We are thus faced with a serious charge. If the old ways of living, the old stereotypes and the old facts are no longer adequate, we must explore the new ways. But we must stand ready with an education which will supply better ways of living, better ways of thinking, and facts more recently found to survive the inquisition of truth seekers. We must meet the challenge of this reconstruction of the public school, and we must meet it in such manner that we build sanely, carefully and effectively for the truly fundamental values in living.

What scientific basis is there for the contention that education should move toward the activity movement or progressive education? There is an erroneous impression abroad—viz., that the activity movement is the outgrowth of sentimentalized reasoning about child life. The activity movement, quite to the contrary, is firmly rooted in the basic sciences of human growth and development. Mental hygiene, as a science of the mind, has for its antecedents all of the basic sciences which deal with life—biology, physiology, hygiene, psychology. Biology demonstrates the self-active character of all growth; physiology emphasizes structural development through activity; hygiene emphasizes the necessity for healthful and restful living; and psychology demonstrates the organic and essentially self-active nature of learning. Mental hygiene, building on all of these, has contributed some of the most essential principles of progressive education—that the attitudes of the child must be of major concern in the educational program; that the activity in which he can engage with whole-souled interest yields better results in personality development (as well as in academic achievement); and that his own active planning, participating in and evaluating of his educational activities are essential steps in the development of his adequacy and security as an individual. These bases are indisputable.[1] The really progressive school attempts to build upon them in planning its educational program. The active interest of the child is directed toward worthy enterprises chosen by child and teacher; the physical life of the child is guarded by adequate muscular exercise, by rest periods, by relaxation, and by wholesome attitudes toward bodily functions; the learning situations are so planned that the child, when psychologically ready, is presented with experiences so connected with his own living and with his own concepts that he learns causes, effects, values and facts in an essential matrix of reality and utility. Therefore, the progressive program wisely planned and carefully guided grows out of the basic facts of the sciences of growth. Moving with them, rather than placing artificial barriers against them, the activity program is fundamentally scientific.

Is there a single method or technique of progressive education? There cannot be a single method or technique of progressive education. Since education is to be conceived as growth, schools must proceed in whatever direction may provide better and better for the education of their communities. No two communities have exactly the same needs; no two schools confront exactly the same problems; no two grades can be taught exactly in the same manner. One objective of education is to start with present realities and move toward future potentialities. The progressive educator, therefore, is the man who studies his community, analyzes the needs of his school, inventories the abilities of teachers and children and then proceeds carefully to meet the needs he has thus discovered. This means that any notion that a program of progressive education can be "put over" by any patent method or technique is erroneous. Any such program is destined for failure at the outset.

Should one attempt to introduce an activity program all at once? It is impossible to present an "even front" in the introduction of a progressive program. The reconstructionist must move slowly to make certain that changes are really assimilated and that they really grow out of the beliefs of and changes in teachers. Much harm has been done in centers where practices have been foisted on teachers who did not understand or did not believe in them. The public school cannot afford to jump ahead of its teachers. Teachers must be given the freedom to forge ahead whenever they are really ready to do so; but teachers must not be forced into practices in which they do not have faith. Some educators, believing that a program could be changed all at once, have relied upon new courses of study made by experts and handed to teachers. This practice is not effective because it does not involve

---

[1] Note pages 162-164 of the *Thirty-Third Yearbook of the National Society for the Study of Education*.

the active growth of teachers. Real course of study revision is synonymous with *changes in teachers* and the best progress is made when they are a simultaneous and cooperative process. Naturally, when the development of the program is dependent upon changes in teachers, the resulting progress is uneven and should reflect much of the unique individual growth of teaching personalities.

What kind of disciplines does the progressive school foster? The progressive school is interested in developing a type of discipline which becomes a part of the child's living. In the old discipline the teacher directed, the child obeyed. In the new discipline, the teacher guides, the child accepts the responsibility for planning and for *taking the consequences* of his own action. The old order included outward appearances of discipline. But when adult-made restrictions were removed real discipline was found to be lacking. In the new, the child helps to establish standards for his behavior, understands *why* such standards are necessary and judges his behavior in the light of consequences. The only restrictions usually necessary for effective discipline are those he and his group impose upon themselves.

Freedom, independence and adaptability are essentials for survival today. But they are not to be confused with irresponsibility, license and vacillation. Freedom and independence come only with well-ordered living. Lives harassed with fears, uncertainties, insecurities and irregularities cannot be free even though every vestige of outer restraint be removed. The progressive school removes unnecessary fears and uncertainties, repudiates the insidious comparisons and attitudes that result in insecurities, and at the same time insists on the regularity and self-control which are so essential to effective self-discipline. Therefore, the progressive school seeks and achieves discipline through the effective assumption of freedom. Only the teacher who lacks a basic understanding of freedom and of child growth lets children live scattered, unorganized lives in the name of freedom. The progressive teacher knows that the building and consistent application of adequate standards of behavior are essential to growth.

Does the progressive school develop real scholarship? The activity movement, properly executed, stimulates scholarship and gives it new depths. The progressive school seizes the opportunity to build real and intrinsic scholarship by releasing children and teachers from narrow academic tracks. There has been, in some quarters, a severe swing away from subject matter because of the stultifying effect its sole emphasis has had upon education. In these quarters scholarship has suffered. Parents have worried—quite properly—about the scattered attack upon knowledge. In these cases the tendency has been to urge a return to the narrow academic limitations of the old school. We **must** correct such faults and avoid any such reaction. A return to the old would involve irretrievable losses. For example, think of the limited scholarship developed in the school in which history is learned chapter by chapter, war by war, from a single textbook; where each child, regardless of his previous knowledge, studies the identical page of a spelling text, the same arithmetic examples or is required to read precisely the same section of the same book with his fellows? This type of study can hardly be dignified by the word "scholarship." This is piece work.

The progressive school aims to build the scholar with a zest for learning; a person who knows how to find and use all possible sources of information and knowledge. The modern school helps children to win a broader and deeper scholarship by leading them to a wider field of experience—a field which cannot be bounded by the covers of textbooks. The child scholar of today even discovers error in textbooks because he goes to sources. Children in a third grade write to an author to question the date of the coinage of the first silver money in this country; children in a fifth grade correct news accounts of the preparations for the Byrd expedition because they have witnessed the preparations and have taken far more accurate notes than the reporters; children in the seventh grade ask for the opportunity to study the origins of superstitions. Why? Because, unbounded by circumscribed texts and courses, but surrounded with books, papers, magazines, materials and experiences with sources, children are left unfettered to be such scholars as they are really capable of being.

Does the progressive school teach the skill subjects? The kind of scholarship the progressive school aims to build demands an independence of attack upon problems with tools adequate for the task. Therefore there can be nothing in progressive belief that repudiates the teaching of the skills. In fact, there is more need for skills, better taught, when children are being given more independence in attacking problems. Progressives do, however, make two changes in the teaching of the skills. First, they give close heed to the scientific disclosures about readiness. For example, because of the symbolic processes involved and because of obscure neurological factors, reading cannot be learned easily before the mental age of six years. Also, recent experimentation has shown that long division, for years the heritage of the fourth grade, is too complex a process for many children of that age and is better learned in the fifth or sixth grade. Sensible and progressive school people save the teaching of such skills until the time that children can learn them readily and in clean-cut fashion. Incalculable harm has been done in teaching complex skills too early and thereby creating an initial confusion from which many children never completely recover.

Second, the progressive teacher makes an effort to see that the skills are learned in such relationships that they have meaning to the children. Because the activity program yields a wide scope of interests, there are equally wide opportunities for the effective use of the skills. The alert teacher, in activity work, can find myriads of opportunities in the course of the day's work. Not all of the drill on skills can come about in the course of activities. Drill, in periods set apart for exercise on needed facts, should be a part of the program. But, skills are taught in the progressive school on an individualized basis. Each child gets drill in the skills he needs, and each child gets such drill at the time in his school career when he is really ready to learn them and understand their use.

Have these things actually been proved in practice? To this point this article has purposely dealt in general terms. Now we present a record of the work of one week in a progressive school.[2] The illustration is taken from a small five-room public school used as a demonstration center for Alabama College, Montevallo. Committees of students constantly observing in the classroom made the following record of the activities and learning occurring during one week of school.

Fourth Grade—Fourth Week

On July 6 the fourth grade went to a fifty-five acre farm about eight miles from the school. Two elderly sisters live alone on this farm. The pupils had discussed this trip and the things they wanted to see: a loom and actual weaving being done. Miss R. had the loom ready for operation when the pupils arrived.

She explained the different parts, their function, and how the thread had been put in. She then showed them how to weave. They looked on with much enthusiasm asking questions as to how and why of this and that. It seemed a bit difficult for one little girl to understand just how the cloth was being made. She was asked if she would like to try. She did and soon understood that it was not such a difficult job, but a rather slow process. The other pupils very systematically arranged themselves in a line and each one took his turn at the loom.

Miss R. then showed them her rabbits, explaining that the fur from the chinchilla and angora rabbit can be used successfully in the textile world.

---

[2] Classroom teacher—Charlotte Peterson. Students who recorded and reported work—Myra T. Barganier, Mrs. Johnnie K. Boykin, Mrs. Gladys Crump, Nellie Davis, and Ada Wimberley—all of Alabama College.

The pupils came back eager to tell what they had seen and to show with pride the sample of their weaving.

Tuesday morning the fourth grade visited a department store:
1. To see cotton materials and to get samples of same
2. To check the spelling of names listed before going and to learn to spell correctly the names of new materials seen.

They found about forty different cotton textiles and brought back many samples which they plan to mount in a scrapbook.

Outcomes of the Work of the Fourth Week

Creative and Appreciative Activities

    Weaving cloth at Miss R's
    Modeling with clay, making masks, animals, figures, etc.
    Planning and thinking out design for woven rug
    Making airplanes, trucks, looms for weaving
    Matching samples of cloth to names
    Making miniature cotton field showing the pickers at work
    Placing news items on bulletin board
    Dramatizing parts of story on cotton
    Improvising conversation for play
    Painting a panel picture of three scenes, thoughtfully carrying out the underlying principles in weaving
    Making miniature bales of cotton for chart on cotton production
    Cutting block letters out of cloth for map of cotton areas
    Making scrapbook for swatches
    Mounting pictures of cotton scenes and textiles
    Appreciation of posters and booklets on cotton made by pupils in Louisiana schools
    Appreciation of poem, "The Fairies Go Shopping," by Milne
    Singing for pleasure, learning "When the Cotton Fields Summer in the Sun"

Reading

    Reading newspaper items on cotton
    Oral reading to find the second parts of the play
    Silent reading to find which character talks first
    Silent reading to see why cotton picker is not successful
    Reading for pleasure by some while others worked on chart and map
    Reading the names of cotton textiles the children had seen at department store as teacher wrote them on the board

Reading, silently, to review their parts in the play, then expressing the conversational part in own words

Reading from book the third part of the play

Reading assignments from Uncle Remus' Basket. The teacher giving remedial instruction to some

Reading from board and deciding on characters for the third scene of play

Reading silently to find what to say and what to do

Arithmetic, Number Concepts

Number of treadles to the loom and age of the shuttle

Number of days required to harness a loom

Price paid for slaves who could weave well

Weight of baby rabbits seen at Miss R's

$28,498,207 amount paid to farmers for land not used in planting cotton. Alabama received $3,136,693; Mississippi, $3,452,714. Finding how much more Mississippi received than Alabama; how much more Alabama received than Georgia. Checked differences found

Cotton picker expensive to operate and lowers the price of cotton for it causes it to be trashy

Quotations on cotton market compared to last week's quotations

Reading thermometer 84 degrees F. and 79 degrees on the one made by the children. Finding difference

Counting by tens on the thermometers

Reviewing number concepts to millions. Writing figures on board as read from news items of number of bales of cotton raised in the States and other countries. Writing dictated numbers on pads. Individualized instructions given

Writing numbers in orderly arrangement

English, Spelling

Oral reports of trip to Miss R's on Friday telling about the shed, the parts of the loom, treadles, bobbin, shuttle, and shaft and how each functioned in making cloth. Compared these with those seen in pictures. Compared the spinning wheel at the farm with the one on which they had tried to spin the week before

One pupil agreeing to write up trip

Discussing unfinished work

Planning for the play, decided about the characters and the scenery in second and third scenes

Dicussing the picnic for Tuesday afternoon at Montebriar

Planning trip to a department store for Tuesday morning to see cotton textiles

Writing questions about what they would like to learn
Listing names of cotton material, teacher writing them on board as pupils spell them, checking the spelling of *voile, organdie, cambric, pique*—the last rhymes with *bouquet* and is French
Describing how these materials looked and for what each was used
Planning a scrapbook to paste samples in for the museum
Learning to pronounce and finding meaning of *figure, boll, crouched, stealthy, burst, creeping cautiously*
Learning the difference between *scene* and *act*
Learning the words *chinchilla* and *angora*

Geography

Locating Enterprise, Alabama, where there will be built a monument to the memory of the boll weevil
Locating cities in Alabama where there are cotton mills
Locating Pepperell Mills in Massachusetts
Comparing output of cotton in Mississippi, Alabama and Georgia

History

The history of the Whithall rug which was displayed in room
The meaning of "Flag of Truce"
The history of early cotton factory shown by pictures

Science

Comparing a small loom to the one seen on Friday, the type of thread used, kind of cloth made, and how thread is taken from loom
Chinchilla and angora fur can be woven into cloth
Coordination of muscles used in weaving is controlled by the brain
Observing "count of thread" through microscope
Discussing the kind of weather suitable for farming, and the name of the best grade of cotton
Discussing how a cotton picker is made

Skills, Habits, Attitudes

Improved use of carpenter's tools
Improved ability to work and play together
Increased skill in painting, modeling, construction work
Improved skill in reading
Better ability to get information through reading
Improvement in organizing information into important episodes

Summary

The true progressive school moves carefully and patiently toward more adequate provisions for education. By study of community needs, by respectful consideration of the abilities of teachers, by careful inventories of the needs of children, the progressive program is planned. Haste, disorder and confusion are foreign to the really progressive school. Rather, serious scholarship, sincere personal relationships, effective self-discipline, and security of personality are its attributes. The activity program, properly initiated, planned to meet the needs of all, is an effective step toward more adequate education. Where it has been carried on with good judgment the attitudes of the children, the results in learnings—in content and even the old live subject matter—have convinced thoughtful, unbiased judges that there are indisputable values inherent in the plan. Progressive education has proved its right to the respectful consideration of all interested in the future of education.

Vol. XIV—p. 58 (Oct. 1937)

Toward a More Democratic Citizenship
BY JAMES S. TIPPETT

Three movements are affecting the development of today's curriculum for the young child, according to Mr. Tippett, curriculum adviser for the Parker School District, Greenville, South Carolina, and author of "Schools for a Growing Democracy." He shows how these movements are affecting curriculum development, points out which one he considers most in line with a philosophy of education which has democratic citizenship as its goal, and names three important principles—cornerstones of curriculum building.

TWENTY-FIVE YEARS AGO THE CURRICULUM APPEARED TO HAVE become fixed in its general aspects. Courses of study were in reasonable agreement as to the quantity of history or geography or poetry or language which should be taught to all the children. The chief emphasis at that time was being placed by educators upon how to make the content of the courses stick by the pupils.

The trend toward a better methodology for mastery of a proposed amount of content still persists, but decreasingly. For young children, concern is not now with how much content is mastered but with the growth of the child as he comes into contact with educative situations.

Trends in Curriculum Making

Three distinct movements are affecting the newer curriculum for young children. All agree that pupils should be active in their learning if it is to be effective. All agree that the schoolroom should be a workshop in which the pupils have freedom to go about their tasks with vigor and understanding. All agree in insisting that working situations as well as materials for carrying work forward are essential. The three movements differ in their emphasis upon the nature of the educative situations which should be prepared or encouraged.

The individual child and his growth based upon his interests: One group of educators says that the interests of children alone need control what is done. The work in the classroom may well be made up of a series of individual small projects. The interests of pupils will control almost totally, except that direction will be given to see that pupils do grow and that the classroom does not become disorganized with poor work habits as an accompaniment. Emphasis is almost wholly upon the individual child and his personal growth. Case studies of the growth of individuals are greatly in evidence. A constant interchange of notes and suggestions is sought between the home and the school. Small concern is shown for the community, except as its affects the child. His effect upon the community is of secondary concern.

The individual child and his growth based upon social situations: A second group of educators is concerned with the child and his growth, but they emphasize that his growth should take place in social situations to which he contributes and which in turn contribute to him. This is the group which has been responsible for the development of units of work or centers of interest, which are based upon child interest, call for the use of many kinds of activity, use the environment, help meet the demands of society, stimulate the use of the skills, provide for individual differences in native capacities and in tastes, and emphasize participation in democratic practices such as cooperating, sharing in responsibilities, adjusting to changing situations, and self-finding. This group is aware of the individual child always, but it feels that he grows best if his individual interests upon many occasions are merged into group interests and if a constant effort is made to bring him into contact with aspects of community life which can be meaningful to him.

The individual child and his growth based on a curriculum more socially functional: The third important movement is toward making the curriculum for young children more socially functional. Units of work or centers of interest, or units of work growing out of centers of interest which are determined beforehand for each school grade, become the core of the curriculum. Educators concerned with this movement would have as a guiding aim the social value of any piece of work carried on. Social values would be determined in advanced in the light of a particular political philosophy—which is designated at present as democratic—and all activities of the schools would be forced as skillfully as possible into that mould. Many of the state-wide programs of curriculum revision show this trend in its most significant aspects. Social values come first, not the child and his normal growth. Social patterning is basic to the program.

Other Trends

Other trends that have a bearing upon the curriculum are for a delay of reading until age seven or later, for an upward shove to the mastery of all skills, such as letter writing, spelling, number combinations, and handwriting, and for greater emphasis upon the introduction of science and of many avenues for creative expression as soon as possible. These trends have small importance in any consideration of a curriculum which leads toward a more democratic citizenship, however significant they may be in making the life of the child more satisfactory and however effective on his level of growth.

Many schoolrooms still show evidence of no move away from the teaching of specific skills and information. The daily schedule is made up of piecemeal bits, and formalized procedure is rampant. The atmosphere in the classroom is unstimulating and dreary. Desks are immovable, and blackboards are dominating. In such classrooms no movement in the direction of any social program except one of regimented procedure can be found.

In an increasingly large number of classrooms, however, significant changes have come about. The significance is with respect to a more democratic form of living in the school and hopefully at least in the home and the community. Specific skills and information are mastered in those classrooms, but in connection with the needs of the learners. Daily schedules are made up of larger working periods and are less inflexible than formerly. A much more informal way of conducting the work of the classroom has come to the teachers and is reflected among the pupils.

The classrooms have been provided with movable furniture, tools and work places, materials of infinite variety and usableness, and books of all kinds and descriptions. Classrooms are pleasant, childlike and beautiful. Bulletin boards for the exhibition of children's work, for clippings, and for countless other purposes have taken the place of the usual expanse of blackboard. The movement in those classrooms is toward democratic citizenship and no amount of concern with methodology for mastery or with specific content can interfere wholly with its progression into democratic living.

Which Movement Will Make for More Democratic Living

An examination, however, of the three distinct movements which are affecting materially the curriculum for the early school years shows some matters for deep concern. Which of the three movements is most in line with a philosophy of democratic living? Each person will have to come to a decision for himself. I choose the second of the three, perhaps because I have worked most closely with those who have put it effectively into operation. It is the movement to develop units of work or centers of interest in which the use of essential skills is plainly evident, which help meet the demands of a democratic society, which are rich in content and draw the whole child into their meaningful progression. Almost lacking in concern for the social order as it is represented by the school group, this second movement seems less likely to make individualists, which can easily be true of the first movement. It lacks a hampering quality imposed upon the third movement of concern with the social function. It calls for more of the child and his interest than the third and less than the first. The first of the movements often ends in selfish absorption in individual matters. The third imposes from without and too early for young children a social pattern that could well be undemocratic just because it is imposed. The second movement concerns itself with the individual and his growth, and it also has the community with individuals and their place in it sufficiently in mind to give children in the early years of school some experience with social living.

Further consideration need not be given to that view of the curriculum which is absorbed in mastery only of skills and content. It is not a trend in any sense of the word but a point of departure. A democracy which has inherited such a conception of the curriculum or which has allowed such a conception to develop as its scheme for education must get away from it. The three movements are faced away from static contentment with mere learning unrelated to doing. The one which seeks to develop the individual without due regard for society is not wholesome. Too much individualism is not truly representative of a democracy. The one which leans toward too early an introduction of social function into child experience is dangerous. All situations in which children work and live together have social meaning, but if the meaning is forced to the front too early or if the meanings are those which adults feel must be forced, then another wall arises. The curriculum becomes fixed and dogmatic. It errs on the side of neglect for the growing child and his interests and possibilities.

Principles To Be Considered

Working together: To learn how to work together seems to me to be the first principle which must be imbedded for the new curriculum and which must have many occasions for practice as the curriculum envelops the child. Cooperation means the opportunity to make plans, and to make those plans in the light of the opinion and desire of others.

Units of work which are based upon the real interests of children offer many opportunities for working together in natural situations. What shall we do? Why shall we do it? How shall we do it? These are constantly recurring questions. Note that the individual has immersed himself in "we." Note further that the real interests of children, and naturally their understanding of the situation, have taken the place of adult conceptions of what should interest them and of what meanings should inhere in the situations which arise. Direction of cooperative effort is essential but not to the point above which the workers can understand its significance or for which they feel a need.

There is clear distinction between the three above-mentioned trends in curriculum making for young children in this matter of cooperation. One neglects it too much. One forces it into unnatural channels. One, like the middle-sized bear, is just right. At least, the one which stands at the middle seems to trend most directly and most surely toward democratic citizenship.

Sharing responsibility: To learn how to share in accepting responsibility and to assume an adequate and proper amount of the responsibilities which a democratic state (or a democratic classroom, which is the nearest approach the young child can make to a state) presents is another cardinal principle for the building of a curriculum. If the curriculum builder concerns himself too much with the individual, the responsibilities which can be assumed must necessarily be tinged with selfish interest. Whether the units of work had preeminently the social function as their guiding star would make little difference as to the number or kind of responsibilities which could be assumed by pupils. Both the second and third trends would meet the requirements for this demand of a democracy. The third might be accused of insisting too soon upon responsibilities which "should" be assumed. This could easily be the case when children are supposed to accept responsibility for doing something about social conditions far out of their realm of experience or understanding. A young child could do nothing about improving the quality of the milk supply in his community just as he could do nothing about a political situation. This would be recognized in the second of the trends toward curriculum making. Those pursuing the third might forget it because of their enthusiasm for a society, which was planned too far in advance.

Growing and developing: Democracy demands that the individuals who compose it should be helped to find themselves as surely as possible and that each individual's abilities be turned not only to his own advancement but to the advancement of the social order. Here plainly is disagreement among the formers of new trends in the education of young children. In one case the individual expresses himself. What is good for him becomes the chief aim. It is, of course, not quite fair to feel that any individual in a schoolroom can live to himself. That can be true also in a curriculum built upon individual interests. Initiative is too easily directed into wholly selfish channels. In a curriculum which has even the most enlightened adult planning back of it, an individual and his possibilities are too easily lost sight of. His initiative, too often directed, becomes warped or crushed into one mould. This is not as likely to be true if the curriculum more surely follows his desires as they become colored by those of his fellows.

To work together, to share properly in assuming responsibility, and to grow at a maximum in all possible directions consistent with the good of others seem to me sufficiently clear and inclusive demands of a society which is moving in democratic ways to furnish accurate guides for those who are making the educative set-up for young children. That trend which makes for their fullest and most democratic expression should be followed.

Vol. XVI—p. 110 (Nov. 1939)

Growth in Social Living Through the Tools of Learning
BY ALICE MIEL

Miss Miel, curriculum counselor in the public schools at Mount Pleasant, Michigan, tells how the tools of learning can be made socially effective without incurring the unfortunate results of the old traditional schools. Teaching that is readiness building rather than rote learning marks today's artist teacher.

IN THESE DAYS WHEN THE SOCIAL JOB OF EDUCATION SEEMS TO BE OF more importance with each fresh burst of news, the spotlight is being thrown on every activity of the school. Even the tool subjects are being subjected to the same searching scrutiny. Are they playing their part in developing socialized individuals, or are they still helping to turn out an ill-assorted lot of individualistic persons, some smug, some defeated, most of them failing to appreciate the value in a democratic social order of equipment for further learning? Does the child in school acquire tools of learning which enable him to be a creative learner and a useful member of society for the rest of his life, or does he merely learn to hate books and decide to have stenographers and adding machines to take care of the unpleasant side of life for him?

Teachers and administrators throughout the country have been conscious for some time that children were not acquiring an efficient use of the tools of learning. However, they have, in many cases, mistakenly supposed that by postponing the teaching of the tool subjects until the later grades and cutting down on time allotments for these subjects, or even cutting them out altogether, they could remedy the situation without making other adjustments. The result has been that much time has been wasted for the children, while the secondary school, the college, and the public have begun to clamor that "standards are being lowered."

The solution to the problem does not lie in the direction of rendering the teaching of the tool subjects more ineffective than ever. In a democracy, particularly in critical times, there is need for a better grasp of the tools of learning than under any other circumstances. More than ever before do individuals need to be equipped with defenses against emotional, irrational reactions. The desire to seek the truth and the knowledge of how to go about seeking it constitute the most effective defenses against such reactions. Therefore, the modern school should place not less but more emphasis upon equipment for learning. But that emphasis must be placed without incurring the unfortunate results of the old school. Increased effectiveness in human beings is desired, not increased inertia.

Weaknesses of the Traditional School

One weakness of the traditional approach was that the children seldom saw the value of what they were learning. They were not helped to gain *insight* into word and letter and number relationships. They were not helped to see the relationships existing between various aspects of their environment. Reading, writing and arithmetic were not presented as magic keys to open exciting doors and solve challenging puzzles; they were something to be done as quickly and as painlessly as possible in order to allow freedom "for living." In other words, in the traditional school, there was satisfaction with a product that could perform glibly, though robot-like, in the field of the three R's. There was not desire to equip a child with tools of learning that would make it possible to continue his own education after school days were over. Furthermore, reading, writing and arithmetic were interpreted very narrowly; they did not include such tools as the ability to use the table of contents and the index, the ability to skim in reading, the ability to apply scientific tests to statements, and the ability to estimate.

There was another weakness of the traditional approach that was even more far-reaching in its effect. That weakness was the failure of the old school to help the child to see the social value of what he was learning. It was enough in the traditional school to secure as near perfection as possible on the part of as many individuals as possible in certain isolated skills. There was little concern that the child become challenged to use his gifts for the benefit of others.

The Problem of Today's School

The problem of present-day education is to correct these faults in the schools of yesterday. The school today must provide experiences through which the children will themselves recognize that they are more effective members of a group if they are equipped with some tools. The teacher's job in this connection becomes larger and more important than ever before. He must so guide the experiences of the children that they will have the opportunity to practice social living. He may help the group to act at all times as a small unit of a democracy in order to provide this opportunity for give-and-take in a social group. Countless situations will then arise which will require the tools of learning. The groups may have to engage in extensive research involving the use of many sources of information and involving record-keeping, or the group may have to depend on a few individual members to find out some facts and report them to the rest. In such a group, engaging in such activities, the valued members will be those who can contribute because they can read, write, speak and figure efficiently.

The little bookworm who loves to read for pleasure but who cannot be persuaded to help clean up the paint or act as secretary for the group will be one of the least valued members.

Emphasis in the school should not be on equipping only the most capable with the tools of learning. We are too likely to use the familiar alibis for not giving much attention to some children. We decide in advance that a certain boy will be "nothing but a ditch-digger." He will, therefore, have little need for reading and writing. Only the simplest arithmetic will be required in his living. Our consciences are clear, then, if we spend most of our time on the "teachables."

Now, it would be most unrealistic to expect that all children could be equipped with learning tools of the same quality. It is folly, of course, not to help our most intelligent children to develop into creative individuals capable of leadership in fields that demand high intellectual capacity. Yet, it is unfair and unsafe in a democracy not to help each individual to obtain the best grasp he can of the tools of learning in order that he may be able to secure at least the minimum amount of information to which the citizen of a free country is entitled. The ditch-digger may not need calculus or trigonometry or even long division, but he needs to appreciate the difference between millions and billions and to understand what a 3 per cent tax on sales does to his total income. "Even the least of these" needs to learn to make simple analyses of propaganda and to find out a few facts on both sides of a question. "Even the least of these" buys goods and casts a ballot.

The course in social studies which was introduced into the elementary curriculum in the hope that it would serve to socialize individuals will not produce that effect as if by magic. Children will have to be helped, as they attempt to solve social problems, to gain mastery over certain tools which will make easier the solutions of the next problem they attack. For example, they should be learning to enjoy reading widely and searchingly to get different points of view; they should be learning to keep records of many kinds; they should be learning to deal with statistics, read maps and graphs, and appreciate the world of number; and they should be learning to express themselves in effective language.

Teaching Which Is Readiness Building

There is no intention, here, of ignoring the many avenues through which, today, an individual may receive information. There is no intention, either, of condoning the excessive attention paid to reading in the old school. However, for many purposes and among them forming considered opinions, there is no adequate substitute for the tool of reading, in which should be included the reading of maps and graphs, tables and charts, as well as of books and periodicals.

The elementary teacher who is doing a good job might be said to be building readiness of different kinds all the time. Instead of teaching the A B C's to babies, the primary teacher lays the groundwork for the development of the dictionary habit in the fourth grade. Instead of meaningless drill on combinations in arithmetic, the primary teacher helps to develop a real appreciation of the difference between *more* and *less* so that in the fourth grade the children do not have to say, "We can do the problem if you will tell us whether to add or take away." Instead of drilling on sounds of letters and phonograms in isolation, the first-grade teacher paves the way for the later use of phonics as one tool for getting the meaning of an unfamiliar word. Instead of serving up graphs or apostrophes as a big, indigestible dish, the skillful teacher sees to it that the children grow up with these things and that they learn their use through seeing others use them and through having opportunity to use them themselves on numerous occasions.

This type of teaching that is readiness-building calls forth the creative ability of the teacher, for it is far more difficult for him to measure his own progress in a readiness-building school than it was in the traditional school where the directives were more specific.

The best guide for the modern teacher is probably the broad aim of doing everything in his power to promote the socialization of children. This may mean doing a better job of teaching reading in the first grade. It may mean helping children to develop good discussion techniques. When the teacher takes it as his goal to help each child in his charge to profit as much by experience as he is capable of profiting at every stage of his development, the children will come out of the elementary school equipped with some basic tools of learning that are suited to their individual abilities. For that reason, these tools will mean much to their possessors and they will be used effectively to make their possessors' lives more satisfactory both to themselves and to others.

Someone has said that education should result in senses quickened and appreciations deepened. It is the tools of learning that make it possible for an individual to become and remain highly sensitive to the needs of people about him and deeply appreciative of the living world. Therein lies the teacher's job.

Vol. XX—p. 345 (Apr. 1944)

Preparing Children for a World Society

BY MARGARET MEAD

To dignify his role upon the earth, twentieth-century man must master ways in which people of different culture or different race or different religion can live together so that each group contributes something positive to the whole. Miss Mead emphasizes the importance of this task, discusses two needs that must be met if it is to be accomplished, and analyzes the contributions of this issue toward fulfilling one of these needs.

ONE WAY OF DIGNIFYING MAN'S ROLE ON THIS EARTH IS TO DIGNIFY the times in which he lives, to identify the special task to be done in his own century. The last century saw man conquer the problem of physical power and harness natural forces so that he no longer needed to toil from dawn to dusk for the barest necessities of life.

In this century a new and perhaps a more difficult task confronts the conscious world—those people in every country who are thinking rather than merely dreaming about a better world life for everyone. We do not have to master the mechanics of travel on sea or land or in the air or the problems of transmitting sound and image through space. All these things have been done. We do have to master ways in which people of different culture or different race or different religion can live together, not merely tolerated or endured but so that each group contributes something positive to the whole.

All through history when two or more peoples have met and exchanged ideas and inventions, works of art and styles of living, something new has resulted. But the something new was not always something good. A Japanese who appreciated Western civilization codified the Japanese Bushido, which became the handbook of Japanese militarism. Hitler, living in an Austrian village, dreamed of a greater Germany. Ezra Pound, after seeking the lovely rhythms of Provençal verse and giving them back to his own people, lived to become an apologist for Fascism. Centuries of conquest in India produced a layering of castes deeply inimical to the development of dignified human living. These instances are conspicuous in the world scene, but equally important are the contacts between children of quite different backgrounds which may set the stage for later hostilities, myths of racial grandeur or religious fanaticism.

Furthermore, we cannot shirk this task of learning how to live together, for there are those with other purposes than ours who know that something can be done with the great unprecedented new contacts between peoples all over the world. In every quiet lane in England American soldiers, accustomed to wider spaces, have driven a jeep or a truck and have been welcomed as allies while the hedgerows trembled. In the United States minority groups from other races and cultures, as well as the young and the old, have suddenly become valuable when every hand was needed for a war job. New jobs have given them a new sense of their own potentialities as they work side by side with people whom they have never known before.

All these heightened contacts, all these new expectations can become either a breeding ground for better understanding or a breeding ground for further wars and revolutions. The technique of exploiting these conflicts is well known to all those who believe that the speediest way to change a bad situation is first to make it worse. The activists of both Right and Left are adept at playing upon the fears and hostilities of peoples who must live together in the same world although they seldom come close together under conditions of friendliness and warmth, except in the schools.

But in the United States the most diverse peoples of every skin color and with many different sound patterns on their tongues sit side by side in the elementary school, share the same drinking fountain, dip their pens in the same ink. At first glance it would seem inconceivable that girls who have gone to the same public school which made no distinctions in creed, nationality or color should suddenly when they become employees at some great war factory object to sharing restrooms and lunchrooms. Yet this does happen and brings sharply into relief two needs: (1) the need for laying a foundation in emotional understanding rather than in formal, verbal understanding of other people, and (2) the need for eliminating the tendency of any group of people, children or adults, to define themselves by the circumstance that they are *not* something else—*not* women, *not* foreigners, *not* Catholics, *not* Protestants, *not* gentiles, *not* Asiatics, *not* white. It will be enough to supply one of these needs without supplying the other.

Children may learn to link arms easily because in school their personal definition of themselves does not include *not* being pigeon-holed with people of another sex, class, race, nationality or religion. If they do not learn as children an easy acceptance of people who are different from themselves, then only too easily the fear or hatred of these differences can be exploited later. But even if children in school do learn to value each other *in school,* this value may all be swept away later if as adults they value themselves mainly in terms of the people with whom they do *not* share jobs or streetcar seats, dinner tables or church pews. . . .

. . . .

Almost every schoolroom in America contains children whose homeways differ if only because they come from another region of the United States. It may be useful to include always some samples of the homeways of different parts of America—May baskets and baked beans from New England, for instance—beside the more sharply contrasting homeways of children from Mexican or Russian or Chinese homes.

When it is possible it will be valuable to emphasize that race and culture are only transitorily and unimportantly connected. Children will know that this is true if they are shown the difference in the homeways of Negro children from the South and from the North, or of Northern and Southern Italians, or of Jewish children from different European countries. In this way children may learn that every group of people has a way of life, compact of tradition and delicate in adjustment to the surrounding physical world, which they carry with them in their words and gestures, their hopes and fears, wherever they go.

The materials which have been collected by the ACE Committee on Intercultural Relations are a particularly fortunate combination because they all invoke the children's emotional response, not merely a textbook comprehension. Songs are perhaps the most successful form of art in bridging every sort of cultural barrier. A snatch of song hummed years afterwards may re-establish contact where it looks as if all had been lost.

Using food as a means of bringing cultural understanding has two purposes. To begin with, in all our European tradition and in most of the world, to eat together of the same food is a sacramental act. To have eaten the food of another still carries an implication of closeness. It is important not only that the foreign food should be brought to school but that where possible it should be cooked at school or brought in still redolent with its peculiar aroma so that the children may share the smell before they eat together.

Differences in food habits are a never-ending source of misunderstanding because people seem to feel that other people *are* what they eat, somehow compounded of the strange, oddly smelling, unfamiliar food. When, however, one eats a bit oneself a bond almost physical in nature is established between the two. Children who bring a little of their homefood into the schoolroom will also have established a bond between home—where all is warmth and kindness and cookies— and school where standards of success often alien to the child's homeways are imposed.

This point is particularly important because so often the question of intercultural or interracial relations is onesided. An attempt is made to make the majority group tolerate or like the minority group without realizing that little love can bloom in the hearts of minority children who have met only routine discrimination and coldness. The school teacher may be the only woman of the majority group whom the children have ever met or will ever meet through their childhood. If they learn to like and trust her and their classmates, they will be ready to respond to the friendliness which is offered them later. It is not enough to make the other children—the children whose names are all American and whose skins are only different degrees of blondness and brunetteness—appreciate their neighbors with strange names and odd tricks of pronunciation and different shades of skin color. Unless this feeling is reciprocated, little will be accomplished.

The third kind of materials which the Committee has collected are games which children have loved and favorite folk tales. Both games and stories have plots—plots which grew from the universal experiences of childhood—of being small while adults are large, of having parents of two sexes, of having to make the best of playing at being grown whenever one wants really to share in the grown-up world. As children join hands and move in a circle, repeating a rhyme which was developed by children bred in a very different culture, some greater understanding of the children whose feet move naturally to that rhythm and whose special hopes and fears are embodied in those words should come to them, inarticulately, below the level that any teacher could verbalize or any child parrot back.

Here it is probably a good thing to do several things: play games which belong to minority children in the school, and play games which belong to some foreign culture of which there is no representative in the school so that all the children—old American, Polish, Italian, Scottish, Irish, Chinese—may experience together how strange a strange rhythm can seem.

The game which is sometimes called "Oranges and Lemons" and sometimes "London Bridge" is played around the world. As children experiment with the different choices: "What do you like best, ice cream or cake?" "What do you like best, coconut hearts or mangoes?" "What do you like best, a leek or a cucumber?"—all the hundred different phrasings which children have given the same game around the world—they will be learning simultaneously that peoples are different and that they have much in common, that comparable and familiar delight can take on many different forms.

Stories are perhaps the most difficult material to use successfully. So often the plot of the wicked stepmother or the proud sister variety may arouse a child's terror without also, as do the folk tales of one's own culture, assuaging some fear that every child in that culture has already known.

Stories from other lands should be chosen very carefully. All frightening situations should be avoided much more carefully than when choosing fairy tales from our own background. And while variants of games from other cultures are a good way of bringing children better understanding, it is probably that variants of our familiar fairy tales,[1] especially the frightening ones like "Snow White" or "Hansel and Gretel," should not be told our children as the way "the little French children tell it." Children who have steeled themselves by long experience to live through the frightening incidents in the familiar tale may be doubly shocked by some new twist of the plot and reject, long after the whole incident is forgotten, the very name of the nation that added that last unbearable bit. For the simplest and most reliable results it will be best to choose stories which emphasize the relationship between children and those parts of the natural environment which happen everywhere—the seasons, the first snow or the first snowdrop, the birth of baby chicks or calves, the full moon.

---

[1] As a corollary of this caution, among a group of children of very mixed nationality, it is probably wise to avoid frightening folk tales of any sort as to some of the children even our familiar ones will include strange and therefore frightening solutions.

As all these materials are used to help the children whose homeways are different feel less strange, to help the children of old American stock to welcome the others, it will be important to suggest to the newcomers that they are also Americans, also valued members of the region, the state, the town, the street where they live. Sometimes well-meant attempts to emphasize the color and beauty of some other national heritage have only resulted in making the children who had a claim on that heritage reject it because they felt that it stood in the way of their becoming full Americans, full citizens of their local world. The extra homeways—the Russian food, the Finnish folk song, the Icelandic folk tale, the accent from Dixie or the lore of a fishing village in New England or of a western ranch—have to be handled as something extra, something plus, and always in such a way that when the children are grown each can be so proud of what he *is* that none will have to rest his sense of security on what he *is not*.

Only so can the children who join hands in some new game today be prepared to take an active and responsible part in the work of this century—the work of orchestrating the cultures of the world so that each may contribute fully to a world culture.

Section VI

*Today's Child —
Tomorrow's World*

Today's Child—Tomorrow's World

Given a provocative environment with sympathetic and wise guidance, today's child will become tomorrow's effective and productive citizen. His todays and tomorrows will merge into his own developing personality, enriched or impoverished by each day's experiences. He will learn through his own explorations, deductions and decisions if afforded the opportunity. His meanings and concepts will broaden and deepen as he encounters and solves perplexing situations. If not hurried, over-pressured and prodded by adults, he will seek rest, relaxation and time to discover the secrets of nature. His play will lead him into vigorous physical activity and his imagination will cause him to ponder, in quietude, the mysteries of life and creation.

The world of 50's and 60's into which today's children have been born and are living has surrounded them with apprehension and fear. The adults have become frightened by the destructive potentialities of technological weapons of war. A resulting power struggle has engendered illogical thinking about children's education. Enrichment has been sacrificed to practice in the learning of skills. A rigid curriculum tends to replace relaxed learning through experimentation and discovery. Homework has displaced recreation for many six- and seven-year-olds. In general, there has been extension downward of prearranged curriculum content.

How much do we understand the obvious portent of tomorrow when we begin to curtail childhood's prerogative to grow according to individual proclivities, when we foreshorten learning rather than extend and deepen it? In a rapidly changing technological society man needs to know himself, to understand his natural and social environment and place value upon changes that will enhance the human individual. He must distinguish between constructive uses of applied technology and those that defeat and destroy human existence. Knowledge is vast, and the future fund of knowledge that will be available is unpredictable except that it is expanding at an ever increasing rate.

Without doubt, the greatest single problem now faced and continuing into tomorrow's world is the wise use of technological knowledge and skills. How to apply the outcomes of scientific effort to the betterment of mankind is the crucial issue. This then must guide education's processes and goals. Even young children should enjoy the stimulus of using their imaginative and creative resources in a social context Educational leadership must find ways to arouse in children a desire and a dedication to these democratic and humanitarian ends.—*By* BERNICE BAXTER, *formerly Director of Human Relations, Oakland Public Schools, California.*

Moving Forward*

BY MARY ESTHER LEEPER

Mary Esther Leeper was Executive Secretary Emeritus and was Chairman of the Steering Committee on securing permanent ACEI headquarters. She served as Executive Secretary of the Association from 1930 to 1952 and continues to contribute creative leadership to ACEI. From 1955 Association members have supported her dream, idea and plan for a center designed for adults working for and with children. Mary Esther Leeper heads the list of "dedicated members" to which she refers in the talk given on Childhood Education Center Dedication Day, August 14, 1960.

THIS IS ACEI'S DEDICATION YEAR! ON AUGUST 14 THE CHILDHOOD Education Center in Washington, D. C., was dedicated to the education and well-being of children. It is designed for use by adults who work with and for children. This building, the first home of an organization now sixty-eight years old, testifies to the ability of the members to:

    recognize a need
    plan for meeting that need
    work to make plans materialize.

This Center means that ACEI work can be done more effectively and that gradually new services can be developed. To the public, it is a constant reminder that children and what happens to them are important.

The building dedication is the result of many people working together for a definite purpose. The human interest stories of this endeavor are varied and often thrilling. There were those individuals who: volunteered a monthly gift "for the duration"; baked bread for friends; gave stock certificates; sent deed for property later sold for several thousand dollars; donated earnings from baby-sitting; sent book royalties; gave money saved by an abbreviated vacation; donated dividends; gave income from guest riders in autos; shared honorariums. Others gave hours and days and weeks and years of volunteer labor. To do this some members traveled far and lived in Washington at their own expense. These gifts and many others were offered in the spirit of the sacrificial first gift of five thousand dollars presented fifteen years ago by the late Isabel Lazarus, then a retired Baltimore teacher. When presenting it

* From *Over the Editor's Desk*, October 1960.

she remarked, "Maybe some day this will help ACEI have its own library."

Many Branches and State Associations gave large cash gifts. Others sent generous earnings from book fairs; dramatic performances for children and adults; movies; family concerts; sales of stationery, candy, nuts, articles to make housekeeping easier; workshop fees; historic and beautiful home tours; fun nights.

Through their own enthusiasm for the Center, members influenced friends and relatives to become "ACEI Builders." A number of business firms also sent generous gifts.

By people working together, ACEI's dream has been realized. The Center has been dedicated. Such efforts will continue until the mortgage is cleared and the Center belongs wholly to ACEI members.

Now that we are in the Center, let us be joyful—yet not satisfied. Occupying the building will mean little to the improvement of opportunities for children unless we look out and beyond. We admire, respect and are grateful to the dedicated kindergarten teachers who had the vision and courage to bring this organization into being sixty-eight years ago. They chose the name, "International Kindergarten Union." We are grateful that we, the members of today, have the privilege of being the "ACEI Builders." But we dare not linger on the early history or even the immediate past. Our concern must be with the present and the future work of this organization. What are we doing today? What are we preparing to do in the years ahead? This responsibility calls for more than dedication of a building! It calls for the dedication or the rededication of every member of this Association.

As members rededicating ourselves to the purposes of the Association, we will recognize the importance of first rereading and meditating on ACEI's purpose as set forth in the Constitution. We will supplement this by also reading the current *Plan of Action*. Let us accept as an over-all working slogan the first statement of the purpose: *To work for the education and well-being of children.* Under this call to action, to what specifics shall we dedicate our efforts? What basic responsibilities are ours? Six areas seem at this time to call for serious dedicated effort by every member and every branch.

As dedicated members we will:

1. Examine continuously and critically the philosophy or beliefs of ACEI as they are being expressed in both words and practices. As individuals and as groups we will participate earnestly in developing and putting into practice the Association's *Plan of Action*. We will give thought to how adequately ACEI's philosophy is expressed in Branch and International conference and workshop programs, publications and

information services. Are beliefs and practices being influenced properly by results of research?

2. Review current research related to the growth of children and how they learn. Whenever possible, apply the results to our work with children. Suggest to ACEI's Executive Board and Staff areas in which research is needed. Welcome opportunities to participate in action research in our community or school or classroom.

3. Encourage the continuance of ACEI's "pioneering spirit" both in Branches and the International Association. Suggest new ways of working, new projects that might be experimented with and evaluated. Recall such examples as: establishment of the kindergarten unit in France (at the close of World War I); study grants for teachers from Norway, Germany, Korea, Australia; sponsorship of and Branch contacts made for Swedish, German, Filipino and South American teachers (at the request of United States Government); joint sponsorship of groups visiting schools abroad; sample toys, school equipment and furniture, photos and bulletins sent to Germany, the Near and the Far East; cooperation of ACEI with American Library Association and National Congress of Parents and Teachers in developing CARE-UNESCO Children's Book Plan; introduction of study and discussion groups at ACEI Conference in 1934, studio or "doing" groups in 1937; change from adoption of the usual resolutions to a *Plan of Action;* initiation of Expansion Service Fund to cover unexpected opportunities for service; introduction of the ACEI Fellow plan whereby each year a teacher from a different region comes to headquarters to keep before Board and Staff reactions and feelings of a teacher of children and Branch member, to enjoy experiences contributing to his own personal and professional development; Functional Display of commercial materials at 1950 Conference (materials approved by ACEI committees and made functional by their use in study and studio groups and by parents and children in the conference community); and the most recent pioneering in the erecting of a headquarters building that is more than an office building—a place where members, parents, children and other community workers, including policemen, may view changing exhibits, examine and use school equipment and materials.

What pioneering projects should ACEI or Branches undertake next? What new ways of working will we suggest to our Branch officers or to the ACEI Executive Board?

4. Extend the use of the democratic process in all phases of ACEI work. Are all members being given an opportunity to make some contribution to their organization's program of service? Are all who need the services of ACEI in our community or state being given op-

portunities to enjoy and participate in such services? Are all those in our community who are concerned with children receiving information about local meetings, ACEI publications, conferences and information services?

5. Use courage, wisdom, tact and determination in support of the quality of education that we believe is good for children. Speak out against the efforts of some zealous individuals and groups that would limit school programs to memorizing, not always learning, facts. Protest when plans for the education of children allow little or no time for individual practice in problem solving, for firsthand learning experiences, and for varied and satisfying creative activities. We will use all our knowledge about how learning takes place and about children to withstand efforts to deprive children of their right to develop to their full potential.

6. Dedication to the improvement of opportunities for children demands looking far ahead, far beyond the walls of the ACEI Center, beyond the children we teach today, beyond our Branch, beyond the International Association. We are told that within ten years man will have conquered interlunar space. We are further told that already technicians have plans on their "dream boards" that can immediately go into effect.

As educators what dreams and plans do we have in the making for the guidance of teachers, parents and others responsible for children in the years ahead? What qualities will be needed in this new space age? Initiative, ability to solve problems, creativeness, scholarship, urge for further knowledge, awareness of resources—these are some of the requisites needed in the new era.

What does such a concept suggest for today's school programs? What dreams does it stimulate regarding school programs in 1970? Dedicated ACEI members have much to do. ACEI Board and staff members need to know of your ideas, your dreams, your plans.

In 1960 ACEI dedicates a building to the education and well-being of children two to twelve years of age. May we, the members, rededicate ourselves to the improvement of opportunities for children through renewed efforts to:

Examine ACEI's philosophy and practices.
Study and use results of recent research related to children and learning.
Foster continuance of the Association's pioneering spirit.
Demonstrate our belief in the value of the democratic process in all
    phases of Association activities.
Use courage, wisdom, tact, determination in support of the quality of
    education we believe is best for children.

Cultivate our dreams and develop plans for education of children in the space age.

These things we can do as individuals, as members of Branches and as members of the International Association. So we shall move forward toward our goals, knowing in our hearts we shall never reach them entirely. Dedicated people who are willing not only to dream and to plan but also to *work* will never have stationary goals for they, like the Association, will always be moving forward.

Vol. XXXVII—p. 356 (Apr. 1961)

Today's Children and Tomorrow's World
BY ROBERT J. HAVIGHURST

This article is based on a talk given in January 1961 at Pacific Oaks Friends School, Pasadena, California, as a Highlight Event in the School's Community Service Program.
Robert J. Havighurst is professor of education, The Committee on Human Development, University of Chicago.

TODAY'S CHILDREN WILL MAKE TOMORROW'S WORLD. BUT WE MAKE today's children and we give them today's world to work with. We are responsible for the children; to some extent we are responsible for today's world in which they live.

I propose to consider today's world and its trends and to indicate the nature of the situation in which children will grow and work. Then I shall suggest the kind of person who can best deal with this world-in-the-making and ask how we can produce that kind of person.

An American View of the World

North Americans tend to see the world in optimistic terms. Our country has grown up in a period when the European-North American segment of the world was growing prosperous and powerful. Our present wealth and abundance lead us to take an optimistic view of history. In the nineteenth century we were inclined to believe that the world was getting better in response to some basic law of historical evolution.

This naive optimism has suffered some rude shocks during the twentieth century: two world wars, a disastrous economic depression and the threat of nuclear extermination. These have tempered the American optimism with some realism. Still, we are basically optimistic.

We now believe that the world can be made better if we work at it.

We also believe in ourselves as makers of history and see history as a product of human achievement. *We are an achievement-oriented people.*

We see *our part of the world as an area of abundance with potentialities for a better society,* even though we recognize our waste of wealth on things which do not produce a better society.

We see the world *becoming interdependent,* and we know our future welfare is bound up with that of the rest of the world. We see ourselves as responsible members of a world organization which must work to produce world order.

Finally, we know the *future will be complex.* The solutions of our domestic, international, social, economic and political problems will have to be worked out on terms which have not yet been drawn up. This will require imagination and flexibility on our part.

The outcome of our competition with Russia can only be guessed. It certainly will not be resolved by military means, unless we or they blunder into war or are drawn in by other nations who are about to join the atomic club. This competition will be resolved in terms of politics and economics, technology and ideology. The result is not likely to be what either we or the Russians would call a victory.

Looking at present and probable events, the historian, Robert Heilbroner, warns us that our usual optimism will be strained by disillusionment to come. We will need two other qualities: fortitude and understanding. These will help us see that although this century is not a period of rapid progress and fulfillment of our social ideals, it is not a time of total loss. There is a job to be done. By doing this job we can influence for the better the vast and impersonal process of worldwide evolution.

. . . For this we need an attitude which accepts the outlook of the historic future without succumbing to false hopes or to an equally false despair; a point of view which sees in the juggernaut of history's forces both the means by which progress painfully made in the past may be trampled underfoot, and the means by which a broader and stronger base for progress in the future may be brought into being.

Such an attitude may retain its kernel of optimism. But more is needed for the display of stoic fortitude than a residual faith in the idea of progress. Above all there is required an understanding of the grand dynamic of history's forces in preparing the way for eventual progress . . . Only from such a sense of historic understanding can come the strength to pass through the gauntlet with an integrity of mind and spirit.[1]

Certainly there are people who will not see the world in this way. Some will seek to turn back the pages of history and recapture a simpler society. These people, calling themselves "conservatives," like to talk

[1] Robert L. Heilbroner, *The Future as History* (New York: Harper & Bros., 1960).

about a need for *positive rebels*. This kind of person, it seems, is one who rebels against all present-day social and educational trends. He seeks to move back to the pre-Revolutionary eighteenth century, when a small minority of "gentlemen" had an easy life.

A good many other people will feel uncomfortable about today and its probable tomorrow but make no effort to do anything about it.

The world of today will destroy itself if it has too many people who either want to go backward in history or don't want to do anything about history.

Needed—a New American

In addition to fortitude and understanding which we Americans must bring to the world of tomorrow, we need a new set of ethical standards which are less parochial than those which served us—after a fashion—in a world dominated by white Europeans and North Americans. Agnes Meyer has stated this proposition:

> Our central problem at this critical juncture of history is to gain a new idea of man and his relationship to his fellow men. . . . In the era of the atomic bomb, human survival depends on new and higher ethical standards than any heretofore achieved—standards acceptable to all mankind that will lead gradually to renunciation of power in human relations and of war in international relations.[2]

The basic theme of this talk is: *The purpose of a nation depends primarily upon the way its children were brought up a generation earlier. The way to improve the nation for tomorrow is to improve the lives of its children today.*

In every newborn child dwells the destiny of society. This not very profound statement contains a burden and a great opportunity.

The burden is the fact that society must repeat endlessly the education of its young. No infant of today is born with any more knowledge or wisdom than the infant born 2500 years ago. Every generation must start anew. The twenty-one-year-olds of this year were born in 1940. They had no advantage over the children born in 1900. They had to learn with the same pain the same things their parents learned before them.

This tired world's opportunity lies in the fact that each generation starts over again. There is the possibility that the new generation will discover better ways of living. That is why we treat children with such respect. They have potentialities for being better than we. And we, in our relative ignorance of how life should be started and carried on, must do our best to give children a good start on paths we ourselves have not trod.

[2] Agnes Meyer, *Education for a New Morality* (New York: The Macmillan Co., 1957).

What should we try to provide for children that will enable them to make a better world tomorrow?

What Kind of People Make a Healthy Society?

A healthy society for this latter half of the twentieth century consists of people with qualities that combine to make them a purposeful, peaceful and productive nation with a positive affirmation of the value of human life.

There are nine personal qualities which make a person who can carry his share of responsibility for making tomorrow's world better than today's.

How do people get these qualities? Primarily through their early experience while they are children. The child is father of the man. *The most enduring and most essential qualities of mind and personality are founded in the early years of life.* Some are determined *before* the usual beginning of school life and others are formed *during* school years. The effort wisely spent on giving children a good start in life is a better investment than the same amount of wise effort spent on the individual later in life.

The kind of person who helps to make a good society:

1. *This person's impulses are basically friendly; he sees the world as a good place and people as good.* He is optimistic and he believes that the world will turn out well. This person can trust his own impulses because he knows they will not get him into trouble. He can give his impulses almost free play, without having to be on guard lest he commit some hostile acts toward others. He has so little unconscious hostility and so little guilt about himself that he can enjoy being an impulsive person. Other people like him that way.

People disillusioned with the contemporary world have said that we should teach young children to fight, hate, kick and scratch so as to prepare them for this world. But we must resist this doctrine with all our might. We must do just the opposite with our children!

As Erik Erikson tells us so persuasively, this first psychosocial task of the child depends largely on the treatment he gets from his mother in the first few months of life. If she satisfies him when he is hungry, comforts him when he is cold and wet, gives him continual experience of physical care; and if during the following years he continues to receive ample evidence of love and support from his family, he will come to trust in the world as a place which is fundamentally hospitable.

2. *This person is intellectually autonomous and therefore prepared to cope intellectually with the unforeseen and unknown world that lies ahead of him.* What we know about personality development tells us that the seeds of autonomy are sown in the second and third years of

life. This is when the child becomes aware of himself as a being separate from his mother and as one who makes decisions, first about his body and later about other activities. If his mental curiosity is allowed to grow by parents and teachers who answer his questions and encourage his questioning mind, he becomes ready to treat the mental disciplines of school as his tools rather than his masters.

3. *He is achievement oriented; he likes to do things well.* This person has a deep, unconscious drive to meet standards of excellence. With so much internal pressure for achievement, he does not need much external pressure. According to work done by Rosen and Winterbottom, the basic drive for achievement results from the child's being trained to do things well and independently. This quality is probably established at least by the age of ten. It is more a result of training at home than elsewhere.

4. *This person has strong inner moral control.* His conscience (or superego) has such positive force that he can stand up for what he knows is right against the pressure of the crowd. This quality comes from his experience of love and punishment from his parents. If they are consistent in their rewards and punishments so that they teach the child clearly the difference between right and wrong and if they give him ample affection, he becomes a person of strong moral character.

5. *This person is creative and spontaneous.* His mind entertains new ideas readily. He makes novel connections between things other people have overlooked. He enjoys putting things and ideas together in new ways. This seems to come naturally to the young child—it is a kind of spontaneous movement of the mind toward what it enjoys. We know less about the conditions under which creativity develops and strengthens itself than we know about the other qualities being considered here. There must be ways of living with children and teaching them which will encourage preservation and development of their early creativity!

6. *This person is rational and foresightful.* This quality is juxtaposed to spontaneity and creativity to remind us that *both* qualities are desirable and compatible. They may *seem* to be in opposition. Rationality means ability to look at facts, draw logical inferences from them and to control one's behavior in light of foreseen consequences. This quality makes moral judgment sounder than it would be if it were simply a set of moral maxims adopted crudely from parents with childish limitations of understanding. This person looks ahead to examine probable outcomes of possible actions and then deliberately chooses what reason tells him is the better course. In a changing world where consequences of individual and national choices cannot always be found in past experiences, this quality of rational foresight separates

the wise and good man from the stupid and good man.

7. *This person can tolerate ambiguity.* In a world of uncertainty, with great risks taken by nations as well as by individuals, this person is not driven by a blind fear of the ambiguous into a rigid demand that only one solution of a problem is correct. Instead, this person can stand to live and work in a situation which is open-ended with many possibilities for solution and which must be worked out flexibly. This person does not need to have everything so neatly and tidily disposed about him that he will not have to take risks.

This quality is related to the basic sense of trust in the world which has previously been mentioned. One can tolerate an uncertain state of affairs if one is basically sure that both the world and one's own drive-impulses can be trusted. This, too, seems to be largely a product of early childhood experience.

8. *He is altruistic.* He enjoys doing things for the welfare of other people. He has a wide moral horizon which includes people far away in space and far ahead in time. World brotherhood is an immediate necessity and a vital reality for him. His altruism has a considerable element of respect for the ways of other cultures and other peoples.

The basis for altruism is probably formed in a family which has plenty of love and affection and trust for every member. The child of such a family can readily extend his moral horizon to take in friends, age-mates, community members, fellow-citizens and all members of the human race.

9. *This person has a world view that is both scientific and religious in the best sense.* His understanding is comprehensive and accurate with respect to the physical world and the nature of man. In a world in which man is gaining more and more control over the atom, space and living cell, it is essential for wise men to understand these things.

This is largely the product of education, formal and informal; most of it comes after the person has emerged from young childhood. But here, too, I would venture the hypothesis that the child's ideology is powerfully influenced by his unconscious imitation of the ideology he sees and hears in the lives of his parents and other significant persons.

How Do We Get More of These People?

The world of today needs more and more people with these qualities. Only people with these qualities can stand up to the tough reality of this world. They can live and be active and beget children in a time of threatened destruction. They can take part as citizens of the world in the multiple and shifting coalitions of nations that lie ahead during the remainder of this century. They can raise their voices against the prevailing tone of moral lethargy and political ambivalence.

People with these qualities can populate islands of excellence in the sea of mass culture that threatens to drown us all. This sea will recede and permit the spread of excellence if enough people support excellence during the next decade.

We doubt that formal education can inculcate these qualities, though it can certainly make them more effective. The basic elements of these qualities are learned through the experience of love and punishment, stimulation and example, which young children get in the family. The school extends and supplements the contribution of the home through the models provided by teachers and age-mates and by means of its environment for learning and living.

The secret of getting more of these people in the coming generation is an open one. We can inculcate these qualities best by doing a much better job of rearing young children. Already we *know* enough to do a better job. Our task as educators is to spread this known knowledge about the formation of personality and character in children. *We want to do a far better job of producing more of these people.* This means doing more research on children—young and older children.

Vol. XXXVI—p. 398 (May 1960)

What Is the Image of Man Tomorrow?
BY EDGAR DALE

Edgar Dale is professor of education, The Ohio State University, Columbus.

As WE PEER INTO THE MIRROR OF THE FUTURE, WHAT IMAGE IS reflected there? How do we picture our role? For purposes of discussion, I shall present these images as opposites, as more sharply different than they could or would normally be.

Somebody or Nobody?

Is your self-image that of an indispensable somebody or a dispensable nobody? How often we hear persons refer to themselves apologetically as "just a teacher." I once asked a group of ministers whether they saw themselves as indispensable persons. Most of them said "no" but later recalled their vote when they began to reflect on what they had recently said in their pulpits.

Is it true that there are social conditions which may lead us to believe that we are insignificant, dispensable nobodies? We must take this into account. For example, I sent a letter to an emeritus professor addressed to the university where he had put in a professional lifetime of distinguished service. It was returned marked, "Not Known Here." Elderly people feel unwanted. An elderly Negro, ill and discouraged, said to me, "I'm a lost boy in the tall weeds."

Many workers are being automated out of their jobs. Indeed, the steel industry lost the recent steel strike because the union workers did not enjoy seeing themselves as dispensable, not even in the short run. Workers do not want to be hands; they prefer to be human beings.

Does the image in the looking glass say, "I am important. I am indispensable. I count for one person"? If it doesn't, we should remember that self-abasement is catching. *A teacher who does not have a high self-regard will reflect this unfavorable image to others.* As teachers we must ask how we can build a sense of strength, an unwillingness to yield to the forces which lead to lowered self-esteem.

No excessive egotism or boasting is involved in a feeling of being important, indispensable. Self-abasement is often an unattractive way of subtly boasting about our modesty, our humility, our meekness.

Creativity or Routine?

Do we have an image of ourselves as interchangeable parts in a social machine, as performers of fixed steps in a routinized process, as organization men, participants in a meaningless ritual over which we have little control?

The image of the cowboy or the sheriff in the Western movie or TV program is popular because it reflects a time when men usually weren't fenced in, and if they were they fought against it. When life became boring they moved to another frontier.

Today the physical frontier is gone but a complex social frontier remains. The social frontier, however, is abstract, less tangible; and we do not clearly see our possible role as innovators, as pioneers in exploring this social and intellectual frontier.

Further, the United States is now a settled society, the richest one the world has ever known. Its work routines may sometimes be boring, but its play routines as reflected in movies and television are pleasantly stupefying. William Dean Howells once said to Edith Wharton: "What the American people want is tragedy with a happy ending."

But we are plagued by doubts. To conform to the routines of the past dooms us to repeat that past with its wars, its depressions, its economic ups and downs, its overt and covert attacks on the richer nations. Our apathy is disturbed by world-sized problems and no easy routines will serve. We must create novel solutions.

Many are now learning that there is something vigorously stimulating about creating, innovating, trying something new. It is invigorating to discover some important things about your own mind and how you can use it to draw intelligent inferences about teaching arithmetic, to analyze the structure of the English language, or to figure out ways of increasing the rigor of one's professional thinking.

Certainly the old ways aren't all wrong and the new ways aren't all right. But as we face the extraordinarily difficult future, we would be greatly strengthened if we teachers were creative and innovative in our approach, less eager for fixed and comfortable routines. "The people I want to hear about," said Robert Frost, "are the people who take risks."

Here we need to think about John Dewey's differentiation between adjustment *to* and adjustment *of*. To adjust *to* a situation may mean that we change ourselves to fit the situation instead of changing the situation to fit us. Margaret Fuller, the transcendentalist, once reluctantly agreed to accept the Universe. "Gad, she'd better," said Carlyle. But still another voice says, "Gad, she'd better not."

Finished or Growing?

The disease in all professions is stagnation, a failure to grow in professional wisdom and competence. The curve of growth is not typically a constantly rising line but one in which plateaus are soon reached. We wonder why children don't want to learn, yet their teachers may exemplify persons who have stopped learning, who have little feeling of the need for disciplining themselves to high standards of professional excellence.

Exhortation won't help much to change the situation. Increased pay will assist but won't get at the central problem. What is lacking is the zest and joy that comes from creative discovery, knowing *why* as well as *how,* trying out something that hasn't been done before.

Power or Weakness?

While many persons may identify themselves with the strong, powerful man in film or television, nevertheless in real life weakness is a hidden but satisfying element of our self-image. We quote with satisfaction the statement of Lord Acton that "power tends to corrupt and absolute power corrupts absolutely." But we might just as easily add that "weakness corrupts and absolute weakness corrupts absolutely."

To be weak is to accept no responsibility, but to be powerful is to accept some responsibility for our strength. Many people run away from power and allow the confident ones to use it for such purposes as they wish. Many teachers covertly and overtly reject power and thus permit thinking about curriculum and educational policy to be taken over by those lacking special competency in this field.

Penetration or Superficiality?

This is the age of the easy answer to the difficult question. A former professor of chemistry at Harvard surveys the American junior high school, but the Carnegie Corporation has not yet given a foundation grant to a junior high school principal for surveying the Harvard curriculum in chemistry.

A careless, shoddy book called *Why Johnny Can't Read* was reprinted by some newspapers of the country. But a series of penetrating studies on the Press in America was given little thoughtful attention by them.

Arguments for and against educational television are presented by persons who have not read the research in the field. Teachers deeply interested in "progressive" practices avidly accept studies which find they work, reject studies which raise doubts.

Sit down with a university scientist and you can get a short, quick answer to the problem of how to teach. The idea that communication is worthy of penetrating study seems not to have occurred to him. One is tempted to ask, "What's the latest dope on phlogiston?"

There is superficiality in the current notion that all you have to do to improve the schools is to add more work in science, in mathematics, in foreign languages. This approach is sometimes needed. But it is of far greater importance to ask why the mathematics or science or foreign language now taught didn't take. We need to discover how to develop a strong foundation on which to build. More and more doesn't necessarily mean better and better. Instead of superficially covering more ground we ought to penetrate more deeply, uncover the ground. It is said that a professor is not smarter than other people, he has his ignorance better organized. To avoid superficiality we need to determine whose ignorance is least dangerous.

We should, however, not be ignorant about the big issues in the curriculum, the nation or the world. We ought to develop some penetration, some wisdom on one or more of these issues. And we can learn how to approach all complex problems in an appropriate mood for study and with a mode of attack. We should learn how to learn and develop a taste for learning.

William James once said that the aim of education is to know a good man when you see him. I have pointed out that *the good man believes that he IS somebody, approaches problems creatively, keeps learning, is willing to accept power, and uses that power insightfully and penetratingly to meet the critical issues of his day.*

Today's World Is Different
BY BEATRICE HURLEY

A rapidly changing global world requires that we help children to live well in the wide house of the world. It requires that we provide problem-centered science programs that afford practice in using aspects of the scientific method. Thus would an open road be provided for children to grow beyond us, the adults, in finding better solutions to emerging problems than are now available. Beatrice Hurley is associate professor of education at New York University.

It requires only a modicum of imagination to foresee that children who live in this bewildering twentieth-century world dwell in a world quite different from that of their elders. The gap between generations widens and the gulf in understanding deepens as time advances. In truth, Gibran's [1] statement of that gulf is an apt one:

> The astronomer may speak to you of his understanding of space, but he cannot give you his understanding.
>
> The musician may sing to you of the rhythm which is in all space, but he cannot give you the ear which arrests the rhythm nor the voice that echoes it.
>
> And he who is versed in the science of numbers can tell of the regions of weight and measure, but he cannot conduct you thither.
>
> For the vision of one man lends not its wings to another man.

Although probably no one denies the validity of the statement that today's world is different, the magnitude of that difference appears to elude many. Among the many are those who hold that the education children need today resembles closely that of an earlier time. The conflict between a dynamic world and a static kind of education of young people cannot long continue without untoward consequences. Today's children need to have the kinds of educational experiences that will make it possible for their growth to extend beyond the horizons of their elders—the adults of yesterday and today. *Children must be liberated from those conformity-ridden customs that dominate much of national life and from the limitations of dogmatic thinking in order to become, in fact, effective citizens of their world.* For only thus does each generation pay its debt to the past.

Predictions as to future discoveries would be ridiculous. Our an-

---

[1] Reprinted from The Prophet, by Kahlil Gibran, by permission of the publisher, Alfred A. Knopf, Inc. Copyright 1923 by Kahlil Gibran. Renewal copyright 1951 by Administrators C.T.A. of Kahlil Gibran Estate and Mary G. Gibran.

cestors could not possibly have conceived, among others, the phenomena of radio, television and atomic bombs. We would be the foremost egotists in the world if we did not believe that our children, with the limitless phenomena of the universe, its array of energy and the enlarging understanding of its controlling laws, will be able to produce many things now thought to be unlikely, if not impossible. Witness the establishment of extraterritorial planets in orbit part way to the moon and the boundless possibilities of extending scientific knowledge attending this achievement. Witness, also, the possibility of extending the area of arable land through perfection of an inexpensive method of producing fresh water from sea water. Or, speculate upon the possibility of using chemistry against illness.

Without attempting any thoroughgoing analysis of the nature of modern civilization, let us now single out for reflection a few distinguishing characteristics of today's world. Then let us speculate upon the nature of the challenge they present to adults interested in the improvement of the education of children in our times.

Characteristics of Today

We live in a global world. This is a new state of affairs. No longer can we think in terms of local, national or continental boundaries. Indeed, we cannot continue to think of the Western Hemisphere as constituting our world. Nor can we afford to envision the minority Caucasian race as special and apart from the great ebb and flow of all mankind. In truth, we are in and of this world—one of all people.

Such thinking has never distinguished itself as good and, in a world now considerably shrunk, to continue to think in such narrow channels is to fail to grasp the realities of our times. The most remote clansmen are our neighbors—a mere matter of hours distant. Their concerns are our concerns; their failures, ours; their successes, a vibrant part of our lives. *We all belong to the family of mankind.* What enhances one, enhances all. Likewise, what diminishes one, diminishes all.

Now it is not change that is new. It is, rather, the rapidity with which change occurs that presents newness. Someone has said that the world almost literally alters as we walk in it. In truth, it does. The life span of a single individual measures not alone small changes but great upheavals in cultural patterns of living. Also, new knowledge of the natural world engulfs, complements or upsets earlier knowledge of that world to such an extent that the human organism finds it difficult to accommodate to the pace of that change.

Yes, within this present generation, *the need for educating our children to be understanding of and appreciative toward the rich cultural diversity of the human family has been sharply accelerated.* Our children must be knowledgeable about remote and diverse peoples. Furthermore, they must become committed to them in terms of brotherhood. Helping children learn to live well in the wide house of the world is a compelling educational need.

Many of the baffling problems of today's world are precipitated by the unprecedented rate of population increase. Each day another 80 to 90 thousand babies are born. Roughly one-third of the world's population retires hungry each night. Countless numbers are woefully ill housed and ill clad. Poverty, disease and needless suffering continue to be enemies of mankind. However, rapid technological and scientific advancement now makes the continuance of such conditions unnecessary.

Utilization of Methods of Science

Therefore, again education today is challenged. *We need to provide the kinds of education whereby scientific advancement will be used to enhance life, not destroy it.* The peacetime use of modern scientific achievement should dominate the thinking of our entire population. The phenomenon of harnessing atomic energy for perfecting instruments of mass suicide leads only to ultimate destruction. True, sharp conflicts in political ideologies presently engage the forces of the free world in combat with the unfree. Moreover, there can be no possible doubt that by fanning the fears of many with the agility of an octopus the advancement of totalitarian control is alarming. However, the long-range goals of mankind must be to provide massive programs of aid and assistance to those uncommitted peoples of the world so that they, too, will not come under the yoke of totalitarianism. Hope is the precious commodity the free world can supply. It is the major sustenance of most people of the world.

Now, modern science education is at the heart of social freedom. That is why science instruction promises so much for today's children. *Through proper utilization of the methods of science, children are encouraged to doubt that the present answers are the final, best possible answers to any problem.* Through science children are encouraged to inquire, when viewing a set of phenomena, "What does this mean in the day-to-day life of people?" Through it children seek, by rational and experimental means, solutions, although tentative and frequently incomplete, to contemporary problems. Through the methods of science tentative hypotheses are tested and, if found valid, are incorporated into a workable body of knowledge with which to view new problems calling for solutions. The over-arching working principle that science educators in the free world must hold and seek to incorporate into the folkways of children is that when confronted with a problem to be solved they can conclude, *"It can be solved."*

In a very real sense, none of the truly enduring contributions of science can function in a totalitarian state. *The methods of science are methods of truth.* Regimentation of ideas and beliefs leaves no room for critical judgment, open-mindedness and individual resourcefulness and responsibleness to flower. *The methods of science prosper only when there is freedom to investigate ideas.* The right of individual dissent, even in the face of accepted truth, is a precious ingredient of scientific thinking. Such a right does not exist when there is danger of punitive retaliation by the state.

Constants in Science

Perhaps the foregoing remarks lead us to consider some of the content of elementary science for today's children. In doing so, it would be an error to overlook the fact that children's urges to understand the natural environment persist as surely today as in the past. *It would also be an error to overlook the fact that countless natural forces and laws of the universe operate today in the identical manner they have always operated.* Children of today receive heat and light from the same sun as did children of countless former generations. The separate members of the solar system are held in their respective orbits today by certain relationships between centrifugal and gravitational forces which have existed for centuries. Evening after evening the same moon that children gazed at ages ago continues to reappear in the sky, and today's children also gaze as it in thoughtful wonderment. Today, wind and water continue to wear away the earth's surface here and build it up there, much as they did in years gone by. The same natural forces that acted then are in action now and in doing so alter the earth's appearance.

Moreover, *children today take note of the same sequences of events that children long ago noted with interest.* Among these might be mentioned that day follows night, season follows season, the water and the nitrogen cycle continue unceasingly to operate, plants and animals continue to compete for the necessities of life as they fulfill their life cycles, iron rusts, clouds form and reform, tides rise and fall.

These operations of natural laws are among the many constants in any modern science program. They constitute a portion of the recurring environmental phenomena with which children of each succeeding generation deal as they attempt to interpret their world. Hence, *providing experiences through which children find opportunities to build concepts and meanings attending these phenomena rightly comprises a major part of the elementary science program.* Among over-arching patterns of the universe which provide focus for insightful science teaching are

concepts concerning the
- age and size of the universe
- interdependence and interrelationships that exist among living and non-living things
- adaptation and variety of plant and animal life
- changes that go on all the time
- interaction and balance of forces in the universe.

Now, of course, it would be folly to think of these as statements to be memorized. They are rather to be thought of as expressions of ideas that represent a growing heritage of man's long search for better understanding of his universe. *It is through countless experiences with these ideas that children gradually come to sense their profoundness.*

Science and Dogmatism

Likewise, the dynamic nature of science constantly demands that all areas of science curriculum content reflect the impact of new knowledge about them. *All areas of science are undergoing change. New ideas must be incorporated and old ones revised.* Science and dogmatism are incompatible. The methods of science are ones of honesty. Throughout life, the honest search for truth requires a disposition on the part of the learner to find explanations for natural phenomena. To this end children profit by the kinds of instruction that utilizes their natural drives and satisfies their persistent urges to understand their world. *Problem-centered science programs provide for practice in using aspects of the scientific method.* Here children pursue tentatively held hypotheses, gather and test data pertinent to their investigations, and subsequently accept or reject their hunches on the basis of their findings.

The ultimate test of the value of science instruction in the elementary school is the use to which the learner puts his newly acquired knowledge. Democracy needs responsible citizens. *Science instruction that encourages children to think through to the consequences of their own actions can help them incorporate intelligent responsibleness into their behavior.* Rendering each learner more sensitive to the idea that his behavior can retard or accelerate the rate at which some of our natural resources are being depleted, assist or upset natural communities in maintaining an equilibrium and balance between plant and animal life, add to or detract from the beauty of the environment is a worthwhile accomplishment in science education in a democracy.

The dynamic quality of modern life necessitates the introduction not alone of new content but the development of more humane attitudes as well. On the one hand, new developments in nuclear energy make possible the perfection of instruments for mass suicide and, on the other, proffer untold possibilities for peacetime improvement of man's future way of life. New knowledge of chemistry hastens the day when those diseases still defying scientific investigation will be harnessed. For example, the dreaded disease called yaws can now be prevented with a single shot of penicillin given at a cost of twenty-five cents a person. Malaria, leprosy, polio have also yielded to modern medical discoveries. Such examples serve to document the fact that the traditional idea of a fixed body of content as an absolute can no longer hold. *The selection of content must be in keeping with goals of democracy.*

Surely now it can be said emphatically that the idea of keeping up with or exceeding the U.S.S.R. in scientific achievement should not be the prime motivation for improving the science education programs in our elementary schools. To fall into such a trap would be calamitous. Our proper point of reference is not to ape the educational goals of a totalitarian regime. *It is rather to develop the kinds of science experiences that will help children develop behavior consonant with democratic values.* It is well to remember that man's manifold accomplishments in the realm of science require that man learn not only to control the instruments he invents but to utilize them to the everlasting benefit of the human race. Hence, social engineering appropriate to the ideals of the free world is important and it is in this area that glaring inequities now exist. For democracy to prosper, the development of a social conscience must keep pace with rapid scientific advancement. Gerald Craig stated this premise in his recent publication:

"For a nation to be free, it is not enough that scientists make discoveries in laboratories, for there are decisions to be made, the complex life of the community must go on, industry and agriculture must maintain their momentum and find ways to improve their operation, and behavior in every walk of life must reflect courage, creativity and responsibility in dealing with the resources of a country. No nation is any stronger than the combined wisdom of its people." [2]

In conclusion, it might well be stated that *the best kind of science instruction is one that offers an open road for children to grow beyond us, the adults, in finding better solutions to emerging problems than are now available.* The methods of science are essentially methods of search for truth. When the dynamic methods of science are coupled with determination to utilize the findings gleaned for the betterment of mankind, the science program in the elementary school will lead children ultimately toward better and more humanitarian living including discovering workable substitutes for violence, a search in which all of today's children must become engaged.

[2] Gerald S. Craig, *Science for the Elementary-School Teacher,* New Edition (Boston: Ginn & Co., 1958), p. 38.

Role of Education in Contemporary Life
BY HAROLD TAYLOR

This is a condensation of a talk given by Harold Taylor, former president of Sarah Lawrence College, Bronxville, New York, at the 1959 Study Conference of the Association for Childhood Education International in St. Louis, Missouri.

I COME BEFORE YOU AS AN UNRECONSTRUCTED PROGRESSIVE WHO believes deeply in progressive education, who is proud to have had a close friendship with John Dewey, who considers Dewey one of the greatest of all educational philosophers, who believes that the trouble with educational thinking in America today is *not* that progressive ideas have undermined the schools and sapped their strength but that there is not enough progressive education in the schools and colleges. It hasn't yet been tried.

America is suffering from conservatism, complacency, and lack of confidence in her own democratic strength. The hard-nosed position about education taken by Admiral Rickover and others who haven't had the privilege of teaching children in a classroom will damage our educational system if taken seriously as a basis for educational planning in the future. A return to progressive ideas in politics, social reform and education is our greatest hope and must be our highest aim.

Fundamental Principle

What is the fundamental principle of democratic education? It is that each child must be encouraged, protected, loved, cherished, respected and taught so that he may become the most that he is capable of becoming. Educational institutions exist to transmit the habits of mind and the social customs of a given society from one generation to the next. The traditional view of education is that the schools are agencies of transmission by which the younger generation is taught what society wants him to do.

Schools and colleges should not be merely the agencies for transmitting American middle-class values, which under community pressure is what they are or will become. They must be agencies for transforming and re-creating the values of each generation.

If each child is to be given a chance to develop fully, the school and society should not simply impose an old set of values upon the new generation. If truth and ethical principle are to be learned by the child, he must rediscover truth and principle for himself with the guidance of sympathetic parents and teachers.

Bringing Powers to Fruition

The progressive idea in education is to consider the child in his own reality, to bring his powers to fruition, and to give him a chance to serve his society in the ways best suited to his talents. The authoritarian idea is to decide what are the needs of society for trained manpower and then to set children to work in school to fill these needs.

Our concern must be for the development of the individual, since we live in a society of massive pressures which are acting to crush the creative element of individual talent.

We are also in a peculiar situation as far as political and intellectual leadership are concerned. Politicians follow the same path as do the television rating systems. They want to know how their ideas are being received before they go on having them. The mass magazines keep trying to find out what their readers think so that they can publish things with which the readers agree, while the readers keep reading the magazines in order to find out what they should think.

We must accept the fact that we live in a mechanized, mobile, collective society. Whether or not our children watch television regularly or read the mass magazines, they are affected by them since the ideas and values of the mass magazines and of television programs permeate the atmosphere in which they and their parents live. Added to this is the general anxiety produced by our living continually in an atmosphere of cold war, with frequent crises and frequent threats of a nuclear war which can destroy us all.

Each generation has its own truth and the chance for a fresh start. Each day is a new one. Each problem can find its own solution. If what I have said is at all accurate as a description of the atmosphere in which today's children are growing up, then we must realize that this situation is one which can create its own cure. The cure suggested by most is that we stiffen our curriculum of academic subjects, clamp down on the young, move more academic subjects into the elementary schools, or do what is called "raising standards" by which is usually meant, making us more like the Russians. The assumption is that more academic material studied for a longer time, particularly if it is material which the student has not chosen to study, will make young men and women better and the country stronger. In my judgment, it will have the effect of making students less interested in learning and more in passing examinations, less interested in the world around them and more in getting ahead in it, less interested in the aims of

Western society and more in the technique of achieving aims already established for them by others.

Pressure for Academic Achievement

There is enormous parental and community pressure already applied to the young to achieve academic standards at the expense of intellectual and human values. While we who believe in the value of learning as a means of developing minds are doing our best to achieve this purpose, parents are urging their children to get good grades and urging their teachers to stop being concerned so much with children's personal growth.

In the vanguard of those who wish to press school children into a cold war curriculum is Admiral Rickover. He is a true nonconformist who isn't afraid to tackle any problem or any person, or even to take on the whole Navy if by doing so he can cut through red tape and release new ideas and new concepts. He does not mind being controversial. He thinks the country's educational system is weak. He finds time wasted on nonessentials, a lack of purpose in the American high school, and a lack of high academic achievement by our students. He also finds that we are not spending enough money on our schools and colleges to achieve the results we must have.

The Admiral has announced that the whole of education lacks a rudder and a compass because John Dewey and the progressives have thrown them both away and have advocated drifting with the tide. Nothing could be further from the truth. Dewey and the progressives have urged and fought for an educational system which can give leadership and direction to American democracy; for an academic program which not only includes the sciences, both social and natural, but which can commit the student to a sense of purpose in his education and to the highest degree of effort to achieve that purpose.

Raise Level of All

The essence of Admiral Rickover's argument is this: We live in an age of technology where the technical expert is necessary for the advancement of our society. The strongest society is the one with the best experts. Therefore, we must use our educational system to produce the technical experts we need if American is to retain its place of leadership in the international community.

I cannot help wishing that a man as intelligent as Admiral Rickover had gone deeper in his social and educational analysis than this.

There is absolutely no doubt that American boys and girls could do more in school and college. They want and will do more if given the education they deserve. But that takes time and money and teachers, not merely for a few brilliant students who have already shown their talents but for the whole mass of children who are presently being classified as the *average* or the *below-average*.

We will gain little by continuing to condemn American schools for the fact that they do not resemble the European or the Russian system. The Russians have discovered that the ten-year academic program produces a very large number of dropouts of those who enter, that it is creating a separate class of youth who think of the farm and the factory as beneath them and who wish the special privileges of an intellectual elite. The steps now taken in the Soviet Union involve two years of vocational training for all, something which should scandalize those in America who argue for an academic American program.

Fundamental to our whole American system is an attitude to life which is democratic and progressive. These attitudes involve moral values. Certainly the arts of communication, reading, writing, spelling are fundamentals. Certainly arithmetic, mathematics, literature, foreign languages, history and science are fundamentals for our American curriculum. But so are the creative arts—music, theatre, dance, painting, drawing, sculpture; and so is the art and science of self-government. These are not frills, they are essentials. Certainly discipline is important, but discipline is not achieved by dictation or installing a purely academic program which all must take merely to undergo "hard subjects."

Current School Problems

How can the ordinary meaning of the word *discipline* be achieved in schools where there are double shifts, forty students in a class, where merely keeping order requires all the emotional and educational power of the teacher? How can teachers learn to discover the talents of individuals and children, give them the guidance they need or raise the level of their academic achievement if they are so overloaded with teaching duties and numbers of children that they can't know the children well enough to help them? How can children learn to respect the rights of others when schools are shut down in order that Negro children should not receive the education they seek and to which they are entitled?

What is needed is a new progressive program of education which actually carries out educational reforms of importance to a new age. The practical administrative problems take our eyes away from the essentials. We talk about immediate needs rather than long-range goals —we discuss the need for scientists and engineers, for educated manpower in industry, for teachers, for buildings, for higher pay. We have become so used to discussing education in these terms that the mind, the spirit, the quality of the American experience are seldom mentioned and seldom missed.

Finally, I wish to comment on some of our material efforts to improve the quality of education and to suggest ways in which these efforts might be improved. The National Defense Education Act is the first little cautious step by Congress toward a solution to educational problems. At a time when ten to fifteen million dollars may be blown up at one single rocket launching, we can muster only six million dollars for loans to the entire college population of the country. In a critical teacher shortage, with an even greater one ahead, we can offer not scholarships for the talented who wish to enter teaching but an inadequate set of loans, half of which may be canceled provided the student enters the teaching profession. At a time when schools are bulging and space is inadequate we find government money-savers who deny the need for classrooms. At a time when we know that modern architecture can give us a school and college environment of beauty and function, we hear talk of minimum budgets, waste of taxpayers' money on the frills of new schools. We can take comfort in the fact that Congress and the administration recognize the fact that we have a real problem, but we need to warn those in charge that unless they develop something bold and imaginative to match the size and depth of our national needs, we are simply not going to have the educational system the times demand.

What is needed is massive federal and state support for our schools and colleges—a federal program of fellowships for graduate students, grants for college buildings, scholarships for those entering the teaching profession, and support for teachers' salaries. Ideas, imagination, the will to create, energy and determination, these are the fundamentals. Money alone will not bring the answer. But money is the necessary condition under which the answer will be obtained, and we will get only the quality of education for which we are prepared to pay.

We as teachers, parents, educators and citizens are the ones who are in touch with the children, who know that there is talent and power beyond belief—in the children we instruct. We can inform the rest of the country that it is time to wake up, that we have a great idea here in the United States, that we have an enormous national talent for progress. It is time to put it to work.

Unreasonable Expectations
BY BOYD McCANDLESS

What are unreasonable expectations? They are not always overexpectation, says Boyd McCandless, director, Iowa Child Welfare Research Station, State University of Iowa.

THE TERM UNREASONABLE EXPECTATIONS IS DOUBLE-EDGED. Typically we think of unreasonable expectations as associated with frustration and failure. Our highly developed sense of social responsibility and strong social motivations are probably responsible for singling out children who cannot compete for the bulk of special service and curricular provisions. These are the slow-learning children, the children with problem behaviors, the children with reading defects. Historically these have been the children who have been neglected by the curriculum, and it is logical, legitimate and necessary that they be helped.

However, a swing too far in that direction results in unreasonable expectations for the generally able and the gifted child. An able child of whom too little is expected and required is as likely to be crippled by *underexpectation* as is a fearful or slow-learning child by overexpectation.

The vast number of undereducated but highly able men I saw among the Maritime Service officer candidates during World War II—sixteen-cylinder minds trained socially and educationally for four-cylinder jobs—suggested the term "occupational neurosis" for a good share of the group. At least a part of these men's difficulties rested in the history of low educational and parental expectations for them.

There are also academically successful children for whom continuous overexpectation has been held by parents and possibly teachers. These children, usually at severe cost, have incorporated their parental overexpectations and need special attention just as much as do those children who suffer from underexpectation. Also requiring careful attention are those bright children who have been relentlessly pressured because of their brightness, yet who remain academically unsuccessful. Frequently it will be found that their academic mediocrity is a defense against parents and teachers—it constitutes their way of "getting even."

The Cultural Role

Unreasonable expectations are just as much the result of social learning as are reading skills and table manners. Our competitive culture leans in the direction of overexpectation. This bias toward too high goals has perhaps been responsible for some tendency for the present-day curriculum to emphasize facilities for the child with "handicaps" as opposed to the generally able child.

Indications of the cultural emphasis on *overexpectation* are very clear. Every American child is touched more or less strongly, as have been his parents and teachers, by such cultural phenomena as "the rags to riches story": "Every boy can be President," "Every girl is a potential Cinderella."

The net result has been to expect great things of children who are average; to regard academic retardation or mediocrity as a tragedy; for the community to expect the schools to work miracles; and for many children to experience what must appear to them as total failure. And while frustration and failure are, at least to some degree, inescapable facts, *total* failure can only be destructive.

What Are Reasonable Expectations?

Research in child development and personality theory provides us with some fairly clear answers to this question. Level of aspiration studies concern goal setting and expectation and have been done with many types of child and adult groups. Typical "adjusted" or "normal" expectations appear to be: after success, the child raises his expectation for himself, for that task at least, somewhat higher than it had been before; after failure he lowers his expectation somewhat; and, consistently, he always expects to do a little better next time than he did last time.

Similar research done with "ill-adjusted" groups shows that they veer irrationally in their expectations of themselves, sometimes lowering expectations drastically after success or raising them after failure and frequently setting consistently negative expectations for themselves (i.e., always expecting to do more poorly next time than they did last time); or consistently expecting quite improbable degrees of success and apparently ignoring entirely their previous performance history. These "ill-adjusted" patterns have been shown to be related to maternal over- and under-protection; to mothers' setting too high goals for their children; and to general personality disturbance. Studies have been done only with mothers, but there is no reason to think that in general fathers are less involved than mothers.

What Is Likely To Result?

Reasonable expectations result in success or reward more frequently than in failure or punishment; and in constructive, realistically modified behavior rather than in unrealistic and maladaptive behavior. Contrariwise, *unreasonable* expectations produce unrealistic goals, failure, lack of satisfaction and nonadaptive behavior.

Failure and frustration, depending on their severity, result in a number of behaviors, some constructive, some nonconstructive. Studies demonstrate that under some circumstances, frustration-failure results in potentially adaptive behaviors, such as increased effort, trying new methods of reaching the goal, and increased drive. However, severe failure, particularly that which is attributed by the child or adult to his own inadequacy, seems to result in such behaviors as withdrawal, passivity, temper outbursts, blaming of "tools" or other persons, fixation on the unadaptive approach already tried, random aggression and fantasy escape.

Only increased effort and new approaches to the goal are generally constructive. They may not be if the goal in question is one impossible to attain; or if the method which the child has already been trying is the correct one. Increased drive may be utilized by the wise teacher constructively but may in turn only add to frustration the child is feeling.

An additional consideration has recently been proposed by two learning theorists (Brown and Farber, writing in November 1951 *Psychological Bulletin*). They set forth the hypothesis that escape from frustration is in itself satisfying and consequently tends to consolidate the behavior that resulted in the escape, without regard to whether that escape-behavior is constructive or not.

As an illustration, the highly traditional and authoritarian schoolroom may be considered: a heavy proportion of child goals is blocked in such a room (e.g., needs for physical activity, communication, individualized goals, self-determination, teacher approval, love and affection). This frustration for many can be escaped only at recess, lunchtime, or release from school in the afternoon. Consequently, no "educational" goals are reinforced for the child but only goals obtainable through free, unsupervised, school-escaping activity. The net result, after years of such school frustration, is likely to be a population hostile to school and schools; suspicious of education, the educator and the educated. The still existing caricature of the old maid schoolteacher, the stereotype of the child mourning over the first day of school, and widespread current attacks on modern education are not totally unrelated to the experiences of great sections of our population during their own schooldays. . . . .

- As a first consideration, the school should not concentrate on reduction of frustration as such. Frustration in and of itself is neither good nor bad but simply inevitable. It is the behavior which results from frustration with which the teacher and the school can work as well as the child's understanding of the cause of frustration. From the developmental point of view, inescapable frustration is probably bad, but escapable frustration is the foundation of education.

- A second basic premise is that teachers should know how children develop in general as well as how the individual child is developing and has developed. In our society, first-graders are desperately eager to go to school and yet are at the same time nearly overwhelmed with anxiety about what is going to happen to them. Late third-graders want desperately to learn cooperative rules and live by them, yet haven't the social and physical skills to do so. Yet a given first-grader may have no anxiety, and another may be so overpowered with worry that his younger siblings at home are displacing him that he can attend to none of the activities of the classroom. A mature third-grader may know all the basketball rules, while another is at the developmental level of "run-sheep-run."

A general knowledge of the process of maturing, of personality development and of physical growth is indispensable for the understanding of either a group of children or a single child. But only study of the individual child can help *him* specifically.

This brings us both to teacher-training programs and to the individual school philosophies. Emphasis on *methods* of teaching is barren unless there is also included a knowledge of *what* we are teaching—or whom! A school management program is incomplete unless it includes provisions for each teacher to study each child and his family. The philosophy of the self-contained classroom, at least in the elementary grades, is an intriguing one and deserves consideration. The self-contained classroom is well described by several authors in *Nations' Schools,* January 1952. The provisions of such a room for home visits, two-year (or more) acquaintance of a given teacher with the group, broadly shared teacher-child activities and interests, relatively complete developmental records for children, all seem to offer possibilities for constructive manipulation of unreasonable expectations in the direction of more reasonable expectations.

- This leads to the third consideration—curricular organization. Ordinarily the American schoolroom takes care of the middle three-fifths of the children in it with reasonable adequacy. But underexpectations exist for the upper one-fifth and overexpectations for the lower one-fifth. Some of the remedies for this lie outside the teacher's power. When classes are too large, only a certain percentage of children can be given adequate attention, and ordinarily the lowest one-fifth monopolizes the attention that perhaps the upper one-fifth could use more profitably. But a carefully thought-out individualized curriculum with varied supplies of reference books and activities, planned in terms of the widely varying needs of *all* the children in the class, can go a long way to counteract this typical "drag toward average-ness." Of course, on the surface, the upper one-fifth demands far less than its lower counterpart. The demand of the upper one-fifth is more subtle yet as important—for challenge!

- Finally, a schoolroom, if it is to meet the demands of adjusting for unreasonable expectations, must possess the attributes of democracy and warmth.

These two terms have become hackneyed and stilted in many circles. Democracy is not pure permissiveness. Studies have demonstrated that permissiveness without purpose is more frustrating to children than any other type of atmosphere, including cold authoritarianism. Full permissiveness is construed all too often by children as being uninterested in their welfare.

Democracy is guidance of a positive sort in terms of carefully thought-out goals, which are communicated to children in terms which they can understand. These goals include such things as academic competence, adequate social skills with other children and adults, assumption of responsibility, internalized discipline, and exploitation of such physical and special attributes as a child may have.

Likewise, warmth is not sentimentality or mawkishness, but is best defined as an honest liking for children, the manifestations of which vary with the needs of a given child. These may range all the way from a staggering slap on the back and the statement, "You were OK," to an independent little boy to holding the shy and dependent child on one's lap while handling a reading section. Warmth must be a part of the teacher, and must be applied in terms of a knowledge of the individual child.

There is a use for permissiveness, too. "Good" permissiveness is that of the mature and well-trained teacher who is secure enough personally and professionally to realize that individual rebellions or failures are not "personally" directed but occur as a result of multiple motivations.

Let us take the positive step of knowledge of child development, of both groups and individuals, in understanding over- and under-expectations. Let us plan to utilize frustration-produced behavior constructively, individualize the curriculum, and include sensible and sound definitions and practices of democracy and warmth in the classroom.

Hurry! Hurry! Hurry! *Why?*

BY ANNIE L. BUTLER

Who feels the need for formalizing instruction for fours and fives? Parents? Teachers? Children? Have basic patterns of child growth and development changed? Who should hurry to assume responsibility for providing functional classrooms with teachable numbers of children, adequate equipment and materials? Who should hurry to assume responsibility for providing fully qualified professional leadership for all aspects of school curriculum? Professional educators? Lay citizens? Annie L. Butler is assistant professor of early childhood education, Indiana University, Bloomington.

ALMOST ANY NEWSPAPER OR TELEVISION NEWSCAST PROVIDES A reminder of the predominant role which speed assumes in our lives today. Our scientists regard successful orbital flights as milestones in the race to put a man on the moon. As a nation we compare our accomplishments to Russia's progress and hurry to keep ahead. Families, too, get caught in the hustle as fathers rush to work and mothers hurry the children to school before going to jobs of their own. From the high school senior competing for admission to his dad's alma mater, down through the junior high school and the elementary grades, children are expected to learn faster. Kindergarten teachers feel this pressure as they hear, "Why waste time with all this play?" "He's so bright, it's time he settled down to do some real learning." Many would create an image of their own education for four- and five-year-old children, moving the more formal structure and primary-grade content into kindergarten. As a consequence, kindergarten teachers are often under pressure to replace the opportunities youngsters have for knowing, thinking and sensing some of the inherent joys and practical uses of learning with prepared readiness materials which are assumed to teach readiness to all children alike.

Learning from Many Experiences

Our concerns about children's learning have changed. Young children amaze us. Responding to all the excitement and adventure of a space shot, they speak glibly of satellites and astronauts in orbit. They can tell us more about Cape Canaveral than about the adjoining town. Five-year-olds appear to understand a few scientific concepts which we learned with difficulty at a much later age—at least they use the right words. Having lived only in the space age, theirs is a space-age language. Not too long ago children in kindergartens built bomb shelters, threw bombs and, incidentally, could identify airplanes which most adults could not identify. Teachers and parents, at that time concerned with the aggressiveness and hostility expressed by the children, wondered whether their emotional experiences would be permanently damaged. But they accepted the intellectual abilities of the children as a matter of fact.

Because we feel different pressures, we notice and value aspects of the child's behavior which previously had less influence. Today's five-year-olds are learning some things faster than others. *Basic patterns of child growth and development, however, have changed little. Children can learn from many different kinds of experiences.* Any desire for better education which manifests itself in formalizing and limiting children's opportunities for learning represents a lack of ability to distinguish between personal preference and quality education. We should broaden rather than narrow the available possibilities.

Early Formalized Learning Misinterpreted

Recent emphasis on science, mathematics and foreign language arising out of the world race for power has caused adults to be aware of their own educational inadequacies as never before. This awareness has precipitated a strong resolution that today's children shall never find themselves in the same predicament. Unspoken, but there nevertheless, are the feelings that children must get an early start in order to enter a profession early, to acquire acceptable status, and to gain sufficient purchasing power to take advantage of the increasing array of new products resulting from the rapid impact of scientific discoveries and technological change. *Beginning formalized teaching at an earlier age is misinterpreted as assuring that the desired learning will occur with greater efficiency and comprehension.*

Under the circumstances it is natural to ask why children should not be taught the fundamental skills in kindergarten so they can begin to master some of this vast knowledge. In the interest of children, it is also natural to ask who feels the need of these skills. The parent, the teacher or the child? Much too often comes the reply that the child should be put through these paces whether he likes it or not. Most five-year-olds show unlimited curiosity for knowledge, but their interest in formal learning is fleeting. We can find many ways to make the knowledge available without insisting on the skills. *Pushing the child to learn skills before he is ready rejects his right to grow in his own way, to take the time he needs.* The possible effect of this rejection on the child's self-concept and his attitudes toward learning deserves serious consideration.

We may forget that in the final analysis children exercise control over their own learning. What is learned may be entirely different from what we think is taught. If the classroom is rife with pressures, the teacher's purpose may be of no value (no matter how worthy the purpose). Children may respond to fear, distrust and pressure toward conformity. Their learning may be the indirect result of anxiety which permeates the atmosphere of their homes or the school. In the rush to master content, the joy, adventure and sense of accomplishment which come from finding out something (which may or may not be new to anyone else) may be lost. We *cannot* possibly foresee the content which four- and five-year-olds must eventually master. We *can* foster their enthusiasm for learning, nourish their growing minds in many directions, facilitate the achievement of their purposes, and offer support as they face inevitable disappointments. *Children must feel a challenge to learn before they can hurry.* Our attempts to hurry them in kindergarten threaten the acceptance of this challenge. So why hurry?

Each Learns at a Different Pace

The hurry-or-you'll-be-late pace of the modern family is completely different from the natural tempo of the three- to six-year-old child. His snowsuit is put on by someone else because there's too little time to wait for him to do it; his play is interrupted without warning because lunch is ready; he is literally dragged along the sidewalk past the interesting window display to go somewhere he doesn't want to go. One advantage of good kindergartens is that children can move at their own pace, both in timing of their activities and in pacing of their learning. Ann can look at a book for fifteen minutes, pointing out and commenting on every detail of the illustrations. Meanwhile Jim can turn quickly through his book, take a ride on the block train and paint a picture all in the same time interval. Later Jim can leave his play easily enough to get cleaned up for morning snack; but he must have time to play with the soap, make faces in the mirror, and maybe take the paper towel back to the wastebasket after having reached the table with both paper towel and wet hands. Both children will eventually learn to read, write and understand number concepts, although they probably will not learn at the same time. They will certainly learn by different routes. The routes may not look efficient and the learning may not appear to have easily identifiable steps. Children show no more readiness and potential for reading after exposure to a formal readiness workbook in the kindergarten than do children who have had an informal activity program.[1]

---

[1] W. Paul Blakely and Erma M. Shadle, "A Study of Two Readiness-for-Reading Programs in Kindergarten," *Elementary English*, #38, November 1961, pp. 502-505.

The learning process takes a long time. The child needs time to grow and practice in using materials, interacting with people and savoring new experiences before he can concentrate on learning in a formalized way.

Viewing Broader Aspects

One way to broaden our view of what the teacher does in a kindergarten is to look at the differences in children which need to be appreciated. All five-year-old children share some needs in common with other five-year-old children, but their differences provide the spark that causes one child to stand out from all the others. A few five-year-olds can read. Others can build highly elaborate and beautifully designed block structures. One child's imagination repeatedly provides ideas for dramatic play. He frequently selects books for the teacher to read, and later his play and his questions reveal how he strives to fit newly acquired information into his already remarkable store of information. Some children who are able to read reject reading as a kindergarten activity, choosing more sociable and creative pursuits which provide a new and different kind of challenge. Children have many talents.[2] If talents (or gifts) are discovered early they can contribute to the child's sense of achievement and open avenues for his abstract learning. The kindergarten teacher is in an enviable position for facilitating development of interests and talents already evident, for widening horizons for children whose abilities are less evident, and for providing an atmosphere in which creativity has a chance to thrive and in which pressures are released whenever possible.

Pressures to formalize the kindergarten also assume a different perspective when examined from the viewpoint of responsibilities assigned to professional educators and to citizens in the community's plan for providing schools. Who has the responsibility for providing functional classrooms—a teachable number of children in each class and adequate equipment and teaching materials? Who has the responsibility for providing fully qualified professional leadership for all aspects of the school's curriculum? Who decides what the program of a particular classroom shall be—or the program of a particular school? If each person concentrates on the responsibility which is his, the hurrying which causes pressures to formalize the kindergarten will be replaced by hurrying which will result in better education.

[2] See ACEI's *All Children Have Gifts.*

Play Is Education
BY N. V. SCARFE

N. V. Scarfe, dean of the Faculty of Education, University of British Columbia, Vancouver, gave this talk at ACEI's Study Conference in Indianapolis in April 1962.

THE PURPOSE OF THIS PRESENTATION IS TO DEMONSTRATE THAT PLAY is the most complete educational process of the mind—Nature's ingenious device for insuring that each individual achieves knowledge and wisdom.

Play may be described as a spontaneous, creative, desired research activity carried out for its own sake. Because it is entirely natural, it is not necessarily moral when judged by the cultural or social ethics of particular people at particular times.

Play is in no sense a simple thing; nor is it explained or interpreted with reference to one or two criteria only. Play, in fact, is a very complex thing, as complex as the human being himself. There have been many theories of play and many criticisms of those theories. The rehearsal theory of Karl Groos, derived from his study of animals, has much to commend it because it postulates play as the means of growth and development and puts great value on it. He noted that play varied according to the level on the scale of evolution at which the various animals stood. The higher animals seemed to have longer periods of infancy and, associated with that, longer periods of more extensive play. Karl Groos's theory is, however, inadequate for the human child, for rehearsal of the complex activity of adulthood is clearly impossible. Further, it does not explain play by adults. Nevertheless, the idea put forward by Karl Groos, that play is a growth mechanism, is still fundamental.

The recapitulation theory of G. Stanley Hall was also an attractive, partial explanation of play; but both child and adult play have an important creative as well as repetitive element.

The superfluous energy theory was the one least able to explain the function of play satisfactorily. While children obviously let off steam at play, the energy expended is simply an incidental concomitant of the pleasure and enthusiasm that play engenders.

The only satisfactory theory is that which views play as an educational research activity. But first it is necessary to discuss the confusions that exist in people's minds about play and work.

Play and Work

Play and work are not opposites. They often coincide but should be measured differently. Work is measured by quantity of physical exertion. Play is measured by quality of emotional involvement. Unfortunately, "work" in public parlance seems to have borrowed emotional connotations. Work apparently is serious and important activity that ought to be done. Play is thought of as a frivolous and worthless waste of time in which weak characters indulge. This is a gross misrepresentation of the fact, because we know that when an activity takes on the characteristics of desired play, then normally more effort is expended and more work done. Work and play are not opposites, and the sooner it is understood that excellent education goes on only when considerable effort is expended in the spirit of serious play, the better it will be for our whole educational system.

Therapy

In the past too much emphasis has been put on the therapeutic value of play in helping to understand the fears, the anxieties and the disturbances of mentally ill children. This emphasis has led some people to suppose that play is necessary only for those who are mentally disturbed or maladjusted as a kind of curative or therapeutic medicine. They overlook the fact that children become ill largely because they have been deprived of the freedom and opportunity to play. Play is as necessary to the child's mental health as food to his physical well-being.

An Educational Process

The concern here is mainly with the positive values of play to the "normal" well child or, put in another way, with the great value of play in education and with the importance that a teacher should attach to using this built-in provision for individual self-education.

Play is the finest form of education because it is, as Lawrence Frank, formerly of the Caroline Zachry Institute of New York, says, "essentially personality development, whereby the individual organism becomes a human being willing to live in a social order and in a symbolic cultural world." [1] A child's play is his way of exploring and experimenting while he builds up relations with the world and with himself. In play he is learning to learn. He is also discovering how to come to terms with the world, to cope with life's tasks, to master skills. In particular he is learning how to gain confidence. In play a child is continually discovering himself anew, for it is not easy for a child to accept the patterned conduct of the social cultural living, and in many cases he must escape into fantasy.

[1] *American Journal of Orthopsychiatry*, Vol. XXV (July 1955), No. 3, pp. 576-90.

Play is a learning activity. It serves the function of a nonverbal mode of communication or a figurative language which satisfies a felt need of young children. Play is educative because while thus employed the child is self-directed, wholly involved and completely absorbed. A child can completely lose himself in play.

Play has, in fact, all the characteristics of a fine and complete educational process. It secures concentration for a great length of time. It develops initiative, imagination and intense interest. There is tremendous intellectual ferment as well as complete emotional involvement. No other activity motivates repetition more thoroughly. No other activity improves the personality so markedly. No other activity calls so fully on the resources of effort and energy which lie latent in the human being. Play is the most complete of all the educational processes, for it influences the intellect, the emotions and the body of the child. It is the only activity in which the whole educational process is fully consummated, when experience induces learning and learning produces wisdom and character.

Creativity

While we are prepared to accept play in preschool education, we neglect at our peril to make sure that the spirit of play continues throughout all school and adult educational studies. To be effective and lasting, all ideas in the mind must somehow be expressed creatively and in some concrete form. This is sometimes called recreation, but it is never exact imitation. All recreation has injected into it the personal creativeness of the doer or play.

An educated person is one whose intellectual efforts have carried over to character formation, attitude development and esthetic sensitivity—or, as Aristotle would have said, "to wisdom and virtue." The late Boyd Bode is quoted as saying that "it is agreed on all hands that education is more than just a matter of learning facts and skills. Public interest is poorly served if attitudes and appreciations do not receive at least equal consideration. The things that are learned must translate themselves into terms of emotion and conduct if they are to be significant." Only by using the spirit and characteristics of play can this be achieved. Unless learning affects the attitudes and emotions it is not good or complete education. The great thing about play is that it totally involves the whole personality of the child; in particular, it modifiies attitudes, character and emotions. It is the carry-over from intellectual activity to emotional involvement which is the true characteristic of a complete education and of play. It is only in creative and artistic activity that this important carry-over takes place. This is why the artistic and creative element of play and of education is so important.

Research

Play is much more than rehearsal or recapitulation or vigorous exuberance, although it may contain all three. Play is essentially a research activity—an adventure, an experiment, a transactional process. It is motivated by innate curiosity and inquiry. It is the expression of a child's urge to find out and discover for himself how to live, how to be. Play has the joy of discovery, the satisfaction of creativity.

If play is thought of as a research activity, then it becomes a most important activity for children and the spirit of play a most important stimulus to mental activity for adults.

Artistry

Sufficient has been said to prove that play is Nature's research activity, Nature's experimental mechanism for enabling a child to discover how to live and how to grow up. But the glory of play is that it is also artistic, spontaneous and often independent of external needs and stimuli. It is probably the spontaneity of play that has caused the general public to use the term "work" as its antithesis, because work in the popular mind is effort required or imposed from outside or an activity determined by someone else. Play is free, because the child's activities in play are still a little tentative and uncommitted, are still capable of exploration and revision, of renunciation and replacement. In play he can manipulate objects, events and even people with less restriction than is imposed on an adult. It is, nevertheless, equally possible for work to have all the qualities of play. Shaw's definition of an educational utopia was, "A place where work was play and play was life."

A child's fantasy is essentially inventive and fancy free. It is a high-handed treatment of inconvenient facts. Nevertheless, a great deal of spiritual and intellectual vigor comes from make-believe. A child investigates the world of things around him by manipulation and direct experiment, whereas he investigates the world of society by a mental experiment called fantasy or make-believe drama.

Thinking

Piaget emphasizes the value of thought in play. He says that symbolic play is egocentric thought in its pure state. He adds that a child wishes to enjoy a private reality of his own. This reality is believed in spontaneously without effort, merely because it is the universe of the ego and the function of play is to protect this universe against forced accommodation to ordinary reality. All play is associated with intense thought activity and rapid intellectual growth.

The highest form of research is essentially play. Einstein is quoted as saying, "The desire to arrive finally at logically connected concepts is the emotional basis of a vague play with basic ideas. This combinatory or associative play seems to be the essential feature in productive thought."

Provides for Play

If play is Nature's means of individual education, how then should a teacher act? In practice, where is the line to be drawn between direct teaching and the child's discovery of the value of a moral order by free experimentation? How can we get discipline or morality into play activity?

Obviously, teaching methods in schools must aim deliberately at feeding the impulse to intellectual play, to experimentation and to the development of concrete modes of self-assertion. It can never be stressed too much that a child must find *his* way to maturity, at *his* own rate, with *his* individualized capacity and limitation. We must provide adequately for play and at the same time respect the dignity of the child so that we do not invade his integrity either by neglect or coercion. A teacher must not stunt or distort personality development or overdevelop it prematurely. How does a teacher encourage animal behavior to become social conduct?

The teacher's task is not that of directing play but of removing obstacles to constructive freedom. Put more positively, the teacher provides materials, space, opportunities and experiences, knowing the children's abilities and interests at different stages of growth. Teaching should exploit the spontaneity of the individual; the teacher should act by suggestion and example, not by precept and command.

The teacher, therefore, provides materials such as building blocks, modeling clay, paint, water, sand, paper; space; time; freedom and affection. He arranges conditions so that children naturally want to learn and want to play, or arranges conditions so that Nature can effect an education. The teacher tries his best not to interfere with the spontaneity, the search, the intellectual curiosity, the creativity or the freedom; instead he encourages dramatic self-expression and artistic growth in a moral atmosphere created by his own example and personality.

The spirit of play is vital to all humanity: the basis of most of the happiness of mankind; the means by which humanity advances creatively, scientifically, intellectually and socially. The spirit of play is vital not only to childhood but to all mankind. In understanding children's play, we understand the key to the processes which educate the whole child. Because we live in a highly civilized world, all play activities need the kindly, sympathetic, understanding teacher who will provide materials, suggestions, kindliness, freedom and space—who, by example, will set standards of behavior and discipline with which children can experiment creatively to their own advantage.

What Price Pressures?
BY GLADYS GARDNER JENKINS

Which pressures produce good results?
Which pressures cause children to retreat in defeat?
What price is paid for "toughening up the curriculum"?

Gladys Gardner Jenkins is lecturer, George Washington University, Washington, D. C.

WHEREVER WE GO IN THE WORLD WE HEAR TALK ABOUT PRESSURES that grownups are under. At the very time we bemoan pressures which bedevil *us,* we do not seem to be fully aware of the pressures we are "pushing" on boys and girls: pressures to behave in a socialized way; to be popular—to belong to the group; to achieve in school and get to college; to hold their own in a competitive world; to take advantage of all the advantages; to live in a world which even grownups cannot say is safe and secure.

Voices of Adults

As if these pressures were not enough for our children to face, many adults are adding to pressures in the name of education: We must see that each child lives up to his potential. We must "toughen up" the curriculum. There must be more homework. We must do away with "frills." The underachiever must be made to achieve. The child must understand his responsibility to society. Children must work harder. They must stay in school longer hours. These are a few of the clichés that keep cropping out in articles, reports, speeches and everyday conversation. These clichés are often used by adults who want their children to have the kind of education which will help prepare them to become creative, constructive citizens—citizens who can best fill our country's need for intelligent, productive manpower. Furthermore, they are often used by adults who understand the seriousness of our times and are sincere in their efforts "to do right by our children." *Their motivation is right, their realization for the need of intelligent and productive manpower is right, but their knowledge of children and how they grow and develop is inadequate.*

Voices of Children

On the other hand, we hear the voices of boys and girls: "I don't want to be in the honors program, I'm afraid I can't carry it." "I can't go to bed yet, my homework isn't done." "Do I have to go to summer school? I told the kids I'd be back at camp." We hear nine-year-old Steve sob himself to sleep because he struck out in the Little League game and lost for his team. When we add to these voices reports from school principals and counselors of mounting tensions in children and the concern in one school system over the many kindergarten children already on tranquilizers, we realize the problem of pressure is mounting and cannot be ignored. We are beginning to ask, "What price pressure?"

Which Are Useful? Destructive?

We know that neither we nor our children can escape from *all* pressures and that it might not be desirable if we could. A certain degree of pressure acts as a driving force to go on to the next step: the desire to learn to read the next word, to finish the job which we want to do, to win the race, to score for the team. What is the difference between useful and destructive pressures?

Constructive pressures are closely allied with other parts of learning: motivation and reward of satisfaction through achievement:

Six-year-old Betty had turned over the pages of books, looked at pictures and listened to stories ever since she was tiny. She wanted to learn to read and was ready to read when she entered first grade. Pressure to exert herself to figure out words, phrases and meanings was wholesome and satisfying. She was rewarded by her own delight and pleasure as she ran home to her mother calling, "I can read, Mummy, I can read!" An added reward was the obvious pleasure of her parents and teacher. Billy, Betty's classmate, didn't have the same success in reading. He struggled along, for reading came hard to him. The pressure of his kindly teacher to have him try just a bit harder, to ask him to pay better attention (the I-know-you-can-do-it kind) resulted in a defeated, distressed and anxious child. Billy had been asked to do something for which he was not ready. In Betty's case, pressure was a spur to work and ended in a feeling of satisfaction and competency—a picture of the self as someone who "can do." But Billy ended first grade with a discouraged picture of himself as someone who was inadequate and as someone who had disappointed his parents and his teacher. Pressure produced increasingly more serious results for Billy.

Pressure put on as pressure alone will almost always fail. Parents who nag a child to do better—without understanding why he is not making progress—may end up with an underachiever. Pressures may be positive if they are combined with motivation which arouses curiosity and interest and makes the child want to exert pressure from within himself to accomplish what he is eager and able to do. *External pressure is of little value. Motivation toward inducing inner pressure is much more effective and infinitely less in danger of backfiring.* Here again we must be sure that the motivation is toward a goal possible to achieve.

A boy scientifically bent—absorbed in pursuing an idea to its conclusion—may put much pressure on himself to dig up material, to find the way to complete his apparatus, and work through to the completion of his project. Another boy may be completely "at sea" about the nature of the experiment. He may see no clear goal, only words, figures and apparatus which confuse and discourage him. One of the greatest challenges to a teacher is to recognize the goal which a Jim or a Sam can achieve. The teacher's job is to motivate inner pressures toward achievement of that goal. If the same goal is used for both boys, one may succeed and the other retreat in defeat.

Toughening Curriculum for Whom?

When we speak of "toughening up the curriculum," we must ask, "How? For whom?" A curriculum "toughened up" to provide stimulus for the out-reaching mind (college-bound child) may boomerang on the child whose goals should be in a different direction, resulting in non-promotion or failure. Stiffer standards with stiffer exams may result in pressure situations which have an ill-assorted array of undesirable outcomes trailing behind. The underachiever is often a child upon whom pressures to succeed have been too heavy; he has pulled out of the race for which he was basically well equipped. Cheating increases in proportion to the emphasis put upon a goal beyond the reach of many children who compete *not* because of personal desire and motivation but because of a situation from which there is no other escape. It takes effort to reach a goal. An adult may press on in spite of difficulties and discouragements because he sees possible results and meanings which will lead to achievement of future goals. But a young child is not an adult. His goal is immediate. His goal is not the career for which his parents would like him to prepare. *When "the going gets hard" for a child, the motivation must have immediate childlike satisfactions and meaning.* He must feel the inner drive to press on rather than turn toward goals which have less meaning and less immediacy.

When pressure is exerted to get a task accomplished (as a step in learning essential for a child's progress), the adult needs to ask himself:

Is this child ready for this step? Or do I just think he *should* be ready? Has he mastered the step which leads to this? Does *he* have a feeling that he is ready to go on? Is the step one that he can be reasonably expected to take? Have I left a way of moving back if he is not ready (to avoid a deep sense of failure)? Have I helped him to see where this is leading?

Positive and Negative Pressures

Intensity and kind are two things to remember about pressure. An intense pressure is never justified unless it is an emergency situation; e.g., when the child's safety is involved. It is never desirable in a classroom learning situation. *Positive pressures bring best results: reward of success and satisfaction of achievement.* Negative pressures of punishment (or lack of reward) may sometimes be used and are occasionally necessary. But, *if continually surrounded with negative pressures, a child will either withdraw into himself or hit back.* There are many subtle negative pressures which can undermine a child's faith in himself and lead to negative results. A parent or teacher's disappointed look, his tight lip over the report card, his sarcastic and undermining remark, his comparison of a child with brothers or sisters (or others) in an attempt to shame him into doing better are negative pressures. These are often used carelessly by those who fail to reach a child through understanding and insight and to find the real causes for lack of success.

If we want children to be creative, pressure is not the answer. *Creativity rarely develops from outward pressure. It may come from the inner pressure of ideas which flow into the mind and demand a way of expression.* We can create an atmosphere in which this can happen. A child who feels comfortable with his parents and teacher—who finds it is safe to ask questions, express ideas, come up with opinions, try doing things even if he makes mistakes—responds to pressures within himself by carrying through to successful performance. This is what we want for children. The child who is told to create may stare at a piece of paper, a hunk of clay or the makings of a science project and leave the paper blank or the material untouched—however filled his mind is with ideas.

Some Can Take It—Others Can't

Some children can take more outside pressure than others. Some do some of their best work under the stimulus of a race or an eagerness to be someone else or to beat their own record. These are the ones who have met success along the way and have developed a confidence in themselves as doers and achievers. They have a chance to win and they know it. Here—as everywhere else in understanding children—we must make room for individual differences which so truly exist. One child may eagerly push ahead while the other may crumple under pressure to compete. An undesirable award such as stars for the number of books read may spur one on and leave another unable to achieve his best. This is because he anticipates failure in relation to others in his family (or class).

"But," we hear it said, "children must get used to being under pressure." No one is more used to being under pressure than the utterly defeated child. What children need is to be helped to respond constructively to pressure. They cannot do this if they are pushed beyond their depth, and they are not likely to do this if they *think* they are beyond their depth.

Positive Motivation Needed

If today's child is to be tomorrow's intelligent, well-informed, creative citizen, he will need motivation to fulfill his potential—not scoldings. Remember that he does not yet see as far as adults. Neither will more hours of schooling nor longer evenings of homework necessarily produce the creative, thoughtful minds we need so desperately. Stimulation that comes from exciting teaching which has meaning for the child (at whatever his level of ability) will go a long way toward stretching his horizons and freeing his potential. Then he will be able to better accept the humdrum parts of school work. Learning will become vital and important to him—not just to his parents or his teacher. *It is not pressure put on children that is needed but better positive motivation.* We find that the child who fails, the one in need of remedial help or the underachiever, usually begins to find himself when the teacher helps him to find himself, when his parents accept him with warmth as himself. When this happens, he can see himself as someone of value, as someone with worth-while interests and ideas, as someone who can do things. He gradually loses his cocoon of self-defense and begins to move outward to take his rightful place.

Rather than add to outward pressures upon boys and girls, we need to release them whenever possible. We need to substitute encouragement to develop a child's own inner drives. This will involve a genuine interest in helping each child to develop his abilities and special gifts, in finding a way to give him more time on his own, not smothering him with things grownups feel are worthwhile; in keeping a balance between the things grownups feel must be accomplished during childhood and the growth needs of children, which demand time and space in which to flourish. Children today are in danger of losing the necessary growing years—growing years at children's pace—because of pressures to grow at adults' pace.

Pressures To Learn Can Be Blocks to Learning

BY JOHN I. GOODLAD

Some pressures in the classroom are: prepackaged content, inappropriate rewards, coverage of subject matter, external standards. What changes are needed to remove these blocks to learning? John I. Goodlad is professor of education, Department of Education, The University of Chicago.

CERTAIN PRESSURES BLOCK CHILDREN'S LEARNING. SOMETIMES THESE pressures stem from beyond the schools; they are part of the larger society. Sometimes these pressures arise inside the classroom; they are part of the teaching-learning environment. We shall concern ourselves here with the latter type.

Prepackaged Content and Inappropriate Rewards

Schools often proceed as though the thinking already had been done. Somebody, somewhere, thought up everything in advance. There's just no more thinking to be done. Or, worse still, nobody had anything to do with it in the first place. Ideas are the product of immaculate conception!

The task of curriculum construction, following this concept of learning, becomes the prepackaging of content into neat, consumable bundles. These bundles are then stored away in a curricular deep-freeze and ultimately displayed before the eager eyes of hopeful pupils. But, alas, once removed from cold-storage, the fast-thawing goods quickly spoil and smell. The pupils are less than enchanted.

Such a concept of learning leads naturally to fixed patterns of teaching. If the purpose of learning is to consume, the purpose of teaching is to dispense. Successful consumption is easily recognized and approved.

In the process of dispensing and consuming, both teacher and learner often become confused over ends. For example, Miss Manton tells a story to her second-grade class. (Of course there's no such thing as a "second-grade" class but we'll abide by the conventions.) Before completing it, she asks, "How do you think this story ends?" So far, so good. The children eagerly pose conclusions. To Tommy's response, Miss Manton answers, "No, I don't quite see how that could be." To Susan's, "No, I don't think so." To Mildred's, "No, that's not *what I'm thinking of*."

A shift has occurred, a subtle but significant shift. A process of inquiry, a process of putting ideas together to infer a logical conclusion, has shifted to a mere guessing game. Guess the right answer and the teacher's warm beam of approval floods down upon you. Learning becomes not a search for meaning, not an exciting pursuit whetted by surprise and the satisfaction of true accomplishment, but a search for responses that bring rewards. Press the right button and gain approval.

Some students learn the process well. They go through high school, college and life burdened with this misguided conception of education. So many nods of approval add up to a B, so many B's add up to an A.B. and an A.B. opens certain doors. In graduate school they ask, "Mr. Professor, what do I need to do [to gain your approval] in your course?" In business they become good organization men.

This is education? I think not. This is pressure to conform, social pressure of the most insidious sort, worming its way like a bacterial infection into the heart of the learning-teaching process, distorting and contaminating it until true education withers and dies.

Some educators writhe in horror over the imminent danger that machines may take over part of the learning-teaching act. Perhaps, for some aspects of learning, machines are more promise than threat. At least they focus on learning for learning's sake. You press the button and you're right or you're wrong. No syrupy words of commendation, no halos, for guessing the teacher's mind. The machines, too, will become monsters to be feared when they dispense peanuts, candy and chewing gum for pressing the right button. Once more the objective ends of education will be contaminated.

Perceptions of Coverage

A distorted perception of coverage often is part of the teaching-learning environment. We must be up to here by Hallowe'en, this much farther by Thanksgiving. Heaven help us if we aren't half-way there by Christmas. Half-way where? Don't ask silly questions. THERE, of course! On to Easter. By May, we're loping out in front, all by ourselves. And the children? Don't be ridiculous. We're almost THERE! A little prodding, a little pushing, a little skipping—and it's June. We're THERE for another year.

Such a concept of coverage creates immeasurable pressures to learn. It, too, is based on a "sacred cow" view of the curriculum. Here are the important things to be learned, laid out in neat order, to be "covered" at a set pace one after the other in the process of getting an education.

There is, indeed, a fairly respectable theory of knowing to support this view of the curriculum. But imagine, for a moment, the problem of selection in today's world! How do teachers determine what is of most worth among all from which to select? The little that can be put into the curriculum in relation to all that is available is as a handful of straw in relation to thousands of silos filled with straw.

And yet, we often act as though *the* most important content already had been selected for all time and appropriately arranged for consumption. We have, indeed, our sacred cow standing stubbornly in the path of reason. Do we dare to kill it?

External Standards

When one troubles to push beyond the criticisms, the panaceas and the slogans mouthed in the name of educational betterment, one sees that many seeking to be heard regard standards as something external to the learning process. "Higher standards, more rigor, better quality," come the pleas. "If they can't learn," says one, "kick 'em out. That's what we did at West Point."

It is difficult (and unwise) for teachers to ignore the clamor, ever mindful as most are of the need to do better. But sometimes we ignore our own beliefs about learning. Short-route methods take on a special attractiveness. Drill replaces the search for meaning. Children repeat their incorrect responses along with correct ones. Teacher presentation replaces pupil exploration. Routes that *appear* to be most direct take precedence.

Learning is seldom the shortest distance between two points. Learning often is oblique and circuitous. The means that appear to be most round-about often lead most directly to the ends sought.

The net result of the pressure of inappropriate standards is likely to be less, not more, learning.

True standards are found within, not outside, the learning process. True standards relate means most appropriately to ends. True standards free rather than restrict the human mind in its search for order and truth. Standards perceived to be outside learning itself are blocks to learning.

Some Ground To Stand On

Each of us readily identifies himself with some part of the foregoing. In recognizing ourselves we can in part right ourselves—but only in part. We're all caught up in a massive piece of machinery that answers not to our commands. Some basic changes are needed.

First, we need a concept of curriculum that better defines our freedoms. Freedom is a disciplined thing. It comes to the individual with increased understanding of his areas of choice as well as his areas of no choice. The sailor who sails strange waters is free to cruise and to explore if he possesses good charts. The sailor who lacks such charts must either pine away on the shore or grope his way cautiously, ever fearful of lurking reefs.

A curriculum plan that better defines our freedoms separates the relatively variable from the relatively constant. A few facts—particularly in the linguistic and mathematical realms—are here for a while, unless the structure of knowing of which they are a part collapses. The learning of them does not call for undue imagination, as though there were wide degrees of choice. In fact, imagination may well be a block to the learning of such facts.

Some facts are transitory or, at best, quite incidental (even accidental) to the learning of larger concepts. Such facts should be subordinated to the larger ends of formulating and employing concepts. The teacher is free to use whatever data seem appropriate to the clarification of larger concepts.

Most curriculum plans now in existence fail to recognize distinctions such as those suggested above. As a result, everything in a plan (even when labelled "for consideration only") becomes relatively constant —to be learned by all. Thus we get our sacred cow.

Second, we need a better understanding of the learner realities before us. We act as though there were only shades of difference among learners —as though, perhaps, the brightest child were twice as bright as the dullest. Actually, the differences in reasoning among slow and bright children almost defy mathematical comparison. One is thousands of times more proficient than the other in certain kinds of abstract reasoning.

In seeking appropriate teaching techniques, we do well to approach these differences as differences in kind (as between a cat and a human being) rather than in degree. Thus, the pedagogical road to learning for the slow may not be more of what was good for the bright. Similarly, the best procedure for the bright may not be just a little less of methods that worked for the average. We need experimental studies designed to find the optimal learning conditions for many kinds and degrees of differences among learners. The studies needed will not be conducted until potential experimenters catch a vision of pupil variability radically different from the view presently in vogue.

Third, we need a concept of learning embracing unlimited expectancy for human creativity. We know little about the potential creativity inherent in the human organism. We know only that our school practices tend to recognize and reward certain abilities out of proportion to other abilities. In a very real sense, then, creativity comes to be defined sociologically rather than biologically and psychologically. What we value most shifts with the ebb and flow of societal tides. What we value in peacetime we value not in time of war.

There is little likelihood of social pressure ceasing to reward only certain kinds of creativity. Social pressure is part of a real world. But the schools can do much to keep open-ended the drive that is human creativity. Schools must avoid like the plague external rewards for certain kinds of learning that freeze the creative process in its infancy. They do well to encourage creativity as an end in itself—creativity is many things—rather than to promote and reward accomplishment in those limited aspects of human activity that happen to be currently popular.

There are appropriate as well as inappropriate pressures to learn. Somewhere along the educative and miseducative road that is life the learner must respond to compelling forces within him, forces seeking to repeat the satisfactory experience of coming to know for one's self. The best way to make sure that these forces never will hold sway is to substitute for them pressures from without—pressures to please, pressures to cover and pressures to conform.

Vol. XXXVII—p. 108 (Nov. 1960)

Do We Push Children?

BY ALICE V. KELIHER

Alice V. Keliher, distinguished service professor, Jersey City State College, New Jersey, points out the difference between "pushing" and "motivating"; shows the injustice to children in five areas in which they are being "pushed." Should there be schemes and devices to go against research findings for the best growth and development of children?

D<small>O WE PUSH CHILDREN</small>? M<small>Y ANSWER IS</small> YES <small>IF WE AGREE ON THE</small> meaning of the word "push" and if we agree that anything we say about schools in the United States cannot be true of *all* schools. There are still those holding the line for the right of children to a period of childhood. Not all of the pressures listed below are generally found in any one school.

As for the word "push"—let's be sure not to confuse it with "challenging" or "mind-stretching" or genuinely "motivating" learning for which children are really ready. There is often too little of the latter approach to learning. The world is indeed "full of a number of things" of great interest to and challenge for children. When we free children for discovery and exploration we do not need to *push* from behind, as it were. A preschool boy, gifted in science, placed a book on his mother's lap saying, "If I could read this I could do what it says."

The best description of "push" is that by Arthur W. Combs:[1]

It is a method familiar to any person who has lived on a farm or has ever driven the cows home from pasture. One goes down the lane from the barn to the pasture, carefully closing the gates where he does not want the cattle to go and opening those where he wants them to go, until he reaches the pasture. In the pasture he irritates the herd in such fashion that they move forward and because the route has been carefully prepared in advance, move up the lane to the barn. . . .

The "fencing in" technique works fine with cattle and sheep . . . it often breaks down in working with people because people, being smarter than cattle or sheep, are always finding gates which we forgot to lock or climbing over the fences we have so carefully erected.

This says so poignantly what I would define as "pushing." Gardner Murphy speaks of what I like to call "mind-stretching" for those who are ready.[2]

One of the great problems of the release of human potentialities is the wise and creative use of this great burst of fresh enthusiasm which seeps like wildfire through the minds of those boys and girls who want to know, to control, who want to get hold of meanings, who want to grow in and through this strange, exciting, challenging environment.

Will these sensitive statements help us not to confuse our criticisms of *pushing* children with our simultaneous plea for genuine *challenge* and *motivation?* Then we can consider what seems to be unwise pushing of children. Is this happening in your community?

1. Pressure To Begin Earlier

A respectable national magazine this past winter carried an article entitled, "Why Waste Our Five-Year-Olds?"[3] Two themes were that five-year-olds should be given an academic program and that they should be toughened up by less "mothering" for the tough age in which they will live. The title, "Why Waste Our Five-Year-Olds?," in itself raises many questions. To what are five-year-olds entitled? To be five and enjoy it?

---

[1] Arthur W. Combs, "Personality Theory and Its Implications for Curriculum Development," *Learning More About Learning* (Washington, D. C.: ASCD, 1959), p. 6.

[2] Gardner Murphy, *Human Potentialities* (New York: Basic Books, Inc., 1958), p. 165.

[3] Virginia C. Simmons, "Why Waste Our Five-Year-Olds?," *Harper's,* April 1960.

We know that a few are ready to read at five but that the great majority are not. *Research has consistently shown that a mental age of six and one-half or over is necessary for reading with understanding.* We are told, again and again, to expect a four-year range of ability when children enter first grade. Oculists warn us that most children's eyes are not mature enough even at six for close application to print and figures.

Yet pressure comes from parents and some school people to start children earlier. A few years ago New York City public school officials lowered the entrance age for first grade to five years, four months (later they changed it). But in July 1960 the announcement appeared that 25,644 boys and girls were not promoted. Could the too-early start of many be partly accountable? The child who starts too young stays too young until that ugly day when a non-promotion policy catches up with him with its consequent damage to his mental health.

2. Pressure To Pare Curriculum Back to Three R's

There is sad confusion in the minds of people who bring this particular pressure on the schools. For example, a committee in San Francisco recommended that the elementary schools spend two-thirds of each day on reading, writing and arithmetic while, at the same time, according to press reports, they urged the schools to reduce "sharing, building Indian villages, and visiting the post office and the fire station." What is there to read about, write about, figure about, if the rich content of experience is to be eliminated? This is certainly "closing the gates" to the real, workable enduring learning of the three R's and "flies in the face" of highly significant research studies of motivation, individual differences and durability of learning.

John E. Anderson, in the 1960 White House Conference study materials, said:[4]

Our information on selection suggests that we should set up environments that permit a wide range of activities in the earlier years. There are two reasons for this. Since traits and abilities show low correlations with one another, it follows that the person needs to explore himself and his environment in order to determine his potentialities. Next, since the process of development is one of organization in which simple units are put together into more complex patterns, it follows that a broad base of experience will facilitate higher levels of final organization. A rich and varied environment offers better possibilities for selection than does a limited and narrow one and permits the person to move from breadth of concern to depth of concern.

Evidence abounds that the richer the environment the better the learning of the three R's. They are so basic to literacy and competency

---

[4] John E. Anderson, "The Development of Behavior and Personality," *The Nation's Children,* Vol. 2 (New York: Columbia University Press, 1960), p. 61.

that we want them learned in the best and the most lasting way possible. Sadly enough we have many people who *can* read but *don't* because they have been taught either to dread it or to think of it as sterile and barren. This is a great injustice to our children who are entitled to learn to love books and to possess growing eagerness for a growing experience with reading as communication.

We'd better watch some of the people who are demanding a cut-back to the three R's with less physical education, less music, less art. Maybe these are the budget cutters who don't care about the cost to children so deprived of their heritage!

3. Pressure To Return to X-Y-Z Grouping or Some Version of It

Here, too, there is marked ignorance of the facts produced by research. Thirty years ago several of us, working with records of tests of thousands of children, showed that you simply cannot get a group that is homogeneous in more than one ability. *Children have important differences within themselves as well as among themselves. They cannot be homogenized.* Get them grouped for one thing and it doesn't hold for the next. A recent summary drawn from a survey of the research states:[5]

> The most important generalization to be drawn from studies of trait variability is that instructional groups formed by general-ability grouping are not sufficiently homogeneous, with reference to achievement or learning capacity in the various curricular areas, to warrant designing a curriculum for uniform mass-instruction procedures. For example, a typical sixth grade will show a range of almost eight years in reading ability. After X-Y-Z sectioning on the basis of educational age, each section will still show a range of from five to seven years.

Indeed all the research put together shows that general X-Y-Z grouping reduces the range only by an average of twenty per cent. This covers only those items included in the measurement. When art, music, handwriting and mechanical skills are included, the reduction is close to zero. What mischief is wrought for so small a reduction of individuality?

The deepest mischief is the damage to the child's assessment of himself. This is equally damaging to the "fast mover" and the "late bloomer." The fast mover is fast only in those things measured. He varies greatly within himself. If he is to make the greatest use of his abilities for the greatest good, then surely he should learn not only a degree of humility but also a sense of obligation to give help and leadership to others. For the slow mover (in those things which have

---

[5] Beck, Cook and Kearney, *Curriculum in the Modern Elementary School* (2d ed., Englewood Cliffs, N. J.: Prentice-Hall, Inc., 1960), p. 43.

been measured) there is the discouragement, the defensiveness, the actual erroneous assessment of his unmeasured abilities and potential contributions.

We have a moral obligation to acquaint ourselves with the new research material on IQ and creativity. There is some indication[6] that IQ and creativity are not synonymous. Indeed there is suspicion that the IQ is a measure of schoolish mental abilities and that creativity often calls for a broader and less-conforming range of intellectual pursuits. It seems possible that children who are able in the non-conforming areas find themselves placed in the slower-moving groups and so their potential is not realized. We cannot afford to lose one iota of creative ability in our society today.

4. Pressure To Return to "Real" Marks

One of the most evil pressures relates to grouping, and that is the practice of governing marks by the group in which the child functions. We are told in many parts of the country that parents demand marks so they can discover where their child "stands" in his group or in a subject. Well, I know of a six-year-old who got a mark of 85 in Religion. What does it mean? What does a mark of 75.6 in History mean? I got such a mark in the eighth grade and I take it to mean that I just squeaked over some mythical line into the passing zone. But what did it really tell my parents? Was it 75.6 per cent of what was in the teacher's mind? In the textbook? In the examination? Would it be the same for me, living in suburbia, as it would be for a child in the one-room rooming house area? No. *We do parents a grave injustice if we let them think that this kind of marking tells them something deep and meaningful about their child.* A mark really obscures what we generally need to communicate in our partnership with parents.

What it does to children is the deeper issue. Now some communities are tying marks to homogeneous grouping. You cannot get a top mark if you are not in the top group. (I suppose the embarrassment of the groupers would be so great if a Z group child came up—not unexpectedly—with top performance.) I asked an administrator about such a hypothetical case. The quick reply was that the child would be moved to the top group so that the paralleling of grouping and marks would go undisturbed.

Then there are those who are giving lower marks for what used to

---

[6] Calvin W. Taylor, *Identification of Creative Scientific Talent* (Salt Lake City: University of Utah Press, 1959).

be the same work in order to "motivate" more effort. A boy I know with an IQ over 120 was promoted to seventh grade in a system where willy-nilly he had to join an accelerated group—to do junior high in two years instead of three. *But* the marking system was to be tailored to the group, a lower mark in this group for the same amount of work expected of those in the non-accelerated groups! What omniscience some presume to have! And what kind of motivation is it to announce (as one principal did) that for the same quality of work performed a year ago marks would be lower this year? Does your heart sink a little as you read it?

We have come a long way in developing sound and wholesome ways of conferring with parents. Schools with strong leaders who know the needs of children are not yielding to this unwise, unknowing pressure for marks that basically have little or no meaning. Here again let us be alert to assess what is called "parent pressure." If there are one or two malcontents, then do be fair to the majority of parents who want the best for their children. Parents *want* the best *if* they are informed on what it is. In one community parents were presented in the public press as being "alarmed" about their children's reading. One father wrote to the newspaper saying, "Indeed, I am an alarmed parent—alarmed lest a system in which my child read 150 books this year might be tampered with and changed!"

5. *Pressure for Subject-Centered Departmentalization*

In some schools children as young as eight are moving from room to room, subject to subject, teacher to teacher, six teachers a day. The high school has moved down. A poor high school at that!

What do the proponents say? "Teachers cannot teach math and science properly to eight- to eleven-year-old children." "Teachers feel more prestige, hold their heads higher if they are teaching subjects." This must mean they are *not* teaching children. "Children can progress at their own rate in each subject and in this way learn more."

Well, if I were an elementary teacher again I would insist that I could teach whatever I expected eight- to eleven-year-olds to learn, knowing how easily and readily they pitch in to help teach each other. What kind of moral professional posture is it to claim that teaching math invites more prestige than teaching children? The greatest Teacher of all said not so.

As for learning more, subject by subject, this brings us back to the core question, "How do children learn?" *They learn best through rich experience woven into a tapestry whose design emerges as the many and varied threads of activity are tied together.* Through the tying together of many approaches to the same concept, the child grips the concept; in Lewin's terms, learnings "adhere," become a usable and useful part of the child's essential equipment for life. Lawrence K. Frank said:[7]

> The child . . . begins to learn, not bit by bit, by analysis of events, by fractionating wholes into parts and trying to understand the relation of two variables, as in our analytically oriented scientific studies; but rather he grasps wholes, approaches the world in patterns that enable him to relate himself cognitively and transactionally to his environment.

I must stop here with this necessarily superficial statement and analysis of only five ways we are pushing children today. Will you mull them over? Study the quotes and the following references. Think deeply before you move in the direction of more schemes and devices that move counter to the best growth and development of children. We used to speak nostalgically of the GOLDEN AGE OF CHILDHOOD. Was there ever? Is there today? Are children entitled to childhood?

References

Association for Childhood Education International, 3615 Wisconsin Avenue, N.W., Washington, D. C. 20016:
  All Children Have Gifts, 1957, 32p., 75¢.
  Arithmetic—Children Use It!, 1954, 56p., 75¢ (out of print).
  Children's Views of Themselves, 1959, 36p., 75¢.
  Continuous Learning, 1951, 40p., 75¢ (out of print).
  Discipline, 1956, 36p., 75¢.
  How Do Children Learn, CHILDHOOD EDUCATION, December 1959.
  How Do Your Children Grow?, 1959, 32p., 75¢.
  How Good Is Our Kindergarten?, 1959, 36p., 75¢.
  Kindergarten Teachers Portfolio, 1954, 12 leaflets, 75¢.
  More About Reading, 1959, 32p., 50¢.
  New Knowledge Requires New Experience, CHILDHOOD EDUCATION, October 1959.
  Pressures in School and Community, CHILDHOOD EDUCATION, October 1960.
  Relating Self to Others, CHILDHOOD EDUCATION, November 1958.
  Reporting on the Growth of Children, 1953, 47p., 75¢ (out of print).
  What Are Kindergartens For?, 1959, 8p., 10¢ ea.; 25 for $2.
  When Children Move from School to School, 1960, 36p., 75¢ (out of print).

Association for Supervision and Curriculum Development, 1201 16th Street, N.W., Washington, D. C. 20006:
  Freeing Capacity To Learn, 1960, 97p., $1.
  Learning and the Teacher, 1959 Yearbook, 222p., $3.75.
  Learning More About Learning, 1959, 88p., $1.

[7] Lawrence K. Frank, *The School as Agent for Cultural Renewal* (Cambridge, Mass.: Harvard University Press, 1959), p. 32.

With Life So Long, Why Shorten Childhood?

BY WINIFRED E. BAIN

The heavy hand presses down from level to level. This is a threat to normal development of childhood. Remember, it takes time to develop young children! Winifred Bain, Cambridge, Massachusetts, is a former president of Wheelock College, Boston, and a former president of the Association for Childhood Education International. She is financial adviser of the Association.

IT IS WELL KNOWN FROM VITAL STATISTICS THAT LIFE EXPECTANCY is longer than ever before in history. Never mind about what it is that keeps us alive so long—vitamins, wonder drugs and regulatory activities —just accept the fact that life stretches ahead for most of us far beyond the age which our grandparents attained. Despite this vista of longevity, there is rife among many who "really want the best" for children the tendency to curtail the period of childhood, not by denial of vitamins and tender loving care, to be sure, but by haste toward getting them into adult patterns. By the age of seven children are supposed to be fully ready to blast off into life space, whereas by seventy-seven or even by eighty-seven they will still be in orbit.

There are some logical reasons for this trend. We have come to accept speed as normal in life processes. In the course of fifteen minutes a man traveled 115 miles into space and back again to earth. Just any ordinary tourist can travel across the United States from the Atlantic to the Pacific in just any ordinary jet plane in four hours, or in comparable time he can cross an ocean or fly over the North Pole. With a little forethought about reserving a time one can be connected in a flash to almost any part of the world by modern telephone. Illustrations could be multiplied, but this is enough to indicate that we have become accelerated in our thinking about life. Furthermore, technical advancements have brought into being great new bodies of knowledge. It is natural to ask, "Shouldn't the children of the coming generation get down to the business of mastering skills? Shouldn't they, above all else, learn the techniques of reading at an early age so as to be able to dig this knowledge out of books?" Another troublesome thought is that the speed of transportation and communication has brought us into direct relationships with people in other lands for whom the older generation was unconcerned and of whom they were even unaware. There is rivalry between nations; a quest for power; a quest for freedom from oppression, strife and misunderstanding.

Acting Their Age

In a large sense the danger is that man will learn to control the elements before he learns to control himself. There is no disputing the fact, of course, that one needs knowledge and reflection on the world's great thinkers, events and discoveries in order to learn how to control himself and his relationship with others. But these things come gradually to children. Children learn to control themselves first of all by being children and behaving like children. An illustration: On the day after the first American took off into space, a group of five-year-olds assembled a helmet, a zipper suit, a scooter and other paraphernalia. One stepped up and said, "I'm Shepard, I'm going to blast off into space." Another said, "No, I want to go." "No," said the first child, "you can be the count-down man and perhaps they will choose you to go next time." These two were boys; but, not to be outdone, up stepped a small girl. She threw her arms passionately around the helmeted figure and said, "I'm Mrs. Shepard. Good-bye, dear, don't get killed. I'll be praying for you." The count-down man began to drone out the numbers, "ten, nine, eight . . ." When he got to "one," away scooted Mr. Shepard into the anteroom and in no time was back to be rescued by all hands with loud acclaim and to receive a resounding kiss from Mrs. Shepard who said with pride, "I knew you'd make it." And Mr. Shepard said, "Boy, what a ride!"

For five-year-olds this is a normal way of behaving—like children who are five years old. Older ones, too, have their own childish ways of behaving, but at no time do they behave in a vacuum. They use the events and concepts of life about them as both stimulus and content for their active pursuits. As they discover the need for more information and skill, they set about to get it. This means that they learn the arts and sciences through living experiences; they experiment, weigh values and ponder a growing philosophy. They learn about man's relationship to man, man's relationship to the physical world and the spiritual realm. They learn to control themselves in the framework of this complex milieu.

Concepts Before Symbols

In contradiction to this theory, one trend in present-day thought is that we must get children ready for each new phase of development by giving them systematic practice in the technical requirements for that phase. This is noticeable in kindergartens where five-year-olds are given practice in technical requirements of the reading process—even graded steps. This is called "reading readiness." But concepts come before symbols, or at least they should. One can master the phonetics of a language and read with fluency without understanding a word of it. But what good does it do? Children need to live savoring the wonders of life, gaining understanding, seeing relationships, following the urge to initiate and create. These are the prerequisites of reading with a purpose and with understanding of vicarious experiences recorded in symbols on the printed page.

A Turnabout Situation

Another contradiction lies in the contrast between the attitude toward requirements for children and the present-day thought about the needs and rights of adults. Adults have shorter work weeks, shorter working days, more do-it-yourself hobbies, more outdoor recreation than in previous times. There are exceptions but this is the trend. At the same time it is thought children must be put through their paces or they will not pass to the next grade or they will not match the achievements of children in other countries or, in the long look ahead, they will not be ready for the competition involved in serious, strenuous times to come. For illustration here is a family of five—father, mother and three children aged twelve, ten and eight. They are musical—each plays an instrument. On occasion they appear in small school or community programs playing simple ensembles or accompaniments for children's choruses. They are normally active in seasonal activities on the playground and they belong to dancing classes. During summer vacations all three learned to swim. No trouble about reading. They learned easily, and when time permits one or another can be found curled up with a book and an apple. But between the dark and the daylight—once known as the "children's hour"—comes homework, more for each child than one child can do alone. All hands pitch in. Father and Mother divide themselves into three parts with major portions assigned to the ten- and twelve-year-olds. By bedtime, hands are trembling over unfinished work and these intelligent, talented, affectionate family members are screaming at each other. Fortunate though, in view of the demands of the children, that Father has short working hours and Mother has labor-saving equipment for the household!

The Top Pushes Down

Childhood is a time of continuous, integrated development charged with activity. At one time, when this concept was stressed in homes, schools and communities, the elementary school was quite generally commended as the best period in the long sequence of children's education since teachers for that level were prepared to concern themselves with the all-round growth and development of little human beings. But recently, since the big push toward mastery for survival, the complaint is frequently heard that children graduating from the elementary grades are not ready for the work of the secondary school. And this refers to those with native endowment necessary for an academic education, not those who for lack of such equipment would formerly have dropped out before the enactment of laws raising the age of compulsory school attendance. Theirs is another long story. But for the usual good child who comes from the usual good elementary school, there is pressure for more knowledge in science, mathematics, social sciences, languages and for greater facility in reading on entering high school than most parents and grandparents had on graduation. No wonder the elementary schools are pushing children! And why are high schools so demanding? They have to get their grist ready to meet the demands of the colleges.

Power and Rivalry Beget Fear

To be sure, many colleges—not all—are flooded with applicants. More young people of college age are going to college than in former generations, and the tidal waves of babies which began flooding the population during the war are now of college age. There is another reason for pressure, too. As noted earlier in this article there are trends in modern thought toward rivalry between nations; a quest for power; a quest for freedom from oppression, strife and misunderstanding. These beget fear. And for survival we look hopefully toward the more mature members of the new generation, the young people of college age. They can be prepared faster to meet the new demands of our times. The younger ones can take longer. But still the heavy hand presses down from level to level—a threat to the normal development of childhood.

Childhood has its own needs and it would be as serious a mistake to fail to challenge children as it is to ply them with requirements beyond their ability. One theory about juvenile delinquency is that it stems from boredom. But why err in either direction? The needs of childhood are simple, really: *growth,* nourishment for growing minds and bodies; *activity* with its own purposes, real to the child; *struggle to attain purposes,* even anguish and disappointments while overcoming obstacles; *play,* with its refreshment and its natural rewards in the discovery of ethical values; *quiet,* with time for rest and reflection, with awe and wonder at the mysteries of creation. Children need in childhood a normal development program in readiness for the courage, judgment, integrity and dedication said to be essential to survival in mature life. In this day and age they will be a long time as adults and "senior citizens."

Who? What? When? Where? How? Why?

BY AGNES SNYDER

Agnes Snyder, professor emeritus, Adelphi College, New York, and now of Wilmington, Delaware, is chairman of CHILDHOOD EDUCATION's Editorial Board. She asks the questions which, if honestly and intelligently answered, give teaching the status of an art.

IN THE EDITORIAL DR. JONAS SALK IS QUOTED AS SAYING THAT IF scientists asked the right questions all the viruses that torment men could be conquered. Although he limits his statement to scientists, it is equally applicable to social scientists. If they asked the right questions it is safe to say we would be much further along the way than we now are toward the solution of the problems of starvation, ignorance, crime, delinquency, war. And if we teachers asked the right questions—of ourselves and of children—we would have more natural and social scientists asking the right questions. Equally important, more people in general would be asked the right questions.

Certainly there never will be a morning on which we will rise to a problemless world; nor should we wish it. We know that every problem solved or even partially solved gives rise to bigger and more challenging ones. In this is the zest of living. No one who loves life ever wants to be problem free; but we do need and should want a more intelligent, less nerve-racking and more humane way of meeting our problems.

The first step is locating our problems. This means asking the right questions.

We all feel the need at times to get away from details that clutter our lives and be off somewhere with trees, mountains, the sea. We want to know what is important, what is fundamental. Young children, before they become entangled in our practical pursuits, often ask the very questions that deep down within us are demanding answers, questions that send us off away from our usual routines to seek solutions.

James Feibleman is quoted in our editorial as saying:

They [children] are eager to learn about everything and they ask the embarrassingly fundamental questions that adults are never able to answer, questions such as: "What is God like, how far does space extend, what is time, why am I here?"

Perhaps, as Feibleman goes on to say, adults will never answer them; but in the *effort* to do so is found that deepening understanding that alone gives meaning to life.

It is in the way that the questioning proclivity of children is used that will determine whether or not our teaching will produce a generation able and eager to ask the questions needed for man's continuous progress. We carry a heavy responsibility: in keeping children from being afraid to ask questions; in teaching them to distinguish between good and poor questions; in having them learn the many different ways of finding answers and of selecting the most suitable; in leading them to understand that although some questions yield to immediate answers the most significant ones take time and hard work, that some may take years and even centuries to explore, and that some may never be fully answered. All this and more are involved.

Simple Words but Basic

Teachers, like journalists, find much of their work centered round simple, one-syllabled words: *Who? What? When? Where? How? Why?* Reporters are not supposed to indulge in the *why;* only editors may do so. But teachers are continuously involved—and often simultaneously—in all six; and it is their answers to the sixth, the *why,* that in a large measure determine the quality of their answers to the other five. In fact, wherever you find schools slavishly following tradition or servile concessions to the demands of ignorant criticism, it is safe to assume that the *why* behind the *who, what, when, where, how* has been neglected. It is just as true that wherever you find a school bubbling with the excitement of adventurous living, with individuality, with originality, you may be sure that the teachers have wrestled with the *why* behind what they are doing.

Why: The Key

The *why* behind all the other *why's* in a teacher's questioning should be: "Why am I teaching?" A young man or woman entering college cannot be expected to give a profound answer to the question. Each is normally more concerned with self-fulfillment than with helping others to realize their potentials.

There is nothing wrong in this and, of course, there are exceptions. There are young people who have successfully withstood the materialistic values of our day and early sense the challenge of teaching. Somehow they have developed a passion for growth in others as well as in themselves; they feel the awesome power of education over both the individual and the race; and for these reasons, they are impelled by an undeniable urge to be one of those who through teaching are striving for a better life for more of man.

Though few young people at the beginning of their careers regard teaching in this light, unless as they become more mature they are stirred by the profound implications of teaching they should choose some other means of livelihood. It is only those who grasp the far-reaching effects of the day-by-day life in the classroom who will have concern over the *why* behind the experiences, the subject matter and the processes of the curriculum.

Because such teachers have achieved a philosophy of life and education, they will not be moved by pressures but proceed unflinchingly along the way their convictions indicate.

Who: The Focus

The answer to *why* is the key that unlocks the door to answers to all the other questions the teacher asks. The *who* is his focus. Who are these children he teaches? Of course, he wants to know how old they are, something of their school achievements, the state of their health, any physical handicaps they may have. The answers can generally be found easily in school records and by superficial observation. They certainly are important; but they are only a beginning. To know the real child—what makes him "tick"—the teacher must penetrate much more deeply.

For the past two hundred years, ever since Rousseau cried out, "Study your child for assuredly you do not know him," thoughtful scientists and lovers of children have heeded his admonition.

As our culture becomes more sophisticated, to know children becomes increasingly difficult. Children soon learn to cover up their real selves just as the adults around them do. Sometimes they are moved to disguise their feelings through fear of punishment or ridicule; sometimes by love, by wanting to do what is expected of them. There is a "school child" who talks school language, who assumes school behavior, who bears little resemblance to the child within the shell.

The questions the teacher will ask himself in order to know his children cannot be prescribed but will vary with the environment. Though specifics cannot be indicated, the questions will have to do largely with relationships and feelings. Who is this child in his innermost being?

Who is he in his home? The petted darling, the scorned one, the ugly duckling, the household drudge, the babysitter for the younger children, a loved child, a wanted child? What image has he of himself? Is he accepting the role assigned him? Is he hostile because of it? How does he see himself as an adult?

Who is he on the street? A boon companion accepted by the group, a leader, a fearful one trying to buy his way into favor, a butt of ridicule? What is the effect of his role on him? Is he belligerent, sneaky, envious, cowed, confident, assured, unhappy, happy?

Such questions are in the teacher's mind but rarely asked aloud—for the knowledge sought lies in that twilight zone where the spoken question is a discordant note, where silence is often golden, where answers are found not through direct questioning but by the listening ear, the seeing eye and the feeling heart. Some of the finest questions the teacher raises are never spoken, never audible to anyone but himself.

What: The Content

The teacher asks, "What shall I teach?" If we were wise enough, the questions children ask us and our own developing philosophy of living and of education would give us the answers. Out of the wonderment of little children could be developed all the knowledge we need to understand our physical and our social worlds and to send us searching for the meaning of life and what makes it of worth.

What makes waves? Where do clouds come from? What is green? What makes the light go on? When is tomorrow? What makes it cold in winter and hot in summer? What is a jet? Where are the stars in the daytime? Must everything die?

What is a president? Why do we vote? Why do people go to jail? Why can't everybody have enough to eat? If there weren't any stores long ago how did people eat? If people can't talk English how do they know what they are saying?

Where is God? What is heaven? Why can't I see God? Why do they put people down in the ground when they die? If God can do anything He wants why does He let some people be bad?

No doubt our own education gives us answers to some of these questions. But are there not gaps in our knowledge that make it difficult for us to answer with depth even some of the simpler ones? How the questions children ask us could send us delving into fields of knowledge to find more precise answers, whereas before we had been satisfied with the superficial!

But we are not wise enough to select curriculum content purely on the basis of children's questions and individual philosophies. Most of us would not qualify even in knowledge. But even if we were, it would not be good. We must make sure that all children share in a common heritage of culture. Otherwise our efforts at understanding among people would be irreparably damaged.

There must be some form of curriculum guide for teachers. It should be universal in approach but local in emphasis, definite but flexible, perennial in its human concerns but subject to continuous modification and revision. There should also be materials in common use comparable in their characteristics to curriculum guides—textbooks, supplementary books, globes, maps, charts, reference material. Over and above these basic materials there should be materials collected by teachers and children representing their specific interests and experiences—pamphlets, pictures, clippings, collections of all sorts.

How: The Process

The teacher's problem is *how* to bring the great masses of available knowledge and the child's questions together. How to do this in such a way that the child's curiosity will be heightened; that he will be stimulated to pursue paths of his own inquiry; that he will, at the same time, share with his fellows the binding force of their common heritage. This is the supreme art of teaching. It can be learned; to a measure, it can be taught; but in the last analysis, like all other arts, it is an expression of the life and aspirations of the artist and therefore he alone can give it form.

In the old days—"the good old days" as our critics would have us think and relive—when teaching was concerned with "subject matter to be taught," with the teacher's responsibility ending there, a definite methodology developed. It found its peak in the late nineteenth century in the work of the McMurry brothers and their associates in what became known as "the five formal steps" in planning. It was based on the psychology and philosophy of the renowned thinker, Johann Friedrich Herbart. It had many merits, particularly in its emphasis on the assimilation of new subject matter by children in terms of their related experiences—an application of Herbart's theory of apperception. But it was subject-matter oriented and developed with little regard for the significance to learning of such concepts as the interaction of the organism and the environment; the interdependence of the physical, mental and emotional; the dynamics of developmental tasks. These are twentieth-century understandings; and they all point to the absolute necessity of considering the "whole child" in his physical, social and spiritual environment if we have concern for any one aspect of his growth.

Any honest appraisal of the work of the schools today will include the acknowledgment that what is being done lags far behind what we know should be done. We have as yet not developed teaching methods which utilize twentieth-century knowledge of human growth and development comparable in the definiteness and thoroughness of "the five formal steps" in its application to teaching of the nineteenth-century psychology. Perhaps we never will, and there are many reasons for this. Beginning with an understanding of children's needs is a more difficult process than beginning with subject matter to be taught. The former is art; the latter, craft. This is one reason for our lag— one reason also why so many school systems are adopting the easier road of formal teaching advised by our critics. Meanwhile the critics attack us, as Harold Taylor so aptly puts it ". . . not for going backward but for not being backward enough. . . ." [1]

When: The Time

One of the most baffling questions of methodology is that of *when*. When to answer a child's question immediately without much ado; when to ignore it; when to answer with another question; when to send a child in pursuit of the answer; when to help and when not to help; when to let an experience simmer and wait for an opportune moment to pick it up.

To everything there is a season, and a time to every purpose under the heaven. *Ecclesiastes 3:1*

This might well be one of the main texts we teachers should carry round with us.

A group of children had been to a puppet show and were eagerly telling the principal, who had not seen it, about it. Bursting with enthusiasm, they totally disregarded sequence, jumping from middle, end, beginning, and all about. Then the teacher, whose adult organization could not bear the topsy-turvy account of the children, stepped in with: "I am afraid Mrs. Brown is not getting a very clear idea of the story; now let's begin at the beginning." What a drop! Here were children reliving their enjoyment, sharing the parts that meant most to them, having fun. Of course, these obliging children tried manfully to comply. The result—a painful classroom exercise.

Of course, organization is important; of course, children should be taught to arrange their thoughts in an orderly manner! But this teacher took the wrong moment; it should have been later.

Every day the teacher in his planning is confronted with the question *when*. In his efforts to combine the children's questions with the proposals of the curriculum guide, he is constantly adapting the order of the guide to the interests of the children. It is practically impossible for any teacher working from inside (of the children) out to follow a curriculum guide step by step as it is outlined. "Strike while the iron is hot"—and be sure to know when it is hot and to strike hard.

In our bow today to the tempo of the times, the question of *when* is particularly crucial. We are being bombarded with insistent demands that we speed up education: teach reading in the kindergarten, even in the nursery; bring high school subjects down in the elementary grades.

[1] Harold Taylor, "What the Family Isn't Teaching," *Saturday Review*, May 18, 1963.

Have we an answer? Can we say definitely *when* each child should be taught *what?* No, most emphatically, we cannot! But we do know with The Preacher that to everything there is a season and that childhood is a season that has its unique purposes and tasks. We know, too, that true growth is slow and that to force it is not good. We know, equally, for a child to work below his ability without challenge to his maximum effort is discouraging and weakening. To have a child work to his greatest potential cannot be done by any wholesale method of prescribing more difficult work earlier. It must be left to the seeing, hearing, sensitive teacher to know *when* each child is ready for his next step.

Where: The Place for Learning Experiences

We know that all education does not take place in the classroom. As rich as it may be with plants, pets, books, aquaria, charts, maps, pictures, it is at best a confining, limiting environment compared with opportunities beyond its walls. But we are so wedded to words, symbols, books as the beginning and end of education that we feel guilty if we use more vital media. In the article quoted earlier, Harold Taylor expresses the anomaly forcefully:

> The direction of learning is from emotion to thought to expression in words, symbols, or symbolic action of some kind—not the reverse as most educators think. Educators think that by exposure to symbols, words, and connected concepts, thoughts will be formed and children will be educated; they will be able to read, write, and speak what they have learned. Education should, then, be formal, academic and confined to the classroom.[2]

Many thinkers in education have decried the formalism and the ineffectiveness of verbalism without experience: Comenius in the early seventeenth century with his dictum, "Things before words"; Pestalozzi with his environment study so well carried out in many German schools in the pre-Hitler days; Dewey in his emphasis on experience.

We need to ask in our planning, *"Where* can this best be taught?" It may be in a lumberyard with the manager as teacher showing the children the different kinds of wood and from where they came; or in a freight station with the children copying the labels on the bales of paper, paper their fathers had helped make, showing the far corners of the earth to which it would be shipped; or in a junk yard where the children enlarge their idea of a magnet as a small bar or horseshoe as they see huge magnets lift parts of wrecked automobiles. It may be in a court as they watch the operation of justice; or in the building where a newspaper passes through the many processes from composition to loading for delivery.

Where? Instead of taking the classroom for granted as the locale for the teaching act, it might be a good thing to ask a reverse question,

---
[2] *Ibid.*

"Is there a better place for this particular experience than the classroom?" If we did ask it, there would be more reality in education. There might even be need for (whisper it) fewer classrooms! !

Not More but Better Questions

Certainly we teachers can never be accused of asking too few questions. If anything, we ask too many. It is a common observation that the further up in the grades you go the fewer questions the children ask and the more the teacher asks. It might be a good idea if some day we carried a pencil and pad around with us and noted the ratio of children's questions to ours. Another day it might be valuable to note the kinds of questions we ask. It is just possible that, in the terms Perry Mason and the District Attorney fling at each other when objecting to the questioning of a witness, some of them just might be "incompetent, immaterial and irrelevant!"

Why do we do it? Why do we ask more and more questions of children? The motive, like teachers' motives generally, is good. It rises out of a conscientious desire that children learn, that we teach them something. We can't just *tell* them; we want to "get it from them." We want to use every crumb of knowledge they have, and we want them to *think*. So, having clearly in mind what *we* want *them* to know, we start off with a nice question about something that we are sure they already know. Then we start in with one question after another leading them through the train of *our* reasoning until someone—often it is just one—comes out with the right answer; that is, the one *we* wanted. In a way this is a distorted version of the application of the Herbartian psychology. It might be interesting after going through such a process to see how many children could repeat it.

We need not deceive ourselves that children learn to think through such a procedure. They do not. To teach thinking we must find a question that the children feel compelled to answer. Then we must guide them through the well-known steps of scientific thinking until they arrive at a tested and satisfying solution. We will not ask many questions along the way. But the children will. Ours will be deliberate; we will be deliberate; we will know *why* we are asking them; therefore, we will know whom, what, where, how and when to ask.

How Valid Are the Criticisms?
BY AFTON DILL NANCE

Teachers would do well to consider the source of criticism and its motivation before allowing themselves to be influenced or troubled by it. Is the person qualified to comment or is he speaking from a background of self-interest, political ambition, ignorance or prejudice? Afton Dill Nance, consultant in elementary education, California State Department of Education, Sacramento, discusses why teachers can no longer afford to be trusting and naive regarding the important issue of criticism.

DURING THE PAST FIFTEEN YEARS THE PUBLIC SCHOOLS OF OUR country have been subjected to a continuous barrage of criticism. They have been criticized for not teaching the fundamentals of reading, writing and arithmetic, for neglecting gifted pupils, for failing to inculcate patriotic ideas, for stifling creativity, for using outmoded methods of instruction and for jumping on the bandwagon of educational faddism. This is but a partial list. During these years schools in many states have been coping with increased enrollments, a shortage of well-qualified teachers, a lack of proper buildings and of provisions for adequate financial support. However, very seldom are the complaints and the problems of adequate support considered together in a rational fashion.

Many of the criticisms are so sweeping and general in character that providing the data which would put them within a proper framework is beyond the power of local educators.

Children Reading Extensively

For example, take the well-publicized comment that "children are not learning to read nowadays." What children? Five-year-olds in a slum environment? Children who have never had a full day of classroom instruction but who have been on half-day sessions during their entire school life? Children in large classes with teachers who are not fully qualified? Children whose families follow the crops? Children from well-established homes whose parents respect the value of education and enjoy reading themselves?

In response to this criticism regarding the efficiency of instruction in reading, teachers and other educators should ask the question, "Does this criticism apply in my classroom or my district?" If it does, the facts should be made known, the reasons explained, and appropriate steps taken to improve the situation. Frequently the appropriate steps will include reduction in class size, in-service education for teachers, improvement in the amount and quality of materials, the establishment of an adequate library, or changes in methods of instruction. No cheap, easy, sure-fire remedies are available to solve complex educational problems.

If, after careful investigation, the criticism is found *not* to apply locally, the public should be informed of this fact through all channels open to public information. The first groups to be well armed with all the facts are the teachers and other educators at all levels. It is also desirable to ascertain whether or not the accusation is valid in areas outside the community.

Evidence is available to disprove the sweeping statement of general failure in the area of reading. Through a nationwide study, A. I. Gates [1] made a comparison of test scores in reading of children in grades five and six in 1937 and in 1957 which indicated that the 1957 children surpassed the 1937 group of the same age and intelligence by at least half a grade. Other studies [2] present similar findings.

Dramatic evidence that today's children are reading extensively may be discovered by a look at the information regarding the number of new books for children which are printed annually. In 1962, 2,328 new books and 256 new editions of books previously published were printed for a total of 2,584. This was 958 more books than were published in 1961, thus marking a substantial increase.[3] It can hardly be possible that the publishing companies are printing books for nonreaders!

However, data such as these will convince only the rational and open-minded members of society. A person who is hostile to public education will reject such information, and direct efforts to influence him will be unsuccessful. Efforts should rather be made to inform the large segments of the public who believe in the American tradition of basing their opinions on ascertainable facts.

Who Criticizes?

Attention may also be directed to the source of the criticism. Is the person qualified to comment, or is he speaking from a background of self-interest, political ambition, ignorance or prejudice? Who is talking?

It may be a well-informed newspaper reporter who has taken time

---

[1] Arthur I. Gates, *"A Review of Tomorrow's Illiterates,* by Charles C. Walcutt and *What Ivan Knows That Johnny Doesn't,* by Arther S. Trace, Jr." Pamphlet printed and distributed by the author (February 1962).

[2] Wendell C. Lanton, *Comparison of the Reading, Arithmetic, Spelling Achievement of Third and Fifth Grade Pupils in 1953 and in 1934.* Dissertation Abstracts, Vol. XIV, No. 10, 1954. See also *The Past-Present Achievement of Evanston School Children.* NEA Research Division, National Education Association of the United States: Washington, D. C. (September, 1954).
Vera Miller and Wendell C. Lanton, "Reading Achievement of School Children—Then and Now," *Elementary English,* Vol. XXXIII (February 1956).

[3] Annual Summary, *Publishers Weekly,* January 21, 1963, Vol. 183, No. 3, p. 40.

to get his facts straight, or it may be an irresponsible headline hunter.

It may be a writer for a magazine honestly committed to the principle that education is of primary importance in a democracy, or it may be a writer or editor who sees a chance for glory if a sensational story causes circulation figures to mount.

It may be an eminent scientist who can speak as an expert on problems of atomic energy or chemistry, but who is not qualified to give advice regarding the teaching of reading to beginners.

It may be someone who sees an opportunity for personal gain if confidence in present methods of instruction can be reduced.

It may be a charlatan seeking cheap publicity whose sole purpose is to discredit the schools so that taxes will more readily be curtailed.

"Is the person presenting the criticism well-informed and honestly concerned with the improvement of education?" This is a question which many teachers ask with difficulty because it implies the possibility of base motives as well as irresponsibility and self-interest on the part of the critics. Most educators have confidence and trust in their fellows. They find it difficult to work effectively to help children fulfill their full potential and at the same time be skeptical of the motivation of members of the adult population. They have been well-schooled to accept criticism and to think that most of it is well-meant and constructive. The idea that much of the present criticism of education stems from irresponsible self-seekers is hard for many educators to accept. However, teachers would do well to consider the source of the criticism and its possible motivation before allowing themselves to be influenced or troubled by it. They can no longer afford to be trusting and naive regarding this important issue. Make no mistake, decreasing the effectiveness of the public school system threatens the very basis of democratic government.

Organized To Criticize

One of the sources of criticism of the public schools is the Council for Basic Education, a nonprofit, lay-oriented group established in 1956, supported by foundation grants and by the dues and payments of its members and subscribers. The Council is well-financed and apparently organized for the purpose of criticizing public education in the name of advancing "quality" education. A well-documented analysis of its arguments is contained in the book *The Ax-Grinders* [4] by Mary Anne Raywid.

Miss Raywid points out the relationships between the Council on Basic Education and such groups as the National Economic Council

---

[4] Mary Anne Raywid, *The Ax-Grinders* (New York: The Macmillan Company, 1962).

and the Foundation for Economic Education, both right-wing political groups. All three groups receive financial assistance from the Volker Fund. The commonality of their interests is indicated by the fact that the National Economic Council has flatly opposed federal aid to education as Socialism;[5] the Foundation for Economic Education publishes articles declaring that education should be a private responsibility;[6] and a statement frequently made in the Bulletin of the Council on Basic Education is that "the correlation between cost and academic achievement is practically zero." [7]

That some of these efforts have been effective in reducing school support is indicated in an article by James E. Bixler entitled, *"School Critics, Influence upon California Legislation."* [8] A quotation follows:

A force having a more serious effect than is apparent is the irresponsible, insidious attacks on public education. It is impossible to say that strident criticism has led directly to curtailment of financial aid to schools. However, it is reasonable to assume that much of the extreme and wholesale criticism might well incline legislators to allot scarce funds elsewhere....

The effect of destructive criticism on the morale of teachers and hence on their efficiency in the classroom cannot be objectively assessed. The continual bombardment of criticism coming from the daily press, from magazines and from other mass media must have its influence. Parents and children may show less respect and understanding for the educational process. Precious time must be taken from instructional duties to interpret and justify professional decisions. However, these efforts to discredit education have not been wholly successful. Raywid again reports as follows:[9]

Despite the fact that there are many severe critics of American education, it appears that a majority of citizens feel that schools are doing a passable, if not always exemplary, job. The last big national poll on education found 79 per cent of the public believing the things taught in the schools of 1950 equal to or more desirable than what was taught in 1930.[10] Of the California citizens polled in 1956, 82 per cent thought public schools were doing a job that was fair or better. In the state of Washington, 79 per cent of those polled thought today's high school graduate is at least as well educated as the graduates of their own day. And in Utah, 81 per cent of those asked were satisfied with the results achieved by their public schools.[11]

Unwarranted Criticism

Certain educators have been remiss in failing to be frank regarding the real problems which face them. Teachers have accepted large classes

[5] *Ibid.*, pp. 114-15.
[6] *Ibid.*, pp. 112-13.
[7] *Ibid.*, p. 102.
[8] James E. Bixler, "School Critics, Influence upon California Legislation," *California Journal of Instructional Improvement* (Burlingame, Calif.: California Association for Supervision and Curriculum Development, Vol. V, No. 3, October 1962), pp. 7-14.
[9] *Ibid.*, p. 207.
[10] Elmo Roper, "What U. S. Thinks About Its Schools," Life XXIX (Oct. 16, 1950), p. 11.
[11] All the studies cited are summarized in the NEA's *Public Opinion Polls on American Education* (Washington: The Association, May 1958), pp. 10-12.

without protest because they considered this their job. They have accepted unwarranted criticism, with its resultant lowering of morale. They have lamented among themselves instead of gathering their facts and formulating a considered and forthright plan attacking the basic underlying problems. They have failed to formulate clearly their own theory and philosophy of education so that they could meet the criticism firmly and objectively.

A defensive attitude is the first line of capitulation; and often a well-planned attack is the best defense. Educators in these days would do well to cultivate a healthy skepticism regarding the motivation of those who make broad and general accusations against the efficiency of today's schools. "He has the right to criticize, who has the heart to help," is an old saying which has application regarding the validity of current criticisms of the schools. Some criticisms are well-meant and constructive, others are motivated solely by ambition and self-interest. Knowing the difference and acting in terms of this knowledge is essential to the continued welfare of "all the children of all the people" whose education is the special charge of the public schools.

Vol. XXVIII—p. 341 (Apr. 1952)

Anthropology — An Integrating Science for an Integrated World
BY ETHEL J. ALPENFELS

"Anthropology holds up a great mirror to man and lets him look at himself in his infinite variety." Clyde Kluckhohn in "Mirror for Man."

How the contributions of anthropology have meaning to everyone working with children is told by Ethel J. Alpenfels, professor of education, New York University.

WHEN I LEFT ELEMENTARY SCHOOL TEACHING TO TAKE UP THE profession of anthropology, many of my friends said: "Why study anthropology? Anthropologists are always talking about abstract ideas and academic concepts. Anthropology isn't practical!"

During the past ten years, however, the word "anthropology," like the word "atomic," has emerged from the ivory towers of the academic world and the pages of obscure textbooks to appear with increasing frequency in the everyday world. Perhaps this is because of its subject

[1] New York: McGraw-Hill Book Company, 1949. P. 11.

matter: the study of man. Perhaps it is because of its early history or its great breadth of interest, but whatever the reason anthropolgy has become one of the most important integrating studies of all the human sciences.

A Science of "Left-overs"

Someone once described anthropology as the "science of left-overs." And so, in one sense, it is. Early scholars chose, for their special field of interest, social and scientific problems neglected by other established fields.

Historians, for example, were interested in written history and in unique events through time; anthropologists sought out cultures that had no written history and pushed time back to study people who lived before recorded history.

Psychology was concerned with individual behavior under controlled conditions; anthropologists engaged in pioneer studies on group behavior.

The student of languages studied grammar and vocabulary; anthropology used languages to help trace the movements of mankind.

Thus, anthropology bridged the gap between history, linguistics and psychology. The contributions from all these fields became fused into one general science of man. Psychologists and psychiatrists, teachers and social workers, geographers and nutritionists, those long accustomed to drawing up findings from many disciplines, are now also using anthropology, the "science of left-overs."

The support that anthropology is receiving from the related sciences and its importance to those who work with children are surprising when you remember its early beginnings, by a handful of practitioners, and its newness as a science. Anthropology is little more than one hundred years old. In its early days, European scholars ventured forth to study customs and habits of almost forgotten people. They brought back reports of outlandish customs and exotic beliefs, bits of broken bone and pottery, and seemed to spend their days measuring skulls of fossil man. No wonder, then, that in this country there grew up a popular picture of the anthropologist as an individual who was as quaint as the people he described.

Learning from the Highways and Byways

Whether it was the lure of far-off places, idle curiosity, or man's endless quest to understand himself better, the anthropologist continued to search for answers along the highways and the byways of both time and space. His search finally led him to a realization of the most important contribution his science has yet made: *that all human beings are more alike than they are different.* All of us have the same biological origin, the same basic needs, and all of us want much the same things out of life.

Yet each one of us is also different. The anthropologist created the term "culture" to express a way of thinking, feeling, believing, that human beings inherit as members of groups. It is our total way of life. Is is a sort of helpful shorthand to distinguish learned behavior from the physical traits we inherit. For children and all those who work with children, however, the concept of culture has important implications. Since culture is learned, it can also be unlearned. The little annoying habits, the superstitions and behavior problems are the result of the environment in which he lives and not because "he was born that way."

The children who come trooping into your classroom each day dress and act and talk very much the same. Yet each one brings different family backgrounds, different life experiences, different tools for learning.

An anthropologist was the first to demonstrate that the chronological and physiological ages of school children do not always coincide. He pointed out the important (and now generally accepted dictum) that a teacher must not demand that all her eight-year-olds, for example, meet a set standard for eight-year-olds. Just as in the growth of a culture, so in the growth of an individual, there are periods when he can acquire a skill more swiftly and efficiently than if he had been forced to do it at an earlier time. Experiments in psychology give ample evidence that children learn and mature at different rates of speed. This knowledge, growing out of the integration of several disciplines, should lessen the anxiety of parents and teachers when a child fails to attain the achievement level prescribed by our culture.

Subculture Patterns Are Important Too

Through pioneer studies of anthropology, no one today doubts the existence of different tribal, ethnic, and national cultures; no one questions the validity of talking about a Samoan culture or an American culture pattern. It is equally important, particularly for those who work with children, to recognize and make use of the new discoveries about the many subcultures right here in the United States.

First and second generation parents, still culturally bound by their national and ethnic groups, often make demands of their children which may contradict the cultural expectations of the classroom. Recent studies of American Indian cultures most dramatically illustrate the differences in racial patterns that often cause conflict in a child. As teachers, we can no longer think of Indians as people who *used to* live where we now do. Nor do they all live on reservations. They may be sitting in your classroom. Last year, a little Hopi Indian girl entered a grade school in Connecticut. One day her teacher complimented her on her beautiful dress. The child burst into tears and ran out of the classroom. The teacher, concerned and confused, wisely began to search for knowledge that would help her understand; she discovered that one must never call attention to a Hopi child in public. In present American culture, public praise by adults is often sought by children; among the Hopi, such praise only embarrasses the child.

Perhaps some of the most important recent research has been done by Allison Davis and W. Lloyd Warner, who found that social classes are actually American subcultures. Families (and children, too) in our society are classified as upper, lower or middle class depending upon the communities in which they live, the family income, the clubs to which they belong, and the type of work the father does. The "wrong" side and the "right" side of town can become a dividing wall over which youngsters cannot climb unless a thoughtful teacher helps them.

Where children are born will help determine how children think. For example, when asked to describe the word "straw," a boy who lived on a farm wrote: "Straw is what you feed cattle." A girl from a middle class family in the city wrote: "Straw is what you use to sip ice cream sodas with." A child from a lower class who kept house for her father wrote: "A straw is something you use to make a broom." Their answers were all correct. That analogy can be applied to more complex problems. An amusing but illuminating definition is the answer one lad gave to the question: "What is a lecture?" He replied: "A lecture is what the policeman gives you when you're bad and when you're really bad, you get the lecture chair." Language, one of our most important tools for learning, can be a barrier between education and "good" education.

An Integrating Science for an Integrated World

Perhaps the newest development—known as the area project—has even greater implications for those who work with children. You will recall that anthropologists of the nineteenth century brought back *single items* of culture; a broken potsherd or an ancient safety pin. Those in the twentieth century brought back monographs on the whole round of life of a *single culture:* the Incas of Peru or the Fijians of the South Pacific. Now, in the 1950's, anthropologists are studying *whole areas* of the world: Southeast Asia or Latin America. In the past, single field workers went out alone to study all aspects of a small group; today, whole teams of specialists from many disciplines are studying societies sharing a common environment but with different culture patterns.

Child Plus Method Plus Subject Matter

This new emphasis has at least three important implications. First, in the field of subject matter, one of the best illustrations can be found in the study of the American Indians. In teaching about the Iroquois, for example, it is not enough to describe the kind of houses, clothes, or food they eat; the Iroquois should be studied in relation to the whole Woodland culture area to which they belonged, and finally their way of life should be compared with that of other Indian tribes in the United States. This is the only way in which children can learn the true picture of Indian life: that all Indians did not live in tepees; that all Indians did not wear feather bonnets and smoke peace pipes; that, until the Spanish came, the Indians did not ride horseback. What is true of Indians is also true of all other people in the world. Upon such seemingly unimportant facts are individual life philosophies built.

The second implication is one that is not new to elementary teachers: we must teach the whole child. A single culture trait will tell us very little about a culture. So it is in our work with children: a single personality trait will not be enough to tell us very much about the whole child. To understand children we must see them as growing, changing, developing human beings. Children, like cultures, are integrated wholes. Both differ in their degrees of integration.

The third implication grows out of the method used in all the sciences. The elementary schools can and must begin to teach and practice the scientific method. For the scientific method is more than a procedure—it is a way of thinking. It is, as Huxley said, organized and trained common sense. It is a search for truth, as applicable in the classroom as in the laboratory. It is a search for facts, and individuals who stay close to facts often end up by thinking for themselves. Elementary school children must be taught to ask: "What is true?" "What is false?" They must learn how to observe and to compare. Teachers can also help them to take one more step: to help them understand the implications of their discoveries. If a fact or a truth is too complex, then the subject matter does not belong in the curriculum at that level.

The Story of Mankind

Anthropology today represents a new emphasis on an old subject: the story of mankind. That new emphasis is reflected in the classroom wherever teachers teach these basic concepts and values and ideas:

• That mankind is one. Wherever differences appear they lie in the cultural pattern, the emotional factors, and in heredity of each individual.

• That part of the past lives in the present. We need to give youngsters a perspective of man's long history if we are to build understanding.

• That we need not go to the old Stone Ages to find out what happens when people are cut off from new ideas. The barriers, the social barriers that man has created, are no less real than oceans that cannot be crossed.

• We must let people grow up. Many ethnic and racial minorities have not grown up because we have not permitted them to do so. We must let all our people grow to their full stature as individuals and to their full responsibility as citizens.

• That all this is a cooperative effort between the teachers, the home, and all the sciences: to teach understanding of common needs of all human beings; to help young people in their thinking to include more people of different backgrounds in the word *American* than we have ever done before; to help students understand that we must learn to live in a changing world.

How to build relationships that contain respect for all human beings is the problem of every discipline. It is particularly urgent in our time because of the potential for destruction that science has uncovered. Yet man travels along his way, saving time by sending cables and using telephones, shrinking space with jet-propelled planes, so fascinated simply by his ability to move fast that he no longer has any time to look where he has been or to find out where he is going.

The United Nations and the Real World
BY CHESTER BOWLES

Address by The Honorable Chester Bowles, Under Secretary of State, at the United Nations Day Luncheon in Washington, D.C., October 24, 1961.

EACH YEAR ON UNITED NATIONS DAY IN LATE OCTOBER WE MEET together to rededicate ourselves to the vision of a world at peace, to a brave, new world in which nations great and small will settle their differences in harmony.

This dream of a united world is an ancient and honorable one, the product of the best in the moral and ethical and religious heritage of every great civilization.

This dream will never die. Eventually, I am sure, it will come true.

But on United Nations Day 1961, against the background of Berlin, Laos, the stepped-up armament race, and the conflicts over the future of the U.N. itself, cooperation and understanding between the great powers seem remote and unrealistic. The world has never appeared so overwhelmingly complex, so agonizingly insecure, and so desperately at odds.

Yet despite its aching conflicts, I believe that the real world of 1961 is no place for a Cassandra. Although the future is exceedingly dangerous, its hopeful possibilities are infinite. If we are to understand the prospects and problems of the United Nations in this world of conflicting danger and hope, we must understand the forces at work in it.

We are contending with two mighty rival tides, running at crosscurrent. At times these two tides seem so contradictory that we are tempted to conclude that one is the reality and the other an illusion.

On the one hand, we have the massive tide of Cold War conflict. This is the world of barbed wire and stone walls, of sneak raids in the jungle and threats of nuclear destruction, the world of violence, distrust and fear, of stand-off and fall-out.

This rampaging tide of Cold War conflict has dominated the headlines since Stalin first threatened Greece and Turkey in 1946.

And yet, parallel to the arms race, coexistent with tension, and largely obscured from public understanding, another tide has been running toward freedom, toward hope, toward increased understanding and justice among nations and men.

What are the components of this less dramatic but perhaps decisive tide of human effort?

First is the movement toward national independence through which 900 million Asians and Africans have thrown off the rule of the old European trading empires to create forty-two new countries within fifteen years. This wave of liberation may earn more pages in the history of our time than the Cold War itself.

When World War II broke out in 1939, more than one-third of all mankind lived in dependent status under the rule of the European countries. Today, less than a generation later, the number is fewer than 2 per cent. Moreover, in large measure this world-wide emancipation has been accomplished without bloodshed.

Today this anti-colonial revolution is entering its final and most difficult stages. It would be folly to assume that the final act of colonial liquidation will be painless. Yet the progress in recent years has been extraordinary.

The *second* aspect of this hopeful tide is the world-wide determination to attack the hunger, disease and despair which for centuries have been the lot of the vast majority of the people of the underdeveloped world.

Although the needs are appalling, an impressive start has been made in providing massive technical and capital aid for their economic and social development.

Until recently, the United States was one of a handful of non-colonial nations engaged in overseas aid. Now some fifteen industrialized nations are offering their capital and technical skills to help speed the progress of economic and social development in the less developed area. Much of this assistance is now being coordinated through regional and international institutions.

So here we have more positive evidence that the counter tide of hope is running strong in world affairs.

A *third* hopeful phenomenon has been the rapid emergence of new international communities of sovereign states which are learning to work in free association for common purposes.

Since the end of World War II there has been a great reaching out across national frontiers, a groping for new forms of international cooperation, and the sudden appearance of new institutions in what remains an unplanned and still embryonic world community.

In the confusion and hurly-burly of the Cold War, it is easy to forget that Western Europe, the cockpit of great wars since the days of the Romans, is now being regionally integrated into a great common market of 350 million skilled peoples, with high and rising standards of living, based on an industrial complex second only to that of the United States.

Moreover, as the United States and Canada reach across the North Atlantic to establish close economic and political cooperation with this vital new European development, we see the institutional framework of an Atlantic Community gradually taking shape.

Meanwhile the institutions of our own Western Hemisphere are expanding in size and becoming more versatile in purpose. The new Alliance for Progress looks forward to hemispheric political, economic and social cooperation on a scale that could scarcely have been imagined before World War II.

In the Act of Bogota and the Declaration of Punta del Este, nineteen Latin American nations have joined in partnership with the United States in all-out effort to hasten their development.

The challenge posed by this Alliance is an enormous one. The Act of Bogota declared, "The success of a cooperative program of economic and social progress will require maximum self-help efforts on the part of the American republics and in many cases the improvement of existing institutions and practices, particularly in the fields of taxation, the ownership and use of land, education and training, health and housing."

This calls for no less than a political, economic and social revolution designed to modernize and invigorate old societies and to bring new opportunities and dignity to their people.

Seven of the Latin American nations are also exploring the possibilities of a common market. Similar economic integration is moving ahead in Central America.

In Southeast Asia regional planning and regional projects, including the vast Mekong River development program, are also moving through the planning stages.

Here in the creation of international agencies and associations we see further evidence of progress toward human betterment and understanding which our grandfathers could scarcely have imagined.

UN and Tides of Conflict and Hope

Now let us consider the United Nations. How does it relate to these twin tides of conflict and hope?

In our frustration with the complex and largely unfamiliar world around us there is a temptation even among the most thoughtful and informed observers to see the possibilities only in terms of the black and white contrasts.

The task of dealing with varying shades of grey is unfamiliar, uncomfortable and unsatisfactory to many Americans. Our experience in building this great nation has conditioned us to believe that there are only two sides to every question, one right and one wrong; that if there are problems, there must be solutions; that if there is struggle, there must be total victory for one and total defeat for the other.

This "all or nothing" attitude is a vital part of the American character and one which has given us much of the special energy and determination which have typified our country since its earliest days.

However, the new world with which we must deal is one of infinite complexity in which simple solutions are rarely available. We represent only 6 per cent of mankind and even with all our great industries and military power there are strict limitations on what we can do.

It is inevitable that Americans who fail to understand the complexities with which the United Nations must deal should charge that this great world organization has failed to do what it was set up to do.

At the same time, however, another aspect of the American character is helping to move us toward the mature understanding of possibilities and limitations which is basic to an effective foreign policy. I refer to our traditional appreciation of variety, to our acceptance of the give-and-take of honest differences, to our belief that a healthy society thrives not on conformity but on diversity.

This is the spirit which we must bring to all we attempt to accomplish in our troubled world. To behave otherwise by creating our own rigid doctrinaire orthodoxy, as do the apostles of modern-day Marxism, would be gravely to weaken our capacity to bring our great influence effectively to bear on the agonizing questions which confront us all.

As President Kennedy said a month ago in his speech to the United Nations General Assembly, "We cannot expect that all nations will adopt like systems, for conformity is the jailer of freedom and the enemy of growth."

An added dimension to the sheer complexity of the challenge is the often overlooked fact that there are not one but many threats to the peace.

In the Middle East, in South Asia, in the Caribbean, even in Africa, there are stubborn and dangerous conflicts and belligerent confrontations which have nothing to do with the Cold War.

If the super powers were by some magic to settle their differences tomorrow, some half dozen conflicts would remain which could produce a very sizable war at any moment. And while missiles which carry thermo-nuclear warheads are incredibly more destructive than World War II field artillery, their aggressive use to promote national ambitions is no easier to justify.

The new nations of Africa and Asia are properly alarmed by the dangerous implications of the big-power nuclear arms race. But they should not forget that they, too, may have contributions to make to the peace of the world in their own backyards.

UN's Record

Now what is the record of the United Nations judged against this complex and difficult background? Certainly its development has not followed the lines laid down in 1945. The hopes for unity among the world's great powers, so tenuously constructed during World War II, failed even to survive the first years of the post-war world.

But in considering the changes of function and emphasis which grew out of the Cold War situation, let us be frank.

If it had not been assumed that the United Nations would be dominated by the Security Council in which we have the veto, the United States Senate never would have voted to join. Yet within a few years the United States and a majority of the members found ways around this veto power; and it was this that made it possible for the United Nations to develop its capacity for executive action.

The Soviet response to this movement to transform the United Nations into a functioning world organization, capable of united action in an emergency, is recorded in its ninety-five vetoes, in its efforts to cripple the Secretariat, and in Mr. Khrushchev's belligerent statement of last spring in which he said he would use armed force to prevent the U.N. from carrying out any decision with which the Soviet Union did not agree.

Under these circumstances it is not surprising that much of what the U.N. has accomplished has been accomplished without the participation and frequently over the opposition of the Soviet Union.

And yet in spite of the determined opposition of one of its most powerful members, the U.N. and its family of specialized agencies have acted with increasing vigor and imagination. Let us briefly consider the remarkable accomplishments of some of these new agencies.

The World Health Organization, for example, is now conducting a world-wide campaign to eliminate malaria, a disease which has caused more deaths and more loss of work than any other in history. It also has launched a campaign to help bring clean water to every village on the globe.

Last year the United Nations Children's Fund, with ninety-eight governments participating, brought better care to 55 million expectant and nursing mothers. It also examined 75 million children for yaws, at an average cost of 15 cents a head.

The World Meteorological Organization is planning a world-wide weather reporting system. The International Telecommunications Union now allocates radio frequencies for the whole world.

In addition there is the equally effective work of the other specialized agencies, of the Technical Assistance program, of the Special Fund, and the new and promising program for recruiting expert personnel for the developing countries. Each of these U.N. agencies is handling tasks which were barely conceivable a generation ago.

Moreover, in every field the regional economic and social cooperation through the bi-national and multi-national agreements of which I spoke earlier is matched by the development of vigorously creative U.N. regional agencies such as ECAFE—the Economic Commission for Asia and the Far East—and ECLA—the Economic Commission for Latin America.

The capacity of the United Nations itself for positive political and economic action was brilliantly demonstrated in the Congo during the past year. Although the final record has not been written and much remains to be done, let us briefly review the progress so far:

When the Congo threatened to fall apart in the summer of 1960, many of the 9,000 European experts who had been managing the productive facilities, the public services, and the technical branches of the economy packed up and went home.

A tiny corps of some 200 United Nations experts, most of them drawn hurriedly from the U.N. Secretariat and the Specialized Agencies, was organized to fill the gap. These international public servants faced a situation in which starvation was claiming scores of people every day, unemployment was rampant, government revenues and exports and reserves were falling, inflation was mounting, and public services were disrupted.

By late 1960 a semblance of order had begun to emerge from the chaos; epidemics were checked, and starvation ended. Somehow, under incredibly difficult circumstances, this United Nations team of technicians and advisers managed to get the wheels turning again.

Then began an even more important task: the long-range job of helping the Congolese to train their own administrative and technical personnel and to create their own institutions. Although this process is in its beginning stages, the results appear promising.

Thus the entire Congo performance has been an extraordinary tribute to the U.N.'s capacity for direct executive action in the complex field of economic and social development.

The Congo also illustrates the U.N. capacity to act politically to create a more solid base for peace and security. There is no need to remind this audience of the remarkable performance of the United Nations in throwing together under the most difficult and urgent circumstances an emergency force of nearly 20,000 men drawn from twenty-eight countries.

The ability of this organization to mobilize, transport, supply and command a major peace-keeping force on short notice exceeded almost everyone's expectations.

The challenge in the Congo is the latest and severest test of the U.N. as peace-maker. In addition there is the record of the U.N. peace-keeping roles in Iran, Greece, Palestine, Suez and Korea.

Finally, in addition to promoting economic and social progress and to keeping the peace, the United Nations has served with considerable effectiveness as an international forum for the airing of disputes.

Although its detractors refer to this function as a debating society, the debates which take place there, in spite of the bitterness and demagoguery with which they are often conducted, are of the utmost importance.

The issues that come before the United Nations are the oldest and most intractable issues of history which cannot be effectively aired in any other arena.

The annual agenda therefore is no less than the agenda of mankind's most pressing problems in the second half of the twentieth century. To mention only a few:

> How can we create machinery for keeping the peace?
> How can we strengthen the concept of international law?
> How can we secure outer space for peaceful use?
> How can we wipe out the poverty that breeds hatred and upheaval?
> How can we better protect human rights and promote a greater measure of justice?

It is true that answers so far have been few and far between. But isn't it a long step toward international sanity to be able to debate them in a world-wide forum in which every viewpoint is represented, and where world opinion can be brought to bear?

Cynics deny even the existence of world opinion, and cynical nations do not hesitate to flaunt it. Yet whatever leader or nation consistently disregards the opinion of mankind will eventually pay, and as time goes on, I believe that the price he pays will become higher.

And here I cannot refrain from replying to the one question which ranks above all others on the agenda of mankind: the question of world disarmament.

If I correctly recall the gospel according to Karl Marx, capitalist societies are kept economically afloat only by war or the prospect of war.

If this is the Communist doctrine, and no good Marxist will deny it, why does the Kremlin not agree to a program of honest disarmament with suitable controls agreeable to all of us?

According to their monolithic creed, would not a sharp reduction of defense spending in the United States bring about the collapse of our economy? Would not millions of unemployed roam the land, and grass grow in our streets? And, in due course, would this not result in the Communists inheriting the earth without a shot being fired?

If this is what the Communists believe to be true, why does the Kremlin refuse to act in accordance with their doctrine? Why do they refuse to accept our challenge to a peaceful competition between their economic, political and social system and our own?

The answer, I believe, lies in the fact that they know that our economy would not collapse and that in such a competition they would be the loser.

Assessing UN and 1961 Real World

How then can we assess the United Nations in the real world of 1961?

Clearly we cannot say that it has abolished the threat of war or even that it has narrowed the gap of disagreement among the world's great powers.

Yet the record is in many ways extraordinary. Although sorely hampered by the vast ideological struggle which commands the unflagging energies of free men everywhere, the United Nations has somehow grown and developed by associating itself ever more effectively with the powerful currents of hope.

Where great issues of justice have been raised, it has served as a meeting house for the opinion of all humanity.

Where violence has threatened, it has time and again proved its growing capacity to divert the pressures and to preserve the peace.

Where peoples have been striving for an end to the tyranny of poverty, it has opened new paths for the indispensable cooperation in the battle against human misery.

We live in a raucous, restless, ill-mannered world in which a Community of Hope exists side by side with a Community of Fear. The Cold War conflict is paralleled by a growing partnership between the United States, the peoples of Asia, Africa and Latin America. It is this evolving world which helps shape the United Nations and which, increasingly, may be shaped by it.

Indeed, I believe there is solid basis for a measured optimism about the future of this great organization.

The new and growing nations, which now form the majority of the United Nations, most urgently need its protection and its help. Why should these nations act to weaken or destroy the international institutional arrangements which are providing them security, economic aid and opportunity to make their views heard?

For them the United Nations Charter is the best guarantee of their right to develop their own nations in their own way.

No, the United Nations is not likely to be destroyed by the majority of its members, however recklessly determined they may sometimes appear to do precisely that. Nor are we likely to destroy or weaken it by our failure to provide the necessary support and the leadership.

President Kennedy put it very simply and directly when he declared to the General Assembly: "Today of all days our dedication to the Charter must be maintained."

Tribute to Hammerskjold

One final word. I cannot close without paying tribute to the man who more than any other of our generation has helped to make the United Nations what we all know it must become.

In his final report to the organization whose voice and conscience he became, Dag Hammarskjold issued this quiet warning:

"The effort through the Organization to find a way by which the world community might, step by step, grow into organized international cooperation within the Charter, must either progress or recede.

"Those whose reactions to the work of the Organization hamper its development or reduce its possibilities of effective action, may have to shoulder the responsibility for a return to a state of affairs which governments had already found too dangerous after the first World War."

In Dag Hammarskjold was combined an inspiring idealism with the hard common sense of the practical politician. The real world of 1961 was precisely the world with which he was concerned, and it was in that world that he enabled the United Nations to operate with growing effectiveness.

We who carry on can do no better than to follow in the course which he charted. We must continue to maintain the vision to which the United Nations has always aspired. Only by so doing can we make the United Nations the instrument of the world-wide Community of Hope which its founders intended it to be.

Vol. XL—p. 73 (Oct. 1963)

The Teacher as a World Citizen*
BY MARION EDMAN

Marion Edman, professor of education, Wayne State University, Detroit, Michigan, who has taught in many countries, states: "Filling the shoes of a teacher in another culture is the best and surest means of learning to understand the world and thereby learning to appreciate it."

READING THE NEWSPAPER OR LISTENING TO NEWS COMMENTATORS today is at times both bewildering and exciting. New names: Basutoland, Laos and Somaliland are mentioned as casually as Indiana, Brooklyn and Hickory Corners. Pictures or words give intimate details of strange regions, unfamiliar peoples and titillating ways of living that make us realize we are part of a world closely and interdependently bound together. Yet in many ways these are far removed from our own particular pattern of life. In such a world, what is the responsibility of the teacher who must help children take for granted and use to advantage what an older generation may find strange or even bizarre?

It is crystal clear that if the teacher relies only on what he himself

---

* This article won the Eleanor Fishburn Award for 1963-64 given by the Educational Press Association of America (EDPRESS) for "outstanding contribution to international understanding."

has learned while in college or on what is written in the average school text, children may learn what is untrue, prejudiced or half-truth. The only alternative is for the teacher to help children keep abreast of what is current, guiding them to interpret what is learned by means of four underlying concepts, basic to the teacher's own understanding of the present world.

Inevitable Change

The *first* of these concepts is the fact of change. Even though change in American life keeps the average citizen almost breathless in trying to keep pace with it, he still finds it hard to comprehend that the same ferment is at work in every corner of the globe. Visitors from a strange land are constantly asked such naive questions as, "Had you ever seen a car before you came to the United States?"

Such questions are offensive to citizens of new nations, who are rightfully proud of their modern cities with all the latest trappings of traffic snarls, elegant public buildings, garish neon lights and blinking advertisements. No matter how "underdeveloped" the country in general may be, change is at work. It is important to the citizens of newly developing countries to demonstrate that they are keeping up with the rest of the world with outward signs of "modern civilization." More basic changes, but perhaps less obvious ones, such as improved economic stability and educational improvement are also happening.

Past Achievements

The *second* concept is that teachers help children understand the pride which many nations take in their achievements of bygone days. Korea, for example, a nation whose progress has been arrested by years of war produced, in very ancient times, a phonetic alphabet (in an area where other nations still use ideographs); movable type (two hundred years before Gutenberg in Germany); celadon pottery (unparalleled for the beauty of its glaze); iron-clad boats (centuries before the Civil War); an observatory for studying the heavens (the world's first); and beautiful architecture, poetry, painting, and choreography.

It is small wonder that Koreans are amazed and disillusioned when they learn that they are generally not given any credit in Western schools for such important contributions to the culture of the world. The same observation could be made for any number of people who today are thought of as "backward" or even "uncivilized." When children understand that the pendulum of civilization has swung in a wide arc during the course of history, their respect will increase for the achievements of the whole human family, and they will realize that most modern practices have very old and deep roots.

It would be good to have it known that the Western world's recent success in orbiting human beings about the earth is due in part to an ancient Korean astronomer looking at the stars in that first crude observatory.

Combination of Forces

The *third* concept is that all cultures develop slowly out of a combination of forces, which are in part environmental and in part the "breakthroughs" achieved by individuals. Some ideas thus developed permeate life completely, particularly the religions of the world.

Children need to ask: *Why* do other people behave as they do? Cultural patterns may seem strange or out of harmony with the way of life familiar to them. Teachers then need to help them look for answers in the physical environment of the people, their history, religion and great leaders.

To understand the passivity of the Oriental which places him outside the fierce competitiveness of Western culture, some knowledge of Hinduism and Buddhism is necessary; to understand the nepotism retarding government and business in many Eastern countries, one must know something of the family organization which Confucianism fosters. A student of modern cultures must understand the fierce loyalties of the Arab world which Islam promotes.

Interdependence in the World

The *fourth* concept is that of the basic interdependence of every part of the world with every other part. Even young children can understand the lack of logic of the gentleman on board ship who was awakened by the news that it had been struck by an iceberg and was rapidly sinking. Said he calmly. "Why should I care, I don't own it."

Children can easily learn how in matters of trade and commerce our own nation relies on countries in remote regions of the globe. It may be somewhat difficult to understand our political and cultural dependence, but a study of the work of the United Nations and its agencies or of our own foreign aid program should emphasize the underlying reasons why such activity is absolutely indispensable in the modern world.

Learning About Other Cultures

By what means shall a teacher achieve understanding and himself keep abreast of change? Obviously the *first* and most important way is to read current discussions of world affairs; to follow all the media of modern communication. The *second* is to be in contact with visitors from foreign lands—students, exchange teachers, travelers. The *third* way, given the opportunity, is to travel. With increased salaries and more varied means of relatively inexpensive transportation, this means of firsthand observation is open to teachers as never before.

Finally, there are a great many opportunities for American teachers to study and to teach abroad. This is by far the most productive way of understanding those who live in cultures other than one's own. The old proverb of the American Indian is in point: "You cannot know your brother until you have walked in his moccasins."

Filling the shoes of a teacher in another culture is the best and surest means of learning to understand and appreciate it.

The recipe for understanding, then, is to read, to discuss, to travel and to teach. The ingredients may be measured to suit the individual teacher.

Vol. XL—p. 390 (Apr. 1964)

The World's Bounty
BY STEWART UDALL

The Honorable Secretary Stewart Udall, United States Department of the Interior, is a conservation enthusiast and author of The Quiet Crisis.

WE LIVE IN AN AGE OF INCREASED GLOBAL INTERDEPENDENCE. EACH week the doors of neighborliness are opened wider through the negotiations of the United Nations, while the birth of new nations and new governments carries hope among established societies of the world that the hard-won lessons of their history will not have been in vain but will be instructive to their fellow men. The educability of the mind of man —its judgment, is discernment, its ultimate wisdom—is the greatest resource of free men. Essential to the progress of free men is how they use the bounty of their environment.

The natural resources of the world are as interdependent as its peoples. The oceans are common waters to all, and the great circulating masses of the atmosphere are not respectors of national boundaries. Oceanographers are still on the outer edge of the secrets of the sea, and atmospheric experts are only beginning to pierce the clouds of global climatology. These two great resources may be demeaned and polluted; or they may be studied, conserved and managed for the good of all mankind—according to the conservation wisdom of this generation.

Exploiting Natural Resources

The history of land utilization reflects man's genius for the extraction and exploitation of natural resources and records the desperate husbandry failures of improvident resource use. The arid wastes of the Middle East were once a fecund and blooming land until overgrazing stripped the soil of its fertility and water retention characteristics. Major agricultural areas of West Pakistan are beset by increased salinity due to generations of harmful irrigation practices. Within a few decades in the nineteenth century, ambitious settlers of continental United States eliminated the pine forests of several northern states; nearly exterminated the fur seal, buffalo and other wildlife species; and turned the grassy prairies into a dustbowl. Today we are national witnesses to the tragic aftermath of the coal-mining harvest of the Appalachians, where pitiful families are clinging to gutted, sterile hillsides and valleys.

Living in Harmony with Nature's Laws

These lessons make plain the necessity of the sound land management programs, undertaken with an ear to the natural rhythms of the earth and an eye to the future. Man has demonstrated an awesome capacity to alter his environment, even to the extent of total self-annihilation; but it is the task of this generation to show that we can live in harmony with nature's laws.

The story of natural evolution is one of greater and greater specialization among creatures—a climatic example of which can be found in the veldt of East Africa, where a panoramic array of dozens of bird and animal species share a delicate, interlocking chain of life. The entry of mankind upon such an environment characteristically severs the links of natural interdependence, simplifies natural diversity, and substitutes the works of technology for the works of nature. The end product of this concept of "progress," we are told, leads to a totally artificial Brave New World of human brood hens feeding upon algae.

One would hope that this technological dream might be repulsive to an informed society and that our heirs would demand a world where all the stimulating majesty of nature's beauties and creatures could be found. In the case of East African wildlife, esthetic sense makes economic sense too, for indigenous wild animals can be harvested for their meat more practically than artificially introduced cattle not adapted to the unique forage and water supplies of the veldt. Preservation of some natural resources for their cultural and inspirational contributions, an essential component of sound conservation anywhere in the world, confers meaning and majesty upon the enterprise of living.

Critical Supply of Living Space

Today's scientists do not foresee critical shortages of mineral, fuel and energy resources, so long as we are efficient in the utilization of what we have and continue our present ability to devise material substitutes. One resource which is in critical supply however is living space itself—that plot of ground and patch of sky in which the individual contacts the elemental world of which he is a part and in which he fulfills his most human attributes. We still have growth room, but the time is coming for thoughtful men and women to ask how much living space the human being needs to function with maximum efficiency and enjoy maximum happiness.

Our mastery over our environment is now so great that the conservation of a region, a metropolitan area or a valley is more important, in most cases, than the conservation of any single resource. Geography has always been a global science, and conservation must now become a truly global concept if the optimum use of resources is to be achieved.

Scientific Discoveries for Advancement of Mankind

In the years ahead, nations can either compete ruthlessly for resources in a context of scarcity or cooperate, respect the laws of nature and share its abundance. Resource interdependence and the common management of those resources owned in common will enlarge the area of unified action and do much to encourage world order. The growth of a worldwide conservation movement might be a gyroscopic force in world politics. The most influential countries of the future surely will be those that bring desalted water to arid lands and use their scientific discoveries to advance the welfare of all mankind.

The creation of a life-giving environment can go hand-in-hand with material progress and higher standards of husbandry if, in the words of the late President Kennedy, we make time "our friend and not our adversary."

For All Children the Teachers Speak

BY AGNES SNYDER

We speak for all children;
For those who falteringly stumble
Along the way—
Lagging, ever lagging behind the footsteps
Of their swifter brothers;
And for those swifter ones—
Restless, curious, leaping ahead,
Anticipating our words, our very thoughts;
And for those we call average—
Who learn what we would have them learn,
Untroubled by their mediocrity,
Amiable, docile to our voice;
We speak for all of them.

We take all children by the hand;
The toil-stained hands of children
Of the farm lands—
Who come to us at nine, the chickens fed,
The milking done;
And the soft rosy hands of girls—
Straight from the arms of mothers at suburban doors
Waving good-byes to their darlings
Walking demurely down the tree-lined streets;
And the grimy hands of children of the slums
Feverishly moving as they furtively eye
The well-brushed suits, the polished shoes,
The well-filled book packs
Of their neighbors;
We take the hands of all of these.

We try to understand all children;
Those quiet ones who forever sit
Pale and withdrawn, who will not play with others,
Who never speak unless you speak to them
And then with but a feeble "yes" or "no"—
More often, "no";
And those who greet you gaily and tell you
All they know—and more—
Of what happened down the street,

The fun, the grief, the latest joke;
And those whose ordered lives
Reflect the order of their homes—
Courteous, disciplined, serene,
Neither forward nor backward;
And yet sometimes we wonder
What might be seething underneath.
We try to understand them all.

We care for all children,
Children whom the unknowing
Call the handicapped;
Children whose sightless eyes
May never know
The green of summer grass,
The rose of sunset;
For those whose twisted bodies
Will never run, or jump, or leap
In childish ecstasy;
For those whose muted lips
May never speak the feeling
That stifled swells within their hearts;
We care for all of them.

We speak for all the children
Of all the nations, all the lands,
Knowing well that in their common human core
Is more of likeness than of difference;
Knowing too that only as we reach that common core
In children
Will men, the world over,
Reach it in each other.
Bright children, slow children,
Black, red, yellow, white,
Privileged children and deprived,
Separate them—one from another—
Segregate them—never!
It is in their young togetherness
Before distrust gives place to fear,
And fear to hate
Wherein alone lies hope
Of that togetherness in man
Which spells the fullness of his destiny.
We speak for all children—
The teachers speak.